Devotional Classics

DEVOTIONAL CLASSICS

SELECTED READINGS FOR
INDIVIDUALS AND GROUPS

Edited by

Richard J. Foster

and

James Bryan Smith

A RENOVARÉ Resource for Spiritual Renewal

HarperSanFrancisco
A Division of HarperCollins*Publishers*

DEVOTIONAL CLASSICS: *Selected Readings for Individuals and Groups.* Copyright © 1990, 1991, 1993 by RENOVARÉ, Inc. All rights reserved. Printed in the United States of America. Unless otherwise noted, no part of this book may be used or reproduced in any manner whatsoever without written permission except in the case of brief quotations embodied in critical articles and reviews. For information address HarperCollins Publishers, 10 East 53rd Street, New York, NY 10022.

Library of Congress Cataloging-in-Publication Data

Devotional classics : selected readings for individuals and groups /
  edited by Richard J. Foster & James Bryan Smith.
      p.   cm.
   Includes bibliographical references and index.
   ISBN: 0-06-066966-7
   1. Devotional literature, English.   2. Devotional exercises.
I. Foster, Richard J.   II. Smith, James Bryan.
BV4801.D39   1993
242—dc20   92–53912
                                                               CIP

01   RRD-H   30 29 28 27 26 25

To

CAROLYNN FOSTER

and

MEGHAN SMITH,

our loving wives, faithful companions, and best friends.

Contents

Introduction

We today suffer from the unexamined notion that the more recent something is, the better, the more true it must be. This book is our attempt to counter this present-day myopia. It brings together fifty-two carefully chosen selections from the great devotional classics.

It is important at the outset to reclaim the words *devotional* and *classic*. For many people today *devotional* means ethereal, otherworldly, irrelevant. To still others it implies sentimentality, superficiality, and an unwillingness to face the hard realities of life. In point of fact, however, genuine devotional writings have nothing to do with these modern misconceptions. Rather, they are writings that aim at the transformation of the human personality. They seek to touch the heart, to address the will, to mold the mind. They call for radical character formation. They instill holy habits.

Likewise, the word *classic* has gotten bad press in our day. If a book is a "classic" we immediately think it must be obscure, hard to read, and most certainly out of touch with modern concerns. As Mark Twain aptly notes, it is the kind of book that "everyone wants to have read but no one wants to read." In reality, however, for a writing to be a classic means simply that many people over a sustained period of time have drawn strength from its insights and witness to its value.

When these two words are brought together—devotional classic—they describe a kind of writing that has stood the test of time and that seeks to form the soul before God.

It is a genuine asset to be soaked in the devotional classics. Pure modernity makes us parochial. But these writings have vintage. They are weaned from the fads of the marketplace. They give us perspective and balance. C. S. Lewis notes, "A new book is still on trial, and the amateur is not in a position to judge it. . . . The only safety is to have a standard of plain, central Christianity ('mere Christianity' as Baxter called it), which puts the controversies of the moment in their proper perspective. Such a standard can only be acquired from old books. It is a good rule, after reading a new book, never to allow yourself another new one till you have read an old one in between."[1] The volume you hold in your hands is our attempt to make available to the average reader just such a "standard of plain, central Christianity."

READING WITH THE HEART

A word of instruction needs to be given about reading these devotional classics. These writers make no attempt to grab you quick and hold you tight. They have no intention of tickling your ears and titillating your fantasies. They promise no easy steps to instant holiness, no guaranteed plan for personal prosperity, no surefire technique for peace of mind.

Since these men and women wrote before the modern notion of speed-reading, they did not know to fill each paragraph with trite clichés and meaningless jargon. As a result, each phrase is pregnant with meaning and it is best to read at a measured pace, pausing often to reread, rethink, reexperience the words until we not only understand their meaning but are shaped by the truth of them. Jean-Pierre de Caussade counsels us: "Read quietly, slowly, word for word to enter into the subject more with the heart than the mind. . . . From time to time make short pauses to allow these truths time to flow through all the recesses of the soul and to give occasion for the operation of the Holy Spirit who, during these peaceful pauses and times of silent attention, engraves and imprints these heavenly truths in the heart. . . . Should this peace and rest last for a longer time it will be all the better. When you find that your mind wanders resume your reading and continue thus, frequently renewing these same pauses."[2]

There is a technical word for this kind of reading and it might be helpful for you to know it—*lectio divina*, "divine reading." This is a kind of reading in which the mind descends into the heart, and both are drawn into the love and goodness of God. We are doing more than reading words; we are seeking "the Word exposed in the words," to use the phrase of Karl Barth. We are endeavoring to go beyond information to formation—to being formed and molded by what we read. We are listening with the heart to the Holy within. This prayerful reading, as we might call it, transforms us and strengthens us.

FIVE GREAT STREAMS

The readings are divided into one preparatory section and then five topical sections: "Preparing for the Spiritual Life," "The Prayer-Filled Life," "The Virtuous Life," "The Spirit-Empowered Life," "The Compassionate Life," and "The Word-Centered Life." It is no accident that these follow the five great streams of Christian life and faith that we have identified in RENO-VARÉ. (RENOVARÉ—a Latin word meaning "to make new"—is an effort working for the renewal of the Church of Jesus Christ in all her multifaceted expressions.) These divisions, however, came after the fact, if you will. We first began developing these readings in an attempt to find helpful material from the recognized classics of faith and devotion for the weekly meetings of our Spiritual Formation groups. It was only later that we realized how well they fit into the five great traditions—Contemplative, Holiness, Charismatic, Social Justice, and Evangelical. And, in fact, we were rather astonished ourselves to see that we had chosen roughly an equal number of selections from each tradition.

We are glad for this because it is our conviction that we need to be experiencing all these traditions if we are to have a balanced vision of faith and life. Each one is a vital dimension of a fully orbed Christian spirituality. Unfortunately, while we may be comfortable, acclimated, or interested in one or two of the five traditions, very few of us are strong in all of them.

We are a little like the gymnast who can excel in the floor exercise, the balance beam, and the parallel bars but who cannot compete on the high bar and the vaulting horse. Such a person is simply not very balanced in gymnastic skills. Likewise, we are imbalanced and ineffective if we excel in, say, evangelism and prayer but lack holiness of life and compassion for the poor. Each tradition—even our favorite one—will throw us out of balance if it is all we know. Balance comes when we strive to learn from all five, when we recognize their importance, and when we set out to make them a part of our lives.

The sections, therefore, are designed to aid you in seeing the major areas of spiritual development. But you may not want to read them in order. After reading through the first section on preparing for the spiritual life, you may find it helpful to skip around the various selections in this book. If, for example, you feel a lack in the area of social justice, you could begin your reading in the fifth section: "The Compassionate Life." Perhaps after two or three readings you will want to focus on the life of prayer—if so, you can go back to the second section, "The Prayer-Filled Life." Always the key is to have a well-rounded diet of spiritual nutrients.

THE EDITING TASK

A brief note now about the abridgment and editing of these writings. Many of these books were written in other centuries, and such things as the archaic style of writing and the length of sentences can discourage the contemporary reader. Therefore, we have shortened sentences and paragraphs. Archaic words have been changed into their modern English equivalents. Material is abridged where there are digressions or allusions that are time-bound. And, on a few occasions, inclusive language has been used where we felt it would enhance the message of the writer.

Always we have worked hard to stay faithful to the essential message of the author and to follow as much as possible the original style and actual words of the author. It is our hope that the abridgment and editing work will help to elicit the same kind of response in the modern reader that these writings did for those who first read them.

Our special thanks to Lynda Graybeal for her editing of our editorial work. She gave countless hours of careful and prayerful labor so that these words from the past might speak to the present with clarity and power.

1. C. S. Lewis, *God in the Dock*, ed. Walter Hooper (Grand Rapids, MI: Eerdmans, 1970), pp. 201–202.
2. Jean-Pierre de Caussade, *The Sacrament of the Present Moment*, trans. Kitty Muggeridge (San Francisco: Harper & Row, 1982), p. xxiii.

Preparing for the
Spiritual Life

THESE FIRST EIGHT selections introduce us to the spiritual life. But notice, they do not follow the pattern we are so accustomed to today of giving people "church lite" with the hope that we can tell them about surrender and abandonment and discipleship later. Vain hope! These authors know better. They know that our God is not a God of half measures. Nothing short of absolute commitment will do.

They speak with one voice. Francis de Sales talks of "true devotion," St. Augustine of "complete surrender," François Fénelon of "a will which is no longer divided," and C. S. Lewis of "giving all to Christ." Jonathan Edwards reminds us that we love God with the affections as well as the mind, and Bernard of Clairvaux urges us to "love God for God's sake" and ultimately to "love self for God's sake." John of the Cross calls us to the purifying bath of the "dark night."

All of this sobers us and reminds us that grace, while free, is not cheap, as Dietrich Bonhoeffer taught us. Our discipleship to Jesus Christ costs nothing less than everything. But as Dallas Willard writes, the cost of nondiscipleship is far greater: "Nondiscipleship costs abiding peace, a life penetrated throughout by love, faith that sees everything in the light of God's overriding governance for good, hopefulness that stands firm in the most discouraging of circumstances, power to do what is right and withstand the forces of evil. In short, it costs exactly that abundance of life Jesus said he came to bring."

With one voice these authors witness to us that the cost of discipleship is a far better bargain than the cost of nondiscipleship.

C. S. Lewis (1898–1963)

INTRODUCTION TO THE AUTHOR

C. S. Lewis will be remembered as one of the most important Christian thinkers of the twentieth century. He was born in Ireland in 1898, and the major part of his adult years was spent as a Fellow of Magdalen College, Oxford, where he taught medieval literature. It was in 1931 that he was "surprised by joy," Lewis's own description of his conversion to Christianity. A brilliant scholar and writer, Lewis used his talents to reach thousands through the printed and spoken word.

He and a group of friends (including J. R. R. Tolkien, author of *Lord of the Rings*) gathered once a week to share their writings. During those years Lewis produced his famous work *The Screwtape Letters*. In the early 1940s he delivered talks on various Christian topics over British radio. His fame grew throughout Great Britain and spread to the United States. Out of those talks came the book *Mere Christianity*, a penetrating work on Christian apologetics. Countless Christians point to this book as an essential part of their faith journey. If sales are an indication of popularity, then C. S. Lewis—even thirty years after his death—is one of the most popular Christian thinkers of the twentieth century. In the following passage Lewis discusses the question, Is Christianity hard or easy?

EXCERPTS FROM *MERE CHRISTIANITY*

1. How Much of Myself Must I Give?

The ordinary idea which we all have before we become Christians is this. We take as the starting point our ordinary self with its various desires and interests. We then admit that something else—call it "morality" or "decent behavior," or "the good of society"—has claims on this self: claims which interfere with its own desires. What we mean by "being good" is giving in to those claims. Some of the things the ordinary self wanted to do turn out to be what we call "wrong": well, we must give them up. Other things turn out to be what we call "right": well, we shall have to do them.

But we are hoping all the time that when all the demands have been met, the poor natural self will still have some chance, and some time, to get on with its own life and do what it likes. In fact, we are very like an honest man paying his taxes. He pays them all right, but he does hope that there will be enough left over for him to live on. Because we are still taking our natural self as the starting point.

2. Two Results

As long as we are thinking that way, one or the other of two results is likely to follow. Either we give up trying to be good, or else we become very unhappy indeed. For, make no mistake: if you are really going to try to meet all the demands made on the natural self, it will not have enough left over to live on. The more you obey your conscience, the more your conscience will demand of you. And your natural self, which is thus being starved and hampered and worried at every turn, will get angrier and angrier.

In the end, you will either give up trying to be good, or else become one of those people who, as they say, "live for others" but always in a discontented, grumbling way—always wondering why the others do not notice it more and always making a martyr of yourself. And once you have become that you will be a far greater pest to anyone who has to live with you than you would have been if you had remained frankly selfish.

3. Harder and Easier

The Christian way is different: harder, and easier. Christ says, "Give me All. I don't want so much of your time and so much of your money and so much of your work: I want You. I have not come to torment your natural self, but to kill it. No half-measures are any good. I don't want to cut off a branch here and a branch there, I want to have the whole tree down. Hand over the whole natural self, all the desires which you think innocent as well as the ones you think wicked—the whole outfit. I will give you a new self instead. In fact, I will give you Myself: my own will shall become yours."

Both harder and easier than what we are all trying to do. You have noticed, I expect, that Christ Himself sometimes describes the Christian way as very hard, sometimes as very easy. He says, "Take up your Cross"—in other words, it is like going to be beaten to death in a concentration camp. Next minute he says, "My yoke is easy and my burden light." He means both. And one can just see why both are true.

4. The Most Dangerous Thing

Teachers will tell you that the laziest boy in the class is the one who works the hardest in the end. They mean this. If you give two boys, say, a proposition in geometry to do, the one who is prepared to take trouble will try to understand it. The lazy boy will learn it by heart because, for the moment, that needs less effort. But six months later, when they are preparing for the exam, that lazy boy is doing hours and hours of miserable drudgery over things the other boy understands, and positively enjoys, in a few minutes.

Laziness means more work in the long run. Or look at it this way. In a battle, or in mountain climbing, there is often one thing which it takes a lot of pluck to do; but it is also, in the long run, the safest thing to do. If you funk it, you will find yourself, hours later, in far worse danger. The cowardly thing is also the most dangerous thing.

5. The Almost Impossible Thing

It is like that here. The terrible thing, the almost impossible thing, is to hand over your whole self—all your wishes and precautions—to Christ. But it is far easier than what we are trying to do instead. For what we are trying to do is to remain what we call "ourselves," to keep personal happiness as our great aim in life, and yet at the same time be "good." We are all trying to let our mind and heart go their own way—centered on money or pleasure or ambition—and hoping, in spite of this, to behave honestly and chastely and humbly.

And that is exactly what Christ warned us you could not do. As He said, a thistle cannot produce figs. If I am a field that contains nothing but grass-seed, I cannot produce wheat. Cutting the grass may keep it short: but I shall still produce grass and no wheat. If I want to produce wheat, the change must go deeper than the surface. I must be ploughed up and resown.

6. Listening to That Other Voice

That is why the real problem of the Christian life comes where people do not usually look for it. It comes the very moment you wake up each morning. All your wishes and hopes for the day rush at you like wild animals. And the first job each morning consists simply in shoving them all back; in listening to that other voice, taking that other point of view, letting that other larger, stronger, quieter life come flowing in. And so on, all day. Standing back from all your natural fussings and frettings; coming in out of the wind.

We can only do it for moments at first. But from those moments the new sort of life will be spreading through our system: because now we are letting Him work at the right part of us. It is the difference between paint, which is merely laid on the surface, and a dye or stain which soaks right through.

He never talked vague, idealistic gas. When He said, "Be perfect," He meant it. He meant that we must go in for the full treatment. It is hard; but the sort of compromise we are all hankering after is harder—in fact, it is impossible. It may be hard for an egg to turn into a bird: it would be a jolly sight harder for it to learn to fly while remaining an egg. We are like eggs at present. And you cannot go on indefinitely being just an ordinary, decent egg. We must be hatched or go bad.

7. The Reason the Church Exists

May I come back to what I said before? This is the whole of Christianity. There is nothing else. It is so easy to get muddled about that. It is easy to think that the Church has a lot of different objects—education, building, missions, holding services. Just as it is easy to think the State has a lot of different objects—military, political, economic, and what not.

But in a way things are much simpler than that. The State exists simply to promote and to protect the ordinary happiness of human beings in this life. A husband and wife chatting over a fire, a couple of friends having a game of darts in a pub, a man reading a book in his own room or digging in his own garden—that is what the State is there for. And unless they are helping to increase and prolong and protect such moments, all the laws, parliaments, armies, courts, police, economics, etc., are simply a waste of time.

In the same way the Church exists for nothing else but to draw men into Christ, to make them little Christs. If they are not doing that, all the cathedrals, clergy, missions, sermons, even the Bible itself, are simply a waste of time. God became Man for no other purpose. It is even doubtful, you know, whether the whole universe was created for any other purpose. It says in the Bible that the whole universe was made for Christ and that everything is to be gathered together in Him.

8. Becoming a Part of the Plan

I do not suppose any of us can understand how this will happen as regards the whole universe. We do not know what (if anything) lives in the parts of it that are millions of miles from this Earth. Even on this Earth we do not know how it applies to things other than men. After all, that is what you would expect. We have been shown the plan only in so far as it concerns ourselves.

What we have been told is how we can be drawn into Christ—can become part of that wonderful present which the young Prince of the universe wants to offer his Father—that present which is Himself and therefore us in Him. It is the only thing we were made for. And there are strange, exciting hints in the Bible that when we are drawn in, a great many other things in Nature will begin to come right. The bad dream will be over: it will be morning.

BIBLE SELECTION: LUKE 14:25–33

25Now large crowds were traveling with him; and he turned and said to them, 26"Whoever comes to me and does not hate father and mother, wife and children, brothers and sisters, yes, and even life itself, cannot be my disciple. 27Whoever does not carry the cross and follow me cannot be my disciple. 28For which of you, intending to build a tower, does not first sit down and estimate the cost, to see whether he has enough to complete it? 29Otherwise, when he has laid a foundation and is not able to finish, all who see it will begin to ridicule him, 30saying, 'This fellow began to build and was not able to finish.' 31Or what king, going out to wage war against another king, will not sit down first and consider whether he is able with ten thousand to oppose the one who comes against him with twenty thousand? 32If he cannot, then, while the other is still far away, he sends a delegation and asks for the terms of peace. 33So therefore, none of you can become my disciple if you do not give up all your possessions."

REFLECTION QUESTIONS

The following questions can be used for discussion within a small group, or used for journal reflections by individuals.

1. C. S. Lewis stresses the need to give all areas of our lives to God. What do you find most difficult about giving all to God?
2. Describe how you would feel if Jesus came to you and spoke the words Lewis quotes in section 3 ("Christ says, 'Give me All. I don't want . . .").
3. According to Lewis, the hardest road we can take in life is the one that appears the easiest (e.g., the boy who waits until the end of the semester to cram for a test). How have your experiences confirmed or denied his claim?

4. The pursuit of personal happiness by being morally good, says Lewis, ends in frustration. What is his reasoning behind this? Do you agree or disagree?

5. In Luke 14:25–33, Jesus encourages those who would follow him to "count the cost" of being one of his disciples. What has being a Christian cost you?

SUGGESTED EXERCISES

The following exercises can be done by individuals, shared between spiritual friends, or used in the context of a small group. Choose one or more of the following.

1. Use a journal this week to reflect on one or more of the following questions:
   a. What are some of the reasons I fear giving my life completely to God?
   b. Which areas of my life am I most reluctant to surrender to God?
   c. In what ways have I experienced the heavy burden of trying to remain in control of my life?

2. C. S. Lewis believes that the way to a surrendered life begins each morning. This week make a conscious effort to push back the clamoring voice of your natural self as soon as you awaken, and, instead, give ear to God, letting him guide and direct your every thought and word. Put three-by-five-inch cards next to your bed and over your bathroom mirror that read, "To whom am I listening?" or "Who's in control?" This will help you begin the day with a peaceful attitude of surrender.

REFLECTIONS

The contrast between God's way of doing things and our way is never more acute than in this area of human change and transformation. We focus on specific actions; God focuses on us. We work from the outside in; God works from the inside out. We try; God transforms.

Jim Smith, my co-worker in these devotional readings, has been greatly helped by the many writings of C. S. Lewis and by this passage in particular. He writes, "When I read this essay, I was brought to my knees. I could hardly finish it. I suddenly knew what was wrong: I had been using my 'natural self' as the starting point. I had been trying to keep my self and its desires intact. Christ was merely an addition to my self. After reading this selection, I resolved to live each day consciously listening to the voice of Christ and letting the new self—the one that Christ gives me—come to life."

May God use this reading to do the same for you and for me.

Richard J. Foster

GOING DEEPER

Lewis, C. S. *The Chronicles of Narnia.* New York: Macmillan, 1953. A collection of seven stories that both delight and instruct. They are wonderful stories to read out loud to your children so that both parent and child can learn and profit from them.

Lewis, C. S. *Mere Christianity.* New York: Macmillan, 1952. A gathering together of three separate series of radio talks: "The Case for Christianity," "Christian Behavior," and "Beyond Personality." This book is a masterful defense of the Christian way. It is must reading.

Lewis, C. S. *Reflections on the Psalms.* New York: Harcourt, Brace & World, 1958. Provides insights and deals with problems in the devotional reading of the Psalms.

Lewis, C. S. *The Screwtape Letters.* New York: Macmillan, 1980. Counsels of a senior devil to a junior devil in the art of temptation. The book contains wonderful insights into the life of faith.

Lewis, C. S. *Space Trilogy.* New York: Macmillan, 1965. Consisting of three volumes, *Out of the Silent Planet, Perelandra,* and *That Hideous Strength,* these books in the science fiction genre are packed with wisdom, theological insight, and great adventure.

Lewis, C. S. *Surprised by Joy.* New York: Harcourt, Brace & World, 1955. The story of Lewis's conversion from atheism to Christianity.

Dallas Willard (1935–)

INTRODUCTION TO THE AUTHOR

Dallas Willard was born in Buffalo, Missouri, on September 4, 1935, and grew up in comparatively poor surroundings. He was married to L. Jane Lakes in 1955, and they have reared two children, John Samuel and Rebecca.

Early on, a life of teaching and scholarship drew Dallas into his chosen field of philosophy. He has taught at the University of Wisconsin and the University of Southern California (his present position) and over the years has distinguished himself as a foremost interpreter of the philosophy of Husserl and, in particular, that philosophic system know as "phenomenology."

Dr. Willard is a distinguished philosopher with over thirty publications. He is also a man of deep faith and Christian conviction. While he can hold his own among any of the great thinkers of our day, I (R. Foster) am most impressed watching him share gospel truths with ordinary folk. For example, when I was pastoring a small church in southern California (where Dallas and Jane attended), I was moved to observe the deep and abiding spiritual friendship that Dallas had with an unschooled but godly construction worker. Even more moving is to be with Dallas Willard at prayer. His intimacy with the Father, his humility of spirit, his compassion for the world is a beautiful thing in which to participate.

The following selection is taken from an appendix to his book *The Spirit of the Disciplines.* The book seeks to lay a foundation for understanding how God changes the inward personality, bringing us into deeper conformity to the way of Christ, and the part we play in that process. This passage deals with the problem in the contemporary church of "undiscipled disciples."

EXCERPTS FROM *THE SPIRIT OF THE DISCIPLINES*

1. Discipleship: For Super-Christians Only?

The word "disciple" occurs 269 times in the New Testament. "Christian" is found only three times and was first introduced to refer precisely to the disciples.... The New Testament is a book about disciples, by disciples, and for disciples of Jesus Christ.

But the point is not merely verbal. What is more important is that the kind of life we see in the earliest church is that of a special type of person. All of the assurances and the benefits offered to humankind in the gospel evidently presuppose such a life and do not make realistic sense apart from it. The disciple of Jesus is not the deluxe or heavy-duty model of the Christian—especially padded, textured, streamlined, and empowered for the fast lane on the straight and narrow way. He stands on the pages of the New Testament as the first level of basic transportation in the Kingdom of God.

2. Undiscipled Disciples

For at least several decades the churches of the Western world have not made discipleship a condition of being a Christian. One is not required to be, or to intend to be, a disciple in order to become a Christian, and one may remain a Christian without any signs of progress toward or in discipleship. Contemporary American churches in particular do not require following Christ in his example, spirit, and teachings as a condition of membership—either of entering into or continuing in fellowship of a denomination or a local church. Any exception to this claim only serves to highlight its general validity and make the general rule more glaring. So far as the visible Christian institutions of our day are concerned, discipleship clearly is optional.... Churches are filled with "undiscipled disciples," as Jess Moody has called them. Most problems in contemporary churches can be explained by the fact that members have not yet decided to follow Christ.

Little good results from insisting that Christ is also supposed to be Lord: to present his lordship as an option leaves it squarely in the category of the white-wall tires and stereo equipment for the new car. You can do without it. And it is—alas!—far from clear what you would do with it. Obedience and training in obedience form no intelligible doctrinal or practical unity with the salvation presented in recent versions of the gospel.

3. Great Omissions from the Great Commission

A different model was instituted in the Great Commission Jesus left the church. The first goal he set forth for the early church was to use his all-encompassing power and authority to make disciples.... Having made disciples, these alone were to be baptized into the name of the Father, and of the Son, and of the Holy Spirit. With this twofold preparation they were to be taught to treasure and keep "all things whatsoever I have commanded you." The Christian church of the first century resulted from following this plan for church growth—a result hard to improve upon.

But in place of Christ's plan, historical drift has substituted: "Make converts (to a particular faith and practice) and baptize them into church membership." This causes two great omissions from the Great Commission to stand out. Most important, we start by omitting the making of disciples or enrolling people as Christ's students, when we should let all else wait for that. We also omit the step of taking our converts through training that will bring them ever increasingly to do what Jesus directed.

The two great omissions are connected. Not having made converts disciples, it is impossible for us to teach them how to live as Christ lived and taught. That was not part of the package, not what they converted to. When confronted with the example and teachings of Christ, the response today is less one of rebellion or rejection than one of puzzlement: How do we relate to these? What have they to do with us?

4. Discipleship Then

When Jesus walked among humankind there was a certain simplicity to being a disciple. Primarily it meant to go with him, in an attitude of study, obedience, and imitation. There were no correspondence courses. One knew what to do and what it would cost. Simon Peter exclaimed: "Look, we've left everything and followed you!" (Mark 10:28). Family and occupations were deserted for long periods to go with Jesus as he walked from place to place announcing, showing, and explaining the governance of God. Disciples had to be with him to learn how to do what he did.

Imagine doing that today. How would family members, employers, and coworkers react to such abandonment? Probably they would conclude that we did not much care for them, or even for ourselves. Did not Zebedee think this as he watched his two sons desert the family business to keep company with Jesus (Mark 1:20)? Ask any father in a similar situation. So when Jesus observed that one must forsake the dearest things—family, "all that he hath," and "his own life also" (Luke 14)—insofar as that was necessary to accompany him, he stated a simple fact: it was the only possible doorway to discipleship.

5. Discipleship Now

Though costly, discipleship once had a very clear, straightforward meaning. The mechanics are not the same today. We cannot literally be with him in the same way as his first disciples could. But the priorities and intentions—the heart or inner attitudes—of disciples are forever the same. In the heart of a disciple there is a desire, and there is decision or settled intent. The disciple of Christ desires above all else to be like him. . . .

Given this desire, usually produced by the lives and words of those already in The Way, there is yet a decision to be made: the decision to devote oneself to becoming like Christ. The disciple is one who, intent upon becoming Christlike and so dwelling in his "faith and practice," systematically and progressively rearranges his affairs to that end. By these actions, even today, one who enrolls in Christ's training, becomes his pupil or disciple.

And if we intend to become like Christ, that will be obvious to every thoughtful person around us, as well as to ourselves. Of course, attitudes that define the disciple cannot be realized today by leaving family and business to accompany Jesus on his travels about the countryside. But discipleship can be made concrete by loving our enemies, blessing those who curse us, walking the second mile with an oppressor—in general, living out the gracious inward transformations of faith, hope, and love. Such acts—carried out by the disciplined person with manifest grace, peace, and joy—make discipleship no less tangible and shocking today than were those desertions of long ago. Anyone who will enter into The Way can verify this, and he or she will prove that discipleship is far from dreadful.

6. The Cost of Nondiscipleship

In 1937 Dietrich Bonhoeffer gave the world his book *The Cost of Discipleship.* It was a masterful attack on "easy Christianity" or "cheap grace," but it did not set aside—perhaps it even enforced—the view of discipleship as a costly spiritual excess, and only for those especially driven or called to it. It was right to point out that one cannot be a disciple of Christ without forfeiting things normally sought in human life, and that one who pays little in the world's coinage to bear his name has reason to wonder where he or she stands with God. But the cost of nondiscipleship is far greater—even when this life alone is considered—than the price paid to walk with Jesus.

Nondiscipleship costs abiding peace, a life penetrated throughout by love, faith that sees everything in the light of God's overriding governance for good, hopefulness that stands firm in the most discouraging of circumstances, power to do what is right and withstand the forces of evil. In short, it costs exactly that abundance of life Jesus said he came to bring (John 10:10). The cross-shaped yoke of Christ is after all an instrument of liberation and power to those who live in it with him and learn the meekness and lowliness of heart that brings rest to the soul. . . . The correct perspective is to see following Christ not only as the necessity it is, but as the fulfillment of the highest human possibilities and as life on the highest plane.

BIBLE SELECTION: MATTHEW 28:16–20

[16]Now the eleven disciples went to Galilee, to the mountain to which Jesus had directed them. [17]When they saw him, they worshiped him; but some doubted. [18]And Jesus came and said to them, "All authority in heaven and on earth has been given to me. [19]Go therefore and make disciples of all nations, baptizing them in the name of the Father and of the Son and of the Holy Spirit, [20]and teaching them to obey everything that I have commanded you. And remember, I am with you always, to the end of the age."

REFLECTION QUESTIONS

The following questions can be used for discussion within a small group, or used for journal reflections by individuals.

1. Dallas Willard makes a strong plea for churches to emphasize discipleship (teaching new converts how to live as Jesus commanded) and not merely

membership (letting new Christians alone once they have joined the church). Describe your church experience in light of these two approaches.

2. According to section 3, what are the two great omissions from the Great Commission? Read the passage from Matthew 28:16–20, noting the exact words that Jesus used.

3. Willard says that the disciple of Christ "desires above all else to be like him [Christ]." Who are some of the people you have desired "to be like," and how did you go about becoming more like each of those people?

4. There has been a lot of discussion about how costly it is to be a disciple. According to section 6, what is the cost of *nondiscipleship?*

5. Willard writes, "If we intend to become like Christ, that will be obvious to every thoughtful person around us, as well as to ourselves." What would change about your life if you were to focus all your energies on becoming like Christ? What kind of reaction would you get from those around you?

SUGGESTED EXERCISES

The following exercises can be done by individuals, shared between spiritual friends, or used in the context of a small group. Choose one or more of the following.

1. This week commit to memory Willard's powerful sentence about the cost of nondiscipleship ("Nondiscipleship costs abiding peace, . . .). Write it on a card and carry it with you. Allow yourself to yearn for peace, love, faith, hopefulness, power, and abundance of life.

2. Willard lists a few things we can do today that are both commanded by Christ and are Christ-like actions (section 5). This week make an effort to love your enemies by praying for them, blessing those who curse you, and walking the second mile with someone who might be oppressing you.

3. Jesus instructed his followers to "obey everything that I have commanded" (Matt. 28:16–20). Go through the Gospel of Matthew and list all the things Jesus commanded us to do. Your list will make up a mosaic of what the basic Christian life should look like according to Jesus.

4. Meditate on the lordship of Christ. Examine your life to see how much of it actually falls under Jesus' authority. Instead of focusing on the cost of giving these areas over to Christ, focus on the high price you have been paying by keeping them under your control.

REFLECTIONS

Perhaps the greatest malady in the Church today is converts to Christ who are not disciples of Christ—a clear contradiction in terms. This malady affects everything in church life and in large measure accounts for the low level of spiritual nutrients in our local congregations.

To counter this sad state of affairs we must determine that, regardless of what others do, our intention is to come under the tutelage of Jesus Christ, our ever-living Savior, Teacher, Lord, and Friend. We seek to undertake the general pattern of life that he undertook—not in slavish mimicking but in overall lifestyle. Disciplines of prayer, solitude, simplicity, and service will mark our overall pattern of life.

There is much more we can do to overcome our "discipleless Christianity"— Jesus, our ever-living Teacher, will show us the way.

GOING DEEPER

Willard, Dallas. *In Search of Guidance.* San Francisco: HarperCollins, 1993. Helps us to live beyond the anxious quest for what God wants us to do and focuses on our becoming the kind of people God wants us to be, which ultimately answers the question of what we are to do.

Willard, Dallas. *Logic and the Objectivity of Knowledge.* Athens: Ohio University Press, 1984. A study and critique of Edmund Husserl's "phenomenology," which Willard significantly differentiates from "linguistic analysis." Only for those interested in serious philosophy.

Willard, Dallas. *The Spirit of the Disciplines.* San Francisco: Harper & Row, 1988. This book shows us how in practical terms we can be conformed to the image of Christ. It explains salvation not only in terms of the forgiveness of sins but also as part of the total transformation of our lives. It makes "following Christ," far from an empty phrase, a vibrant reality filled with specific content. It invites us to undertake the easy yoke and light burden of Christ, which stands in direct contrast to the hard yoke and heavy burden of nondiscipleship.

Jonathan Edwards (1703–1758)

INTRODUCTION TO THE AUTHOR

Jonathan Edwards was a Congregational pastor and a key figure in the eighteenth-century "Great Awakening." He is considered one of America's greatest theologians. Born in Connecticut and educated at Yale, he ministered for twenty-three years at a church in Northampton, Massachusetts. He later became a missionary to the Indians at Stockbridge. In 1758 he was named president of Princeton University but died only a few weeks after taking office.

Edwards produced a theology of Christian spirituality for his age that blended together Lockean philosophy and his own Calvinist theology. His main concern was the question, How do we distinguish the presence of the Holy Spirit? Christian experience, according to Edwards, is a gift of God, but he spent his life working out the ways in which we define that experience. A central theme of his writings—evidenced in the following selection—is the importance of religious "affections," which he defined as the passions that move the will to act.

EXCERPTS FROM *RELIGIOUS AFFECTIONS*

1. Engagement of the Heart

The kind of religion that God requires, and will accept, does not consist in weak, dull, and lifeless "wouldings"—those weak inclinations that lack convictions—that raise us but a little above indifference. God, in his word, greatly insists that we be in good earnest, fervent in spirit, and that our hearts be engaged vigorously in our religion: "Be fervent in spirit, serving the Lord" (Rom. 12:11, modified KJV).

"And now, O Israel, what does the Lord your God require of you? To fear the Lord your God, to walk in his ways, and to love him, and to serve the Lord your God with all your heart and with all your soul" (Deut. 10:12). This fervent, vigorous engagement of the heart is the fruit of a real circumcision of the heart that alone has the promise of life: "And the Lord your God will circumcise your heart, and the heart of your children, to love the Lord your God with all your heart and with all your soul that you may live" (Deut. 30:6).

2. Holy Affection

If we are not earnest in our religion, and if our wills and inclinations are not strongly exercised, we are nothing. The importance of religion is so great that no halfhearted exercise will suffice. In nothing is the state of our heart so crucial as in religion, and in nothing is luke-warmness so odious.

True religion is a powerful thing. The power of it appears, first, in the inward exercises of the heart (which is the seat of all religion). Therefore, true religion is called "the power of godliness," in contrast to the external appearances of it, i.e., the mere "form": "Having the form of godliness but denying the power of it" (2 Tim. 3:5). The Spirit of God is a spirit of powerful holy affection in the lives of those who have a sound and solid religion. This is why it is written that God has given his people the spirit of power, and of love, and of a sound mind (2 Tim. 1:7).

When we receive the Spirit of God, we receive the baptism of the Holy Ghost who is like "fire," and along with it the sanctifying and saving influences of God. When this happens, when grace is at work within us, it sometimes "burns" within us, as it was for Jesus' disciples (Luke 24:32).

3. The Exercising of the Will

The work of religion has been compared to the doing of exercises, wherein we desire to have our hearts engaged in God. Metaphors like "running the race," "wrestling with God," "striving for the great prize," and "fighting with strong enemies" are often used to describe the exercises we engage in.

But true grace has varying degrees. There are some who are new in the faith—"babes in Christ"—in whom the inclination to engage in these exercises is weak. Yet every one of us who has the power of godliness in our heart will be inclined to seek the things of God. And

whatever our state, this power will give us strength enough to overcome our weak inclinations so that these holy exercises will prevail over our weaknesses.

For every true disciple of Christ loves him above father and mother, sister and brother, spouse and children, houses and land—yes, even above his own life. From this it follows that wherever true religion is, there is a will that moves that person to spiritual exercises. But what we said before must be remembered: the exercising of the will is nothing other than the affections of the soul.

4. The Spring of Action

The nature of human beings is to be inactive unless influenced by some affection: love or hatred, desire, hope, fear, etc. These affections are the "spring of action," the things that set us moving in our lives, that move us to engage in activities.

When we look at the world, we see that people are exceedingly busy. It is their affections that keep them busy. If we were to take away their affections, the world would be motionless and dead; there would be no such thing as activity. It is the affection we call covetousness that moves a person to seek worldly profits; it is the affection we call ambition that moves a person to pursue worldly glory; it is the affection we call lust that moves a person to pursue sensual delights. Just as worldly affections are the spring of worldly actions, so the religious affections are the spring of religious actions.

5. A Heart Deeply Affected

A person who has a knowledge of doctrine and theology only—without religious affection—

has never engaged in true religion. Nothing is more apparent than this: our religion takes root within us only as deep as our affections attract it. There are thousands who hear the Word of God, who hear great and exceedingly important truths about themselves and their lives, and yet all they hear has no effect upon them, makes no change in the way they live.

The reason is this: they are not affected with what they hear. There are many who hear about the power, the holiness, and the wisdom of God; about Christ and the great things that he has done for them and his gracious invitation to them; and yet they remain exactly as they are in life and in practice.

I am bold in saying this, but I believe that no one is ever changed, either by doctrine, by hearing the Word, or by the preaching or teaching of another, unless the affections are moved by these things. No one ever seeks salvation, no one ever cries for wisdom, no one ever wrestles with God, no one ever kneels in prayer or flees from sin, with a heart that remains unaffected. In a word, there is never any great achievement by the things of religion without a heart deeply affected by those things.

6. True Religion

The Holy Scriptures clearly see religion as a result of affections, namely, the affections of fear, hope, love, hatred, desire, joy, sorrow, gratitude, compassion and zeal.

The Scriptures see religion as the result of *holy fear*. Truly religious persons tremble at the Word of God. It is his holiness that makes them fear. The fear of God is a great part of godliness.

So also, *hope* in God and in the promises of God, according to the Scriptures, is a very important part of true religion. It is mentioned as one of the three great things of which religion consists (1 Cor. 13:13). "Happy is the one whose hope is in the Lord" (Ps. 146:5). It is spoken of as the helmet of the Christian soldier, "the hope of salvation" (1 Thess. 5:8). It is a sure and steadfast anchor of the soul (Heb. 6:19).

7. Participation in the Blessings

So also, *love* is given a high place in the Scriptures as a proper affection. We are called to love God, and the Lord Jesus Christ, and our neighbor. The texts that speak of the importance of love are too many to mention. The contrary affection—hatred—is also a part of true religion, but in the sense that we hate sin and evil: "The fear of the Lord is to hate evil" (Prov. 8:13).

Also, *holy desire*, which finds its expression in longing and thirsting after God, is also a part of true religion. "As the deer pants after the watering stream, so my soul pants after you, O Lord" (Ps. 42:1–2). Jesus also said, "Blessed are they who hunger and thirst after righteousness, for they shall be filled" (Matt. 5:6). This holy thirst is spoken of as a condition of participation in the blessings of eternal life.

Also, the Scriptures speak of *joy* as a great part of true religion. "Delight yourself in the Lord, and he shall give you the desires of your heart" (Ps. 37:4). It is mentioned among the principal fruits of the Spirit of grace: "The fruit of the Spirit is love, joy, . . ." (Gal. 5:22).

8. A Pleasing and Acceptable Sacrifice

Religious sorrow, mourning, and brokenness of heart are also frequently spoken of as a great part of true religion, a distinguishing quality of the saints. "Blessed are they that mourn," said Jesus, "for they shall be comforted" (Matt. 5:4).

It is also a pleasing and acceptable sacrifice to God: "The sacrifices of God are a broken spirit; a broken and contrite heart, O God, you will not despise" (Ps. 51:17).

Another affection often mentioned is *gratitude,* the exercise of which much of true religion consists, especially as exercised in thankfulness and praise to God. This is spoken of so much in the Book of Psalms and other parts of the Bible I need not mention any particular texts.

In addition, the Holy Scriptures also speak of *compassion* as an essential affection in true religion, so much so that all of the good characters in the Bible demonstrate it. The Scriptures choose this quality as the one which will determine who is righteous: "The righteous show mercy" (Ps. 37:21). It is our way of honoring God: "He that honors the Lord shows mercy to the poor" (Prov. 14:31). Jesus himself said it is the way we obtain mercy: "Blessed are the merciful, for they shall receive mercy" (Matt. 5:7).

9. Missing from the Lukewarm

Finally, *zeal* is spoken of as a very essential part of true religion. It is spoken of as something which Christ had in mind for us when he paid for our redemption: "Who gave himself for us, that he might redeem us from all iniquity, and purify unto himself a peculiar people, zealous of good works" (Titus 2:14). It was also the essential thing missing from the lukewarm Laodiceans (Rev. 3:15–16).

I have mentioned only a few texts out of an innumerable multitude to show that throughout the Bible, true religion is placed in the affections. The only way to deny this claim is to use some rule other than the Bible by which to measure the nature of true religion.

BIBLE SELECTION: DEUTERONOMY 10:12–22

[12]So now, O Israel, what does the LORD your God require of you? Only to fear the LORD your God, to walk in all his ways, to love him, to serve the LORD your God with all your heart and with all your soul, [13]and to keep the commandments of the LORD your God and his decrees that I am commanding you today, for your own well-being. [14]Although heaven and the heaven of heavens belong to the LORD your God, the earth with all that is in it, [15]yet the LORD set his heart in love on your ancestors alone and chose you, their descendants after them, out of all the peoples, as it is today. [16]Circumcise, then, the foreskin of your heart, and do not be stubborn any longer. [17]For the LORD your God is God of gods and Lord of lords, the great God, mighty and awesome, who is not partial and takes no bribe, [18]who executes justice for the orphan and the widow, and who loves the strangers, providing them food and clothing. [19]You shall also love the stranger, for you were strangers in the land of Egypt. [20]You shall fear the LORD your God; him alone you shall worship; to him you shall hold fast, and by his name you shall swear. [21]He is your praise; he is your God, who has done for you these great and awesome things that your own eyes have seen. [22]Your ancestors went down to Egypt seventy persons; and now the LORD your God has made you as numerous as the stars in heaven.

REFLECTION QUESTIONS

The following questions can be used for discussion within a small group, or used for journal reflections by individuals.

1. According to Edwards, what is "the spring of action," the source of motivation behind everything we do?
2. Think of a time when you decided to get involved in some activity (e.g., joining a club, learning a new sport, going to a church). What were the "affections" that led to it?
3. Edwards believes that "no one is ever changed, either by doctrine, by hearing the Word, or by the preaching or teaching of another, unless the affections are moved by these things." Describe a time when you were suddenly moved by a doctrine or a Bible verse or a sermon, and were subsequently changed.
4. According to Deuteronomy 10:12–13, what are the "affections" and what are the "actions" that are required of us?
5. Beginning in section 6, Edwards lists and describes nine affections that Scripture encourages us to have: holy fear, hope, love, holy desire, joy, religious sorrow, gratitude, compassion, and zeal. Which of these affections have you felt the most? In which would you most like to see growth?

SUGGESTED EXERCISES

The following exercises can be done by individuals, shared between spiritual friends, or used in the context of a small group. Choose one or more of the following.

1. In section 4, Edwards writes that all of us would be inactive were it not for affections. Examine your actions this week, simply writing down the things you do without any judgment. At the end of the week sit down and pencil in a probable motivation for each action. Try to be honest as you examine why you did what you did.
2. Use the list of nine holy affections in sections 6–9, focusing on the one in which you would like to see growth in your life. Notice that each affection is based on a scriptural foundation. Do a personal Bible study on that particular affection (e.g., hope), paying attention to the theology and doctrine that undergirds it (e.g., the promise of salvation).
3. In Deuteronomy 10:20ff., Moses exhorts his hearers to fear God, to cling to God and praise him, because of what God has done for them. As Edwards

notes, there must be a motivation (or affection) behind the action, and in this case the motivation for reverence, adherence, and praise is reflecting on all that God has done. Make a list of all the things that God has done for you. The list will likely be quite long. Look over this list and let praise begin to fill your mouth.

4. Worship this week. Really worship. Use Saturday evening to begin preparing for worship. Set aside a time of solitude when you can reflect on the power and the glory of God. Meditate on his love for you. Go early to church and spend time worshiping and thanking God. Pray for those around you that they might be moved by God during the service. Above all, allow yourself to truly feel the presence of God moving among the people.

REFLECTIONS

Jonathan Edwards teaches us that the intellectual life and the passionate life should be friends, not enemies. Without the slightest contradiction it is possible to be both tough-minded and tenderhearted. What we learn to do is to descend with the mind into the heart and there wait in anticipation for the heavenly Whisper. We worship God with brain and viscera!

We today desperately need this lesson because a modern myth abounds that true objectivity must be passionless. As a result, we analyze and dissect the spiritual life without the slightest personal involvement or commitment and think we understand it. But the spiritual life cannot be understood in this detached way. We understand by commitment. And we enter into commitment and sustain commitment by what Edwards rightly calls "holy affections."

GOING DEEPER

Edwards, Jonathan. *The Nature of True Virtue.* Ann Arbor, MI: University of Michigan Press, 1960. For those interested in a more philosophically oriented essay.

Edwards, Jonathan. *The Works of Jonathan Edwards.* Edited by Perry Miller. 5 vols. New Haven, CT: Yale University Press, 1959. This series (which you should be able to locate in most libraries) is the best compilation of Edwards's writings and contains more than most people are ever able to read. Volume 2 is his five-hundred-page treatise on *Religious Affections* from which the excerpt for this reading has been taken. You should also know about an edition of *Religious Affections* that was edited by James Houston of Regent College, Vancouver, B.C. It is part of an excellent series of devotional classics edited by Houston and published by Multnomah Press (Portland, OR, 1990).

Simonson, Harold. *Jonathan Edwards: Theologian of the Heart.* Grand Rapids, MI: Eerdmans, 1974. A serious interpretation of Edwards from both a literary and a theological point of view. Contrary to many scholars who focus on the influence of John Locke, Simonson insists that the deeper influences on Edwards were Calvin, Augustine, and ultimately the Bible itself. And Simonson takes seriously the heartfelt piety of Edwards as foundational for his life and thought.

Francis de Sales (1567–1622)

INTRODUCTION TO THE AUTHOR

Francis de Sales was born into a noble family at the castle of Sales and later attended a Jesuit school in Paris. The Jesuits taught him the classics, Hebrew, Greek, and the life of discipline. His training also included the study of law and the humanities. He was ordained a priest in 1591 despite opposition from his family. In 1602 he became the bishop of Geneva.

Francis was a prolific writer whose works had a great influence on the church. He combined spiritual depth with ethical concern in a way that few writers, before or after him, have been able to do. He was a master of metaphor, describing the mysteries of the spiritual life through simple, everyday images like bees and milk, birds and sugar. Because of his considerable influence, Francis is considered to be one of "the doctors of the Western Church."

In the following excerpts, Francis addresses "Philothea," a name meaning one who loves God.

EXCERPTS FROM *INTRODUCTION TO THE DEVOUT LIFE*

1. Only One True Devotion

You wish to live a life of devotion, dearest Philothea, because you are a Christian and you know that it is a virtue most pleasing to God's majesty. Since little faults committed in the beginning of a project grow infinitely greater in its course and finally are almost irreparable, above all else you must know what the virtue of devotion is.

There is only one true devotion, but there are many that are false and empty. If you are unable to recognize which kind is true, you can easily be deceived and led astray by following one that is offensive and superstitious.

2. Phantoms of Devotion

In his pictures Arelius painted all faces after the manner and appearance of the women he loved, and so too everyone paints devotion according to his own passions and fancies. Someone given to fasting thinks himself very devout if he fasts although his heart may be filled with hatred. Much concerned with sobriety, he doesn't care to wet his tongue with wine or even water but won't hesitate to drink deep of his neighbor's blood by detraction and gossip.

Another person thinks himself devout because he daily recites a vast number of prayers, but after saying them he utters the most disagreeable, arrogant, and harmful words at home and among the neighbors. Another gladly takes a coin out of his purse and gives it to the poor, but he cannot extract kindness from his heart to forgive his enemies.

Another forgives his enemies but never pays his creditors unless compelled to do so by force of law. All these individuals are usually considered to be devout, but they are by no means such. Saul's servants searched for David in his house but David's wife, Michal, had put a statue on his bed, covering it with David's clothes, and thus led them to think that it was David himself who was lying there sick and sleeping. In the same manner, many persons clothe themselves with certain outward actions connected with holy devotion, and the world believes that they are truly devout and spiritual whereas they are in fact nothing but copies and phantoms of devotion.

3. Spiritual Agility

Genuine, living devotion, Philothea, presupposes love of God, and hence it is simply true love of God. Yet it is not always love as such. Inasmuch as divine love adorns the soul, it is called grace which makes us pleasing to his Divine Majesty. Inasmuch as it strengthens us to do good, it is called charity. When it has reached a degree of perfection at which it makes us not only do good, but also do this carefully, frequently, and promptly, it is called devotion.

Ostriches never fly; hens fly in a clumsy fashion, near the ground and only once in a while, but eagles, doves, and swallows fly aloft, swiftly and frequently. In like manner, sinners in no way fly up toward God but make their whole course here upon the earth and for the earth. Good people who have not as yet attained to devotion fly toward God by their good works but do so infrequently, slowly, and awkwardly.

Devout souls ascend to God more frequently, promptly, and with lofty heights. In short, devotion is simply that spiritual agility by which charity works in us or by aid of which we work quickly and lovingly. Just as it is the function of charity to enable us to observe all God's commandments in general and without exception, so it is the part of devotion to enable us to observe them more quickly and diligently.

Hence anyone who does not observe all God's commandments cannot be held to be either good or devout. To be good a person must have charity, and to be devout, in addition to charity, he must have great zeal and readiness in performing charitable actions.

4. The Fire of Charity

Since devotion consists in a certain degree of eminent charity, it not only makes us prompt, active, and faithful in observance of God's commands, but in addition it arouses us to do quickly and lovingly as many good works as possible, both those commanded and those merely counseled or inspired. A person just recovered from illness walks only as far as he must and then slowly and with difficulty; so also a sinner just healed of an iniquity walks as far as God commands him, but he walks slowly and with difficulty until such time as he has attained to devotion. Then like someone in sound health he not only walks but runs and leaps forward "on the way of God's commandments." Furthermore, he moves and runs in the paths of his heavenly counsels and inspirations.

To conclude, charity and devotion differ no more from one another than does the flame from the fire. Charity is spiritual fire, and when it bursts into flames, it is called devotion. Hence devotion adds nothing to the fire of charity except the flame that makes charity prompt, active, and diligent not only to observe God's commandments but also to fulfill his heavenly counsels and inspirations.

5. The World Distorts Holy Devotion

Those who discouraged the Israelites from going into the Promised Land told them that it was a country that "devoured its inhabitants." In other words, they said that the air was so malignant it was impossible to live there for long, and its natives such monsters that they ate humans like locusts. It is in this manner, my dear Philothea, that the world distorts holy devotion as much as it can. It pictures devout persons as having discontented, gloomy, sullen faces and claims that devotion brings on depression and unbearable moods.

But just as Joshua and Caleb held both that the Promised Land was good and beautiful and that its possession would be sweet and agreeable, so too the Holy Spirit by the mouths of all the saints and our Lord by his own mouth assure us that a devout life is sweet, happy, and lovable.

6. They Change It into Honey

The world sees devout people as they pray, fast, endure injuries, take care of the sick, give alms to the poor, keep vigils, restrain anger, control their passions, give up sensual pleasures, and perform other actions that are rigorous in themselves and by their very nature.

But the world does not see the heartfelt inward devotion that renders all such actions pleasant, sweet, and easy. Look at the bees amid the banks of thyme. They find there a very bitter juice, but when they suck it out, they change it into honey because they have the ability to do so.

O worldly people! It is true that devout souls encounter great bitterness in their works of mortification, but by performing them they change them into something more sweet and delicious. Because the martyrs were devout men and women, fire, flame, wheel, and sword seemed to be flowers and perfume to them. If devotion can sweeten the most cruel torments and even death itself, what must it do for virtuous actions?

7. Spiritual Sugar

Sugar sweetens green fruit and in ripe fruit corrects whatever is crude and unwholesome. Now devotion is true spiritual sugar for it removes bitterness from discipline and anything harmful from our consolations. From the poor it takes away discontent, care from the rich, grief from the oppressed, pride from the exalted, melancholy from the solitary, and facturedness from those who live in society.

It serves with equal benefit as fire in winter and dew in summer. It knows how to use prosperity and how to endure want. It makes both honor and contempt useful to us. It accepts pleasure and pain with a heart that is nearly always the same, and it fills us with a marvelous sweetness.

8. Various Degrees of Charity

Consider "Jacob's ladder," for it is a true picture of the devout life. The two sides between which we climb upward and to which the rungs are fastened represent prayer, which calls down God's love, and sacraments, which confer it. The rungs are the various degrees of charity by which we advance from virtue to virtue, either by descending by deeds of help and support for our neighbor or by contemplation ascending to a loving union with God.

9. Angelic Hearts

I ask you to regard attentively those who are on this ladder. They are either people with angelic hearts or angels in human bodies. They are not young, although they seem to be so because they are so full of vigor and spiritual agility. They have wings to soar aloft in holy prayer and they also have feet to walk among people in a holy and loving way of life.

Their faces are beautiful and joyous because they accept all things meekly and mildly. Their legs, arms, and heads are uncovered because in their thoughts, affections, and deeds they have no purpose or motive but that of pleasing God. The rest of their body is clothed but only by a decent light robe because they use the world and worldly things but do so in a most pure and proper way, taking of them only what is necessary for their condition. Such are devout persons.

10. The Scent of Sweetness

Believe me, my dear Philothea, devotion is the delight of delights and queen of the virtues since it is the perfection of charity. If charity is milk, devotion is its cream; if it is a plant, devotion is its blossom; if it is a precious stone, devotion is its luster; if it is rich ointment, devotion is its beautiful scent, yes, the scent of sweetness which comforts humans and rejoices angels.

11. Every Vocation Dipped in Honey

Devotion must be exercised in different ways by the gentleman, the worker, the servant, the prince, the widow, the young girl, and the married woman. Not only is this true, but the practice of devotion must also be adapted to the strength, activities, and duties of each particular person.

Philothea, true devotion does us no harm whatsoever, but instead perfects all things. When it goes contrary to one's lawful vocation, it is undoubtedly false. "The bee," Aristotle says, "extracts honey out of flowers without hurting them" and leaves them as whole and fresh as it finds them. True devotion does better still. It not only does no injury to one's vocation or occupation, but on the contrary adorns and beautifies it. All kinds of precious stones take on greater luster when dipped into honey, each according to its color. So also every vocation becomes more agreeable when united with devotion. Care of one's family is rendered more peaceable, love of husband and wife more sincere, service of one's prince more faithful, and every type of employment more pleasant and agreeable.

12. Someone to Lead You

When commanded to go to Rages, young Tobias answered, "I do not know the way," and his father replied, "Go then and find someone to lead you." I say the same thing to you, Philothea. Do you seriously wish to travel the road to devotion? If so, look for a good person to guide and lead you. This is the most important of all words of advice. As the devout Avila says, "Although you seek God's will, you will never find it with such certainty as on the path of that humble obedience so highly praised and practiced by all devout writers."

Who shall find such a friend? The Wise Man answers, "Those who fear the Lord," that is, humble souls who sincerely desire to make spiritual progress. Since it is important for you, Philothea, to have a guide as you travel on this holy road to devotion, you must most insistently beseech God to provide you with one after his own heart. Have no misgivings in this regard for he who sent down an angel from heaven, as he did to young Tobias, will give you a good and faithful guide.

BIBLE SELECTION: ROMANS 13:8–10

[8]Owe no one anything, except to love one another; for the one who loves another has fulfilled the law. [9]The commandments, "You shall not commit adultery; You shall not murder; You shall not steal; You shall not covet"; and any other commandment, are summed up in this word, "Love your neighbor as yourself." [10]Love does no wrong to a neighbor; therefore, love is the fulfilling of the law.

REFLECTION QUESTIONS

The following questions can be used for discussion within a small group, or used for journal reflections by individuals.

1. "Everyone paints devotion according to his own passions and fancies," writes Francis de Sales, meaning that we tend to emphasize the doing of certain spiritual disciplines with which we are comfortable while neglecting others. What are some of your favorite devotional practices? Which do you find the most difficult to do?

2. Francis speaks of three stages of spiritual growth (a beginning awareness— grace; strength to do good works—charity; and the ability to do good frequently and promptly—devotion) and compares them to three types of birds (those that cannot fly—ostriches; those that fly clumsily—hens; and those that soar—eagles). Which stage (or bird!) best describes you? Why?

3. What does the nonbeliever see as he or she looks at the life of a devout person? What does the nonbeliever not see?

4. In Romans 13:10, Paul proclaims, "Love does no wrong." Francis de Sales writes in a similar fashion, "True devotion does . . . no harm whatsoever." When have you seen religious devotion actually do harm to others? Describe. When have you seen religious devotion "adorn and beautify" others?

5. Francis reminds us that devotion "must be exercised in different ways" and that it "must be adapted to the strength, activities, and duties of each particular person." Given your level of spiritual energy, your weekly activities and duties, what kind of devotional habits fit your needs?

SUGGESTED EXERCISES

The following exercises can be done by individuals, shared between spiritual friends, or used in the context of a small group. Choose one or more of the following.

1. Practice the spiritual discipline with which you are least familiar, the one you have yet to engage in with joy or regularity. Take a week to discover the joys of that spiritual discipline. Use Richard Foster's *Celebration of Discipline* or Dallas Willard's *Spirit of the Disciplines* as a guide in these uncharted waters.

2. Paul encouraged us to keep all the commandments by keeping this one: Love your neighbor as yourself (Rom. 13:9). This week do something loving for your neighbor. Treat the people around you as you would wish to be treated.

3. Find a spiritual friend. Francis encourages us to seek the help of a "good person to guide and lead you." Look for a person who shares your love and commitment to God, and ask that person to meet with you for regular prayer and encouragement and guidance.

4. The world distorts holy devotion, says Francis, because it sees only the outer actions, which appear bitter and unbearable. This week begin changing these false opinions by sharing the joy of prayer, fasting, solitude, etc., with those who do not know God. Be bold as you proclaim the joy you receive in your spiritual life.

REFLECTIONS

I'm glad for the teaching of Francis de Sales because it helps to clarify a major point of confusion in our day. It is generally assumed today that devotion means a series of religious duties to add to an already overcommitted schedule. But such is simply not the case. By themselves, the externals of religion are dry, dead, dusty stuff. No, we all need the heartfelt habit that Francis calls "charity," by which he simply means the ability to do good to all people.

Francis de Sales reminds us that on the vertical plane "true devotion" means a head-over-heels, white-hot love of God. On the horizontal plane it means a strength free of guile to serve others. May God stir up within us deep-seated yearnings for this one and only "true devotion."

GOING DEEPER

Camus, Jean Pierre. *The Spirit of Saint François de Sales.* New York: Harper & Bros., 1952.

de Sales, Francis. *Introduction to the Devout Life.* Garden City, NY: Image, 1966. This book has been recognized as a masterpiece of devotional literature for three and a half centuries. It is written for Christians of all walks of life. Its greatness lies in its originality, its completeness, its sincerity, its balance, and its penetration into spiritual reality.

de Sales, Francis. *On the Love of God.* Garden City, NY: Doubleday, 1963.

de Sales, Francis. *On the Preacher and Preaching.* Chicago: Henry Regnery, 1962.

John of the Cross (1542–1591)

INTRODUCTION TO THE AUTHOR

Born in Fantiveros, Castile, in Spain, John became a Carmelite monk in 1564. He studied philosophy and theology at the Carmelite college in Salamanca, one of Europe's leading universities. In 1567, the year he was ordained, he met with Teresa of Avila. Teresa saw great potential in John and put him in charge of the order. She admired his rigorous life-style and leadership ability. She was not disappointed, as John was able to establish several new orders.

It was during this time that he was named "John of the Cross," as a result of his suffering and commitment. He spent the rest of his life in the service of the Catholic Reform through his leadership and many writings. He was eventually arrested and put in confinement by those who opposed the reform. It was in confinement that his most famous work, *The Dark Night of the Soul,* was written. It describes the work of God upon the soul—not through joy and light, but through sorrow and darkness. The concept of the "dark night" has become an integral part of understanding the spiritual journey. Though he died four centuries ago, John of the Cross continues to exercise a significant influence on Christian spirituality.

EXCERPTS FROM *THE DARK NIGHT OF THE SOUL*

1. To Purify the Soul

At a certain point in the spiritual journey God will draw a person from the beginning stage to a more advanced stage. At this stage the person will begin to engage in religious exercises and grow deeper in the spiritual life.

Such souls will likely experience what is called "the dark night of the soul." The "dark night" is when those persons lose all the pleasure that they once experienced in their devotional life. This happens because God wants to purify them and move them on to greater heights.

After a soul has been converted by God, that soul is nurtured and caressed by the Spirit. Like a loving mother, God cares for and comforts the infant soul by feeding it spiritual milk.

Such souls will find great delight in this stage. They will begin praying with great urgency and perseverance; they will engage in all kinds of religious activities because of the joy they experience in them.

But there will come a time when God will bid them to grow deeper. He will remove the previous consolation from the soul in order to teach it virtue and prevent it from developing vice. The following sections deal with the seven capital sins. In each of the sins it becomes clear how the soul has begun to misuse its spiritual consolation and why God must take it away in order to purify the soul from these imperfections.

2. Secret Pride

Beginners in the spiritual life are apt to become very diligent in their exercises. The great danger for them will be to become satisfied with their religious works and with themselves. It is easy for them to develop a kind of secret *pride,* which is the first of the seven capital sins.

Such persons become too spiritual. They like to speak of "spiritual things" all the time. They become content with their growth. They would prefer to teach rather than to be taught. They condemn others who are not as spiritual as they are. They are like the Pharisee who boasted in himself and despised the publican who was not as spiritual as he.

The devil will often inflame their fervor so that their pride will grow even greater. The devil knows that all of their works and virtues will become valueless and, if unchecked, will become vices. For they begin to do these spiritual exercises to be esteemed by others. They want others to realize how spiritual they are. They will also begin to fear confession to an-other for it would ruin their image. So they soften their sins when they make confession in order to make them appear less imperfect.

They will beg God to take away their imperfections, but they do this only because they want to find inner peace and not for God's sake. They do not realize that if God were to take away their imperfections from them, they would probably become prouder and more presumptuous still.

But those who are at this time moving in God's way will counter this pride with humility. They will learn to think very little of themselves and their religious works. Instead, they will focus on how great and how deserving God is and how little it is that they can do for him. The Spirit of God dwells in such persons, urging them to keep their treasures secretly within themselves.

3. Attached to the Feelings

Many of these beginners will also begin to have spiritual *greed,* the second capital sin. They will become discontented with what God gives them because they do not experience the consolation they think they deserve. They begin reading many books and performing many acts of piety in an attempt to gain more and more spiritual consolation.

Their hearts grow attached to the feelings they get from their devotional life. They focus on the affect, and not on the substance of devotion. Quite often these souls will attach themselves to particular religious objects or holy places and begin to value visible things too highly.

But those who are on the right path will set their eyes on God and not on these outward things nor on their inner experiences. They will enter the dark night of the soul and find all of these things removed. They will have all the pleasure taken away so that the soul may be purified. For a soul will never grow until it is able to let go of the tight grasp it has on God.

4. Three Causes

The third sin is spiritual *luxury*. It is from this sin that all of the others proceed, and thus, it is the most important. Here is what happens: a soul which is deep in prayer may experience profound temptations and find itself powerless to prevent them. Sometimes this even happens during holy communion, or when saying confession. This happens from one of three causes.

The first cause is the physical pleasure the body takes in spiritual things. The lower part of our nature, the flesh, is sometimes stirred up during times of devotion. But it cannot possess and lay hold upon the experience, and so, begins to stir up what it can possess, namely, the impure and the sensual.

The second cause is the devil. In order to disturb and disquiet the soul the devil will try to stir up impurity within the soul, hoping that it will give heed to these temptations. The soul will begin to fear these temptations and become lax in prayer, and if they persist, it may even give up on prayer altogether.

The third cause is an inordinate fear of impure thoughts. Some souls are so tender and frail that they cannot stand such thoughts and live in great fear of them. This fear in itself can cause their downfall. They become agitated at the least disturbance and thus are too easily distracted.

When the soul enters into the dark night, all these things are put under control. The flesh will be quieted, the devil will be silent, and the fear will subside, all because of the fact that God takes away all of the sensory pleasure, and the soul is purified in the absence of it.

5. Saints in a Day

When the soul begins to enjoy the benefits of the spiritual life and then has them taken away, it becomes angry and embittered. This is the sin of spiritual *wrath*, the fourth capital sin, and it, too, must be purged in the dark night.

When their delight comes to an end, these persons are very anxious and frustrated just as an infant is angry when it is taken away from its mother's breast. There is no sin in this natural disappointment, but if it is left to itself, it may become a dangerous vice.

There are some who become angry with themselves at this point, thinking that their loss of joy is a result of something they have done or have neglected to do. They will fuss and fret and do all they can to recover this consolation. They will strive to become saints in a day. They will make all kinds of resolutions to be more spiritual, but the greater the resolution, the greater is the fall.

Their problem is that they lack the patience that waits for whatever God would give them and when God chooses to give them. They must learn spiritual meekness which will come about in the dark night.

6. Beyond the Limits of Moderation

The fifth sin is spiritual *gluttony*. Many souls become addicted to the spiritual sweetness of the devotional life and strive to obtain more and more of it. They pass beyond the limits of moderation and nearly kill themselves with spiritual exercises.

They will often try to subdue their flesh with great acts of submission, lengthy fasts, and painful penances. But note: these are one-sided penances; they do not come from God. Such persons are working their own will, and thus, grow in vice rather than in virtue.

They are not walking in true obedience, but rather, are doing what they want in the time and measure that they have chosen. They do these things not for God but for themselves, and for this reason they will soon grow weary in them. For this reason, it is probably better for these persons to give up their devotions entirely.

The problem is this: when they have received no pleasure for their devotions, they think they have not accomplished anything. This is a grave error, and it judges God unfairly. For the truth is that the feelings we receive from our devotional life are the least of its benefits. The invisible and unfelt grace of God is much greater, and it is beyond our comprehension.

It may be said that through their efforts to obtain consolation such souls actually lose their spirituality. For true spirituality consists in perseverance, patience, and humility. The sin of spiritual gluttony will prompt them to read more books and say more prayers, but God, in his wisdom, will deny them any consolation because he knows that to feed this desire will create an inordinate appetite and breed innumerable evils. The Lord heals such souls through the aridity of the dark night.

7. Weary with Spiritual Exercises

The last two sins are the vices of spiritual *envy* and spiritual *sloth*. People who fancy themselves as spiritual are quite often not pleased to hear about the spiritual growth of others. Their chief concern is to be praised themselves. They are not pleased that such attention is being given to someone else and would prefer to be thought of as the most spiritual of all. This is contrary to love, which, as Paul says, rejoices in goodness.

Spiritual sloth happens when the pleasure is removed from the spiritual life. Such souls become weary with spiritual exercises because they do not yield any consolation, and thus, they abandon them. They become angry because they are called to do that which does not fit their needs. They begin to lose interest in God for they measure God by themselves and not themselves by God. Such souls are too weak to bear the crosses that are given to us to help us grow, crosses we face in the dark night of the soul.

8. God Works Passively

Let it suffice to say, then, that God perceives the imperfections within us, and because of his love for us, urges us to grow up. His love is not content to leave us in our weakness, and for this reason he takes us into a dark night. He weans us from all of the pleasures by giving us dry times and inward darkness.

In doing so he is able to take away all these vices and create virtues within us. Through the dark night pride becomes humility, greed becomes simplicity, wrath becomes contentment, luxury becomes peace, gluttony becomes moderation, envy becomes joy, and sloth becomes strength. No soul will ever grow deep in the spiritual life unless God works passively in that soul by means of the dark night.

BIBLE SELECTION: PSALM 42

As a deer longs for flowing streams,
so my soul longs for you, O God.
²My soul thirsts for God,
for the living God.
When shall I come and behold the face
    of God?
³My tears have been my food day and night,
while people say to me continually,
"Where is your God?"

⁴These things I remember,
as I pour out my soul:
how I went with the throng,
and led them in procession to the house
    of God,
with glad shouts and songs of thanksgiving,
a multitude keeping festival.
⁵Why are you cast down, O my soul,
and why are you disquieted within me?
Hope in God; for I shall again praise him,
my help ⁶and my God.

My soul is cast down within me;
therefore I remember you

from the land of Jordan and of Hermon,
from Mount Mizar.
⁷Deep calls to deep
at the thunder of your cataracts;
all your waves and your billows
have gone over me.
⁸By day the LORD commands his steadfast
        love,
and at night his song is with me,
a prayer to the God of my life.

⁹I say to God, my rock,
"Why have you forgotten me?
Why must I walk about mournfully
because the enemy oppresses me?"
¹⁰As with a deadly wound in my body,
my adversaries taunt me,
while they say to me continually,
"Where is your God?"

¹¹Why are you cast down, O my soul,
and why are you disquieted within me?
Hope in God; for I shall again praise him,
my help and my God.

REFLECTION QUESTIONS

The following questions can be used for discussion within a small group, or used for journal reflections by individuals.

1. According to John of the Cross, why does God impose a "dark night of the soul" upon a person?
2. Of the "seven capital sins," which one do you struggle with the most?
3. Have you ever experienced what might be called a "dark night" in your spiritual journey, a time when the joys and delights seemed to vanish? Describe.
4. The psalmist cries out to God, "Why have you forgotten me?" (Ps. 42:9). What advice or encouragement would John of the Cross give to the psalmist?

5. Of the virtues mentioned by John (humility, simplicity, contentment, peace, moderation, joy, and strength), which do you feel most in need of?

SUGGESTED EXERCISES

The following exercises can be done by individuals, shared between spiritual friends, or used in the context of a small group. Choose one or more of the following.

1. Go through each of the seven capital sins, noting the characteristics of those who are struggling with it (i.e., pride: a desire to teach and not be taught, a contentment with their growth, etc.). Note which of the seven categories best describes your situation at present.

2. Ask a close friend to identify your spiritual strengths. Using the counsel of John of the Cross, examine these virtues and resolve to keep them in check, lest they become vices. By giving thanks for these strengths as gifts and not as your personal accomplishments you will enable God to use them even more in the future.

3. Abandon your spiritual disciplines for one week. While this may seem like a radical exercise, it may serve to free you from several hidden demons, such as the performance trap, pride in your spiritual works, religious addiction, and the judging of those who do less than you. Use the time to relax and enjoy God.

4. Be patient with God this week. John of the Cross consistently counsels us not to fuss and fret and take our spiritual lives into our own hands, but simply to receive what God would have us receive, no more, no less. Learn the discipline of gratitude for the small things.

REFLECTIONS

What John of the Cross calls "the dark night of the soul" is a universal experience for the great writers of devotion. To desire spiritual maturity without the dark night is like an athlete hoping to become a champion without training or an author expecting to produce a great book without thinking.

The results of this work on the soul are altogether good. In the passage you read, John of the Cross shows how the dark night helps us to be free from the "seven capital sins." He could just as well have shown how it operates in developing within us the "seven great virtues," i.e., fortitude, prudence, justice, temperance, faith, hope, and love. The point is that this is one of the key means that God uses to transform the human personality. For us, the crucial issue is our responsiveness to this passive moving of the Holy Spirit.

GOING DEEPER

Hardy, Richard. *Search for Nothing: The Life of John of the Cross.* New York: Crossroad, 1982. Useful if you are looking for a biography of this remarkable man.

John of the Cross: Selected Writings. Edited by Kieran Kavanaugh. New York: Paulist, 1987. This volume is part of the excellent series on *The Classics of Western Spirituality.* There is no better one-volume source. You should also be aware of the three-volume reference edition on *The Complete Works of Saint John of the Cross* published by Newman Press.

Wojtyla, Korl. *Faith According to Saint John of the Cross.* Translated by Jordan Aumann. San Francisco: Ignatius, 1981. This is a sample of the many articles and books that explore St. John's ideas and teaching.

Bernard of Clairvaux (1090–1153)

INTRODUCTION TO THE AUTHOR

Bernard was one of the great leaders in the history of the Church. He was an eloquent speaker and considered by many to be one of the holiest individuals who ever lived. He grew up in Dijon, France, and at the age of twenty-two entered as a novice in the monastery of Cîteaux. Three years later he was appointed to supervise a group of his fellow monks in the newly founded monastery at Clairvaux. Though he was offered high positions in the church, Bernard remained at Clairvaux until his death.

Thanks to careful preservation over the centuries, many of Bernard's writings have survived today. His works had a profound influence on both Martin Luther and John Calvin. The following reading is taken from his well-known work, his treatise *On the Love of God.* In it Bernard incisively outlines his famous "four degrees of love."

EXCERPTS FROM *ON THE LOVE OF GOD*

1. Why God Should Be Loved

You ask me, "Why should God be loved?" I answer: the reason for loving God is God himself. And why should God be loved for his own sake? Simply because no one could be more justly loved than God, no one deserves our love more. Some may question if God deserves our love or if they might have something to gain by loving him. The answer to both questions is yes, but I find no other worthy reason for loving him except himself.

God is entitled to our love. Why? Because he gave himself for us despite the fact that we are so undeserving. What better could he have given? If we ask why God is entitled to our love, we should answer, "Because he first loved us." God is clearly deserving of our love especially if we consider who he is that loves us, who we are that he loves, and how much he loves us.

And who is God? Is he not the one to whom every spirit bears witness: "Thou art my God"? God has no need of our worldly possessions. True love is precisely this: that it does not seek its own interests. And how much does he love us? He so loved the world that he gave his only Son; he laid down his life for us.

2. The First Degree of Love: Love of Self for Self's Sake

Love is a natural human affection. It comes from God. Hence the first and greatest commandment is, "Thou shalt love the Lord thy God." But human nature is weak and therefore compelled to love itself and serve itself first. In the human realm people love themselves for their own sake. This is planted within us for who ever hated his own self?

But if this love of ourselves becomes too lavish, it will overflow its natural boundaries through excessive love of pleasure. People can easily become slaves to the soul's enemy: lust. This love of self is held in check by the command to love our neighbor. If we cannot love our neighbor because of our love of self, then we must restrain our lusts and give to our neighbor's needs. Your love will then be temperate when you take from yourself and give to your neighbor.

But what will you do if your own needs are not met? Will you look to God to meet your needs? God promises that those who seek first the kingdom and his righteousness will have all things added unto them. God promises that to those who restrict themselves and give to their neighbor, he will give whatever is necessary. Seeking first the kingdom means to prefer to bear the yoke of modesty and restraint rather than allow sin to reign in your mortal body.

In order to love our neighbor we must see that God is the cause of our love. How can we have a pure love for our neighbor if we do not love him in God? And you cannot love your neighbor unless you love God. God must be loved first in order that we may love our neighbor in God.

3. The Second Degree of Love: Love of God for Self's Sake

God, therefore, who makes everything that is good, makes himself to be loved. He does it as follows: first, God blesses us with his protection. When we live free from trouble we are happy, but in our pride we may conclude that we are responsible for our security. Then, when we suffer some calamity, some storm in our lives, we turn to God and ask his help, calling upon him in times of trouble. This is how we who only love ourselves first begin to love God. We will begin to love God even if it is for our own sake. We love God because we have learned that we can do all things through him, and without him we can do nothing.

4. The Third Degree of Love: Love of God for God's Sake

In the first degree of love we love ourselves for our own sake. In the second degree of love we love God for our own sake, chiefly because he has provided for us and rescued us. But if trials and tribulations continue to come upon us, every time God brings us through, even if our hearts were made of stone, we will begin to be softened because of the grace of the Rescuer. Thus, we begin to love God not merely for our own sakes, but for himself.

In order to arrive at this we must continually go to God with our needs and pray. In those prayers the grace of God is tasted, and by frequent tasting it is proved to us how sweet the Lord is. Thus it happens that once God's sweetness has been tasted, it draws us to the pure love of God more than our needs compel us to love him. Thus we begin to say, "We now love God, not for our necessity, for we ourselves have tasted and know how sweet the Lord is."

When we begin to feel this, it will not be hard to fulfill the second commandment: to love our neighbor. For those who truly love God in this way also love the things of God. Also, it becomes easier to be obedient in all of the commands of God. We begin to love God's commands and embrace them.

This love is pure because it is disinterested (i.e., not offered in order to obtain something). It is pure because it is not merely in our words that we begin to serve, but in our actions. We love because we are loved. We care for others because Jesus cares for us.

We have obtained this degree when we can say, "Give praise to the Lord for he is good, not because he is good to me, but because he is good." Thus we truly love God for God's sake and not for our own. The third degree of love is the love by which God is now loved for his very self.

5. The Fourth Degree of Love: Love of Self for God's Sake

Blessed are we who experience the fourth degree of love wherein we love ourselves for God's sake. Such experiences are rare and come only for a moment. In a manner of speaking, we lose ourselves as though we did not exist, utterly unconscious of ourselves and emptied of ourselves.

If for even a moment we experience this kind of love, we will then know the pain of having to return to this world and its obligations as we are recalled from the state of contemplation. In turning back to ourselves we will feel as if we are suffering as we return into the mortal state in which we were called to live.

But during those moments we will be of one mind with God, and our wills in one accord with God. The prayer, "Thy will be done," will be our prayer and our delight. Just as a little drop of water mixed with a lot of wine seems to entirely lose its own identity as it takes on the taste and color of the wine; just as iron, heated and glowing, looks very much like fire, having lost its original appearance; just as air flooded with the light of the sun is transformed into the same splendor of the light so that it appears to be light itself, so it is like for those who melt away from themselves and are entirely transfused into the will of God.

This perfect love of God with our heart, soul, mind, and strength will not happen until we are no longer compelled to think about ourselves and attend to the body's immediate needs. Only then can the soul attend to God completely. This is why in the present body we inhabit this is difficult to maintain. But it is within God's power to give such an experience to whom he wills, and it is not attained by our own efforts.

6. Entering into the First, Second, and Third Degrees of Love

What are the four degrees of love? First, we love ourselves for our own sake; since we are unspiritual and of the flesh we cannot have an interest in anything that does not relate to ourselves. When we begin to see that we cannot subsist by ourselves, we begin to seek God for our own sakes. This is the second degree of love; we love God, but only for our own interests. But if we begin to worship and come to God again and again by meditating, by reading, by prayer, and by obedience, little by little God becomes known to us through experience. We enter into a sweet familiarity with God, and by tasting how sweet the Lord is we pass into the third degree of love so that now we love God, not for our own sake, but for himself. It should be noted that in this third degree we will stand still for a very long time.

7. Can We Attain the Fourth Degree of Love?

I am not certain that the fourth degree of love in which we love ourselves only for the sake of God may be perfectly attained in this life. But, when it does happen, we will experience the joy of the Lord and be forgetful of ourselves in a wonderful way. We are, for those moments, one mind and one spirit with God.

I am of the opinion that this is what the prophet meant when he said: "I will enter into the power of the Lord: O Lord I will be mindful of Thy justice alone." He felt, certainly, that when he entered into the spiritual powers of the Lord he would have laid aside self and his whole being would, in the spirit, be mindful of the justice of the Lord alone.

When we attain the fourth degree of love, then the net of charity which now, drawn through this great and vast sea, does not cease to gather together fish of every kind, when brought at last to the shore casting forth the bad, will retain only the good. Still, I do not know if we can attain this degree in this life. We live in a world of sorrow and tears and we experience the mercy and comfort of God only in that context. How can we be mindful of mercy when the justice of God alone will be remembered? Where there is no place for misery or occasion for pity, surely there can be no feeling of compassion.

BIBLE SELECTION: 1 JOHN 4:7–21

[7]Beloved, let us love one another, because love is from God; everyone who loves is born of God and knows God. [8]Whoever does not love does not know God, for God is love. [9]God's love was revealed among us in this way: God sent his only Son into the world so that we might live through him. [10]In this is love, not that we loved God but that he loved us and sent his Son to be the atoning sacrifice for our sins. [11]Beloved, since God loved us so much, we also ought to love one another. [12]No one has ever seen God; if we love one another, God lives in us, and his love is perfected in us.

[13]By this we know that we abide in him and he in us, because he has given us of his Spirit. [14]And we have seen and do testify that the Father has sent his Son as the Savior of the world. [15]God abides in those who confess that Jesus is the Son of God, and they abide in God.

[16]So we have known and believe the love that God has for us.

God is love, and those who abide in love abide in God, and God abides in them. [17]Love has been perfected among us in this: that we may have boldness on the day of judgment, because as he is, so are we in this world. [18]There is no fear in love, but perfect love casts out fear; for fear has to do with punishment, and whoever fears has not reached perfection in love. [19]We love because he first loved us. [20]Those who say, "I love God," and hate their brothers or sisters, are liars; for those who do not love a brother or sister whom they have seen, cannot love God whom they have not seen. [21]The commandment we have from him is this: those who love God must love their brothers and sisters also.

REFLECTION QUESTIONS

The following questions can be used for discussion within a small group, or used for journal reflections by individuals.

1. Which of the four stages of love have you experienced in your spiritual journey? Describe.
2. What are the motivating factors that move us from stage 1 to stage 2? Stage 2 to stage 3? Stage 3 to stage 4?
3. In your opinion, which is the most common stage of love? Why?
4. The writer of 1 John proclaims that we are able to love because God first loved us. How does the love that God has for you enable you to love God? Love yourself? Love others?
5. The fourth degree of love, writes Bernard, is a powerful moment, a sense of oneness, wherein we are "entirely transfused into the will of God." Have you ever been blessed by one of these special moments? Describe. Why are they only "temporary"?

SUGGESTED EXERCISES

The following exercises can be done by individuals, shared between spiritual friends, or used in the context of a small group. Choose one or more of the following.

1. The first stage of love is a love of ourselves for our own sake. To get beyond this stage, according to Bernard, we must see God as the one who created us and protects us. Spend some time this week reflecting on your birth, noting how you did not create yourself. Also, reflect on how your life is a gift, that even your continued existence is not your own doing.
2. The second stage of love is a love of God for self's sake, wherein we love God for all that he does, though we do not love God for who God is. Bernard believes that after years of being brought through trials by God we can begin to love God for God's sake. Why wait for tribulation? Make a list of all the times that God has brought you through trials. Use this list to help you move into that third degree of love.
3. Loving our neighbor, says Bernard, keeps our self-love in check. This week make an effort to lighten the burden of those around you, beginning with those with whom you live. The invaluable gift of listening is a great way to start.
4. Meditate on Psalm 139. This marvelous song of the glory of creation, of God's miraculous love and our miraculous existence, will help you focus on the God whose love reaches into the farthest regions of our hearts.

REFLECTIONS

If anyone deserves to stand beside St. John as an "apostle of love," it has to be Bernard. He wrote some eighty-six sermons on the Song of Solomon as an allegory of divine/human love. His beautiful hymn, "Jesus the Very Thought of Thee," reverberates with the language of divine love.

> *O hope of every contrite heart, O joy of all the meek;*
> *To those who fall, how kind thou art! How good to those who seek!*
> *But what to those who find? Ah, this No tongue nor pen can show;*
> *The love of Jesus, what it is None but His loved ones know.*

How very appropriate of Bernard to remind us of the centrality of love. We so easily elevate other things to the place of first importance: our big budgets and impressive buildings, our dedicated service to the world, our doctrinal eccentricities. But Bernard cuts through all our ego-strutting activity and calls us again to love God in purity of heart, in sincerity of soul, in holiness of life.

GOING DEEPER

Bernard of Clairvaux. Translated by Gillian Evans and edited by Richard Payne. New York: Paulist, 1987. From *The Classics of Western Spirituality.* This volume contains a very helpful introduction to Bernard by Jean LeClercq, possibly the best available. The foreword was written by the translator, Gillian Evans, who is an Oxford-trained medieval scholar.

Bernard of Clairvaux. *The Love of God.* Portland, OR: Multnomah, 1983. From the *Classics of Faith and Devotion* series. A book designed for devotional reading and introduced by James M. Houston, a former lecturer at Oxford and chancellor of Regent College. Also includes selec-

tions by Bernard's friend, William of St. Thierry.

Bernard of Clairvaux. *On the Song of Songs.* Kalamazoo, MI: Cistercian, n.d.

Bernard of Clairvaux. *Sermons on Conversion.* Kalamazoo, MI: Cistercian, n.d.

Bernard of Clairvaux. *Treatises I, Treatises II, and Treatises III.* Kalamazoo, MI: Cistercian, n.d.

Evans, Gillian. *The Mind of St. Bernard of Clairvaux.* Oxford: Oxford University Press, 1983.

James, Bruno S. *Saint Bernard of Clairvaux.* London: Hodder & Stoughton, 1957. A penetrating short biography.

LeClercq, Jean. *Bernard of Clairvaux and the Cistercian Spirit.* Kalamazoo, MI: Cistercian, n.d.

François Fénelon (1651–1715)

INTRODUCTION TO THE AUTHOR

François de Salignac de La Mothe Fénelon was a prominent member of the court of Louis XIV, serving as the tutor of the duke of Burgundy. A man of high esteem in the church, Fénelon was appointed archbishop of Cambrai in 1695. During this time he became acquainted with Madame Guyon and was greatly influenced by her and others of the Quietist movement in France. (Quietism stressed the importance of complete detachment from the things of this world.)

Fénelon's defense of Quietism (in his work *Maxims of the Saints*) created a controversy that eventually led to his denunciation by Pope Innocent XII (for "having loved God too much, and man too little"), his banishment by Louis XIV, and his appointment to a local church where he earned the reputation of being an ideal pastor.

Fénelon corresponded with many prominent figures of his day, serving as their spiritual director. His letters were compiled and published for the edification of others. The major theme of François' writing is complete love of God. The following selection reflects his constant emphasis that the spiritual life, far from being a life of drudgery, is the only way to joy.

EXCERPTS FROM *CHRISTIAN PERFECTION*

1. A Hundredfold Happiness

Christian perfection is not so severe, tiresome, and constraining as we think. It asks us to be God's from the bottom of our hearts. And since we thus are God's, everything that we do for him is easy. Those who are God's are always glad, when they are not divided, because they only want what God wants and want to do for him all that he wishes. They divest themselves of everything, and in this divesting find a hundredfold return.

Peace of conscience, liberty of heart, the sweetness of abandoning ourselves in the hands of God, the joy of always seeing the light grow in our hearts, finally, freedom from the fears and insatiable desires of the times, multiply a hundredfold the happiness which the true children of God possess in the midst of their crosses, if they are faithful.

2. A Will That Is No Longer Divided

They sacrifice themselves, but to what they love most. They suffer, but they want to suffer, and they prefer the suffering to every false joy. Their bodies endure sharp pain, their imagination is troubled, their spirit droops in weakness and exhaustion, but their will is firm and quiet in their deepest and most intimate self.

What God asks of us is a will which is no longer divided between him and any creature. It is a will pliant in his hands which neither seeks nor rejects anything, which wants without reserve whatever he wants, and which never wants under any pretext anything which he does not want. When we are in this disposition, all is well, and the most idle amusements turn to good works.

3. So Desirable a State

Happy are they who give themselves to God! They are delivered from their passions, from the judgments of others, from their malice, from the tyranny of their sayings, from their cold and wretched mocking, from the misfortunes which the world distributes to wealth, from the unfaithfulness and inconstancy of friends, from the wiles and snares of the enemy, from our own weakness, from the misery and brevity of life, from the horrors of a profane death, from the cruel remorse attached to wicked pleasures, and in the end from the eternal condemnation of God.

We are delivered from this countless mass of evils, because placing our will entirely in the hands of God, we want only what God wants, and thus we find his consolation in faith, and consequently hope in the midst of all sufferings. What weakness it would be then to fear to give ourselves to God and to undertake too soon so desirable a state!

4. Transported with Joy

Happy are they who throw themselves with bowed head and closed eyes into the arms of the "Father of mercies," and the "God of all consolation," as St. Paul said! Then we desire nothing so much as to know what we owe to God, and we fear nothing more than not to see enough what he is asking for.

As soon as we discover a new insight into our faith, we are transported with joy like a miser who has found a treasure. The true Christian, whatever the misfortunes which Providence heaps upon him, wants whatever comes and does not wish for anything which he or she does not have. The more one loves God, the more one is content. The highest perfection, instead of overloading us, makes our yoke lighter.

5. Wings to Fly on His Way

What folly to fear to be too entirely God's! It is to fear to be too happy. It is to fear to love God's will in all things. It is to fear to have too much courage in the crosses which are inevitable, too much comfort in God's love, and too much detachment from the passions which make us miserable.

So let us scorn earthly things, to be wholly God's. I am not saying that we should leave them absolutely, because when we are already living an honest and regulated life, we only need to change our heart's depth in loving, and we shall do nearly the same things which we were doing. For God does not reverse the conditions of his people, nor the responsibilities which he himself has given them, but we, to serve God, do what we were doing to serve and please the world and to satisfy ourselves.

There would be only this difference, that instead of being devoured by our pride, by our overbearing passions, and by the malicious criticism of the world, we shall act instead with liberty, courage, and hope in God. Confidence will animate us. The expectation of the eternal good things which are drawing near, while those here below are escaping us, will support us in the midst of our suffering. The love of God, which will make us conscious of God's love for us, will give us wings to fly on his way and to raise us above all our troubles. If we have a hard time believing this, experience will convince us. "Come, see and taste," said David, "how sweet is the Lord."

6. The Spirit of Love Which Makes Everything Easy

Jesus Christ said to all Christians without exception, "Let him who would be my disciple carry his cross, and follow me." The broad way leads to perdition. We must follow the narrow way which few enter. We must be born again, renounce ourselves, hate ourselves, become a child, be poor in spirit, weep to be comforted, and not be of the world which is cursed because of its scandals.

These truths frighten many people, and this is because they only know what religion exacts without knowing what it offers, and they ignore the spirit of love which makes everything easy. They do not know that it leads to the highest perfection by a feeling of peace and love which sweetens all the struggle.

Those who are wholly God's are always happy. They know by experience that the yoke of the Lord is "easy and light," that we find in him "rest for the soul," and that he comforts those who are weary and overburdened, as he himself has said.

7. Eternity Advances to Receive Us

But woe unto those weak and timid souls who are divided between God and their world! They want and they do not want. They are torn by passion and remorse at the same time. They fear the judgments of God and those of others. They have a horror of evil and a shame of good. They have the pains of virtue without tasting its sweet consolations. O, how wretched they are! Ah, if they had a little courage to despise the empty talk, the cold mockings, and the rash criticism of others, what peace they would enjoy in the bosom of God!

How dangerous it is for our salvation, how unworthy of God and of ourselves, how pernicious even for the peace of our hearts, to want always to stay where we are! Our whole life was only given us to advance us by great strides toward our heavenly country. The world escapes like a delusive shadow. Eternity already advances to receive us. Why do we delay to advance while the light of the Father of mercies shines for us? Let us hasten to reach the kingdom of God.

8. This Jealous and Dominant Love

The one commandment suffices to blow away in a moment all the excuses which we could make for having reservations from God. "Thou shalt love the Lord thy God with all thy heart, with all thy soul, with all thy mind, and with all thy strength." See how the terms were joined together by the Holy Spirit, to prevent all the reservations which a person could wish to make to the prejudice of this jealous and dominant love.

All is not too much for God. He suffers no division, and he allows us no longer to love outside of God except what God himself commands us to love for love of him. We must love only him not only with all the stretch and strength of our hearts, but also with all the concentration of our thought. How then could we believe that we love him if we cannot resolve to think on his law and to bend all our energy to doing his will?

9. Follow with a Brave Heart

Those who fear to see too clearly what this love asks fool themselves by thinking that they have this watchful and devoted love. There is only one way to love God: to take not a single step without him, and to follow with a brave heart wherever he leads.

All those who live the Christian life, and yet would very much like to keep a little in with the world, run great risk of being among the lukewarm of whom it is said they will be "spewed out of the mouth of God."

God has little patience with those weak souls who say to themselves, "I shall go this far and no farther." Is it up to the creature to make the law for his Creator? What would a king say of a subject, or a master of a servant, who only served him in his own way, who feared to care too much for his interests, and who was embarrassed in public because of belonging to him? What will the King of Kings say to us if we act like these cowardly servants?

10. This Principle of Pure Love

Why would we prefer to see the gifts of God in ourselves rather than in others, if this is not attachment to self? Whoever prefers to see them in himself than in others, will also feel badly to see them more perfect in others than in himself. Hence comes jealousy. Then what must we do? We must rejoice that God has performed his will in us, and that he reigns within us, not for our happiness, nor for our perfection because it is ours, but for God's good pleasure and for his pure glory.

This is not a fantastic subtlety, because God, who wants to strip the soul to perfect it, and will pursue it relentlessly toward a purer love, makes it really pass these tests of itself, and does not let it rest until it has taken away all reversion and all self-support from its love. Nothing is so jealous, so severe, and so sensitive as this principle of pure love. It is like the gold which is purified in the crucible. The fire consumes all that is not pure gold. We must also make crucibles of our entire hearts, to purify the divine love.

BIBLE SELECTION: 1 PETER 4:1–6

Since therefore Christ suffered in the flesh, arm yourselves also with the same intention (for whoever has suffered in the flesh has finished with sin), [2]so as to live for the rest of your earthly life no longer by human desires but by the will of God. [3]You have already spent enough time in doing what the Gentiles like to do, living in licentiousness, passions, drunkenness, revels, carousing, and lawless idolatry. [4]They are surprised that you no longer join them in the same excesses of dissipation, and so they blaspheme. ⁵But they will have to give an accounting to him who stands ready to judge the living and the dead. ⁶For this is the reason the gospel was proclaimed even to the dead, so that, though they had been judged in the flesh as everyone is judged, they might live in the spirit as God does.

REFLECTION QUESTIONS

The following questions can be used for discussion within a small group, or used for journal reflections by individuals.

1. What is the one disposition (attitude or approach) that Fénelon believes is necessary in order to move from a miserable to a joyful spiritual life?
2. Those who give themselves to God, writes Fénelon, are delivered from a "countless mass of evils." From what things has God delivered you?
3. The divided souls are those who are weak and timid, who desire to "stay where we are." Describe a time in your life when you wanted to stay where you were but God was calling you to move ahead.
4. In the Bible selection, Peter reminds his readers of their past. Consider your own past, and answer this question: How is your life different as a result of your faith?
5. Peter also addresses the problem of "peer pressure," which is a problem even among adults. As new Christians, Peter's hearers were being ridiculed by those who had known them before they changed. How have you dealt with those who knew you before you became a follower of Christ?

SUGGESTED EXERCISES

The following exercises can be done by individuals, shared between spiritual friends, or used in the context of a small group. Choose one or more of the following.

1. Make the disposition of surrender your chief aim this week. Cultivate the habit of seeking nothing but God in all you do. Use Fénelon's admonition as your guide: Do not take a single step without God.
2. Fénelon writes, "God has little patience with those weak souls who say to themselves, 'I shall go this far and no farther.'" Define your "comfort zone" this week. Examine the limits of your obedience. Ask yourself why you would only "go this far and no farther."
3. Fénelon also notes that we are often afraid of being too committed to God, afraid of being too happy. Though it sounds strange, this fear is a reality for many. Use your journal to answer the question, Why am I afraid to be happy?

4. Peter exhorts the young church, "Since therefore Christ suffered in the flesh, arm yourselves also with the same intention . . ." This week, arm yourself with the thought of Christ's suffering for you. In times of struggle, call to mind the glorious love of the Savior who willingly suffered for you.

REFLECTIONS

I like the focus Fénelon places upon the gains of a faithful discipleship. Those on the outside see only loss in following Christ. They miss entirely the great freedoms: the freedom from a stifling self-absorption; the freedom from a plotting and scheming one-upmanship; the freedom from the insecure systems of this world. And so much more.

Oh, and joy—I like the way Fénelon parses the joys of Christian living: the joy of a growing power to do the right; the joy of a peaceful conscience; the joy of "seeing the light grow in our hearts." Listen to his stirring words from a passage not in the reading, "God is so good that he only awaits our desire to overwhelm us with this gift which is himself. If we feed ourselves with Jesus Christ and his word, we shall be like a vessel in full sail with a fair wind." It almost makes you want to rush headlong into obedience, doesn't it!

GOING DEEPER

Fénelon, François. *Christian Perfection.* Minneapolis: Bethany House, 1975. This is the best known and the most important of Fénelon's writings. The essays are brief and cover a wide range of spiritual direction from "The Use of Time" to "Helps in Sadness." I must warn you not to attempt to read this book quickly. It is best read by living for days, even weeks, with one small essay before going on to the next.

Fénelon, François. *Let Go.* Springdale, PA: Whitaker House, 1973. This small book is a collection of forty letters that Fénelon wrote.

They are addressed to several earnest people at the court of Louis XIV who sought to live a life of true spirituality in the midst of a court life that was shamelessly immoral.

Fénelon, François. *The Royal Way of the Cross.* Translated by H. Sidney Lear and edited by Hal McElwaine Helms. Orleans, MA: The Community of Jesus, 1980. This book is a series of letters and spiritual counsels by Fénelon. The topics are wonderfully wide and practical.

St. Augustine (354–430)

INTRODUCTION TO THE AUTHOR

St. Augustine, the bishop of Hippo, was the great doctor of the Latin church. He was born in North Africa in 354, the son of a pagan father and a devoutly religious mother. He was brought up as a Christian and at the age of sixteen went to Carthage to complete his education in law. In 375 he became interested in philosophy and abandoned his Christian heritage. A skilled orator, Augustine was offered a professorship in Rome, where he founded his own school of rhetoric.

There he came under the influence of the philosophy of Plato and the teachings of St. Ambrose. After a long inner struggle he renounced his earlier philosophical beliefs and embraced the Christian faith. He then returned to Africa where he formed a religious community. In 391 he was ordained a priest (against his wishes) as the Vandals began an invasion of Hippo.

For thirty-four years he lived in this monastic community. He wrote a vast number of books and became known for his eloquence, logic, and spiritual passion. These three combined to make Augustine one of the most significant thinkers in the history of the Christian Church. Perhaps no one except St. Paul has been so widely read for so long. His theological insights shaped not only the age he lived in, but all the subsequent centuries of Christianity. It is difficult to find a theologian—from any age—who has not been influenced by the teachings of St. Augustine.

The following selection comes from Augustine's autobiographical work, *Confessions*. In this passage he sheds light on the eternal struggle of the will and its surrender to Christ by retelling his own conversion to the life of faith.

EXCERPTS FROM *CONFESSIONS*

1. A House Divided

My inner self was a house divided against itself. Why does this strange phenomenon occur? The mind gives an order to the body and is at once obeyed, but when it gives an order to itself, it is resisted. What causes it? The mind commands the hand to move and is so readily obeyed that the order can scarcely be distinguished from its execution. Yet the mind is mind and the hand is part of the body. But when the mind commands the mind to make an act of will, these two are one and the same and yet the order is not obeyed.

Why does this happen? The mind orders itself to make an act of will, and it would not give this order unless it willed to do so; yet it does not carry out its own command. But it does not fully will to do this thing and therefore its orders are not fully given. It gives the order only in so far as it wills, and in so far as it does not will, the order is not carried out.

2. Weighed Down by Habit

For the will commands that an act of will should be made, and it gives this command to itself, not to some other will. The reason, then, why the command is not obeyed is that it is not given with the full will. For if the will were full, it would not command itself to be full, since it would be so already.

It is therefore no strange phenomenon partly to will to do something and partly not to will to do it. It is a disease of the mind which does not wholly rise to the heights where it is lifted by the truth, because it is weighed down by habit. So there are two wills in us, because neither by itself is the whole will, and each possesses what the other lacks.

3. Torn Between Conflicting Wills

When I was trying to reach a decision about serving the Lord my God, as I had long intended to do, it was I who willed to take this course and again it was I who willed not to take it. It was I and I alone. But I neither willed to do it nor refused to do it with my full will. So I was at odds with myself. I was throwing myself into confusion. All this happened to me

although I did not want it, but it did prove that there was some second mind in me besides my own. It only meant that my mind was being punished. My action did not come from me but from the sinful principle that dwells in me (Rom. 7:17). It was part of the punishment of a sin freely committed by Adam, my first father.

When we try to make a decision, we have one soul which is torn between conflicting wills. Some say that there are two opposing minds within us, one good and the other bad, and that they are in conflict because they spring from two opposing substances or principles.

For you, O God of truth, prove that they are utterly wrong. You demolish their arguments and confound them completely. It may be that both the wills are bad. For instance, a person may be trying to decide whether to spend his money extravagantly or hoard it like a miser, or, whether to commit murder or adultery—or even a third, whether to commit theft instead. Since he cannot do all at once, his mind is torn between these wills which cannot be reconciled.

4. The Full Force of the Will

It is just the same when the wills are good. If I am trying to decide between reading one of St. Paul's epistles or one of the Psalms—or perhaps one of the gospels—some will say that in each case the will is good. Supposing, then, that a person finds all these things equally attractive and the chance to do all of them occurs at the same time, is it not true that as long as he cannot make up his mind which of them he most wants to do, his heart is torn between several different desires? All these different desires are good, yet they are in conflict with each other until he chooses a single course to which the will may apply itself to a single whole, so that it is no longer split into several different wills.

The same is true when the higher part of our nature aspires after eternal bliss while our lower self is held back by the love of temporal pleasure. It is the same soul that wills both, but it wills neither of them with the full force of the will. So it is wrenched in two and suffers great trials because while truth teaches it to prefer one course, habit prevents it from relinquishing the other.

5. On the Brink of the Resolution

This was the nature of my sickness. I was in torment, reproaching myself more bitterly than ever as I twisted and turned in my chain. I hoped that my chain might be broken once and for all, because it was only a small thing that held me now. All the same it held me. And you, O Lord, never ceased to watch over my secret heart. In your stern mercy you lashed me with the twin scourge of fear and shame in case I should give way once more and the worn and slender chain should not be broken but gain new strength and bind me all the faster.

In my heart I kept saying, "Let it be now, let it be now!" and merely by saying this I was on the point of making the resolution. I was on the point of making it, but I did not succeed. Yet I did not fall back into my old state. I stood on the brink of the resolution, waiting to take fresh breath. I tried again and came a little nearer to my goal, and then a little nearer still, so that I could almost reach out and grasp it.

But I did not reach it. I could not reach out to grasp it, because I held back from the step by which I should die to death and become alive to life. My lower instincts, which had taken hold of me, were stronger than the higher, which were untried. And the closer I came to

the moment which was to mark the great change in me, the more I shrank from it in horror. But it did not drive me back or turn me from my purpose: it merely left me hanging in suspense.

6. My State of Indecision

I was held back by all my old attachments. They plucked at my garment of flesh and whispered, "Are you going to dismiss us? From this moment we shall never be with you again, for ever and ever. From this moment on you will never again be allowed to do this thing or that." What was it, my God, when they whispered "this thing or that"? Things so sordid and shameful that I beg you in your mercy to keep the soul of your servant free from them!

These voices, as I heard them, seemed less than half as loud as they had been before. They no longer barred my way, but their mutterings seemed to reach me from behind, trying to make me turn my head when I wanted to go forward. Yet, in my state of indecision, they kept me from tearing myself away, from shaking myself free of them and leaping across the barrier to the other side where you were calling me. Habit was too strong for me when it asked, "Do you think you can live without these things?"

7. Trembling at the Barrier

But by now the voice of habit was very faint. I had turned my eyes elsewhere, and while I stood trembling at the barrier, on the other side I could see the chaste beauty of Continence in all her serene, unsullied joy, as she modestly beckoned me to cross over and to hesitate no more. She stretched out loving hands to welcome and embrace me, holding up a host of good examples to my sight.

She smiled at me to give me courage, as though she were saying, "Can you not do what these men and women do? Do you think they find the strength to do it in themselves and not in the Lord their God? It was the Lord their God who gave me to them. Why do you try to stand in your own strength and fail? Cast yourself upon God and have no fear. He will not shrink away and let you fall. Cast yourself upon him without fear, for he will welcome you and cure you of your ills."

I was overcome with shame, because I was still listening to the futile mutterings of my lower self and I was still hanging in suspense. And again Continence seemed to say, "Close your ears to the unclean whispers of your body, so that it may be mortified. It tells you of things that delight you, but not such things as the law of the Lord your God has to tell."

8. Why Not Now?

I probed the hidden depths of my soul and wrung its pitiful secrets from it, and when I mustered them all before the eyes of my heart, a great storm broke within me. Somehow I flung myself down beneath a fig tree and gave way to the tears which now streamed from my eyes. For I felt that I was still the captive of my sins, and in misery I kept crying, "How long shall I go on saying, 'Tomorrow, tomorrow'? Why not now? Why not make an end of my ugly sins at this moment?"

I was asking myself these questions, weeping all the while with the most bitter sorrow in my heart, when all at once I heard the singing of a child in a nearby house. Whether it was the voice of a boy or girl I cannot say, but again and again it repeated the refrain, "Take it and read, take it and read." At this I looked up, thinking hard whether there was any kind of game in which children used to chant words like these, but I could not remember ever hearing them before.

I stemmed my flood of tears and stood up, telling myself that this could only be a divine command to open my book of Scripture and read the first passage on which my eyes should fall. So I hurried back to the place where I had put down the book containing Paul's epistles. I seized it and opened it, and in silence I read the first passage on which my eyes fell: *Not in revelling and drunkenness, not in lust and wantonness, not in quarrels and rivalries. Rather, arm yourselves with the Lord Jesus Christ; spend no more thought on nature and nature's appetites* (Rom. 13:13, 14, editor's trans.).

I had no wish to read more and no need to do so. For in an instant, as I came to the end of the sentence, it was as though the light of confidence flooded into my heart and all the darkness of doubt was dispelled. I marked the place with my finger and closed the book. You converted me to yourself, so that I no longer placed any hope in this world but stood firmly upon the rule of faith.

BIBLE SELECTION: ROMANS 7:14–25

[14]For we know that the law is spiritual; but I am of the flesh, sold into slavery under sin. [15]I do not understand my own actions. For I do not do what I want, but I do the very thing I hate. [16]Now if I do what I do not want, I agree that the law is good. [17]But in fact it is no longer I that do it, but sin that dwells within me. [18]For I know that nothing good dwells within me, that is, in my flesh. I can will what is right, but I cannot do it. [19]For I do not do the good I want,

but the evil I do not want is what I do. [20]Now if I do what I do not want, it is no longer I that do it, but sin that dwells within me.

[21]So I find it to be a law that when I want to do what is good, evil lies close at hand. [22]For I delight in the law of God in my inmost self, [23]but I see in my members another law at war with the law of my mind, making me captive to the law of sin that dwells in my members. [24]Wretched man that I am! Who will rescue me from this body of death? [25]Thanks be to God through Jesus Christ our Lord!

So then, with my mind I am a slave to the law of God, but with my flesh I am a slave to the law of sin.

REFLECTION QUESTIONS

The following questions can be used for discussion within a small group, or used for journal reflections by individuals.

1. St. Augustine says that he felt like "a house divided," torn between two opposing desires. Have you ever had this experience? Describe.

2. A strong force that works against our inner unity, writes Augustine, is that we are weighed down by habit. What role have habits played in your struggle of commitment to God?

3. In Romans 7:19, Paul confesses that he is unable to do what he wants to do, what he knows is right and good, and yet he finds himself doing that which he does not want to do, what he knows is wrong and evil. How is Jesus Christ the solution to his problems?

4. Augustine writes about the whispers of his old habits, and how they tried to persuade him until, in time, their voices grew faint. Which voices of habit would cry out the loudest if you were to try and break that habit?

5. In the final section, Augustine asks himself, "How long shall I go on saying, 'Tomorrow, tomorrow'? Why not now? Why not make an end of my ugly sins at this moment?" How would you answer his question?

SUGGESTED EXERCISES

The following exercises can be done by individuals, shared between spiritual friends, or used in the context of a small group. Choose one or more of the following.

1. Resolve this week to bring an end to one of your bad habits. Refuse to be mastered by anything other than God. Use Augustine's story to draw encour-

agement. Do not try to master the habit by yourself; instead, rely on the strength of God.

2. Near the end of the journey, Augustine is visited by Continence, who strengthens him by showing him how other men and women have overcome their temptations. This week read about the lives of people like Jim Eliott, Hudson Taylor, and Elizabeth Fry, or any other person whose life will be an encouragement to you.

3. Continence also urged Augustine to close his ears to unclean whispers. Each time you face temptation this week, turn your attention away from its plea. In its place, turn your attention to that which is beautiful, honorable, and truthful.

4. Allow Christ to rescue you, as he did Paul, from the war within. Resolve not to resolve, but instead, resign. Let Christ have control of the struggle within.

REFLECTIONS

Few can match St. Augustine for insight into moral theology. In these selections he uncovers for us the dilemma of conflicting wills that we all experience. We are at odds with ourselves, a house divided. Because we are stamped with the image of God, we long for the good, the true, the beautiful. Because we live in a good world gone bad, we hanker after the distortions of God's good creation. We try by sheer willpower to seek the good but we fail, always fail, because the will is in conflict with itself and is in need of redemption. Merely to think good thoughts or to desire good things is not enough. We need—as did Augustine and Paul before him—the transforming power of Jesus Christ alive and present among us. Then our conflicting wills can come under the rule of the divine Arbitrator.

GOING DEEPER

Brown, Peter. *Augustine of Hippo*. Berkeley and Los Angeles: University of California Press, 1967. The best of the biographies—lively and engaging.

St. Augustine. *The Confessions*. Various editions. This book is must reading. It is one of the finest examples of the autobiographical genre, omitting as it does the trivialities and egomania that dominate contemporary autobiographies. Understanding that the evolution of the heart is the true stuff of autobiography, Augustine traces his own intellectual and spiritual pilgrimage from Manichaeanism to "the Academics" to Neoplatonism to Christ.

St. Augustine. *On Free Choice of the Will*. Translated by Anna S. Benjamin and L. H. Hackstaff. Indianapolis, IN: Bobbs-Merrill, 1964. This book has been called the "high water mark" of Augustine's philosophical writings. Using Socratic dialogue, he tackles the toughest issue for the Christian faith—the problem of evil.

The Prayer-Filled Life

THE CONTEMPLATIVE TRADITION (the Prayer-Filled Life) gives special attention to loving God. "True, whole prayer is nothing but love," says St. Augustine. Each of the following selections deals with prayer in one form or another. But what is interesting is the tremendous variety in the writers' approaches. There is Julian of Norwich, who invites us to "pray according to the goodness of God," and Douglas Steere, who reminds us to be open to "tiny promptings" and "gentle whispers"; Evelyn Underhill, who urges us to "[rise] out of the vanity of time into the riches of eternity," and George Buttrick, who calls us to "a regimen of private prayer." The variations are wide and yet they complement one another in innumerable ways.

Three of the selections are written prayers: those by Lancelot Andrews, Søren Kierkegaard, and John Baillie. It is interesting to hold them side by side and see the variety amidst unity in them. You will immediately catch the sense of utter dependence and the stress upon God's tender love that pervade all the prayers.

Notice how Martin Luther in the sixteenth century, Jean-Nicholas Grou in the eighteenth century, and Thomas Merton in the twentieth century each express concern over our attempts to manipulate God through prayer. At times we can "sin upon the right hand" through legalism (Luther), or we can avoid heart prayer by "reciting [a] set of words" (Grou), or we can try to master God through the "tricks of the spiritual life" (Merton).

Two authors who are often linked together even though they come from different centuries and widely divergent backgrounds are Brother Lawrence and Frank Laubach. The comparison is valid, for both had a profound experience of "an habitual sense of God's presence." And arching over all the teachings is Henri Nouwen's invitation to solitude, where we create an open, empty space in our hearts for God to work.

Thomas Merton (1915–1968)

INTRODUCTION TO THE AUTHOR

Born in Prades, France, Thomas Merton had a trying and painful childhood—his mother died when he was six, and his father (an artist who moved from place to place, often leaving young Thomas unattended) died when he was fifteen. In his teens and early twenties Merton led a prodigal, sensual life in his search for fulfillment.

In his mid-twenties Merton experienced a profound conversion while attending Columbia University, and he joined the Roman Catholic church. At the age of twenty-six he entered Gethsemane Abbey in Kentucky where he would live the rest of his life as a Trappist monk.

In 1948 he published *The Seven Storey Mountain,* an autobiography that mirrored the spiritual climate of the times. It quickly became an international best-seller. Merton went on to write many more books that made a significant impact on the face of Western spirituality. Known for his journal writing, meditations, and social critique, Merton continues to influence the late twentieth century in many ways.

Some criticize his attempts to bridge the gap between Eastern and Western spirituality, but he never surrendered his belief in the importance of a relationship with God through Jesus Christ. In the same vein, Merton also held a delicate balance between the inner and the outer life—contemplation and action. Because of this he was able to have an influence not only in the Church, but in the secular world as well.

His accidental death in 1968 was a tragic loss, yet Merton continues to inspire countless men and women. The following excerpts come from a little book he wrote for fellow monks, but it contains priceless wisdom for all Christians who long to go deeper in the spiritual life.

EXCERPTS FROM *CONTEMPLATIVE PRAYER*

1. Magical Methods

In meditation we should not look for a "method" or a "system," but cultivate an "attitude," an "outlook": faith, openness, attention, reverence, expectation, supplication, trust, joy. All these finally permeate our being with love in so far as our living faith tells us we are in the presence of God, that we live in Christ, that in the Spirit of God we "see" God our Father without "seeing." We know him in "unknowing." Faith is the bond that unites us to him in the Spirit who gives us light and love.

Some people may doubtless have a spontaneous gift for meditative prayer. This is unusual today. Most people have to learn to meditate. There are *ways* of meditation. But we should not expect to find magical methods, systems which will make all difficulties and obstacles dissolve into thin air.

2. Hardship in Prayer

Meditation is sometimes quite difficult. If we bear with hardship in prayer and wait patiently for the time of grace, we may well discover that meditation and prayer are very joyful experiences. We should not, however, judge the value of our meditation by "how we feel." A hard and apparently fruitless meditation may in fact be much more valuable than one that is easy, happy, enlightened, and apparently a big success.

There is a "movement" of meditation, expressing the basic "paschal" rhythm of the Christian life, the passage from death to life in Christ. Sometimes prayer, meditation, and contemplation are "death"—a kind of descent into our own nothingness, a recognition of helplessness, frustration, infidelity, confusion, igno-

rance. Note how common this theme is in the Psalms (see Pss. 39, 56).

Any effort and sacrifice should be made in order to enter the kingdom of God. Such sacrifices are amply compensated for by the results even when the results are not clear and evident to us. But effort is necessary, *enlightened, well-directed,* and *sustained.*

3. Mere Good Will

Right away we confront one of the problems of the life of prayer: that of learning when one's efforts are enlightened and well-directed and when they spring simply from our confused whims and our immature desires. It would be a mistake to suppose that mere good will is, by itself, a sufficient guarantee that all our efforts will finally attain to a good result. Serious mistakes can be made even with the greatest good will.

Certain temptations and delusions are to be regarded as a normal part of the life of prayer. But when we think we have attained a certain degree of skill in contemplation, we may find ourselves getting all kinds of strange ideas. We may even cling to them with a fierce dedication, convinced that they are supernatural graces and signs of God's blessing upon our efforts when, in fact, they simply show that one has gone off the right track and is perhaps in serious danger.

4. Guiding the Beginner

For this reason, humility and docile acceptance of sound advice are very necessary in the life of prayer. Though spiritual direction may not be necessary in the ordinary Christian life, and though a monk may be able to get along to some extent without it (many have to!), it becomes a moral necessity for anyone who is trying to deepen his or her life of prayer.

The spiritual director is someone who is capable of guiding the beginner in the ways of prayer and detecting any sign of misguided zeal and wrong-headed effort. Such a one should be listened to and obeyed, especially when the director cautions against the use of certain methods and practices which he sees to be out of place or harmful in a particular case, or when he declines to accept certain "experiences" as progress.

5. Resisting God

The right use of effort is determined by the indications of God's will and grace. When one is simply obeying God, a little effort goes a long way. When one is in fact resisting him (though claiming to have no other intention than that of fulfilling his will), no amount of effort can produce a good result.

On the contrary, the stubborn ability to go on resisting God in spite of ever clearer indications of his will is a sign that one is in great spiritual danger. Quite often we are not able to see this in ourselves. This is another reason why a spiritual director may be really necessary.

The work of the spiritual director consists not so much in teaching us a secret and infallible method for attaining to esoteric experiences, but in showing us how to recognize God's grace and his will, how to be humble and patient, how to develop insight into our own difficulties, and how to remove the main obstacles keeping us from becoming people of prayer.

6. The "Tricks" of the Spiritual Life

These obstacles may have very deep roots in our character, and in fact we may eventually learn that a whole lifetime will barely be sufficient for their removal. For example, many people who have a few natural gifts and a little ingenuity tend to imagine that they can quite easily learn, by their own cleverness, to master the methods—one might say the "tricks"—of the spiritual life.

The only trouble is that in the spiritual life there are no tricks and no shortcuts. Those who imagine that they can discover spiritual gimmicks and put them to work for themselves usually ignore God's will and his grace. They are self-confident and even self-complacent. They make up their minds that they are going to attain to this or that and try to write their own ticket in the life of contemplation.

They may even appear to succeed to some extent. But certain systems of spirituality—notably Zen Buddhism—place great stress on a severe, no-nonsense style of direction that makes short work of this kind of confidence. One cannot begin to face the real difficulties of the life of prayer and meditation unless one is first perfectly content to be a beginner and really experience himself as one who knows little or nothing and has a desperate need to learn the bare rudiments. Those who think they "know" from the beginning will never, in fact, come to know anything.

7. Imprisoned in Themselves

People who try to pray and meditate above their proper level, who are too eager to reach what they believe to be "a high degree of prayer," get away from the truth and from reality. In observing themselves and trying to convince themselves of their advance, they become imprisoned in themselves. Then when they realize that grace has left them, they are caught in their own emptiness and futility and remain helpless. *Acedia* (sloth, or apathy in spirit) follows the enthusiasm of pride and spiritual vanity. A long course in humility and compunction is the remedy!

We do not want to be beginners. But let us be convinced of the fact that we will never be anything else but beginners.

8. A Brave and Absurd Attempt to Evade Reality

Another obstacle—and perhaps this one is most common—is spiritual inertia, inner confusion, coldness, lack of confidence. This may be the case of those who, after having made a satisfactory beginning, experience the inevitable let-down which comes when the life of meditation gets to be serious.

What at first seemed easy and rewarding suddenly comes to be utterly impossible. The mind will not work. One cannot concentrate on anything. The imagination and the emotions wander away. Sometimes they run wild. At this point, perhaps, in the midst of a prayer that is dry, desolate, and repugnant, unconscious fantasies may take over. These may be unpleasant and even frightening. More often, one's inner life simply becomes a desert which lacks all interest whatever.

This may no doubt be explained as a passing trial, but we must face the fact that it is often more serious than that. It may be the result of a wrong start in which a blockage has appeared, dividing the "inner life" from the rest of one's existence. In this case, supposed "inner life" may actually be nothing but a brave and absurd attempt to evade reality altogether.

9. Firmly Rooted in Life

Under the pretext that what is "within" is in fact real, spiritual, supernatural, etc., one cultivates neglect and contempt for the "external" as worldly, sensual, material, and opposed to grace. This is bad theology and bad asceticism. In fact, it is bad in every respect because instead of accepting reality as it is, we reject it in order to explore some perfect realm of abstract ideals which in fact has no reality at all.

Very often the inertia and repugnance which characterize the so-called "spiritual life" of many Christians could perhaps be cured by a simple respect for the concrete realities of every-day life, for nature, for the body, for one's work, one's friends, one's surroundings, etc.

A false supernaturalism which imagines that "the supernatural" is a kind of realm of abstract essences (as Plato imagined) that is totally apart from and opposed to the concrete world of nature offers no real support to a genuine life of meditation and prayer. Meditation has no point unless it is firmly rooted in life.

BIBLE SELECTION: PSALM 39

I said, "I will guard my ways
that I may not sin with my tongue;
I will keep a muzzle on my mouth
as long as the wicked are in my presence."
²I was silent and still;

I held my peace to no avail;
my distress grew worse,
³my heart became hot within me.
While I mused, the fire burned;
then I spoke with my tongue:

[4]"LORD, let me know my end,
and what is the measure of my days;
let me know how fleeting my life is.
[5]You have made my days a few handbreadths,
and my lifetime is as nothing in your sight.
Surely everyone stands as a mere breath.
[6]Surely everyone goes about like a shadow.
Surely for nothing they are in turmoil;
they heap up, and do not know who will
      gather.

[7]"And now, O Lord, what do I wait for?
My hope is in you.
[8]Deliver me from all my transgressions.
Do not make me the scorn of the fool.
[9]I am silent; I do not open my mouth,
for it is you who have done it.

[10]Remove your stroke from me;
I am worn down by the blows of your hand.

[11]You chastise mortals
in punishment for sin,
consuming like a moth what is dear to them;
surely everyone is a mere breath.

[12]"Hear my prayer, O LORD,
and give ear to my cry;
do not hold your peace at my tears.
For I am your passing guest,
an alien, like all my forebears.
[13]Turn your gaze away from me, that I may
      smile again,
before I depart and am no more."

REFLECTION QUESTIONS

The following questions can be used for discussion within a small group, or used for journal reflections by individuals.

1. Describe your previous experiences with meditation.

2. Merton speaks harshly against those who would try to draw near to God through a system or a method. In what ways have you tried to manipulate God with "magical methods"?

3. Natural gifts such as ingenuity or cleverness, writes Merton, can present great problems in the spiritual life as we look for "tricks" and "shortcuts." What is wrong with this approach to spiritual growth?

4. Merton thought that Psalm 39 was a good example of how our life before God can become "a kind of descent into our own nothingness, a recognition of helplessness, frustration, infidelity, confusion, ignorance." Have you ever experienced a feeling of helplessness and frustration in your spiritual life? Describe.

5. Effort and exertion in the spiritual life, Merton believes, are helpful only if we are being led by God; if we are in fact resisting God's leading, "no amount of effort can produce a good result." If Thomas Merton were your spiritual director, and heard you share your present practices, would he describe you as one who is led, or one who is still trying to lead? Why?

SUGGESTED EXERCISES

The following exercises can be done by individuals, shared between spiritual friends, or used in the context of a small group. Choose one or more of the following.

1. Set aside fifteen minutes a day for solitude and meditation. Relax from strain and stress and simply rest in God's presence.

2. Merton believes that we need to cultivate an "attitude" in our life before God. He lists eight attitudes that unite us to God: faith, openness, attention, reverence, expectation, supplication, trust, and joy. During your times of reflection, choose one of these attitudes and nurture it by concentrating on offering short, simple prayers. For example, in *faith,* simply say, "Lord, I believe in you. I know that you can do all things, . . ."

3. Take an inventory of your bag of spiritual tricks. Which magical methods have you relied on in the past, or used as a way of manipulating God? Refuse to come before God with a false sense of control, and confess to God the sin of having reduced your relationship to mere formalism.

4. The psalmist pledges, "I will guard my ways that I may not sin with my tongue; I will keep a muzzle on my mouth as long as the wicked are in my presence." Make a similar pledge, by going through a portion of the day in silence. Silence will free you from the compulsion to control others.

REFLECTIONS

I am constantly pleased at how applicable Merton's writings are to the nonmonastic world in which most of us live. The guidance he gives on meditative prayer is practical and "bite-sized." It is something I can actually do. And the difficulties to which he alludes describe where I have been.

I am glad for this because prayer is one of those areas where we need all the help we can get. With prayer we are entering holy ground, and we simply must confess our poverty of spirit. No single denomination, or church, or group of people contains so much of the truth on this matter that it can succeed while isolating itself from the rest of the Christian community. We need the wealth of experiences and hard-won insights of all who are seeking to follow Christ and become his friend.

GOING DEEPER

Merton, Thomas. *Contemplative Prayer.* New York: Doubleday, 1969. I think this is Merton's best book. Written out of the rough texture of lived experience, it describes for us the creative and healing work of prayer that is "accomplished in silence, in nakedness of spirit, in emptiness, in humility." You should also be aware of his book *Spiritual Direction and Meditation* (Collegeville, MN: Liturgical, 1960), which covers many of the same themes.

Merton, Thomas. *Seeds of Contemplation.* New York: Dell, 1959. This was not intended to be a "popular" book and yet we can be thankful that it has become so. It is a series of mature reflections on the interior life that are just as useful to those outside the monastery walls as for those inside.

Merton, Thomas. *The Seven Storey Mountain.* New York: Harcourt, Brace, 1948. This autobiographical work is the book that brought Merton to the attention of the reading public. Merton not only thought carefully and experienced deeply, he also wrote well—a rare combination.

Merton, Thomas. *The Sign of Jonas.* New York: Harcourt, Brace, 1953. Good, solid, prophetic writing.

Julian of Norwich (1343–1413)

INTRODUCTION TO THE AUTHOR

Julian is the most popular of the English mystics. She lived as a Benedictine nun in Norwich, beside the St. Julian Church, from which she most likely took her name. Little is known about Julian's life, although she is mentioned by her contemporary, Margery Kempe.

Julian's book *Revelations of Divine Love* entitled her to become the first great female writer in the English language. Despite her disclaimers of being unskilled as an author, she wrote lively prose in a style all her own. She was well trained in the Bible as well as the teachings of the Church.

Her theology is based on her mystical experiences. She became seriously ill at the age of thirty and in the midst of her suffering prayed for a vision of Christ's passion. Once in a time of prayer Julian heard the words, "I am the foundation of your praying"—words that greatly influenced her spiritual life. She always pointed to the goodness and love of God, a light in a time of darkness for Julian, who lived in an age of social unrest and fear of the Black Plague.

Joy is perhaps the keynote in her writings. She penned the famous saying, "All shall be well and all shall be well, and all manner of things shall be well." Her writings have been called "the most perfect fruit of later medieval mysticism in England." The following selection shows both her intense desire and her sane reasoning. While her "revelations" may be hard for us today to identify with completely, they contain significant insights from which we all can learn.

EXCERPTS FROM *REVELATIONS OF DIVINE LOVE*

1. Still I Desired More

In the year 1373, on May 13, God gave me a three-fold revelation. This was his gracious gift to me in response to my desire to know him more.

The first was a deep recollection of his passion. The second was a bodily sickness. The third was to have, of God's gift, three wounds.

As to the first, it seemed to me that I had some feeling for the Passion of Christ, but still I desired to have more by the grace of God. My wish was to have been present with those who loved Christ and were with him at his passion so that I, with my own eyes, might have seen the passion which our Lord suffered for me, and so that I might have suffered with him as the others did who loved him. I never desired any other sight or revelation of God.

2. Purged by God's Mercy

As to the second grace, there came into my mind a desire of my will to have by God's gift a bodily sickness. I wished that the illness might be so severe that it seemed mortal. This was so that I might receive all the rites of the Church and to think that indeed I was about to die.

I wanted to experience every kind of pain, bodily and spiritual, which I would have if I were to die—every fear and temptation. I intended this because I wanted to be purged by God's mercy and afterwards live more to his glory because of that sickness.

These two desires about the Passion and the sickness which I desired from him were with a condition because it seemed to me that this was no ordinary kind of prayer. Therefore I prayed, "Lord, you know what I want. If it is your will that I have it, or if it is not your will, do not be displeased with my prayer, for I do not want anything that you do not want."

3. Three Wounds

As to the third, by the grace of God and the teaching of the Church I conceived a great desire to receive three wounds in my life. They were: the wound of true contrition; the wound of loving compassion; and the wound of longing with my will for God.

Though I asked for the other two conditionally, I asked urgently for this third without any condition. The two desires which I mentioned first passed from my mind, but the third remained there continually.

4. To Live to Love God Better

When I was thirty years old, God sent me a bodily sickness in which I was confined to the bed for three days and nights. On the third night I received all the rites of the Church, and I did not expect to live until morning.

After this I remained in bed for two more days, and on the sixth night I thought that I was on the point of death as did those who were with me. And yet, I felt a great reluctance to die, not because of any thing on earth which held me here or because of any fear or pain, for I trusted the mercy of God. But it was because I wanted to live to love God better and longer so that I might through the grace of that living have more knowledge and love of God than I might have even in heaven!

I realized that all the time that I had lived here was very little and short in comparison with the bliss of eternal life in heaven. I thought, "Good Lord, can my living no longer be to your glory?" With all the will of my heart I assented to be wholly God's.

5. The Image of Your Savior

I lasted until the seventh day, and by then my body felt dead from the inside. My curate was sent for to be present at my death. Before he came into the room, my eyes were fixed upwards, and I could not speak. He set the Cross before my face and said, "I have set the image of your Savior before you; look at it and take comfort from it."

It seemed to me that I was well, though my eyes were still fixed upwards, as it seemed to me that it was upwards to heaven that I was going. Nevertheless, I agreed to fix my eyes on the face of the Crucifix if I could. I did, but soon after my sight began to fail, and the room grew dark around me. As my eyes focused on the Cross, everything around it appeared ugly as if all around it were terrifying demons.

After this the upper part of my body began to die. I could not feel anything. My greatest pain was the shortness of breath. I truly believed that I was on the point of my death when suddenly, at that moment, all the pain was taken away and I was well, as well as I had ever felt before. I felt uneasy, though, wishing that I would have been delivered from this world to be with God, as my heart had longed for.

6. Hot and Flowing Freely

Then suddenly it came into my mind that I ought to wish for that first grace, that my body might be filled with a recollection of Christ's passion. It seemed to me that I might also receive the wounds which I had been praying for as well. Yet I never asked for any kind of revelation or vision from God—I only wanted to have the compassion I thought a loving soul would have for Jesus by witnessing his suffering.

It was at that moment that I saw red blood running down from under the crown, hot and flowing freely, just as it must have been beneath the crown of thorns that pressed upon his head. I fully perceived at that moment that it was Jesus, both God and man, who suffered for me, for I now knew it directly without anyone telling me.

In that same revelation, suddenly the Trinity filled my heart full of the greatest joy, and I understood that it will feel like that in heaven.

For the Trinity is God; God is the Trinity. The Trinity is our maker, the Trinity is our protector, the Trinity is our everlasting lover, the Trinity is our endless joy and bliss, by our Lord Jesus Christ and in our Lord Jesus Christ.

Where Jesus appears, the blessed Trinity is understood. I said, "Blessed be the Lord!" in a loud voice. I was astonished that our God who is to be feared and revered would be so intimate with a sinful creature such as I.

7. No Bigger Than a Hazelnut

At the same time as I saw this sight of the head bleeding, our good Lord showed a spiritual sight of his familiar love. I saw that he is to us everything which is good and comforting for our help. He is our clothing who wraps and enfolds us for love, embraces us and shelters us, surrounds us for his love which is so tender that he may never desert us. And so in this sight I saw that he is everything which is good, as I understand.

And in this he showed me something small, no bigger than a hazelnut, lying in the palm of my hand, as it seemed to me, and it was as round as a ball. I looked at it with the eye of my understanding and thought: What can this be? I was amazed that it could last, for I thought that because of its littleness, it would suddenly have fallen into nothing. And I was answered in my understanding: It lasts and always will, because God loves it; and thus everything has being through the love of God.

In this little thing I saw three properties. The first is that God made it, the second is that God loves it, the third is that God preserves it. But what did I see in it? It is that God is the Creator and the protector and the lover. For until I am substantially united to him, I can never have perfect rest or true happiness, until, that is, I am so attached to him that there can be no created thing between my God and me.

And also our good Lord revealed that it is very greatly pleasing to him that a simple soul should come naked, openly and familiarly. And lovingly I pray to thee O' God, by your goodness give me yourself, for you are enough for me.

And these words of the goodness of God are very dear to the soul and very close to touching our Lord's will, for his goodness fills all his creatures and all his blessed works full and endlessly overflows in them. For he is everlastingness, and he made us only for himself and restored us by his precious Passion and always preserves us in his blessed love; and all this is of his goodness.

8. The Highest Form of Prayer

This revelation was given to my understanding to teach our souls wisely to adhere to the goodness of God. At the same time, our habits of prayer were brought to my mind, and how, in our ignorance of love, we are accustomed to use intermediaries in our prayers. It was then I saw that it brings more honor to God and more true delight if we faithfully pray to him for his goodness than if we employ all the intermediaries in the world. Why? Because his goodness is full and complete, and in it there is nothing lacking.

We pray to God to know his passion, death, and resurrection—which come from the goodness of God. We pray to God for the strength that comes from his Cross—which also comes from the goodness of God. We pray to God with all the help of the saints who have gone before us—which, again, comes from the goodness of God. All of the strength that may come through prayer comes from the goodness of God, for he is the goodness of everything.

For the highest form of prayer is to the goodness of God. It comes down to us to meet our humblest needs. It gives life to our souls and makes them live and grow in grace and virtue. It is near in nature and swift in grace, for it is the same grace which our souls seek and always will.

9. Immeasurable Love

Just as our flesh is covered by clothing, and our blood is covered by our flesh, so are we, soul and body, covered and enclosed by the goodness of God. Yet, the clothing and the flesh will pass away, but the goodness of God will always remain and will remain closer to us than our own flesh.

God only desires that our soul cling to him with all of its strength, in particular, that it clings to his goodness. For of all of the things our minds can think about God, it is thinking upon his goodness that pleases him most and brings the most profit to our soul.

For we are so preciously loved by God that we cannot even comprehend it. No created being can ever know how much and how sweetly and tenderly God loves them. It is only with the help of his grace that we are able to persevere in spiritual contemplation with endless wonder at his high, surpassing, immeasurable love which our Lord in his goodness has for us.

Therefore we may ask from our Lover to have all of him that we desire. For it is our nature to long for him, and it is his nature to long for us. In this life we can never stop loving him.

I learned a great lesson of love in this blessed vision. For of all things, contemplating and loving the Creator made my soul seem less in its own sight and filled it full with reverent fear and true meekness and with much love for my fellow Christians.

BIBLE SELECTION: PSALM 8

O Lord, our Sovereign,
how majestic is your name in all the earth!

You have set your glory above the heavens.
[2]Out of the mouths of babes and infants
you have founded a bulwark because of your
    foes,
to silence the enemy and the avenger.

[3]When I look at your heavens, the work of
    your fingers,
the moon and the stars that you have
    established;
[4]what are human beings that you are mindful
    of them,
mortals that you care for them?

[5]Yet you have made them a little lower than
    God,
and crowned them with glory and honor.
[6]You have given them dominion over the
    works of your hands;
you have put all things under their feet,
[7]all sheep and oxen,
and also the beasts of the field,
[8]the birds of the air, and the fish of the sea,
whatever passes along the paths of the seas.

[9]O Lord, our Sovereign,
how majestic is your name in all the earth!

REFLECTION QUESTIONS

The following questions can be used for discussion within a small group, or used for journal reflections by individuals.

1. Have you ever experienced anything like what Julian calls a "revelation"? If so, describe. If not, do you believe that these experiences are real?

2. Julian's prayer, as she notes, was no ordinary prayer, and thus she added a disclaimer ("if it is not your will . . ."). What kinds of things have you yearned for and yet felt reluctant to ask them of God, uncertain of whether you were in line with God's desires?

3. Why did Julian long for her illness? What did it accomplish in her spiritual life? Has an illness ever led you or someone you know to a greater awareness of God?

4. What do you think it means to pray according to "the goodness of God," as Julian prescribes? If this were the foundation of your prayers, how might they be changed from the way you currently pray?

5. What does Psalm 8 teach us about the nature of God? About the nature and importance of human beings?

SUGGESTED EXERCISES

The following exercises can be done by individuals, shared between spiritual friends, or used in the context of a small group. Choose one or more of the following.

1. Julian was inspired at a young age with a desire for three things from God. Spend some time reflecting on this question: What three things do I most desire from God? Make them the subject of your prayers this week.

2. Experiencing the Passion or death of Jesus was a central desire of Julian, and has been the fruitful object of Christian reflection for centuries. This week center your prayer time on the passion of Christ, focusing each day on a different aspect of Christ's death.

3. Julian's meditation on the "hazelnut" led her to consider how God is the one who creates, loves, and preserves. Take a nature walk; allow yourself to marvel at creation, at how God was pleased to make each tree, each blade of grass, and how God, in his grace, preserves all that is.

4. Julian writes, "It is thinking upon [God's] goodness that pleases him most." This week focus your thoughts on the goodness of God. Seize every opportunity to speak about God's goodness among your friends. Keep thoughts of the goodness of God present wherever you go.

REFLECTIONS

Did you notice that the end result of Julian's experiences was to be drawn into a deep understanding of the goodness of God? She, in fact, called the experience of the goodness of God "the highest form of prayer."

This is a hard reality for us moderns to enter into. We have been taught that "the good life" resides in everything and anything but God. Discipleship, the cross, obedience—these are hardly words that we associate with goodness. And because we cannot see the goodness of rightness, we fail to see the goodness of God. But perhaps, just perhaps, we can take a cue from Julian—and the psalmist—to "taste and see that the Lord is good."

GOING DEEPER

Julian of Norwich. *Showings.* Translated by Edmund Colledge and James Walsh. New York: Paulist, 1978. This is part of *The Classics of Western Spirituality* series. It contains both the short and the long text and is the best in English. The Introduction is especially valuable, as are many of the Introductions throughout this series. (Sometimes this book is titled *Revelations of Divine Love.*)

Lancelot Andrews (1555–1626)

INTRODUCTION TO THE AUTHOR

Although as a young man Lancelot Andrews was a member of the Puritans, he is now remembered as one of the outstanding figures in the history of the Anglican church. Andrews became the bishop of Ely, Winchester, and Chichester, then the chaplain to Queen Elizabeth, and later, served as an apologist for King James I in his debates with Cardinal Bellarmine. He was a Fellow of Pembroke Hall, Cambridge, and one of the scholars who was appointed in 1607 to prepare the King James Version of the Bible.

Andrews was widely known as an eloquent preacher because of his wordplays and sense of humor, which contrasted starkly with the popular Puritan style of plainness.

Andrews greatly influenced author and poet T. S. Eliot, who was inspired to write a book about him. Eliot's poem "Journey of the Magi" begins with a quotation from one of Andrews's sermons.

It has been said that Andrews's great genius was his ability to compose prayers that "lift the mind up to God." The following selection is taken from a book that Andrews wrote for his own "private devotions" and never intended to publish. It consists of written prayers that Andrews used as daily devotional aids. We suggest that you use this selection as Andrews intended it, namely, as your personal prayer.

EXCERPTS FROM *PRIVATE DEVOTIONS*

1. A Light That Never Sets

Through the tender mercy of our God, the dayspring from on high has visited us. Glory be to Thee, O Lord; glory to you, Creator of the light, Enlightener of the world. God is the Lord who has shown us the light.

Glory be to you for the visible light: the sun's radiance, the flame of fire; day and night, evening and morning. For the light invisible and intellectual: that which may be known of God, that which is written in the law, oracles of prophets, melody of psalms, instruction of proverbs, experience of histories—a light which never sets.

By your resurrection raise us up into newness of life, supplying to us frames of repentance. The God of peace that brought again from the dead our Lord Jesus, that great Shepherd of the sheep, through the blood of the everlasting covenant, make us perfect in every good work to do his will. Work in us that which is pleasing in his sight, through Jesus Christ, to whom be glory for ever and ever.

You who sent down on your disciples your Thrice-Holy Spirit, do not take the gift from us, but renew it, day by day, in us who ask you for it.

2. I Have Sinned, Lord

Merciful and pitiful Lord, long-suffering and full of compassion: I have sinned, Lord, I have sinned against Thee. O wretched man that I am, I have sinned, Lord, against you grievously, as I have participated in false vanities.

I conceal nothing from you, Lord. I make no excuses. I denounce against myself my sins. Indeed, I have sinned against the Lord in the following ways, and call to mind those particular sins I wish to confess.

I have sinned and perverted that which was right, and it profited me nothing. And what shall I say now? Without plea, without excuse, I am self-condemned. I have destroyed my own self.

O Lord, righteousness belongs to you, but in me there is only confusion. You are just in bringing sentence upon me. And now, Lord, what is my hope? Is it not you, Lord? Truly my hope is in you, if I have hope left, if your loving-kindness will abound in the face of all my sins.

O Lord, remember what I am made of and who made me, for I am the work of your hands. I was made in your image, I am the reward of your blood, a name from your Name, a sheep of your pasture, a son of your Covenant.

Do not forsake the work of your own hands. Have mercy upon me, O God, according to your loving-kindness, according to the multitude of your tender mercies, blot out my transgressions.

3. Incline My Heart

I will lift up my hands into your commandments which I have loved. Open my eyes and I shall see, incline my heart and I shall desire, order my steps and I shall walk in the way of your commandments.

O Lord, be my God, and let there be no other before you. Grant me to worship you and serve you according to your commandments: with truth in my spirit, with reverence in my body, with the blessing upon my lips—both in private and in public.

Help me to show honor and submission to those who have been put over me. Help me to show affection for and care for those who have been put in my charge. Help me to overcome evil with good, to be free from the love of money, and to be content with what I have. Help me to speak the truth in love, to be desirous not to lust, or to walk after the lusts of my flesh.

O Lord, help me: To bruise the serpent's head. To consider the end of my days. To cut off occasions to sin. To be sober. Not to sit idle. To shun the company of the wicked. To make a covenant with my eyes. To bring my body into subjection. To give myself to prayer. To come to repentance.

Hedge up my way, O Lord, with thorns that I may avoid the false path of vanity. Hold me steady with the bit and the bridle so that I do not pull away from you. O Lord, compel me to come in to you.

4. This Most Holy Faith

I believe in you, O God, Father, Word, Spirit—one God. I believe that by your Fatherly love all things were created; that by your goodness and love all things have been gathered into one in your Word, who for us and for our salvation became flesh, was conceived, born, suffered, was crucified and was buried, descended, rose again, ascended, sat down, and will return and judge.

I believe that by the operation of your Holy Spirit you have called the whole world into a commonwealth of faith and holiness. I believe in the communion of saints, the forgiveness of sins in this world, and the resurrection of the flesh and life everlasting in the world to come. I believe this most holy faith, once delivered to the saints. O Lord, help me in my unbelief.

Help me to receive faith from his miraculous conception, humility from his lowly birth, patience from his suffering, power to crucify the sin in my life from his Cross, burial of all my evil thoughts in good works from his burial. Grant that I might be able to meditate on hell from his descent, to find newness of life in his resurrection, to set my mind on things above from his ascension, to judge myself in preparation of his returning judgment.

5. One Heart and One Soul

O God of truth, establish all who stand in truth, and restore all who are sick with sin and false beliefs. Remember your congregation which you purchased and redeemed long ago. Grant to all who believe that we may be of one heart and one soul.

O Lord of the harvest, send forth laborers into the field. Grant unto our clergy the ability to proclaim your word of truth and to live their lives according to those truths. Grant that these ministers who love you would obey and submit to your word of truth.

6. Profound and Perpetual Peace

O Lord, King of all nations, strengthen all the states and the leaders of the inhabited world who have been given authority from you. Scatter all the people who delight in war. Make all war cease unto the ends of the earth.

And remember especially our divinely guarded king, and work with him more and more. Prosper his ways in all things; speak good things to his heart for your Church and your people. Grant to him profound and perpetual peace, that in his tranquility we, too, may lead a quiet and peaceable life.

Grant unto farmers good seasons. Grant unto the fishermen good weather. Grant unto the tradesmen a desire not to compete with one another. Grant unto all merchants to pursue their business with lawful integrity.

O Lord, you have called us to overcome evil with good and to pray for our enemies. I ask, Lord, that you have pity on my enemies, just as you have pity on me. Lead them, together with me, into your heavenly kingdom.

7. Remember My Family and My Kin

O God, not of us only, but also of our seed, bless our children that they may grow in wisdom as in stature, in favor with you and with all people. You have called us to provide for our families, and you despise those who do not care for their households. Remember my family and my kin according to the flesh. Grant me to do all I can for their good.

Bless all who have blessed me, Lord; bless all from whom I have received blessing. Grant me, Lord, to love those who love me: my friends and my family's friends, and all of the children of my friends. Never forsake them.

8. Remember the Lonely

Remember, Lord, all the infants, the children, the youth, the young, the middle-aged, and the elderly who are hungry, sick, thirsty, naked, captive, or friendless in this world. Be with those who are tempted with suicide, those who are sick in soul, those who are in despair.

Remember those who are in prison, all those who are under sentence of death. Remember the widows and widowers, the orphans, and those who travel in a foreign land. Remember all who this day will work under oppressive conditions. Remember the lonely.

9. You Are the Fountain of Life

It is right and good that we, for all things, at all times, and in all places, give thanks and praise to you, O God. We worship you, we confess to you, we praise you, we bless you, we sing to you, and we give thanks to you: Maker, Nourisher, Guardian, Healer, Lord, and Father of all.

You are the Fountain of Life, the Treasure of everlasting goods to whom the heavens sing praise—all the angels and heavenly powers, crying out to one another—while we, the weak and unworthy join with them singing:

"Holy, holy, holy, Lord God of Hosts, the whole earth is full of the majesty of your glory."

Blessed be the glory of the Lord for his Godhead, his mysteriousness, his sovereignty, his almightiness, his eternity, and his providence.

The Lord is my strength, my strong rock, my defense, my deliverer, the horn of my salvation, and my refuge. Amen.

BIBLE SELECTION: 2 SAMUEL 7:18–29

[18]Then King David went in and sat before the LORD, and said, "Who am I, O Lord GOD, and what is my house, that you have brought me thus far? [19]And yet this was a small thing in your eyes, O Lord GOD; you have spoken also of your servant's house for a great while to come. May this be instruction for the people, O Lord GOD! [20]And what more can David say to you? For you know your servant, O Lord GOD! [21]Because of your promise, and according to your own heart, you have wrought all this greatness, so that your servant may know it. [22]Therefore you are great, O LORD God; for there is no one like you, and there is no God besides you, according to all that we have heard with our ears. [23]Who is like your people, like Israel? Is there another nation on earth whose God went to redeem it as a people, and to make a name for himself, doing great and awesome things for them, by driving out before his people nations and their gods? [24]And you established your people Israel for yourself to be your people forever; and you, O LORD, became their God. [25]And now, O LORD God, as for the word that you have spoken concerning your servant and concerning his house, confirm it forever; do as you have promised. [26]Thus your name will be magnified forever in the saying, 'The LORD of hosts is God over Israel'; and the house of your servant David will be established

before you. [27]For you, O LORD of hosts, the God of Israel, have made this revelation to your servant, saying, 'I will build you a house'; therefore your servant has found courage to pray this prayer to you. [28]And now, O Lord GOD, you are God, and your words are true, and you have promised this good thing to your servant; [29]now therefore may it please you to bless the house of your servant, so that it may continue forever before you; for you, O Lord GOD, have spoken, and with your blessing shall the house of your servant be blessed forever."

REFLECTION QUESTIONS

The following questions can be used for discussion within a small group, or used for journal reflections by individuals.

1. What has been your experience with using prayers written by another for your own devotions?

2. Lancelot Andrews offers several different types of prayer in this selection: praise, confession, petition, intercession. Which type of prayer fits your current feelings as you come before God?

3. In section 4, Andrews proclaims both his faith in God and his unbelief, pleading to God, "Help me to receive faith. . . ." How have you dealt with your own lack of faith? How might Andrews's courage to pray for faith where it is lacking provide encouragement for you?

4. Lancelot Andrews prays for God to act in significant ways, in his life and in the lives of others. How has prayer changed you? How have your prayers affected others?

5. David's original request was not denied, but it was modified by God (see 2 Sam. 7:4–16 in light of the passage listed above). What does this prayer reveal about David? About God? About prayer?

SUGGESTED EXERCISES

The following exercises can be done by individuals, shared between spiritual friends, or used in the context of a small group. Choose one or more of the following.

1. Use Lancelot Andrews's prayers as your own this week. Pray them slowly, as if they were your own words. Stay with each sentence until you can lift it to God from your own heart.

2. Write out your own prayers this week. Let the mood of your heart dictate the style of your prayer: if you feel remorse and guilt, write a prayer of confession; if you feel joy, write a prayer of praise, etc.

3. In the same manner as King David, pray on the basis of what God has promised you (see 2 Sam. 7:27–28). As in the old hymn, try "Standing on the Promises of God."

4. Take time to pray for others in the manner of Lancelot Andrews. Write out a list of all those who need your prayers. Intercede on their behalf this week.

REFLECTIONS

We can be profoundly grateful that Andrews went through the disciplines necessary to bequeath to us this legacy of devotional prayer. You may not be accustomed to written prayers. Along with the many written prayers in the Bible, the Private Devotions *of Andrews is a good place to start.*

A few suggestions may be helpful. Begin by praying the written prayers, allowing the Holy Spirit to move you beyond the words themselves. Then too, you may be drawn into composing prayers of your own. And finally, allow the Spirit to direct you to a phrase or single word that he would like to use to instruct your heart.

GOING DEEPER

Andrews, Lancelot. *Lancelot Andrews and His Private Devotions.* Translated by Alexander Whyte. Grand Rapids, MI: Baker, 1981. This classic of devotional literature was written out of the complexities of court problems in England. From the selection you have just read, you can see that the book consists of prayers composed by Andrews. The areas covered are many: meditation and adoration, confession of sin, prayer for grace, confession of faith, and many prayers of intercession.

Brother Lawrence (1611–1691)

INTRODUCTION TO THE AUTHOR

Born into a poor family in Lorraine, France, Nicholas Herman (later known as Brother Lawrence) grew up and became a soldier and a household servant. He never received any formal education, and yet he left behind one of the classic memoirs of the devotional life.

In 1666 he became a lay brother in the Discalced Carmelite order in Paris. He worked there in the kitchen, calling himself "a servant of the servants of God." He remained there until his death at the age of eighty. In his own life he determined to be an experiment of living every moment in "the presence of God." His attempts to create an habitual state of communion led to new heights of spiritual living. Like a pioneer, he discovered a new world of spiritual living that others, notably Frank Laubach and Thomas Kelly, have since traveled.

No task was too trivial for Brother Lawrence, for he was able to transform the mundane chores of the kitchen into glorious experiences of heaven. Like Benedict and Bernard of Clairvaux, he blended work with prayer.

The following selection comes from a book that was compiled after his death. His abbot, Joseph de Beaufort, collected Lawrence's letters and notes, which were found in Beaufort's room along with added accounts of conversations he had had with Lawrence. Perhaps no other writing in all of Christian literature so beautifully and simply expresses the joy of living in the presence of God.

EXCERPTS FROM *THE PRACTICE OF THE PRESENCE OF GOD*

1. An Habitual Sense of God's Presence

I write this only because you have so earnestly requested that I explain to you the method by which I have learned how to develop an habitual sense of God's presence which our Lord, in his mercy, has been pleased to grant to me.

I must tell you that it is with great difficulty that I am obliged to share this with you, and I share it only with the agreement that you show this letter to no one. If I knew that you would let it be seen, all the desire I have for your advancement would not force me to send it. Nonetheless, the account I can give to you is as follows. . . .

2. My All for God's All

I have found in many books many different ways of going to God and many different practices in living the spiritual life. I began to see that this was only confusing me, as the only thing I was seeking was to become wholly God's.

Thus, I resolved to give my all for God's all. After having given myself wholly to God that he might take away my sin, I renounced, for the love of God, everything that was not God, and I began to live as if there was none but God and I in the world.

Sometimes I imagined myself standing before him as a poor criminal at the feet of the judge. At other times I beheld him in my heart as my Father and as my God. I worshiped him as often as I could, keeping my mind in his holy presence and recalling it back to God as often as I found it had wandered from him.

3. The Difficulties That Occurred

I found a great deal of pain in this exercise, and yet I continued it even in the midst of all the difficulties that occurred, trying not to trouble myself or get angry when my mind had wandered involuntarily. I made this my business throughout the entire day in addition to my appointed times of prayer.

At all times, every hour, every minute, even at my busiest times, I drove away from my mind everything that was capable of interrupting my thought of God.

This has been my practice since the first days I entered into religion. Though I have done it imperfectly, I have found great advantages in this practice. I am aware, however, that all of these advantages are to be attributed to the mercy and goodness of God, because we can do nothing without him—especially me!

4. A Familiarity with God

But when we are faithful in keeping ourselves in his holy presence, keeping him always before us, this not only prevents our offending him or doing something displeasing in his sight (at least willfully), but it also brings to us a holy freedom, and if I may say so, a familiarity with God wherein we may ask and receive the graces we are so desperately in need of.

In short, by often repeating these acts they become *habitual,* and the presence of God becomes something that comes naturally to us. Give God thanks with me for his great goodness toward me, which I can never sufficiently admire, and for the many favors he has done for so miserable a sinner as I am.

5. The Very Best Return

I have never found this method I am describing in any books, and yet I seem to have no difficulty with it. I had a conversation a few days ago with a very devout person who told me the spiritual life was a life of grace. He said it begins with a holy fear, is increased by the hope of eternal life, and is consummated by the pure love of God. He said that each of these states has different stages and different methods by which one arrives at that blessed consummation.

I have not followed all of these methods he describes. On the contrary, I found that they discouraged me. This was the reason why I made this resolution to give myself wholly to God as the very best return I could to him for his love. Because of my love for God, I then renounced all.

6. Faith Alone Was Enough

For the first year I spent much of the time set apart for devotions thinking about death, judgment, hell, heaven, and my sins. I continued this for a few years, applying my mind to these thoughts in the morning and then spending the rest of the day, even in the midst of all my work, in the presence of God. I considered that he was always with me, that he was even within me.

After a while I accidently began doing the same thing in my set times of devotion as I had been doing the rest of the day. This produced great delight and consolation. This practice produced in me so high an esteem for God that faith alone was enough to satisfy all my needs.

7. The Source and Substance of My Suffering

This was how I began. And yet, I must tell you that for the first ten years I suffered a great deal. The awareness that I was not as devoted to God as I wanted to be, the awareness of my past sins which were always present in my mind, and the great yet unmerited favors God did for me were the source and substance of my suffering.

During this time I sinned often only to rise again soon. It seemed to me that all the creatures of the world, all reason, and even God were against me. All that was in my favor was

faith. I was troubled and sometimes with the thought that all of my blessings in this endeavor were merely my own presumption, pretending to have arrived at this state so easily while others arrive with great difficulty. At other times I thought that this was all merely a willful delusion and that, in attempting this, I had lost my hope of salvation.

8. An Habitual, Silent, and Secret Conversation

When I finally reached a point where I wanted to quit, I found myself changed all at once. In my soul, which until that time was in distress, I suddenly felt a profound inward peace as if it were in its true place of rest.

Ever since that time I have walked before God in simple faith, with humility and with love, and I apply myself diligently to do nothing and think nothing which might displease him. I hope that when I have done what I can, he will do with me what he pleases.

As for what happens to me these days, I cannot express it. I no longer have any pain or difficulty because I have no will except that of God's, which I endeavor to do in all things, and to which I am so resigned that I would not pick up a straw from the ground against his will, or for any other motive than out of pure love for God.

I have since given up all forms of devotions and set prayers except those which are suitable to this practice. I make it my business only to persevere in his holy presence wherein I keep myself by a simple attention and a general fond regard to God, which I refer to as an *actual presence* of God. Or, to put it another way, an habitual, silent, and secret conversation of the soul with God. This often causes me to have feelings of inward rapture—and sometimes outward ones! They are so great that I am forced to have to moderate them and conceal them from others.

9. Full of Mercy and Goodness

In short, I am assured beyond any doubt that my soul has been with God for nearly thirty years. I have not shared it all so as not to bore you, but I think it is proper that I tell you what manner I imagine myself before God whom I behold as king.

I imagine myself as the most wretched of all, full of sores and sins, and one who has committed all sorts of crimes against his king. Feeling a deep sorrow, I confess to him all of my sins, I ask his forgiveness, and I abandon myself into his hands so that he may do with me what he pleases.

This king, full of mercy and goodness, very far from chastening me, embraces me with love, invites me to feast at his table, serves me with his own hands, and gives me the key to his treasures. He converses with me, and takes delight in me, and treats me as if I were his favorite. This is how I imagine myself from time to time in his holy presence.

10. The Inexpressible Sweetness

My most useful method is this simple attention, done with a passionate regard toward God to whom I find myself often attached with greater sweetness and delight than that of an infant at its mother's breast. So much so that— if I dare use this expression—I choose to call this state the bosom of God because of the inexpressible sweetness which I taste and experience there.

If sometimes my thoughts wander from God because of necessity, I am recalled back to God soon after by inward sensations so charming and delicious that I am afraid to speak of them. I desire you to see and know my great wretchedness rather than the great favors which God does for me, unworthy and ungrateful as I am.

11. A Stone Before a Sculptor

As for my set hours of prayer, they are only a continuation of the same exercise. Sometimes I imagine myself as a stone before a sculptor from which he will carve a beautiful statue. Presenting myself before God, I ask him to form his perfect image in my soul and make me entirely like himself.

At other times when I apply myself to prayer, I feel all of my spirit and all of my soul lift itself up without any care or any effort on my part. It continues as if it were suspended and firmly fixed in God, as in its center and place of rest.

I know that some will accuse me of inactivity, of delusion, and of self-love. I confess that it is a holy inactivity, and would be a happy self-love if the soul in that state were capable of it, because in reality, while I am in this state of repose, I cannot be disturbed by such emotions which were formerly my strength and support, but which in that state hinder rather than assist.

I cannot allow this state to be called a delusion because the soul which enjoys God in this manner desires nothing except God. If this is a delusion in me, it belongs to God to remedy it. Let him do what he pleases with me; I desire only him and to be wholly devoted to him.

BIBLE SELECTION: PSALM 108

My heart is steadfast, O God, my heart is
        steadfast;
I will sing and make melody.
Awake, my soul!
[2]Awake, O harp and lyre!
I will awake the dawn.
[3]I will give thanks to you, O LORD, among the
        peoples,
and I will sing praises to you among the
        nations.
[4]For your steadfast love is higher than the
        heavens,
and your faithfulness reaches to the clouds.

[5]Be exalted, O God, above the heavens,
and let your glory be over all the earth.
[6]Give victory with your right hand, and
        answer me,
so that those whom you love may be rescued.

[7]God has promised in his sanctuary:
"With exultation I will divide up Shechem,
and portion out the Vale of Succoth.
[8]Gilead is mine; Manasseh is mine;
Ephraim is my helmet;
Judah my scepter.
[9]Moab is my washbasin;
on Edom I hurl my shoe;
over Philistia I shout in triumph."

[10]Who will bring me to the fortified city?
Who will lead me to Edom?
[11]Have you not rejected us, O God?
You do not go out, O God, with our armies.
[12]O grant us help against the foe,
for human help is worthless.
[13]With God we shall do valiantly;
it is he who will tread down our foes.

REFLECTION QUESTIONS

The following questions can be used for discussion within a small group, or used for journal reflections by individuals.

1. Brother Lawrence speaks of his confusion over the "many different ways of going to God" that he read about in books, until finally he resolved to relate to God in a way that fit his needs. What personal approach to living with God have you found most helpful?

2. In his early attempts at practicing the presence of God, Brother Lawrence was hindered by a wandering mind. What has helped you as you have endeavored to overcome this struggle?

3. In section 8, Brother Lawrence confesses, "I finally reached a point where I wanted to quit." What happened at that very moment that changed his life forever?

4. Brother Lawrence abandoned "all forms of devotions and set prayers" because he wanted all his life, not simply an hour here and there, to be lived in an attitude of prayer. Can you relate to this desire? How might "practicing the presence of God" help you?

5. The psalmist proclaims God's faithfulness and gives God praise for his steadfast love. What attributes of God move you to praise and adoration?

SUGGESTED EXERCISES

The following exercises can be done by individuals, shared between spiritual friends, or used in the context of a small group. Choose one or more of the following.

1. Experiment with practicing the presence of God this week. Develop the habit of returning to God even in the midst of your daily tasks.

2. Brother Lawrence wrote this selection to a friend as a means of helping that person grow closer to God. Write a letter to a friend this week, sharing some of the things that have helped you in your devotional life.

3. Allow yourself to abandon your set times of prayer in favor of developing the holy habit of a continuous sense of God's presence for one week.

4. Memorize Psalm 108. Repeat it while you are at work, thus helping you to glorify God in all that you do.

REFLECTIONS

It is quite amazing that such an ordinary person could produce such an extraordinary book. Lawrence called himself "the lord of all pots and pans" in honor of his regular employment in the kitchen. Yet he took this simple work and turned it into "the sacrament of the present moment."

I hope his experience will encourage us. Most of us are in jobs largely devoid of glamour, status, or prestige. Seldom will our daily decisions make much difference on the world scene. Yet we too can know this habitual practice of the presence of God. And perhaps that experience is the most important of all.

GOING DEEPER

Brother Lawrence. *The Practice of the Presence of God.* Translated by John J. Delaney. New York: Doubleday, 1977. This is a fresh English translation and contains an in-depth Introduction and a brief Foreword by Henri J. M. Nouwen. This simple book shows us how to "trust God once and for all and abandon ourselves to Him alone." The universal appeal is found in the fact that this ordinary man, Lawrence of the Resurrection, found a way to be always in the presence of God, and he shows that we too can live in this way.

Douglas V. Steere (1901–)

INTRODUCTION TO THE AUTHOR

Douglas Steere was educated at Michigan State, Harvard, and Oxford in the early decades of the twentieth century. A Rhodes scholar, brilliant thinker, and skilled author of many fine devotional books, Steere has spent most of his life teaching philosophy at Haverford College and is a member of the Society of Friends (Quakers).

He is one of the few American authors in the past century who has combined academic integrity with spiritual authenticity. He also holds a delicate balance between contemplation (the inner life) and action (the outer life). He and his wife, Dorothy, have traveled on many missions to Africa, Europe, and Asia as members of the American Friends Service Committee.

The following selection comes from a book first published in 1938 titled *Prayer and Worship*. This particular selection deals with the subject of "intercessory prayer," that is, praying for people and/or events. As is his style, Steere invites us to engage in this highly important work of prayer while keeping in mind the necessity of responding to God's call through action.

EXCERPTS FROM *PRAYER AND WORSHIP*

1. The Inner Springs of Prayer

Prayer for others is a form of petitional prayer that makes deep demands on the faith of an individualistic generation that has so largely lost its sense of inner community. Yet, at no point, do we touch the inner springs of prayer more vitally than here.

For when we hold up the life of another before God, when we expose it to God's love, when we pray for its release from drowsiness, for the quickening of its inner health, for the power to throw off a destructive habit, for the restoration of its free and vital relationship with its fellows, for its strength to resist temptation, for its courage to continue against sharp opposition—only then do we sense what it means to share in God's work, in his concern; only then do the walls that separate us from others go down and we sense that we are at bottom all knit together in a great and intimate family.

2. No Greater Intimacy

There is no greater intimacy with another than that which is built through holding him or her up in prayer. The firm bond that existed between John Frederic Oberlin and his parish was laid each morning in the hour that he devoted to prayer for his individual parishioners. We are told that as they went past his house at this hour in the morning, they did so in quiet, for they knew what was happening there.

Forbes Robinson's *Letters to His Friends* reveals his constant use of this form of prayer for his Cambridge associates. He remarks in one letter that if he really would reach some need in his friend's life, he would always prefer a half-hour's silent petition for him to an hour's conversation with him.

3. The Power of Renovation

An unbeliever once mockingly begged Catherine of Siena that she pray for his soul. She prayed by day and by night, and the power of renovation disarmed and brought him to his knees. I know of a Japanese girl whose father had found a whole chain of reverses too much for him to meet normally and who had taken the alcoholic shortcut. She prayed for him hour after hour until the time came when he yielded, gave up drink, committed his life to the center of Divine love he had experienced, and with the help and love of his devoted family he has continued a new way of life.

4. Lapping at the Shores of Our Lives

It is not a question of changing God's mind or of exercising some magical influence or spell over the life of another. Before we begin to pray, we may know that the love of the One who is actively concerned in awakening each life to its true center is already lapping at the shores of that life. We do not do it at all.

Such prayer is only cooperation with God's active love in besieging the life or new areas of the life of another, or of a situation. If you pray for something other than what is in keeping with that cooperation, you go against the grain, and if you remain in prayer and are sensitive, you will realize this and be drawn to revise it. As in all petitional prayer, the one who really prays must be ready to yield.

5. You Are Called

You may pray for the release of some area of life in a friend and find that you are called upon to set right something in your own life that has acted as a stumbling block to him. You may pray that your friend be given courage to endure certain hardships and find that you are drawn to pack your bag and go and join him or that you are to give up your pocket money for the next month or even perhaps to give a fortnight's or a month's salary to help along his cause. In intercessory prayer one seldom ends where one began.

6. Tiny Promptings, Gentle Whispers

During these active forms of work in the silence: in contrition, in purification, in simplification and refreshment, in petition, and in intercession, frequently, if we were sensitive and listening, there come clear insights of things to be done. Often they come in that receptive silent waiting after we have opened our needs and where we do nothing but wait for direction. Again, they may come during the day and push their way in between events that seem to bear no connection with them.

These insights are precious and to be heeded if we are to live in response to that which we feel in prayer. When they involve some real adjustments that may be costly to effect, the Quakers have called these *concerns*. They lack a word for the tiny promptings, the gentle whispers that are equally as important and that may represent concerns in the forming.

7. The Molten Freedom of the Person

"Prayer is incipient action," and these clues are the lines along which the molten freedom of the person in prayer is to be cast. "Mind the Light" reads an inscription on a sundial. Come under holy obedience.

Here is the unformed side of life's relationships—the letters to be written, the friends to be visited, the journey to be undertaken, the suffering to be met by food, or nursing care, or fellowship. Here is the social wrong to be resisted, the piece of interpretive work to be undertaken, the command to "rebuild my churches," the article to be written, the wrong to be forgiven, the grudge to be dropped, the relationship to be set right, the willingness to serve God in the interior court by clear honest thinking, and the refusal to turn out shoddy work.

8. Established in the Power

Yet we need more than the intimations. We need spiritual staying power to carry them out. "Profession of truth, without the life and power, is but a slippery place, which men may easily slide from," wrote Isaac Penington. He commends his own practice of praying to be established in the power that will enable him to carry out these leadings. "I wait on him for the strength to fulfill it."

Here in the silence, as that power gathers, it is well to face the difficulty one will meet in carrying out this concern. Here in the silence it is well to see the only semi-inflammable character of the bridge you mean to burn; to face the inertia, the resistances, the amused smiles of friends; the coldness and want of under-

standing on the part of many who resent having their attention called to social justice in which they are involved—the strangling doubts of your own later hours—doubts that led Teresa of Avila to say: "I see few people who have not too much sense for everything they have to do." These need to be met and overcome in the silence.

9. The Precious Chain of Influence

If we ignore these leadings, they poison future prayer. Katherine Mansfield wrote, "I went upstairs and tried to pray, but I could not, for I had done no work." And if they are ignored, they break the precious chain of influence that this act may have set going. You become a link in this chain when you begin to pray. If you fail, it must wait for another. "Were you faithful? Did you yield?"

There is nothing greater than this constant fidelity. "The world goes forward," wrote Harold Gray, who served a term in Leavenworth during the war for his conscientious objection, "because in the beginning one man or a few were true to the light they saw and by living by it enabled others to see." Holy obedience to the insights, the concerns that come, that persist, and that are in accord with cooperation with God's way of love is not only the active side of prayer, but is the only adequate preparation for future prayer.

10. Loving Back

There can be no complete prayer life that does not return to the point from which we began—the prayer that is a response to the outpouring love and concern with which God lays siege to every soul. When that reply to God is most direct of all, it is called *adoration*. Adoration is "loving back." For in the prayer of adoration we love God for himself, for his very being, for his radiant joy.

"Religion is adoration," was a favorite remark of that veteran of prayer, Friedrich von Hügel. "The most fundamental need, duty, honor, and happiness of men is not petition or even contrition, nor again, even thanksgiving . . . but *adoration*." Adoration is not alone a special stage in prayer, although it may be that, too. All the truest prayer is shot through with it and its mood is the background to all real contrition, petition, and intercession.

In adoration we enjoy God. We ask nothing except to be near him. We want nothing except that we would like to give him all. Out of this kind of prayer comes the cry "Holy! Holy! Holy!" In the school of adoration the soul learns why the approach to every other goal had left it restless.

BIBLE SELECTION: DEUTERONOMY 9:12–21

[12]Then the LORD said to me, "Get up, go down quickly from here, for your people whom you have brought from Egypt have acted corruptly. They have been quick to turn from the way that I commanded them; they have cast an image for themselves." [13]Furthermore the LORD said to me, "I have seen that this people is indeed a stubborn people. [14]Let me alone that I may destroy them and blot out their name from under heaven; and I will make of you a nation mightier and more numerous than they."

[15]So I turned and went down from the mountain, while the mountain was ablaze; the two tablets of the covenant were in my two hands. [16]Then I saw that you had indeed sinned against the LORD your God, by casting for yourselves an image of a calf; you had been quick to turn from the way that the LORD had commanded you. [17]So I took hold of the two tablets and flung them from my two hands, smashing them before your eyes. [18]Then I lay prostrate before the LORD as before, forty days and forty nights; I neither ate bread nor drank water, because of all the sin you had committed, provoking the LORD by doing what was evil in his sight. [19]For I was afraid that the anger that the LORD bore against you was so fierce that he would destroy you. But the LORD listened to me that time also. [20]The LORD was so angry with Aaron that he was ready to destroy him, but I interceded also on behalf of Aaron at that same time. [21]Then I took the sinful thing you had made, the calf, and burned it with fire and crushed it, grinding it thoroughly, until it was reduced to dust; and I threw the dust of it into the stream that runs down the mountain.

REFLECTION QUESTIONS

The following questions can be used for discussion within a small group, or used for journal reflections by individuals.

1. When a friend comes to you with a problem, which are you most likely to do: pray for the friend, help the friend, or a combination of the two?

2. Steere notes that when we pray for people we will, on many occasions, be led to do something for them in addition to praying for them. How do you know when God wants you to do more than pray for a person?

3. Steere also notes that during our times of prayer we will often be led to make amends in our own lives before offering a prayer of petition. How does this compare with your own experience?

4. Steere describes the work of prayer as "cooperation with God's active love." Why is this awareness so crucial?

5. Moses tells the people, in Deuteronomy 9:19, that it was his prayer that saved them from destruction. In what instances have you become aware of the power of prayer to effect real changes in particular situations?

SUGGESTED EXERCISES

The following exercises can be done by individuals, shared between spiritual friends, or used in the context of a small group. Choose one or more of the following.

1. Steere relates the story of John Frederic Oberlin and how he prayed for members of his church each morning. Whether or not you are a pastor, set aside some time each morning for intercessory prayer for the members of your church.

2. Steere also tells the stories of Catherine of Siena and the young Japanese girl, both of whom prayed for people and saw dramatic changes. Commit one person to prayer this week that you know needs to experience God's love.

3. Listen for "the tiny promptings, the gentle whispers" of God during your times of prayer. Be open to hearing what you can do in the situations for which you are praying.

4. Become a living prayer this week by writing a letter, donating food, visiting the sick, or setting a relationship right. In doing so you might just become someone else's answer to prayer.

REFLECTIONS

No human activity draws us more deeply into the heart of God than prayer. And no way of prayer places us more solidly into the affairs of human life than intercessory prayer. This is as it should be. Love of God, of necessity, leads to love of neighbor. They are not two commands, but one.

As we learn to love people—truly love them—we will desire for them far more than it is within our power to give them, and that will drive us all the more deeply into prayer for them. The converse is also true: the more we pray for people the more we will come to love them. Here, then, is a penetrating test of our devotion: if we do not pray for people—truly pray for them—how can we say that we love them?

GOING DEEPER

Steere, Douglas V. *On Beginning from Within—On Listening to Another.* New York: Harper & Row, 1964. Essays concerned with the intensification of the life of God in the individual hearts of men and women.

Steere, Douglas V. *Prayer and Worship.* Richmond, IN: Friends United Press, 1978. A slender volume well worth many readings. It addresses the question of why so many Christians "atrophy away on the early plateaus of the religious life" and offers a prescription for spiritual growth rooted in private prayer and corporate worship.

Steere, Douglas V. *Together in Solitude.* New York: Crossroad, 1982. Here, selected essays by Douglas Steere are brought together to compose a lovely and varied bouquet on the interior life. Among the best chapters is the case study of Baron Friedrich von Hügel as spiritual director.

Steere, Douglas V. *Work and Contemplation.* New York: Harper & Bros., 1957. A book that shows Steere's deep conviction that the interior life must be fused with a concern for action.

Henri J. M. Nouwen (1932–)

INTRODUCTION TO THE AUTHOR

Henri Nouwen was born in Nijkerk, Holland, and came to the United States in 1964. A Roman Catholic priest and psychologist, he has taught at several prestigious universities, including Yale, Harvard, and Notre Dame. He is the author of over twenty books, among them *The Genesee Diary*, *The Wounded Healer*, and *With Open Hands*, with the more recent ones being *Gracias* and *The Road to Daybreak*.

Nouwen's spiritual pilgrimage has brought him in recent years to serve the mentally handicapped in L'Arche, an international network of communities. After spending one year in Trosly, France, he has been at Daybreak in Richmond Hills, Ontario, Canada, since 1986. At a L'Arche home, the mentally handicapped and their assistants live together as God's children trying to enflesh the gospel. Assistants provide basic care for their charges: cooking, cleaning, encouraging, and praying.

Henri Nouwen's spiritual sensitivity is both refreshing and prophetic. The following selection invites us to intimacy, invites us to the spiritual life.

EXCERPTS FROM *MAKING ALL THINGS NEW*

1. Hard Work

The spiritual life is a gift. It is the gift of the Holy Spirit, who lifts us up into the kingdom of God's love. But to say that being lifted up into the kingdom of love is a divine gift does not mean that we wait passively until the gift is offered to us.

Jesus tells us to set our hearts on the kingdom. Setting our hearts on something involves not only serious aspiration but also strong determination. A spiritual life requires human effort. The forces that keep pulling us back into a worry-filled life are far from easy to overcome.

"How hard it is," Jesus exclaims, ". . . to enter the kingdom of God!" (Mark 10:23, JB). And to convince us of the need for hard work, he says, "If anyone wants to be a follower of mine, let him renounce himself and take up his cross and follow me" (Matt. 16:24, JB).

2. The Small, Gentle Voice

Here we touch the question of discipline in the spiritual life. A spiritual life without discipline is impossible. Discipline is the other side of discipleship. The practice of a spiritual discipline makes us more sensitive to the small, gentle voice of God.

The prophet Elijah did not encounter God in the mighty wind or in the earthquake or in the fire, but in the small voice (see 1 Kings 19:9–13). Through the practice of a spiritual discipline we become attentive to that small voice and willing to respond when we hear it.

3. From an Absurd to an Obedient Life

From all that I said about our worried, over-filled lives, it is clear that we are usually surrounded by so much outer noise that it is hard to truly hear our God when he is speaking to us. We have often become deaf, unable to know when God calls us and unable to understand in which direction he calls us.

Thus our lives have become absurd. In the word *absurd* we find the Latin word *surdus*, which means "deaf." A spiritual life requires discipline because we need to learn to listen to God, who constantly speaks but whom we seldom hear.

When, however, we learn to listen, our lives become obedient lives. The word *obedient* comes from the Latin word *audire*, which means "listening." A spiritual discipline is necessary in order to move slowly from an absurd to an obedient life, from a life filled with noisy worries to a life in which there is some free inner space where we can listen to our God and follow his guidance.

Jesus' life was a life of obedience. He was always listening to the Father, always attentive to his voice, always alert for his directions. Jesus was "all ear." That is true prayer: being all ear for God. The core of all prayer is indeed listening, obediently standing in the presence of God.

4. The Concentrated Effort

A spiritual discipline, therefore, is the concentrated effort to create some inner and outer space in our lives, where this obedience can be practiced. Through a spiritual discipline we prevent the world from filling our lives to such an extent that there is no place left to listen. A spiritual discipline sets us free to pray or, to say it better, allows the Spirit of God to pray in us.

5. A Time and a Space

Without solitude it is virtually impossible to live a spiritual life. Solitude begins with a time and a place for God, and him alone. If we really believe not only that God exists but also that he is actively present in our lives— healing, teaching, and guiding—we need to set aside a time and a space to give him our undivided attention. Jesus says, "Go to your private room and, when you have shut your door, pray to the Father who is in that secret place" (Matt. 6:6, JB).

6. Inner Chaos

To bring some solitude into our lives is one of the most necessary but also most difficult disciplines. Even though we may have a deep desire for real solitude, we also experience a certain apprehension as we approach that solitary place and time. As soon as we are alone, without people to talk with, books to read, TV to watch, or phone calls to make, an inner chaos opens up in us.

This chaos can be so disturbing and so confusing that we can hardly wait to get busy again. Entering a private room and shutting the door, therefore, does not mean that we immediately shut out all our inner doubts, anxieties, fears, bad memories, unresolved conflicts, angry feelings, and impulsive desires. On the contrary, when we have removed our outer distractions, we often find that our inner distractions manifest themselves to us in full force.

We often use these outer distractions to shield ourselves from the interior noises. It is thus not surprising that we have a difficult time being alone. The confrontation with our inner conflicts can be too painful for us to endure.

This makes the discipline of solitude all the more important. Solitude is not a spontaneous response to an occupied and preoccupied life. There are too many reasons not to be alone. Therefore we must begin by carefully planning some solitude.

7. Write It in Black and White

Five or ten minutes a day may be all we can tolerate. Perhaps we are ready for an hour every day, an afternoon every week, a day every month, or a week every year. The amount of time will vary for each person according to temperament, age, job, lifestyle, and maturity.

But we do not take the spiritual life seriously if we do not set aside some time to be with God and listen to him. We may have to write it in black and white in our daily calendar so that nobody else can take away this period of time. Then we will be able to say to our friends, neighbors, students, customers, clients, or patients, "I'm sorry, but I've already made an appointment at that time and it can't be changed."

8. Bombarded by Thousands of Thoughts

Once we have committed ourselves to spending time in solitude, we develop an attentiveness to God's voice in us. In the beginning, during the first days, weeks, or even months, we may have the feeling that we are simply wasting our time. Time in solitude may at first seem little more than a time in which we are bombarded by thousands of thoughts and feelings that emerge from hidden areas of our minds.

One of the early Christian writers describes the first stage of solitary prayer as the experience of a man who, after years of living with open doors, suddenly decides to shut them. The visitors who used to come and enter his home start pounding on his doors, wondering why they are not allowed to enter. Only when they realize that they are not welcome do they gradually stop coming.

This is the experience of anyone who decides to enter into solitude after a life without much spiritual discipline. At first, the many distractions keep presenting themselves. Later, as they receive less and less attention, they slowly withdraw.

9. Tempted to Run Away

It is clear that what matters is faithfulness to the discipline. In the beginning, solitude seems so contrary to our desires that we are constantly tempted to run away from it. One way of running away is daydreaming or simply falling asleep. But when we stick to our discipline, in the conviction that God is with us even when we do not yet hear him, we slowly discover that we do not want to miss our time alone with God. Although we do not experience much satisfaction in our solitude, we realize that a day without solitude is less "spiritual" than a day with it.

10. The First Sign of Prayer

Intuitively, we know that it is important to spend time in solitude. We even start looking forward to this strange period of uselessness.

This desire for solitude is often the first sign of prayer, the first indication that the presence of God's Spirit no longer remains unnoticed.

As we empty ourselves of our many worries, we come to know not only with our mind but also with our heart that we were never really alone, that God's Spirit was with us all along. Thus we come to understand what Paul writes to the Romans, "Sufferings bring patience . . . and patience brings perseverance, and perseverance brings hope, and this hope is not deceptive, because the love of God has been poured into our hearts by the Holy Spirit which has been given to us" (Rom. 5:4–6, JB).

11. The Way to Hope

In solitude, we come to know the Spirit who has already been given to us. The pains and struggles we encounter in our solitude thus become the way to hope, because our hope is not based on something that will happen after our sufferings are over, but on the real presence of God's healing Spirit in the midst of these sufferings.

The discipline of solitude allows us gradually to come in touch with this hopeful presence of God in our lives, and allows us also to taste even now the beginnings of the joy and peace which belong to the new heaven and the new earth.

The discipline of solitude, as I have described it here, is one of the most powerful disciplines in developing a prayerful life. It is a simple, though not easy, way to free us from the slavery of our occupations and preoccupations and to begin to hear the voice that makes all things new.

BIBLE SELECTION: 1 KINGS 19:9–13

⁹At that place he came to a cave, and spent the night there.

Then the word of the LORD came to him, saying, "What are you doing here, Elijah?" ¹⁰He answered, "I have been very zealous for the LORD, the God of hosts; for the Israelites have forsaken your covenant, thrown down your altars, and killed your prophets with the sword. I alone am left, and they are seeking my life, to take it away."

¹¹He said, "Go out and stand on the mountain before the LORD, for the LORD is about to pass by." Now there was a great wind, so strong that it was splitting mountains and breaking rocks in pieces before the LORD, but the LORD was not in the wind; and after the wind an earthquake, but the LORD was not in the earthquake; ¹²and after the earthquake a fire, but the LORD was not in the fire; and after the fire a sound of sheer silence. ¹³When Elijah heard it, he wrapped his face in his mantle and went out and stood at the entrance of the cave. Then there came a voice to him that said, "What are you doing here, Elijah?"

REFLECTION QUESTIONS

The following questions can be used for discussion within a small group, or used for journal reflections by individuals.

1. Henri Nouwen refers to the twofold nature of the spiritual life: it is both a gift and hard work on our part. How has your journey been like receiving a gift? In what ways has it been hard work?

2. We engage in the spiritual disciplines, writes Nouwen, in order to "prevent the world from filling our lives to such an extent that there is no place left to listen." What things are currently filling your life and preventing you from listening?

3. Solitude, according to Nouwen, creates space for God, but it also removes our protective distractions, forcing us to deal with our inner chaos. Why does this make solitude all the more important for us?

4. The thoughts that bombard us during times of solitude may be compared with visitors who are no longer welcome. How does Nouwen use this analogy to help us feel encouraged as we do battle with distractions?

5. God could have spoken to Elijah in the violent wind, the earthquake, or the fire, but instead chose to speak in a still small voice. How has God used silence to speak to you?

SUGGESTED EXERCISES

The following exercises can be done by individuals, shared between spiritual friends, or used in the context of a small group. Choose one or more of the following.

1. This week make the move from an absurd to an obedient life by actively listening to God in solitude. Begin to push aside the distractions as you engage in the discipline of solitude.

2. Do not run from distractions but, rather, turn them into prayers. Keep a pad and pencil by your chair as you relax in solitude; when a distracting thought comes into your mind, write it down and then commit it to prayer.

3. Schedule appointments with God. Nouwen suggests that we actually write our devotional times in our daily calendars. This will help us keep our appointments with God, and it will prevent others from usurping this precious time.

4. Get up early next Sunday and go to the sanctuary for a time of solitude before worship. Spend an hour or so listening to God, and praying for the people who will share this space with you.

REFLECTIONS

Solitude is one of the deepest disciplines of the spiritual life because it crucifies our need for importance and prominence. Everyone—including ourselves at first—will see our solitude as a waste of good time. We are removed from "where the action is." That, of course, is exactly what we need. In silence and solitude God slowly but surely frees us from our egomania.

In time we come to see that the really important action occurs in solitude. Once we have experienced God at work in the soul, all the blare and attention of the world seem like a distant and fragmentary echo. Only then are we able to enter the hustle and bustle of today's machine civilization with perspective and freedom.

GOING DEEPER

Nouwen, Henri J. M. *The Genesee Diary: Report from a Trappist Monastery.* New York: Walker, 1985. A journal record of Nouwen's stay at the upstate New York monastery near Rochester.

Nouwen, Henri J. M. *Making All Things New: An Invitation to the Spiritual Life.* San Francisco: Harper & Row, 1981. This slender volume calls us into the depths of a spiritual life. It tries to answer the twin questions, "What does it mean to live a spiritual life?" and "How do we live it?"

Nouwen, Henri J. M. *The Road to Daybreak: A Spiritual Journey.* New York: Doubleday, 1988. The story of Nouwen's journey to the L'Arche community. He writes: "The noncompetitive life with mentally handicapped people, their gifts of welcoming me regardless of name or prestige, and the persistent invitation to 'waste some time' with them opened in me a place that until then had remained unavailable to me, a place where I could hear the gentle invitation of Jesus to dwell with Him. My sense of being called to L'Arche was based more on what I had to receive than on what I had to give."

Nouwen, Henri J. M. *The Wounded Healer: Ministry in Contemporary Society.* New York: Doubleday, 1979. A living exegesis on how we can minister healing and wholeness in today's broken world.

George A. Buttrick (1892–1980)

INTRODUCTION TO THE AUTHOR

Born in England in 1892, George Buttrick was educated at Lancaster Independent College. He later came to the United States and was ordained by the Congregational church in 1915. Five years later he entered the Presbyterian ministry. In 1927 he became the pastor of Madison Avenue Presbyterian Church in New York City and served there until his death in 1980.

During his ministry Buttrick delivered many lectures and addresses at colleges and universities around the world. He was also a gifted writer on the spiritual life. His book *Prayer* is considered to be one of the most thorough and comprehensive works on prayer ever written. The following selection deals with the actual practice of prayer, offering the reader, in his words, "detailed guidance." May God use these "hints," as Buttrick calls them, to better your life of prayer.

EXCERPTS FROM *PRAYER*

1. A Simple Regimen of Private Prayer

We now attempt to give some clear and detailed guidance in private prayer. There can be no rules, certainly no binding rules, but only hints. Yet no one need travel an unmarked path. The saints are our teachers; and other people, versed in prayer, who would be aghast to be called saints. Jesus himself is *the* Teacher.

Prayer is friendship with God. Friendship is not formal, but it is not formless: it has its cultivation, its behavior, its obligations, even its disciplines; and the casual mind kills it. So we offer here, as a guide-map not as a chain, a simple regimen of private prayer.

2. An Orderly Quietness

Prayer begins, not in asking, but in *a silent self-preparation*. We should not rush into the Presence; the church of private devotion should be entered through the vestibule in an orderly quietness. This comes best as a by-product of a mind focused on God. We say to ourselves, "His light fills the world. It fills this room." Thus we meditate.

The next step is an *act of faith*, on which Jesus laid the constant stress: "All things, whatsoever ye ask in prayer, believing, ye shall receive." In this initial silence of prayer we say to ourselves that whatever we ask "in the nature of Christ" is ours, granted only our earnestness in prayer and life. Always prayer is prefaced by an act of faith. We take counsel with our certitudes, not with our doubts and fears.

3. The Widespread Mercy

In prayer itself there is no fixed order, but both a primary impulse and the experience of praying people show that the first stage may be *thanksgiving*.

A lecturer to a group of businessmen displayed a sheet of white paper on which was one blot. He asked what they saw. All answered, "A blot." The test was unfair: it invited the wrong answer. Nevertheless, there is an ingratitude in human nature by which we notice the black disfigurement and forget the widespread mercy.

We need deliberately to call to mind the joys of our journey. Perhaps we should try to write down the blessings of one day. We might begin: we could never end: there are not pens or paper enough in all the world. The attempt would remind us of our "vast treasure of content."

4. Rooted in Life Beyond Life

Therefore the prayer of thanksgiving should be quite specific: "I thank thee for *this* friendship, *this* threat overpassed, *this* signal grace." "For all thy mercies" is a proper phrase for a general collect, but not a private gratitude. If we are "thankful for everything," we may end by being thankful for nothing.

The thanksgiving should also probe deep, asking, "What are life's *abiding* mercies?" Thus gratitude would be saved from earthliness and circumstance, and rooted in Life beyond life.

"Count your many blessings," says the old hymn, "and it will surprise you what the Lord hath done." This prayer should end in glad and solemn resolve: "Lord, seal this gratitude upon my face, my words, my generous concern for my neighbors, my every outward thought and act."

5. Setting Hooks into the Facts

Prayer may next become *confession*. A rebound of nature hints that this is a wise order: "God has been exceedingly kind, and I have given him selfishness for love." True confession is neither self-excoriation—"To be merciless with anyone, even ourselves, is no virtue"—nor casual evasion. Overconscientiousness becomes morbid: underconscientiousness becomes indifference and decay.

Confession to those we have wronged is sometimes, not always, wise: there are circumstances in which such confession would spread and aggravate the hurt. But confession to God, whom we have more deeply wronged, is always wise: he has understanding and love.

Our sin is against the Living Order, and we have neither inward peace nor inward power until we have offered prayers of penitence. Confession, like thanksgiving, should be specific. It should not be ruthless, but it should not excuse: it should set hooks into the facts. "I confess *this* sharp judgment, *this* jealousy, *this* cowardice, *this* bondage of dark habit, *this* part in the world's evil."

6. New Freedom in His Grace

Contrition is not easy work: it is surgery. But, like surgery, it is not an end in itself: the wise prayer of confession always leads to an acceptance of God's pardon ... God does not wish us to remember, except as a reminder of our dependence, for he is willing to forget anything.

It might be wise to rise from kneeling at this point in the prayer as a token of our acceptance of God's pardon, our sure faith in his absolution, and our new freedom in his grace. That standing erect might also symbolize both our resolve to make wise restoration insofar as we have power to mend our blunders, and our sincere renunciation of our sins.

Confession is incomplete without that resolve. Our will, however feeble it may be, must descend squarely on the side of a new life. Otherwise even our penitence may become a self-deceit and an abuse of God's goodness. But true confession is a cleansing of the soul.

7. Love Sees Faces

Then may follow a prayer of *intercession*, without which the most earnest prayer might sink into selfishness. *The Lord's Prayer* in almost every phrase keeps us mindful of our neighbors: *"Our* Father" ... *"our* daily bread" ... *"our* trespasses."

Private intercession should be specific. "We humbly beseech Thee for all sorts and conditions of people," is an appropriate phrase in a collect—which, as the very word indicates, draws all worshipers into one act of devotion, and provides a form into which each worshiper may pour his secret prayer—but it is out of place in individual petition.

Genuine love sees faces, not a mass: the good shepherd "calleth his own sheep by name." Intercession is more than specific: it is pondered: it requires us to bear on our heart the burden of those for whom we pray.

8. Its Heart Entreaty

Whose name should come first? Perhaps the name of our enemies. The injunction of Jesus is plain: "Pray for them which despitefully use you." He told us that worship is vain if we are embittered; that we should be wise to leave our gift before the altar, go to make peace with our neighbor, and then worship. Only then can we truly worship. So the first intercession is, "Bless So-and-so whom I foolishly regard as an enemy. Bless So-and-so whom I have wronged. Keep them in Thy favor. Banish my bitterness."

Intercession also names the leaders of mankind in statecraft, medicine, learning, art, and religion; the needy of the world; our friends at work or play, and our loved ones. A sense of responsibility may prompt us to prepare a chart of intercession, so that day by day we may enter earnestly into the needs of the world, and not forget nor fail anyone who closely depends upon our prayers.

So true intercession is specific and pondered. It is also daring: it carries on its heart-entreaty the crisis of the world. Like thanksgiving, it is not complete without our vow. Sincere prayer-in-love is never in vain.

9. Before Eternal Eyes

The fourth order in our prayer may be *petition*. It comes last, not because it is most important, but because it needs the safeguard of earlier prayer. We should not fear to lift *our* earthly needs before Eternal Eyes, for we are held in Eternal Love.

But we should fear the encroachment of a selfish mind. Petition is defended against that threat if first we give thanks, confess our sins, and pray for our neighbors. Then the petition may have free course.

Sometimes, in sorrow, dread, or helplessness, it will be a crisis cry of creaturehood—a beating on heaven's door with bruised knuckles in the dark. Sometimes it will be friendship-talk with God about the affairs of everyday. Surely both prayers would be approved by Christ: his disciples cried in their extremity, "Lord, save us"; and day by day they spoke with him about their struggles, enigmas, and joys of the journey.

To try to thwart the prayer of petition is to deny human nature. The New Testament has better wisdom: "Be overanxious for nothing; but in everything by prayer and supplication with thanksgiving let your requests be made known unto God." Yet petition should grow in grace so as to "covet earnestly the best gifts"; and it should always acknowledge that our sight is dim and that our purposes are mixed in motive. It should always conclude with, "Nevertheless not my will, but thine, be done."

10. Friendship Held in Reverence

The intervals of these four prayers should be filled by *meditation*. After thanksgiving we should contemplate God's abounding goodness, and await his word concerning his own gifts. After confession we should adore the pardoning Love made known in Christ, and listen for his guidance. After intercession we should pause to try to see the whole world's need as Christ saw it from his cross. After petition we should wait again to meditate upon the Will.

Prayer is listening as well as speaking, receiving as well as asking; and its deepest mood is friendship held in reverence. So the daily prayer should end as it begins—in adoration. The best conclusion is, "In the name of Jesus Christ: Amen." For in the name or nature of Jesus is our best understanding of God, and the best corrective of our blundering prayers. The word "Amen" is not idle: it means "So let it be." It is our resolve to live faithfully in the direction of our prayers, and our act of faith in God's power.

BIBLE SELECTION: LUKE 6:27–36

27"But I say to you that listen, Love your enemies, do good to those who hate you, 28bless those who curse you, pray for those who abuse you. 29If anyone strikes you on the cheek, offer the other also; and from anyone who takes away your coat do not withhold even your shirt. 30Give to everyone who begs from you; and if anyone takes away your goods, do not ask for them again. 31Do to others as you would have them do to you.

32"If you love those who love you, what credit is that to you? For even sinners love those who love them. 33If you do good to those who do good to you, what credit is that to you? For even sinners do the same. 34If you lend to those from whom you hope to receive, what credit is that to you? Even sinners lend to sinners, to receive as much again. 35But love your enemies, do good, and lend, expecting nothing in return. Your reward will be great, and you will be children of the Most High; for he is kind to the ungrateful and the wicked. 36Be merciful, just as your Father is merciful."

REFLECTION QUESTIONS

The following questions can be used for discussion within a small group, or used for journal reflections by individuals.

1. Buttrick cautions us against being either too formal or too formless in our prayer life. On which side are you more likely to err?

2. It is easy, says Buttrick, to forget "the widespread mercy" of God and focus instead on all our personal problems. How might his recommendation that we set aside time for thanksgiving help you see more of the "white paper" and less of the "blot"?

3. In all four aspects of prayer, Buttrick urges us to be specific. Why is this so important?

4. Do you ever feel guilty praying for yourself? What would George Buttrick say to those who do?

5. If you were to follow Jesus' command to pray for your enemies, who would you begin praying for today?

SUGGESTED EXERCISES

The following exercises can be done by individuals, shared between spiritual friends, or used in the context of a small group. Choose one or more of the following.

1. Use Buttrick's guide-map of prayer this week. Move gently from silent self-preparation to thanksgiving to confession to intercession to petition.

2. Even if you do not follow Buttrick's regimen, follow his advice about being specific when you pray. Make your thanksgiving visible by writing down all the things for which you are thankful; make petition more tangible by seeing faces, not merely the masses, as you pray.

3. This week pray for your enemies, for those who have wronged you. Make them the central focus of your intercession. Notice how difficult it is to pray for someone and retain those angry feelings.

4. Beyond praying for our enemies, Jesus admonishes us to do good, not only to people who are kind to us, but also to those who are not. This week do something helpful or kind to someone you do not know, to someone who has not done anything for you.

REFLECTIONS

I am helped by George Buttrick's words on prayer. It isn't so much that he is giving me new insights into prayer—in one form or another I have heard it all before. It is that when I read him, I want to pray. Many authors help me understand prayer; few help me practice it.

I'm glad for this feature in Buttrick for I am in need of constant encouragement to keep in the experience of prayer. It is so easy for me to fall back into analysis and debate and avoid "the practice of the Presence." Maybe you experience the same difficulty. Certainly we can all be grateful for Buttrick's "hints" on prayer, which nudge us onward in the Way.

Richard J. Foster

GOING DEEPER

Buttrick, George Arthur. *God, Pain and Evil.* Nashville, TN: Abingdon, 1966. Buttrick was a pastor and as a pastor was concerned to communicate the Christian faith to modern men and women conditioned by the skepticism of our day. To respond to this pastoral need he wrote three books on apologetics, of which this is one. The other two are *The Christian Fact and Modern Doubt* and *Christ and History.*

Buttrick, George Arthur. *The Parables of Jesus.* Garden City, NY: Doubleday, Doran, 1928. This series of sermons shows Buttrick at his preacherly best. He was a great preacher and even wrote a book on the sermon craft—*Jesus Came Preaching.*

Buttrick, George Arthur. *Prayer.* New York: Abingdon-Cokesbury, 1942. This is a very substantial and comprehensive book. Not for speed reading but don't be afraid of it either.

Søren Kierkegaard (1813–1855)

INTRODUCTION TO THE AUTHOR

Søren Kierkegaard was born in Copenhagen in the early nineteenth century. He graduated from the University of Copenhagen and then spent two years in Germany before returning to Copenhagen, where he would spend the rest of his life. In 1843 he wrote and published his first book, *Either/Or,* which startled the religious world with its denouncement of watered-down Christianity.

In fact, Kierkegaard's life and works were a serious challenge to the institutional church that he believed had removed the necessary leap of faith and the individual's (as opposed to the masses') responsibility of commitment. All his writings served as a kind of judgment against a church that minimized the distance between the human and the divine. Kierkegaard believed that there was a great chasm between God and human beings and that the only bridge was Jesus Christ. In the period of history we call the Enlightenment (when reason seemed to triumph over faith and human potential over human weakness), Kierkegaard's philosophy served as a corrective to a world and a church that had lost its identity.

The following selection is a series of prayers found throughout Kierkegaard's many writings. Quite often he would interject a prayer in the midst of his discourses. These prayers reflect not only his thought, but also his heart, for behind the keen intellect was a heart that longed for God.

EXCERPTS FROM *THE PRAYERS OF KIERKEGAARD*

1. Moved in Infinite Love

You who are unchangeable, whom nothing changes! You who are unchangeable in love, precisely for our welfare, not submitting to any change: may we too will our welfare, submitting ourselves to the discipline of Your unchangeableness, so that we may in unconditional obedience find our rest and remain at rest in Your unchangeableness. You are not like us; if we are to preserve only some degree of constancy, we must not permit ourselves too much to be moved, nor by too many things. You on the contrary are moved, and moved in infinite love, by all things. Even that which we human beings call an insignificant trifle, and pass by unmoved, the need of a sparrow, even this moves You; and what we so often scarcely notice, a human sigh, this moves You, You who are unchangeable! You who in infinite love do submit to be moved, may this our prayer also move You to add Your blessing, in order that there may be brought about such a change in us who pray as to bring us into conformity with Your unchangeable will, You who are unchangeable!

2. You Have Loved Us First

Father in Heaven! You have loved us first, help us never to forget that You are love so that this sure conviction might triumph in our hearts over the seduction of the world, over the inquietude of the soul, over the anxiety for the future, over the fright of the past, over the distress of the moment. But grant also that this conviction might discipline our soul so that our heart might remain faithful and sincere in the love which we bear to all those whom You have commanded us to love as we love ourselves.

You have loved us first, O God, alas! We speak of it in terms of history as if You have only loved us first but a single time, rather than that without ceasing You have loved us first many times and every day and our whole life through. When we wake up in the morning and turn our soul toward You—You are the first—You have loved us first; if I rise at dawn and at the same second turn my soul toward You in prayer, You are there ahead of me, You have loved me first. When I withdraw from the distractions of the day and turn my soul toward You, You are the first and thus forever. And yet we always speak ungratefully as if You have loved us first only once.

3. Have Then a Little Patience

Father in Heaven! Show us a little patience; for we often intend in all sincerity to commune with You and yet we speak in such a foolish fashion. Sometimes, when we judge that what has come to us is good, we do not have enough words to thank You; just as a mistaken child is thankful for having gotten his own way. Sometimes things go so badly that we call upon You; just as an unreasoning child fears what would do him good. Oh, but if we are so childish, how far from being Your true children You who are our true Father, ah, as if an animal would pretend to have a man as a father. How childish we are and how little our proposals and our language resemble the language which we ought to use with You, we understand at least that it should not be this way and that we should be otherwise. Have then a little patience with us.

4. Hold Us Up Against Our Sins

Father in Heaven! Hold not our sins up against us but hold us up against our sins so that the thought of You when it wakens in our soul, and each time it wakens, should not remind us of what we have committed but of what You did forgive, not of how we went astray but of how You did save us!

5. The Promise and the Pain

Father in Heaven! We know indeed that seeking is never without its promise, how then could we fail to seek You, the author of all promises and the giver of all good gifts! We know well that the seeker does not always have to wander far afield since the more sacred the object of his search, the nearer it is to him;

and if he seeks You, O God, You are of all things most near!

But we know also that the seeking is never without its pains and temptations, how then would there not be fear in seeking You, who are mighty! Even he who trusts in thought to his kinship with You does not venture forth without fear upon those crucial decisions of thought where, through doubt, he seeks to trace Your presence in the wise order of existence or, through despair, he seeks to trace You in the obedience under providence of rebellious events.

Those, whom You call Your friends, who walk in the light of Your countenance, they, too, not without trembling, seek the meeting of friendship with You who alone are mighty. People of prayer who love with their whole heart—it is not without anxiety that they venture into the conflict of prayer with their God. The dying man, for whom You shift the scene, does not relinquish the temporal without a shudder when You call him. Not even the child of woe, for whom the world has nothing but suffering, flees to You without fear, You who do not merely alleviate, but are all in all! How then should the sinner dare to seek You, O God of righteousness! But therefore he seeks You, not as these others do, but seeks You in the confession of sins.

6. The Sickness Unto Death

Father in Heaven! To You the congregation often makes its petition for all who are sick and sorrowful, and when someone among us lies ill, alas, of mortal sickness, the congregation sometimes desires a special petition; grant that we may each one of us become in good time aware what sickness it is which is the sickness unto death and aware that we are all of us suffering from this sickness.

O Lord Jesus Christ, who came to earth to heal them that suffer from this sickness, from which, alas, we all suffer, but from which You are able to hear only those who are conscious they are sick in this way; help us in this sickness to hold fast to You, to the end that we may be healed of it.

O God the Holy Spirit, who comes to help us in this sickness if we honestly desire to be healed; remain with us so that for no single instant we may to our own destruction shun the Physician, but may remain with Him—delivered from sickness. For to be with Him is to be delivered from our sickness, and when we are with Him we are saved from all sickness.

7. To Will One Thing

Father in Heaven! What are we without You! What is all that we know, vast accumulation though it be, but a chipped fragment if we do not know You! What is all our striving, could it ever encompass a world, but a half-finished work if we do not know You: You the One, who is one thing and who is all!

So may You give to the intellect, wisdom to comprehend that one thing; to the heart, sincerity to receive this understanding; to the will, purity that wills only one thing. In prosperity may You grant perseverance to will one thing; amid distractions, collectedness to will one thing; in suffering, patience to will one thing.

You that gives both the beginning and the completion, may You early, at the dawn of day, give to the young the resolution to will one thing. As the day wanes, may You give to the old a renewed remembrance of their first resolution, that the first may be like the last, the last like the first, in possession of a life that has willed only one thing.

Alas, but this has indeed not come to pass. Something has come in between. The separation of sin lies in between. Each day, and day after day something is being placed in between: delay, blockage, interruption, delusion, corruption. So in this time of repentance may You give the courage once again to will one thing.

True, it is an interruption of our ordinary tasks; we do lay down our work as though it were a day of rest when the penitent is alone before You in self-accusation. This is indeed an interruption. But it is an interruption that searches back into its very beginnings that it might bind up anew that which sin has separated, that in its grief it might atone for lost time, that in its anxiety it might bring to completion that which lies before it.

You that gives both the beginning and the completion, give your victory in the day of need so that what neither our burning wish nor our determined resolution may attain to, may be granted unto us in the sorrowing of repentance: to will only one thing.

8. Each Morning Broken

Lord! Make our heart Your temple in which You live. Grant that every impure thought, every earthly desire might be like the idol Dagon—each morning broken at the feet of the Ark of the Covenant. Teach us to master flesh and blood and let this mastery of ourselves be our bloody sacrifice in order that we might be able to say with the Apostle: "I die every day."

BIBLE SELECTION: 1 SAMUEL 5

When the Philistines captured the ark of God, they brought it from Ebenezer to Ashdod; [2]then the Philistines took the ark of God and brought it into the house of Dagon and placed it beside Dagon. [3]When the people of Ashdod rose early the next day, there was Dagon, fallen on his face to the ground before the ark of the LORD. So they took Dagon and put him back in his place. [4]But when they rose early on the next morning, Dagon had fallen on his face to the ground before the ark of the LORD, and the head of Dagon and both his hands were lying cut off upon the threshold; only the trunk of Dagon was left to him. [5]This is why the priests of Dagon and all who enter the house of Dagon do not step on the threshold of Dagon in Ashdod to this day.

[6]The hand of the LORD was heavy upon the people of Ashdod, and he terrified and struck them with tumors, both in Ashdod and in its territory. [7]And when the inhabitants of Ashdod saw how things were, they said, "The ark of the God of Israel must not remain with us; for his hand is heavy on us and on our god Dagon." [8]So they sent and gathered together all the lords of the Philistines, and said, "What shall we do with the ark of the God of Israel?" The inhabitants of Gath replied, "Let the ark of God be moved on to us." So they moved the ark of the God of Israel to Gath. [9]But after they had brought it to Gath, the hand of the LORD was against the city, causing a very great panic; he struck the inhabitants of the city, both young and old, so that tumors broke out on them. [10]So they sent the ark of the God of Israel to Ekron. But when the ark of God came to Ekron, the people of Ekron cried out, "Why have they brought around to us the ark of the God of Israel to kill us and our people?" [11]They sent therefore and gathered together all the

lords of the Philistines, and said, "Send away the ark of the God of Israel, and let it return to its own place, that it may not kill us and our people." For there was a deathly panic throughout the whole city. The hand of God was very heavy there; [12]those who did not die were stricken with tumors, and the cry of the city went up to heaven.

REFLECTION QUESTIONS

The following questions can be used for discussion within a small group, or used for journal reflections by individuals.

1. In section 1, Kierkegaard begins his prayer by acknowledging God's unchangeableness. Why is the changelessness of God important?

2. Kierkegaard writes that God not only loved us first once but loves us first all the time. How does this affect your understanding of who you are in God's eye? How does this affect your prayers?

3. Seeking God, writes Kierkegaard, is filled with promises and pain. What pains have you experienced as a result of seeking God? How have they shaped your life?

4. Just as the idol Dagon (see 1 Sam. 5) was crushed at the feet of the Ark of the Covenant, so Kierkegaard prays that every impure thought, every earthly desire, might be destroyed each morning. What earthly desires would you want God to destroy within you so that you could be fully committed to God?

5. God is more powerful than any of our idols, according to the story of Dagon in 1 Samuel 5. How has the power of God been at work in your life recently? Where has "the hand of God [been] very heavy" in your life?

SUGGESTED EXERCISES

The following exercises can be done by individuals, shared between spiritual friends, or used in the context of a small group. Choose one or more of the following.

1. Turn Kierkegaard's prayers into your prayers during your times of devotion. Pray them slowly, savoring each phrase, considering its meaning, and lifting it to God as the cry of your own heart.

2. The fact that God first loved us, and continues to love us first, was important to Kierkegaard. Write out the three simple words *I love you* on a card or scrap of paper. Carry it with you wherever you go, and each time you look at it remember that wherever you are, whatever you are doing, God is there, loving you first.

3. A central theme of Kierkegaard's writings is that of willing one thing. That one thing for Kierkegaard was to seek first the kingdom of God, to remain committed to God in all that he did. Simplify your life this week by concentrating on this one thing, knowing that all that you need will be added unto you.

4. Read the Bible stories of the Ark of the Covenant this week. Notice how central the ark was in the life of Israel, and how it represented the presence and power of God.

REFLECTIONS

It is a wonderful thing to see a first-rate philosopher at prayer. Tough-minded thinking and tenderhearted reverence are friends, not enemies. We have for too long separated the head from the heart, and we are the lesser for it.

We love God with the mind and we love God with the heart. In reality, we are descending with the mind into the heart and there standing before God in ceaseless wonder and endless praise. As the mind and the heart work in concert, a kind of "loving rationality" pervades all we say and do. This brings unity to us and glory to God.

GOING DEEPER

Kierkegaard, Søren. *A Kierkegaard Anthology.* Edited by Robert Bretall. Princeton, NJ: Princeton University Press, 1946. A representative selection of Kierkegaard's major writings. Covering seventeen works, it includes material from *The Journals, Either/Or,* and *The Attack upon "Christendom."*

Kierkegaard, Søren. *The Prayers of Kierkegaard.* Edited by Perry D. LeFevre. Chicago: University of Chicago Press, 1956. Nearly one hundred of Kierkegaard's prayers are gathered here from his published works and private papers, not only to illuminate his life of prayer, but also to serve as a book of personal devotions for Christians today.

Kierkegaard, Søren. *Purity of Heart Is to Will One Thing.* New York: Harper & Bros., 1938. One of the best books on the classic discipline of self-examination. It was written, as Kierkegaard states, as a "spiritual preparation for the feast of confession." The "one thing" we are to will is, of course, the good that ultimately is God.

Lowrie, Walter. *A Short Life of Kierkegaard.* Princeton, NJ: Princeton University Press, 1970. An excellent, readable introduction by the foremost biographer of the great Danish thinker.

Evelyn Underhill (1875–1941)

INTRODUCTION TO THE AUTHOR

Few women of the twentieth century have done more to further our understanding of the devotional life than Evelyn Underhill. Her scholarly research and writing have helped saints and skeptics alike in the study of religion and spirituality. Her highly praised book *Mysticism: A Study in the Nature and Development of Man's Spiritual Consciousness* has gone through many editions and continues to be a foundational text for all students of spirituality.

Underhill was educated at King's College for Women in London, where she spent much of her time writing and lecturing. She was the Upton lecturer at Manchester College, Oxford, from 1921 to 1922. However, her enduring contribution comes not from her academic achievements but from her personal insights into the devotional life. After a religious conversion at the age of thirty-two, she practiced this devotional life with great intensity.

Underhill's personal spiritual journey intersected with her intellectual capability, producing the much needed combination of authentic spirituality and academic integrity. As a result, she was a highly sought after spiritual director. In addition, she became well known as the conductor of retreats at various Anglican religious centers.

In the following selection Underhill describes the inner mechanics of prayer, shedding light on the place of the mind, the emotions, and the will in the life of prayer.

EXCERPTS FROM *THE ESSENTIALS OF MYSTICISM*

1. Stretching Out the Tentacles

In the first place, what do we mean by prayer? Surely just this: that part of our conscious life which is deliberately oriented towards, and exclusively responds to, spiritual reality. God is that spiritual reality, and we believe God to be immanent in all things: "He is not far from each one of us: for in him we live and move and have our being."

"Prayer," says Walter Hilton, "is nothing else but an ascending or getting up of the desire of the heart into God by withdrawing it from earthly thoughts." It is "ascent," says Ruysbroeck, of the Ladder of Love. In the same spirit William Law defines prayer as "the rising of the soul out of the vanity of time into the riches of eternity."

It entails, then, a going up or out from our ordinary circle of earthly interests. Prayer stretches out the tentacles of our consciousness not so much towards that Divine Life which is felt to be enshrined within the striving, changeful world of things; but rather to that "Eternal truth, true Love, and loved Eternity" wherein the world is felt to be enshrined.

2. This Double Situation

The whole of a person's life consists in a series of balanced responses to this Transcendent-Immanent Reality. Because we live under two orders, we are at once a citizen of Eternity and of Time. Like a pendulum, our consciousness moves perpetually—or should move if it is healthy—between God and our neighbor, between this world and that.

The wholeness, sanity, and balance of our existence depend entirely upon the perfection of our adjustment to this double situation; on the steady alternating beat of our outward adoration, and our homeward-turning swing of charity. Now, it is the outward swing which I want to consider: the powers that may be used in it, and the best way in which these powers may be employed.

3. Three Faculties

First, there are three capacities or faculties which we have under consideration—the thinking faculty, the feeling faculty, and the willing or acting faculty. These practically cover all the ways in which the self can react to other selves and other things. From the combination of these three come all the possibilities of self-expression which are open to us.

In our natural life we need to use all of them. Do we need them in our spiritual life, too? Christians are bound to answer this question in the affirmative. It is the *whole person* of intellect, of feeling, and of will which finds its only true objective in the Christian God.

4. Work and Rest

Prayer should take up and turn towards the spiritual order all the powers of our mental, emotional, and volitional life. Prayers should be the highest exercise of these powers; for here they are directed to the only adequate object of thought, of love, and of desire. It should, as it were, lift us to the top of our condition, and represent the fullest flowering of our consciousness. For here we breathe the air of the supernatural order, and attain according to our measure that communion with Reality for which we were made.

Prayer will include many different kinds of spiritual work; and also—what is too often forgotten—the priceless gift of spiritual rest. It will include many kinds of intercourse with Reality—adoration, petition, meditation, contemplation—and all the shades and varieties of these which religious writers have named and classified.

As in the natural order the living creature must feed *and* grow, must suffer *and* enjoy, must get energy from the world *and* give it back again if it is to live a whole and healthy life. So, too, in the spiritual order. All these things—the giving and the receiving, the work and the rest—should fall within the circle of prayer.

5. The Transition from Inaction to Action

Now, when we do anything consciously, the transition from inaction to action unfolds itself in a certain order. First, we form a concept of that which we shall do; the idea of it looms up in our minds. Second, we feel that we want to do it, or must do it. Third, we determine that we will do it. These phases may follow on another so swiftly that they seem to be fused into one; but when we analyze the process which lies behind each conscious act, we find that this is the normal sequence of development.

First we think, then we feel, then we will. This little generalization must not be pressed too hard; but it is broadly true, and gives us a starting-point to trace out the way in which the three main powers of the self act in prayer. It is important to know how they act or should act.

6. An Active and Disciplined Intelligence

Prayer, as a rule, should begin with something we usually call an intellectual act, with thinking of what we are going to do. All the great writers on prayer take it as a matter of course that "meditation" comes before "oration" (or spoken prayer). Meditation is simply the art of thinking steadily and methodically about spiritual things. So, too, most modern psychologists assure us that instinctive emotion does its best work when it acts in harmony with our reasoning powers.

There are some who believe that when we turn to God we ought to leave our brains behind us. True, they will soon be left behind by necessity if we go far on the road towards God who is above all reason and all knowledge, for

the Spirit swiftly overpasses these imperfect instruments. But those whose feet are still firmly planted upon earth gain nothing by anticipating this moment when reason is left behind; they will not attain the depths of prayer by the mere annihilation of their intelligence.

In saying this—in insisting that reason has a well-marked and necessary place in the soul's approach to God—I am not advocating a religious intellectualism. I am well aware that it is "by love," as the old mystic said, "God may be gotten and beheld; by thought never." It is humility and love that are essential for successful prayer. But surely it is a mistake to suppose that these qualities cannot exist side by side with an active and disciplined intelligence.

7. Preparing the Consciousness

Prayer, then, begins by an intellectual adjustment. By thinking of God earnestly and humbly to the exclusion of other objects of thought, by deliberately surrendering the mind to spiritual things, by preparing the consciousness for the inflow of new life.

But having thought of God, the self, if it stops there, is no more in touch with God than it was before. We may think as long as we like, but nothing happens; thought unhelped by feeling ever remains apart from its object. The intellect is an essentially static thing: we cannot think our way along the royal road which leads to heaven.

8. The Industrious Will and the Passionate Heart

Where the office of thought ends, there the office of will and feeling begins: "Where the intellect must stay without," says Ruysbroeck, "these may enter in." Desire and intention are the most dynamic of our faculties; they do work. They are the true explorers of the Infinite, the instruments of our ascents to God. Reason comes to the foot of the mountain; it is the industrious will urged by the passionate heart which climbs the slope.

Experience endorses this emphasis on will and desire as central facts of our personality, the part of us which is supremely our own. In turning our will and desire towards Spiritual Reality we are doing all that we can of ourselves, we are selecting and deliberately concentrating upon it our passion and our power.

9. The Very Center and Art of Prayer

Now, intellect and feeling are not wholly in our control. They fluctuate from day to day, from hour to hour; they are dependent on many delicate adjustments. Sometimes we are mentally dull, sometimes we are emotionally flat. On such occasions it is notoriously useless to try to beat ourselves up to a froth: to make ourselves think more deeply or make ourselves care more intensely.

If the worth of our prayer life depended upon the maintenance of a constant high level of feeling or understanding, we would be in a dangerous place. Though these often seem to fail us, the reigning will remains. Even when our heart is cold and our mind is dim, prayer is still possible to us. "Our wills are ours, to make them Thine."

The determined fixing of our will upon God, and pressing toward him steadily and without deflection; this is the very center and the art of prayer. The most theological of thoughts soon becomes inadequate; the most spiritual of emotions is only a fairweather breeze. Let the ship take advantage of it by all means, but not rely on it. She must be prepared to beat to windward if she would reach her goal.

BIBLE SELECTION: ACTS 17:22–34

[22]Then Paul stood in front of the Areopagus and said, "Athenians, I see how extremely religious you are in every way. [23]For as I went through the city and looked carefully at the objects of your worship, I found among them an altar with the inscription, 'To an unknown god.' What therefore you worship as unknown, this I proclaim to you. [24]The God who made the world and everything in it, he who is Lord of heaven and earth, does not live in shrines made by human hands, [25]nor is he served by human hands, as though he needed anything, since he himself gives to all mortals life and breath and all things. [26]From one ancestor he made all nations to inhabit the whole earth, and he alloted the times of their existence and the boundaries of the places where they would live, [27]so that they would search for God and perhaps grope for him and find him—though indeed he is not far from each one of us. [28]For 'In him we live and move and have our being'; as even some of your own poets have said,

'For we too are his offspring.'

[29]Since we are God's offspring, we ought not to think that the deity is like gold, or silver, or stone, an image formed by the art and imagination of mortals. [30]While God has overlooked

the times of human ignorance, now he commands all people everywhere to repent, [31]because he has fixed a day on which he will have the world judged in righteousness by a man whom he has appointed, and of this he has given assurance to all by raising him from the dead."

[32]When they heard of the resurrection of the dead, some scoffed; but others said, "We will hear you again about this." [33]At that point Paul left them. [34]But some of them joined him and became believers, including Dionysius the Areopagite and a woman named Damaris, and others with them.

REFLECTION QUESTIONS

The following questions can be used for discussion within a small group, or used for journal reflections by individuals.

1. What are the three faculties that Evelyn Underhill encourages us to use in our times of prayer? Give concrete examples of how these three faculties work in our daily life (see sections 3 and 5).

2. The mind, according to Underhill, should not be left out of the act of prayer, because it is the faculty that prepares the way for prayer. How has your intellect helped or hindered your prayer life?

3. The mind may be dull now and then, and the emotions may be flat at times, but what, according to Underhill, is always under our control? Why is this important in prayer?

4. St. Paul tells the Athenians, "[God] is not far from each one of us." Do you sometimes feel that God is far from you? When have you felt the closest to God? Who do you believe actually moved in each case, you or God?

5. Underhill stresses that although our reasoning faculties are limited, we do not have to leave our brains behind in the life of prayer. Why do you think there is a tendency to devalue the intellect in the spiritual life?

SUGGESTED EXERCISES

The following exercises can be done by individuals, shared between spiritual friends, or used in the context of a small group. Choose one or more of the following.

1. Use Evelyn Underhill's three-part movement of prayer this week. Begin in the mind, making space for God by reflecting on spiritual truths; move to the emotions by concentrating on your desire for God; hold yourself in his presence by a deliberate act of your will.

2. Prayer also includes times of rest, writes Underhill. Perhaps you have been pressing too hard in your times of prayer. Allow yourself to experience a little holy leisure this week, knowing that there is a time to work and a time to rest. To deny this is to work against the rhythms of God.

3. Underhill encourages us to think "steadily and methodically about spiritual things." Make a list of the attributes of God (e.g., God is all-knowing, all-powerful, unchangeable, loving, etc.). Think steadily on these things, making them the object of your contemplation.

4. St. Paul knew that his audience consisted of intellectual types and therefore altered his style without changing the content of his preaching. This week reach out to someone whose faith background is different from yours. Be careful to speak in that person's language, being mindful of the way he or she sees the world, and yet do not compromise your own convictions about Christ and his gospel.

REFLECTIONS

In these selections Evelyn Underhill gives us substantial help in our understanding of the life of prayer. It is so easy for us to fall into the unexamined assumption that either God gifts us with the spirit of prayer or he doesn't, and that our contribution to the process is essentially negligible. To be sure, without the active agenting of the Holy Spirit, our prayer work would be so much babble.

We have an important part to play, however, and Underhill stresses our active participation in God's work. She helps us see how our minds and wills and emotions can all be brought into the service of prayer. How often we fail to enlist our wonderful rational faculties in this holy work! How often we refuse to allow our feelings to lead us higher up and deeper in! How often we lack the will to persevere just when we were on the verge of slipping into the Holy of Holies! How much better to harness all our mental, volitional, and emotional powers for the service of Christ.

GOING DEEPER

Armstrong, Christopher J. R. *Evelyn Underhill: An Introduction to Her Life and Writings.* Grand Rapids, MI: Eerdmans, 1975. This book places Evelyn Underhill in her own historical setting between the two great wars and assesses her influence. It contains a helpful bibliography of about one hundred of her essays and articles.

Underhill, Evelyn. *The Essentials of Mysticism.* New York: Dutton, 1960. Underhill has been able to give intellectual and theological underpinnings for the profound but sometimes perplexing tradition of Christian mysticism. In the same genre she has written *The Mystic Way* (1913), *Practical Mysticism* (1915), and *The Life of the Spirit and the Life of Today* (1922).

Underhill, Evelyn. *Worship.* New York: Crossroad, 1982 (out of print). This book explores the primary realities of our relationship to God, which our devotional action is intended to express.

Frank Laubach (1884–1970)

INTRODUCTION TO THE AUTHOR

In 1915 Frank Laubach went with his wife to the Philippine Islands as a missionary. After founding churches on the island of Mindanao, he established and became dean of Union College in Manila. In 1930 he returned to Mindanao to work with the Mohammedan Moros who regarded the Christian Filipinos as their enemies. Laubach, however, went with a heart filled with the presence of God and sought only to live among them, not trying to coerce them into Christianity but living each moment with a sense of God's presence.

It is estimated that through his educational efforts he was responsible for teaching one-half of the ninety thousand people in that area to read and write. More than that, he has brought thousands of people to a richer experience of God. The following reading comes from the letters he wrote during his Mindanao days.

EXCERPTS FROM *LETTERS BY A MODERN MYSTIC*

1. Open Windows

January 3, 1930

To be able to look backward and say, "This, *this* has been the finest year of my life"— that is glorious! But anticipation! To be able to look ahead and say, "The present year can and *shall* be better!"—that is more glorious! I have done nothing but open windows—God has done the rest. There has been a succession of marvelous experiences of the friendship of God. I resolved that I would succeed better this year with my experiment of filling every minute full of the thought of God than I succeeded last year. And I added another resolve—to be as wide open toward people and their need as I am toward God. Windows open outward as well as upward. Windows open *especially* downward where people need the most!

2. Submission: The First and Last Duty

January 20, 1930

Submission is the first and last duty of man. That is exactly what I have been needing in my Christian life. Two years ago a profound dissatisfaction led me to begin trying to line up my actions with the will of God about every fifteen minutes or every half hour. Other people to whom I confessed this intention said it was impossible. I judge from what I have said that few people are trying even that. But this year I have started out trying to live all my waking moments in conscious listening to the inner voice, asking without ceasing, "What, Father, do you desire said? What, Father, do you desire done this minute?"

3. Feeling God in Each Movement

January 26, 1930

For the past few days I have been experimenting in a more complete surrender than ever before. I am taking by deliberate act of will, enough time from each hour to give God much thought. Yesterday and today I have made a new adventure, which is not easy to express. I am feeling God in each movement, by an act of will—willing that He shall direct these fingers that now strike this typewriter—willing that He shall pour through my steps as I walk—willing that He shall direct my words as I speak, and my very jaws as I eat!

You will object to this intense introspection. Do not try it, unless you feel unsatisfied with your own relationship with God, but at least allow me to realize all the leadership of God I can. I am disgusted with the pettiness and futility of my unled self. If the way out is not more perfect slavery to God, then what is

the way out? I am trying to be utterly free from everybody, free from my own self, but completely enslaved to the will of God every moment of this day.

4. Moment by Moment

We used to sing a song in the church in Benton which I liked, but which I never really practiced until now. It runs:

> "Moment by moment, I'm kept in His
>   love;
> Moment by moment I've life from above;
> Looking to Jesus till glory doth shine;
> Moment by moment, O Lord, I am Thine."

It is exactly that "moment by moment," every waking moment, surrender, responsiveness, obedience, sensitiveness, pliability, "lost in His love," that I now have the mind-bent to explore with all my might. It means two burning passions: First, to be like Jesus. Second, to respond to God as a violin responds to the bow of the master. Open your soul and entertain the glory of God and after a while that glory will be reflected in the world about you and in the very clouds above your head.

5. Only One Thing Now

January 29, 1930

I feel simply carried along each hour, doing my part in a plan which is far beyond myself. This sense of cooperation with God in the little things is what astonishes me. I seem to have to make sure of only one thing now, and every other thing "takes care of itself," or I prefer to say what is more true, God takes care of all the rest. My part is to *live in this hour in*

continuous inner conversation with God and in
perfect responsiveness to his will. To make this hour
gloriously rich. This seems to be all I need to
think about.

6. Undiscovered Continents of
Spiritual Living

March 1, 1930

The sense of being led by an unseen hand
which takes mine while another hand reaches
ahead and prepares the way, grows upon me
daily. I do not need to strain at all to find opportunity. Perhaps a man who has been an
ordained minister since 1914 ought to be
ashamed to confess that he never felt the joy of
complete hourly, minute by minute—now
what shall I call it?—more than surrender.

It is a will act. I compel my mind to open
straight out toward God. I wait and listen with
determined sensitiveness. I fix my attention
there, and sometimes it requires a long time
early in the morning to attain that mental state.
I determine not to get out of bed until that
mind set, that concentration upon God, is settled. It also requires determination to keep it
there. After a while, perhaps, it will become a
habit, and the sense of effort will grow less. But
why do I harp on this inner experience? Because I feel convinced that for me and for you
who read there lie ahead undiscovered conti-
nents of spiritual living compared with which
we are infants in arms.

But how "practical" is this for the average
man? It seems now to me that yonder plow-
man could be like Calixto Sanidad, when he
was a lonesome and mistreated plowboy,
"with my eyes on the furrow, and my hands on
the lines, but my thoughts on God." The millions at looms and lathes could make the hours

glorious. Some hour spent by some night
watchman might be the most glorious ever
lived on earth.

7. How Infinitely Richer

March 15, 1930

Every waking moment of the week I have
been looking toward Him, with perhaps the exception of an hour or two. How infinitely
richer this direct first hand grasping of God
himself is, than the old method which I used
and recommended for years, the endless reading of devotional books. Almost it seems to me
now that the very Bible cannot be read as a
substitute for meeting God soul to soul and
face to face.

8. Can It Be Done?

March 23, 1930

We can keep two things in mind at once.
Indeed we cannot keep one thing in mind more
than half a second. Mind is a flowing something. It oscillates. Concentration is merely the
continuous return to the same problem from a
million angles. So my problem is this: Can I
bring God back in my mind-flow every few
seconds so that God shall always be in my
mind as an after image, shall always be one of
the elements in every concept and precept? I
choose to make the rest of my life an experiment in answering this question.

I do not invite anybody else to follow this
arduous path. I wish many might. We need to
know, for example, Can a laboring man successfully attain this continuous surrender to
God? Can a man working at a machine pray
for people all day long, and at the same time
do his task efficiently? Can a mother wash

dishes, care for the babies, continuously talking to God?

If you are like myself, this has been a pretty strong diet. So I will put something simpler and more attainable: "Any hour of any day may be made perfect by merely choosing. It is perfect if one looks to God that entire hour, waiting for his leadership all through the hour and trying hard to do every tiny thing exactly as God wishes it done."

9. Difficulty and Failure

April 19, 1930

If this record of a soul [sic] struggle to find God is to be complete it must not omit the story of difficulty and failure. I have not succeeded very well so far. This week, for example, has not been one of the finest in my life, but I resolve not to give up the effort. Yet strain does not seem to do good. At this moment I feel something "let go" inside, and lo, God is here! It is a heart melting "here-ness," a lovely whispering of father to child, and the reason I did not have it before was because I failed to let go.

10. Letting God Control

April 22, 1930

This morning I started out fresh, by finding a rich experience of God in the sunrise. Then I tried to let him control my hands while I was shaving and dressing and eating breakfast. Now I am trying to let God control my hands as I pound the typewriter keys. There is nothing that we can do excepting to throw ourselves open to God. There is, there must be, so much more in Him than He can give us. It ought to be tremendously helpful to be able to acquire the habit of reaching out strongly after God's thoughts, and to ask, "God, what have you to put into my mind now if only I can be large enough?" That waiting, eager attitude ought to give God the chance he needs.

Oh, this thing of keeping in constant touch with God, making him the object of my thought and the companion of my conversations, is the most amazing thing I ever ran across. *It is working.* I cannot do it even half a day—not yet, but I believe I shall be doing it some day for the entire day. It is a matter of acquiring a new habit of thought. Now I *like* God's presence so much that when for a half hour or so he slips out of mind—as he does many times a day—I feel as though I had deserted him, and as though I had lost something very precious in my life.

11. Poetry Far More Beautiful

May 24, 1930

The day had been rich but strenuous, so I climbed "Signal Hill" back of my house talking and listening to God all the way up, all the way back, all the lovely half hour on the top. And God talked back! I let my tongue go loose and from it there flowed poetry far more beautiful than any I ever composed. It flowed without pausing and without ever a failing syllable for a half hour. I listened astonished and full of joy and gratitude. I wanted a dictaphone for I knew that I should not be able to remember it—and now I cannot. "Why," someone may ask, "did God waste his poetry on you alone, when you could not carry it home?" You will have to ask God that question. I only know He did and I am happy in the memory.

BIBLE SELECTION: PSALM 139:1–10, 17–18, 23–24

O LORD, you have searched me and
    known me.
[2]You know when I sit down and when
    I rise up;
you discern my thoughts from far away.
[3]You search out my path and my lying down,
and are acquainted with all my ways.
[4]Even before a word is on my tongue,
O LORD, you know it completely.
[5]You hem me in, behind and before,
and lay your hand upon me.
[6]Such knowledge is too wonderful for me;
it is so high that I cannot attain it.

[7]Where can I go from your spirit?
Or where can I flee from your presence?
[8]If I ascend to heaven, you are there;

if I make my bed in Sheol, you are there.
[9]If I take the wings of the morning
and settle at the farthest limits of the sea,
[10]even there your hand shall lead me,
and your right hand shall hold me fast.

[17]How weighty to me are your thoughts,
    O God!
How vast is the sum of them!
[18]I try to count them—they are more than
    the sand;
I come to the end—I am still with you.

[23]Search me, O God, and know my heart;
test me and know my thoughts.
[24]See if there is any wicked way in me,
and lead me in the way everlasting.

REFLECTION QUESTIONS

The following questions can be used for discussion within a small group, or used for journal reflections by individuals.

1. What led Frank Laubach to experiment with practicing God's presence? (See section 2.) Describe how you feel about your spiritual life right now.

2. Laubach refers to this practice as an act of the will. To what is he directing his will? What thoughts? What actions?

3. The author describes this practice as a habit. What thoughts are you in the habit of thinking? How does your thought life shape who you are?

4. Laubach writes, "There is . . . so much more in Him than He can give us." Over the past few years, what things has God given you? What keeps God from being able to give you more?

5. According to Psalm 139, is there any place we can go to escape the presence of God? How do you feel about the constant presence of God?

SUGGESTED EXERCISES

The following exercises can be done by individuals, shared between spiritual friends, or used in the context of a small group. Choose one or more of the following.

1. Try Laubach's experiment of thinking of God each moment. Try it for ten minutes. Try it for an hour. Try it for a whole day. Record your experiences.
2. Submission, according to Laubach, was central to his experiment. As you go about your tasks this week, deliberately pause to listen for God's counsel, and attempt to line up your actions with God's will as often as you think of it.
3. Put some reminder (e.g., a note, a cross, a Bible passage) in your work space that will trigger thoughts of God's presence each time you glance at it throughout your workday.
4. Make the prayer of the psalmist (Ps. 139:23–24) your prayer this week. Ask God to search your heart and mind as you endeavor to live a whole and complete life.

REFLECTIONS

I marvel at the prayer experiences of Frank Laubach. Here is a giant of a man, a man who developed a method of literacy training that has been used worldwide, compassionately declaring, "I want to learn how to live so that to see someone is to pray for them." He has helped me tremendously.

Even today, I like to thumb through his letters and journals until I encounter one of his prayer experiments that seems right for me for now. Perhaps it is an experiment in praying for people on a plane, inviting Jesus Christ to go from passenger to passenger, bringing his love into their lives. Then I'll try it for a while and see what I learn. It's a great adventure, this life of prayer, and Frank Laubach has pioneered the way for many of us.

GOING DEEPER

New Reader's Press has undertaken the task of republishing some of Frank Laubach's works in *The Heritage Collection* (Syracuse, NY, 1990). To date they have done *The Story of Jesus* in three parts: *Jesus' Birth and Ministry, Jesus' Death and Resurrection,* and *The Parables of Jesus.* The only other Laubach writings in print include portions of his diary (*Practicing His Presence,* edited by Gene Edwards, Auburn, ME: Seed Sowers, 1973) and *School Prayers* (Washington, DC: Public Affairs Press, 1969). For other works, scour libraries and used book stores. Look for titles such as *Letters by a Modern Mystic, Game with Minutes, Learning the Vocabulary of God,* and *Prayer: The Mightiest Force in the World.*

John Baillie (1886–1960)

INTRODUCTION TO THE AUTHOR

John Baillie was born in Gairloch, Scotland, and attended the Inverness Royal Academy in Edinburgh. He also studied at the universities of Jena and Marburg. He later taught at Edinburgh as well as at Toronto, Union Theological Seminary, and Auburn Theological Seminary. He served as the moderator of the General Assembly of the Church of Scotland in 1943.

Baillie was well known and highly respected as a theologian, teacher, and author. Though he was a professor of systematic theology by trade, Baillie was not a theologian for whom God was merely speculative. Few theologians have done better at combining the mind and the heart than John Baillie. His devotional life was at the center of all his academic endeavors, and, like Evelyn Underhill, he was able to find that delicate balance between faith and reason.

The following selection comes from one of Baillie's most popular writings—a collection of prayers designed to be used mornings and evenings. The following Morning Prayers are best used each day as you rise. Read each one slowly, praying it and making it your own.

EXCERPTS FROM *A DIARY OF PRIVATE PRAYER*

1. First Morning: "My First Thought"

Eternal Father of my soul, let my first thought today be of You, let my first impulse be to worship You, let my first speech be Your name, let my first action be to kneel before You in prayer.

For Your perfect wisdom and perfect goodness:

For the love with which You love mankind:

For the love with which You love me:

For the great and mysterious opportunity of my life:

For the indwelling of Your Spirit in my heart:

For the sevenfold gifts of Your Spirit:

I praise and worship You, O Lord.

Yet let me not, when this morning prayer is said, think my worship ended and spend the day in forgetfulness of You. Rather from these moments of quietness let light go forth, and joy, and power, that will remain with me through all the hours of the day;

Keeping me chaste in thought:

Keeping me temperate and truthful in speech:

Keeping me faithful and diligent in my work:

Keeping me humble in my estimation of myself:

Keeping me honorable and generous in my dealings with others:

Keeping me loyal to every hallowed memory of the past:

Keeping me mindful of my eternal destiny as a child of Yours.

Through Jesus Christ my Lord. Amen.

2. Second Morning: "Continued Dependence upon You"

O God my Creator and Redeemer, I may not go forth today except You accompany me with Your blessing. Let not the vigor and freshness of the morning, or the glow of good health, or the present prosperity of my undertakings, deceive me into a false reliance upon my own strength. All these good gifts have come to me from You. They were Yours to give and they are Yours also to curtail. They are not mine to keep; I do but hold them in trust; and only in continued dependence upon You, the Giver, can they be worthily enjoyed.

Let me then put back into Your hand all that You have given me, rededicating to Your service all the powers of my mind and body, all my worldly goods, all my influence with others. All these, O Father, are Yours to use as You will. All these are Yours, O Christ. All these are Yours, O Holy Spirit. Speak in my words today, think in my thoughts, and work in all my deeds. And seeing that it is Your gracious will to make use even of such weak human instruments in the fulfillment of Your mighty purpose for the world, let my life today be the channel through which some little portion of Your divine love and pity may reach the lives that are nearest to my own.

In Your solemn presence, O God, I remember all my friends and neighbors, my fellow townsfolk, and especially the poor within our gates, beseeching You that You would give me grace, so far as in me lies, to serve them in Your name. Amen.

3. Third Morning: "Joyous and Helpful Labor"

Lord of my life, whose law I fain would keep, whose fellowship I fain would enjoy, and to whose service I would fain be loyal, I kneel before You as You send me forth to the work of another day.

This day, O Lord—

give me courtesy:

give me meekness of bearing, with decision of character:

give me longsuffering:

give me chastity:

give me sincerity of speech:

give me diligence in my allotted task.

O You who in the fullness of time raised up our Lord and Savior Jesus Christ to enlighten our hearts with the knowledge of Your love, grant me the grace to be worthy of His name. Amen.

4. Fourth Morning: "Your Waiting Presence"

Almighty and eternal God,

You are hidden from my sight:

You are beyond the understanding of my mind:

Your thoughts are not as my thoughts:

Your ways are past finding out.

Yet You have breathed Your Spirit into my life:

Yet You have formed my mind to seek You:

Yet You have inclined my heart to love You:

Yet You have made me restless for the rest that is in You:

Yet You have planted within me a hunger and thirst that make me dissatisfied with all the joys of earth.

O You who alone know what lies before me this day, grant that in every hour of it I may stay close to You. Let me be in the world, yet not of it. Let me use this world without abusing it. If I buy, let me be as though I possessed not. If I have nothing, let me be as though possessing all things. Let me today embark on no undertaking that is not in line with Your will for my life, nor shrink from any sacrifice which Your will may demand. Suggest, direct, control every movement of my mind; for my Lord Christ's sake. Amen.

5. Fifth Morning: "The Lord and Giver of Life"

God of my forefathers, I cry unto You. You have been the refuge of good and wise people in every generation. When history began, You were the first enlightener of minds, and Yours was the Spirit that first led them out of their brutish estate and made them human. Through all the ages You have been the Lord and giver of life, the source of all knowledge, the fountain of all goodness.

The patriarchs trusted You and were not put to shame:

The prophets sought You and You committed Your word to their lips:

The psalmist[s] rejoiced in You and You were present in their song[s]:

The apostles waited upon You and they were filled with Your Holy Spirit:

The martyrs called upon You and You were with them in the midst of the flame:

Forbid it, Holy Lord, that I should fail to profit by these great memories of the ages that are gone by, or to enter into the glorious inheritance which You have prepared for me; through Jesus Christ my Lord. Amen.

6. Sixth Morning: "This Your Greatest Gift"

O God, who has proven Your love for all humanity by sending us Jesus Christ our Lord, and has illuminated our human life by the radiance of His presence, I give You thanks for this Your greatest gift.

For my Lord's days upon the earth:

For the record of His deeds of love:

For the words he spoke for my guidance and help:

For His obedience unto death:

For His triumph over death:

For the presence of His Spirit within me now:

I thank you, O God.

Grant that the remembrance of the blessed Life that once was lived out on this common earth under these ordinary skies may remain with me in all the tasks and duties of this day. Let me remember—

His eagerness, not to be ministered unto, but to minister:

His sympathy with suffering of every kind:

His bravery in the face of His own suffering:

His meekness of bearing, so that, when reviled, He reviled not again:

His steadiness of purpose in keeping to His appointed task:

His simplicity:

His self-discipline:

His serenity of spirit:

His complete reliance upon You, His Father in Heaven.

And in each of these ways give me grace to follow in His footsteps. Amen.

7. Seventh Morning: "O Lord and Maker of All Things"

O Lord and Maker of all things, from whose creative power the first light came forth, who looked upon the world's first morning and saw that it was good, I praise You for this light that now streams through my windows to rouse me to the life of another day.

I praise You for the life that stirs within me:

I praise You for the bright and beautiful world into which I go:

I praise You for earth and sea and sky, for scudding cloud and singing bird:

I praise You for the work You have given me to do:

I praise You for all that You have given me to fill my leisure hours:

I praise You for my friends:

I praise You for music and books and good company and all pure pleasures.

Amen.

BIBLE SELECTION: LUKE 12:22–31

[22]He said to his disciples, "Therefore I tell you, do not worry about your life, what you will eat, or about your body, what you will wear. [23]For life is more than food, and the body more than clothing. [24]Consider the ravens: they neither sow nor reap, they have neither storehouse nor barn, and yet God feeds them. Of how much more value are you than the birds! [25]And can any of you by worrying add a single hour to your span of life? [26]If then you are not able to do so small a thing as that, why do you worry about the rest? [27]Consider the lilies, how they grow: they neither toil nor spin; yet I tell you, even Solomon in all his glory was not clothed like one of these. [28]But if God so clothes the grass of the field, which is alive today and tomorrow is thrown into the oven, how much more will he clothe you—you of little faith! [29]And do not keep striving for what you are to eat and what you are to drink, and do not keep worrying. [30]For it is the nations of the world that strive after all these things, and your Father knows that you need them. [31]Instead, strive for his kingdom, and these things will be given to you as well."

REFLECTION QUESTIONS

The following questions can be used for discussion within a small group, or used for journal reflections by individuals.

1. Baillie's first prayer asks, among other things, that "[this prayer] will remain with me through all the hours of the day." Have you ever felt the energy of your morning prayer begin to fade as the day goes on? What things can we do to help our prayers remain with us through the day?

2. Baillie gives thanks for his many blessings—health, prosperity, material possessions, worldly influence, etc.—and asks that God help him put them in
God's service. Which of your blessings is most difficult for you to place in the
service of God? Why?

3. Baillie draws strength from the "cloud of witnesses" who have gone before
him: the saints and apostles and martyrs who have walked the road and left
us markers. Think of some of the people from the past who have given you
insight and encouragement in your spiritual journey. What blessings have
they provided you?

4. Jesus Christ is the focus of the sixth morning prayer. For Baillie, Jesus is not
only the focus of prayer but a model for Christian living to which he aspires.
Name some of the ways in which Christ is an inspiring example to you.

5. Jesus encourages us to consider the ravens and the lilies who do not worry
and yet are cared for by God. What are some of the things you have trouble
not worrying about? How can prayer enable you to gain victory over your
worries?

SUGGESTED EXERCISES

The following exercises can be done by individuals, shared between spiritual
friends, or used in the context of a small group. Choose one or more of the following.

1. Let John Baillie's morning prayers guide you in your times of prayer for the
next seven days. Read them slowly, meditating on each phrase, letting the
words dwell within you until they become your own.

2. Many of Baillie's prayers ask God to nurture certain values in his life. Choose
one or more of these virtues (e.g., chastity in thought, temperance in speech,
faithfulness in work) and make them the object of your special prayers this
week.

3. The greatest gift, according to Baillie, is the blessed life of Christ. He asks
God to help him remember all that Jesus said and did. This week, focus
your attention on the words and actions of Jesus as you read one of the
Gospels.

4. In the prayer of the seventh morning, Baillie offers a litany of praise to God
for the many things that make him grateful. Compose your own prayer of
praise, thanking God for the many things with which you have been blessed,
but that so often go unnoticed or are taken for granted.

REFLECTIONS

There is no better way to learn about prayer than by praying, and we can have no better human teacher than John Baillie. It is good to debate the mysteries of prayer, to ponder the profundities of prayer, to learn the methods of prayer. It is better to pray.

Prayer is a little like an automobile: you do not have to understand everything about its inner workings for it to get you somewhere. I have found that if we simply pray—even if we pray in wrong ways—God is pleased with our feeble efforts and Jesus lovingly guides us into more excellent ways. Also, we can be assured that the blessed Holy Spirit will adjust, correct, and interpret our prayer before the throne of God.

GOING DEEPER

Baillie, John. *A Diary of Private Prayer.* New York: Walker, 1986. Thirty days of written prayers for both morning and evening. With blank pages facing each written prayer for our own notations, reflections, and prayers, the form is well suited for leading us into the spirit of worship and prayer.

Baillie, John. *A Diary of Readings.* New York: Collier/Macmillan, 1955. Brief daily readings that draw on a great variety of sources from Athanasius to Bonhoeffer.

Baillie, John. *The Sense of the Presence of God.* New York: Scribner, 1962. This is the last book from the creative pen of Dr. Baillie. It was written to be delivered as the Gifford Lectures, and, although death prevented Baillie from delivering the lectures, the Gifford Committee recognized the manuscript's worth and gave it the status of Gifford Lectures, publishing it posthumously. It deals with the knotty problem of how finite human beings can know the infinite God and, in doing so, interacts with the prevailing philosophical movements of our day: logical positivism, linguistic analysis, existentialism, and others.

Martin Luther (1483–1546)

INTRODUCTION TO THE AUTHOR

Martin Luther is best known as the father of the Protestant Reformation. Born into a peasant family in Eisleben, Germany, Luther sought to better himself by becoming a scholar. However, at the age of twenty he suffered a deep anxiety about his own salvation and entered an Augustinian monastery to soothe his religious conscience. Soon afterward he felt called into the priesthood and was ordained in 1507. While serving as a professor of biblical literature at Wittenberg in 1512, he lectured on Paul's letter to the Romans, an exercise that shaped his theological thinking—especially concerning salvation. In 1517 he composed the famous ninety-five theses and nailed them on the door of the castle church in Wittenberg, registering his complaints with the Roman Catholic church and providing the impetus for the Protestant Reformation.

Luther was not only a brilliant theologian but also a man of deep piety. The following selection, compiled from three sources, demonstrates his insight into the subject of prayer. He was deeply influenced by the writings of St. Augustine and Bernard of Clairvaux. Luther's faith was lively, earthy, and practical; his logic was powerful; and his leadership skill unparalleled. As you read the following devotional selection you will be sitting at the feet of one of the most influential men in the history of the Church. More importantly, his experience of God was deep and abiding.

EXCERPTS FROM *TABLE TALK*, "EPISTLE SERMON, FOURTH SUNDAY IN ADVENT," AND "TREATISE ON GOOD WORKS"

1. Prayer and Supplication

By "prayer" we understand simply formal words or expressions—as, for instance, the Lord's Prayer and the psalms—which sometimes express more than our request. In "supplication" we strengthen prayer and make it effective by a certain form of persuasion; for instance, we may entreat one to grant a request for the sake of a father, or of something dearly loved or highly prized. We entreat God by his Son, his saints, his promises, his name. Thus

Solomon says, "Jehovah, remember for David all his affliction." And Paul urges, "I beseech you therefore, brethren, by the mercies of God"; and again, "I . . . entreat you by the meekness and gentleness of Christ."

2. Petition and Thanksgiving

"Petitioning" is stating what we have at heart, naming the desire we express in prayer and supplication. In the Lord's Prayer are seven petitions, beside prayer proper. Christ says: "Ask, and it shall be given you; seek, and ye shall find; knock, and it shall be opened unto you: for every one that asketh receiveth; and he that seeketh findeth; and to him that knocketh it shall be opened." In "thanksgiving" we recount blessings received and thus strengthen our confidence and enable ourselves to wait trustingly for what we pray.

3. Prayer Made Vigorous

Prayer is made vigorous by petitioning; urgent by supplication; by thanksgiving, pleasing and acceptable. Strength and acceptability combine to prevail and secure the petition. This, we see, is the manner of prayer practiced by the Church; and the holy fathers in the Old Testament always offered supplication and thanks in their prayers. The Lord's Prayer opens with praise and thanksgiving and the acknowledgment of God as a Father; it earnestly presses toward him through filial love and a recognition of fatherly tenderness. For supplication, this prayer is unequaled. Hence it is the sublimest and the noblest prayer ever uttered.

4. Unceasing Prayer

There is no Christian who does not have time to pray without ceasing. But I mean the spiritual praying, that is: no one is so heavily burdened with his labor, but that if he will he can, while working, speak with God in his heart, lay before Him his need and that of other men, ask for help, make petition, and in all this exercise and strengthen his faith.

5. What to Expect from Prayer

We should pray by fixing our mind upon some pressing need, desiring it with all earnestness, and then exercise faith and confidence toward God in the matter, never doubting that we have been heard. St. Bernard said, "Dear brothers, you should never doubt your prayer, thinking that it might have been in vain, for I tell you truly that before you have uttered the words, the prayer is already recorded in heaven. Therefore you should confidently expect from God one of two things: either that your prayer will be granted, or, that if it is not granted, the granting of it would not be good for you."

6. Praying in Faith

Prayer is a special exercise of faith. Faith makes the prayer acceptable because it believes that either the prayer will be answered, or that something better will be given instead. This is why James says, "Let him who asks of God not waver in faith, for if he wavers, let him not think that he shall receive anything from the Lord." This is a clear statement which says directly: he who does not trust will receive nothing, neither that which he asks nor anything better.

7. Jesus' Teaching on Prayer

Jesus himself has said, "Therefore I say unto you, What things soever ye desire, when ye pray, believe that ye receive them, and ye shall have them" (Mark 11, KJV). And in Luke 11 (editor's trans.) he said, "Ask, and it shall be given; seek, and you shall find; knock, and it shall be opened unto you. For everyone that asks receives, everyone who seeks finds, and to everyone who knocks it shall be opened. For what father among you, if his son asks for bread, will give him a stone? or if he asks for an egg, will give him a scorpion? If you know how to give good gifts to your children, how much more shall your Father who is in heaven give the Holy Spirit to all them that ask Him!"

Are we so hard of heart that these words of Jesus do not move us to pray with confidence, joyfully and gladly? So many of our prayers must be reformed if we are to pray according to these words. To be sure, all of the churches across the land are filled with people praying and singing, but why is it that there is so little improvement, so few results from so many prayers? The reason is none other than the one which James speaks of when he says, "You ask and do not receive because you ask amiss" (James 4:3). For where this faith and confidence is not in the prayer, the prayer is dead.

8. Laying the Need—Not Prescribing the Answer

From this it follows that the one who prays correctly never doubts that the prayer will be answered, even if the very thing for which one prays is not given. For we are to lay our need before God in prayer but not prescribe to God a measure, manner, time, or place. We must leave that to God, for he may wish to give it to us in another, perhaps better, way than we think is best. Frequently we do not know what to pray as St. Paul says in Romans 8, and we know that God's ways are above all that we

can ever understand as he says in Ephesians 3. Therefore, we should have no doubt that our prayer is acceptable and heard, and we must leave to God the measure, manner, time, and place, for God will surely do what is right.

9. Sinning on the Left or the Right

The true worshipers are those who worship God in Spirit and in truth. All who believe their prayers will not be heard sin upon the left hand against this Scripture in that they go far astray with their unbelief. But those who set times, places, measures, and limits for God sin upon the right hand and come too close with their tempting of God. So God has forbidden us to err from his commandment on either the left or the right, that is, either with unbelief or with tempting. Instead, we are to come to God in simple faith, remaining on the straight road, trusting him, and yet setting him no bounds.

10. What Should We Pray For?

What are the things we should lay before the Almighty God in prayer? Answer: First, our personal troubles. In Psalm 32, David cried out, "You are my hiding place; you will protect me from trouble and surround me with songs of deliverance" (v. 7, NIV). Likewise, in Psalm 142, "I cry aloud to the Lord . . . I pour out my complaint before him; before him I tell my trouble." When we pray we should keep in mind all of the shortcomings and excesses we feel, and pour them out freely to God, our faithful Father, who is ready to help. If you do not know or recognize your needs, or think you have none, then you are in the worst possible place. The greatest trouble we can ever know is thinking that we have no trouble for we have become hard-hearted and insensible to what is inside of us.

11. The Ten Commandments: A Mirror for the Soul

There is no better mirror in which to see your need than the Ten Commandments. In them you will find what you lack and what you should seek. You may find in them that you have a weak faith, small hope, and little love toward God. You may see that you do not praise and honor God as much as you praise and honor yourself. You may see that you do not love the Lord, your God, with all of your heart. When you see these things you should lay them before God, cry out to him and ask for help, and with all confidence expect help, believing that you are heard and that you will obtain mercy.

12. What a Great Gift We Have in Prayer

No one can believe how powerful prayer is and what it can effect, except those who have learned it by experience. It is important when we have a need to go to God in prayer. I know, whenever I have prayed earnestly, that I have been heard and have obtained more than I prayed for. God sometimes delays, but He always comes.

It is amazing that a poor human creature is able to speak with God's high Majesty in heaven and not be afraid. When we pray, the heart and the conscience must not pull away from God because of our sins and our unworthiness, or stand in doubt, or be scared away. When we pray we must hold fast and believe that God has heard our prayer. It was for this reason that the ancients defined prayer as an *Ascensus mentis ad Deum*, "a climbing up of the heart unto God."

BIBLE SELECTION: MARK 11:22–25

22Jesus answered them, "Have faith in God. 23Truly I tell you, if you say to this mountain, 'Be taken up and thrown into the sea,' and if you do not doubt in your heart, but believe that what you say will come to pass, it will be done for you. 24So I tell you, whatever you ask for in prayer, believe that you have received it, and it will be yours.

25"Whenever you stand praying, forgive, if you have anything against anyone; so that your Father in heaven may also forgive you your trespasses."

REFLECTION QUESTIONS

The following questions can be used for discussion within a small group, or used for journal reflections by individuals.

1. Prayer, according to Luther, involves stating what is in our hearts. How open and honest, would you say, is your prayer life? Do you find it difficult to be yourself before God?

2. According to Luther, one of two things is certain to happen each time we lift up a prayer to God. What are these two things?

3. Of all the attitudes necessary for true prayer, perhaps none is more essential for Luther than trust. In what areas in your life do you find it difficult to trust God?

4. Luther believes that we sin on the left when we lack faith and that we sin on the right when we prescribe specific measures and times to God. On which of the two sides are you prone to lean in your prayers?

5. Jesus said, "Whatever you ask for in prayer, believe that you have received it, and it will be yours." How does this compare or contrast with what Martin Luther teaches concerning prayer?

SUGGESTED EXERCISES

The following exercises can be done by individuals, shared between spiritual friends, or used in the context of a small group. Choose one or more of the following.

1. Strive to be more honest in your prayer life this week. State what is in your heart; allow yourself the freedom to be who you are as you stand in the presence of God.

2. Try using Luther's advice about not prescribing manner, measure, time, and place in your prayers. Learn the joy of faith that trusts God to answer your prayers in the best possible manner, measure, time, and place.

3. Use the Ten Commandments in your prayer time. As Luther recommends, use them—as one who gazes into a mirror—to help you see your life more clearly.

4. Jesus connects prayer and forgiveness in an inseparable way, not only in the passage from Mark 11, but also in the Lord's Prayer. This week make the forgiveness of others not merely a part of your prayers but an essential aspect of your life with God.

REFLECTIONS

Nothing is more central to the spiritual life than prayer, for prayer ushers us into perpetual communion with the heart of God. And there are many things to learn about this life of constant conversation with the Holy One.

But we must beware of making things too complicated. Like children coming to their parents, so we come to God. There is awe to be sure, but there is also intimacy. We bring our heart cries to a loving Father. Like the mother hen who gathers her chicks under her wings, so our God cares for us, protects us, comforts us (Matt. 23:37).

So no matter how much we study the labyrinthine realities of prayer, let us forever come as children to a loving Abba who delights to give and to forgive.

GOING DEEPER

Bainton, Roland H. *Here I Stand: A Life of Martin Luther.* New York: Abingdon, 1950. Popular history, superbly done without sacrificing scholarship or precision.

Dillenberger, John, ed. *Martin Luther: Selections from His Writings.* Garden City, NY: Anchor Books, 1961. Contains Luther's three Reformation treatises of 1520 ("Open Letter to the Christian Nobility," "The Babylonian Captivity of the Church," and "The Freedom of a Christian"), along with carefully selected works that show the historical and theological development of Luther's thought.

Luther, Martin. *Day by Day We Magnify Thee.* Minneapolis: Augsburg, 1982.

Luther, Martin. *Sermons of Martin Luther.* Edited by John N. Lenker. 8 vols. Grand Rapids, MI: Baker, 1983.

Luther, Martin. *The Table-Talk of Martin Luther.* Edited by T. S. Kepler. New York: World, 1952. A delightful collection of wit and wisdom (and some things not so wise) from Luther.

Jean-Nicholas Grou (1730–1803)

INTRODUCTION TO THE AUTHOR

Jean-Nicholas Grou lived in France and Holland. He was a Jesuit priest who entered into a deeper life with God on a retreat in 1767 where he learned to live his life in the spirit of prayer and complete abandon to God's will. He spent most of his time writing and speaking on the subject of spiritual growth, particularly the practice of prayer.

The following passage comes from his famous work *How to Pray*. In it he urges us to look to God alone to teach us to pray. Grou calls us to abandon our many methods and focus upon the object of our prayer: God. Many times we struggle in prayer because our focus is on the act of praying, i.e., the proper methods, formulae, and words. Grou teaches us to pray "in spirit and in truth" by letting our hearts, not our lips, do most of our praying. His writing is simple and precise, yet full of enthusiasm and warmth. When reading Grou one feels the presence of God in his words.

EXCERPTS FROM *HOW TO PRAY*

1. God Alone Teaches Us to Pray

One day the disciples said to Jesus Christ: "Lord, teach us to pray." It was the Holy Spirit who inspired them to make this request. The Holy Spirit convinced them of their inability to pray in their own strength, and he moved their hearts to draw near to Jesus Christ as the only Master who could teach them how they ought to pray. It was then that Jesus taught them the Lord's Prayer.

There is no Christian who is not in the same case as the disciples. Every Christian ought to say to the Savior as humbly as they:

"Lord, teach us to pray." Ah! if we were only convinced of our ignorance and of our need of a Teacher like Jesus Christ! If we would only approach him with confidence, asking him to teach us himself and desiring to be taught by his grace how to converse with God! How soon we should be skilled in it and how many of its secrets we should discover! Do not let us say that we know how to pray the prayer they learned from him. We may know the words, but without grace we cannot understand the meaning and we cannot ask or receive what it expresses.

2. Who Prevents Us?

Who prevents us from receiving the gift of prayer? Can we doubt that Jesus Christ is willing to give it to us? But do we desire it? Do we ask it? Do we think we need it? How many Christians do not even know what it is? And how many others instead of desiring it are afraid of it because it would commit them to a new way of life?

We know by heart a few forms of prayer. We find others to choose from in books. This is where many people stop, and when they have read these or recited them by heart, they imagine that nothing else is required. How grievously we deceive ourselves! With all these forms, however beautiful the sentiments expressed, we do not know how to pray. Perhaps we are praying in our own way, but we are not praying in God's way. Where is the woman whose chief prayer is to ask God to teach her how to pray?

God must teach us everything concerning the nature of prayer: its object, its characteristics, the disposition it requires, and the personal application we must make of it according to our needs. In the matter of prayer we are as ignorant of the theory as of the practice.

3. A Supernatural Act

We know in general that prayer is a religious act, but when it comes to praying we easily forget that it is a supernatural act which is therefore beyond our own strength and can only be performed by the inspiration and help of grace. As St. Paul says: "Not that we are competent to claim anything for ourselves, but our competence comes from God" (2 Cor. 3:5, NIV).

Do we have the feeling of our own insufficiency in our mind and in our heart? Are we conscious of it when we place ourselves in God's presence? Do we begin our prayers with this secret confession? I am not saying that we must always vocally ask God's help, but such a request ought to be in our hearts and such an attitude should govern the whole course of our prayer.

But if we are to look for everything from God, all our good thoughts and feelings, how is it that we are often so dull and indifferent, satisfied to say our prayers coldly and without any preparation? Why do others try so hard to inflame their imagination as if prayer depended on their own efforts, as if it were not necessary that God's action should govern and direct their prayer? Since prayer is a supernatural act, we must earnestly ask God to produce it in us, and then we must perform it tranquilly under his guidance. We must draw down divine grace by our favor and then we must cooperate with it without interfering with its effects. If God does not teach us, we shall never know thoroughly the nature of prayer.

4. A Wholly Spiritual Act

"God is a Spirit," said Jesus, "and they that worship him must worship him in spirit and in truth" (John 4:24, KJV). Prayer, then, is a wholly spiritual act, addressed to God who is the Supreme Spirit, the Spirit who sees all things and is present in all things. As St. Augustine says, God is closer to us than we are to ourselves. Knowing this is the essence of prayer. The posture of our body and the words we use have no significance in themselves and are only pleasing to God as they express the feelings of the heart. For it is the heart that prays, it is to the voice of the heart that God listens, and it is the heart that he answers. When we speak of the heart, we mean the most spiritual part of us. In the Scriptures, prayer is always ascribed to the heart, for it is the heart that God teaches and it is through the heart that he enlightens the mind.

5. From the Heart

If this is true, why do we pray so much with our lips and so little with our heart? Why in meditation do we work so hard in the search for considerations and use our wills so little to move them to acts of affections? Why do we not lay open our heart to God and beg him to put into it whatever is most pleasing to him? Who could call it a bad method if it springs from humility, from a deep sense of our own inability, and from a lively faith and trust in God? Such is the method suggested by the Holy Spirit to those souls who ask him to teach them how to pray.

"But my heart says nothing to me when I am in the presence of God," you say. "In the silence I find nothing but emptiness, dryness, distractions. If I try to fix my mind, to arouse in myself some feelings of devotion, to drive off distracting thoughts, it is absolutely essential for me to use a prayer book." Your heart says nothing?! In so far as it is silent, you are not praying at all, but is it any less so when your mouth is uttering words? Do you not see that these fine feelings you borrow from books only affect your imagination? They are not your words, but someone else's, and they become yours only for the moment that you are reading them; once the book is closed, you are as dry and as cold as you were before. "Nevertheless," you say, "I was praying while I was reciting or reading that set of words." So you think and you are satisfied, but is that God's point of view? Is God equally satisfied? What do your words matter to him, to him who only listens to the heart?

6. The Voice of the Heart

You ask me what this voice of the heart is. It is love which is the voice of the heart. Love God and you will always be speaking to him. The seed of love is growth in prayer. If you do not understand that, you have never yet either loved or prayed. Ask God to open your heart and kindle in it a spark of his love, and then you will begin to understand what praying means.

If it is the heart that prays, it is evident that sometimes, and even continuously, it can pray by itself without any help from words, spoken or conceived. Here is something which few people understand and which some even entirely deny. They insist that there must be definite and formal acts. They are mistaken, and God has not yet taught them how the heart prays. It is true that thoughts are formed in the mind before they are clothed in words. The proof of this is that we often search for the right word and reject one after another until we find the right one which expresses our thoughts accurately. We need words to make ourselves intelligible to other people but not to the Spirit. It is the same with the feelings of the heart. The heart conceives feelings and adopts them without any need of resorting to words unless it wishes to communicate them to others or to make them clear to itself.

For God reads the secrets of the heart. God reads its most intimate feelings, even those which we are not aware of. And if these are feelings about God, how could he fail to see them, since it is God who plants them in us by his grace and helps our will to adopt them? It is not necessary to make use of formal acts to make ourselves heard by God. If we do make use of them in prayer, it is not so much for God's sake as our own in that they help us to keep our attention fixed in his presence. Our weakness often calls for the help of such acts, but they are not of the essence of prayer.

7. The Prayer of Silence

Imagine a soul so closely united to God that it has no need of outward acts to remain attentive to the inward prayer. In these moments of silence and peace when it pays no heed to what is happening within itself, it prays and prays excellently, with a simple and direct prayer that God will understand perfectly by the action of grace. The heart will be full of aspirations towards God without any clear expression. Though they may elude our own consciousness, they will not escape the consciousness of God. This prayer, so empty of all images and perceptions, apparently so passive and yet so active, is, so far as the limitations of this life allow, pure adoration in spirit and in truth. It is adoration fully worthy of God in which the soul is united to him as its ground, the created intelligence to the uncreated, without anything but a very simple attention of the mind and an equally simple application of the will. This is what is called the prayer of silence, or of quiet, or of bare faith.

8. God Is Teaching Your Heart

If you feel any attraction for the simple and general prayer of which I have been speaking, do not reject it on the excuse that it has no definite aim and that you rise from your knees without having asked for anything. Let me say it again, you are mistaken. In reality, you have asked for everything, both for yourself and for those whom you love, and far more effectually than if you had made the detailed requests whose many words would only have exhausted you and hindered the action of God.

After this brief explanation, you must see that you have not until now understood what prayer really is. If, after reading this you are beginning to have a new understanding of prayer, thank God for it; for it is he who is teaching your heart and what I am writing here for your instruction comes from him.

BIBLE SELECTION: MATTHEW 6:5–13

[5]"And whenever you pray, do not be like the hypocrites; for they love to stand and pray in the synagogues and at the street corners, so that they may be seen by others. Truly I tell you, they have received their reward. [6]But whenever you pray, go into your room and shut the door and pray to your Father who is in secret; and your Father who sees in secret will reward you.

[7]"When you are praying, do not heap up empty phrases as the Gentiles do; for they think that they will be heard because of their many words. [8]Do not be like them, for your Father knows what you need before you ask him.

[9]"Pray then in this way:

> Our Father in heaven,
> hallowed be your name.
> [10]Your kingdom come.
> Your will be done,
> on earth as it is in heaven.
> [11]Give us this day our daily bread.
> [12]And forgive us our debts,
> as we also have forgiven our debtors.
> [13]And do not bring us to the time of trial,
> but rescue us from the evil one."

REFLECTION QUESTIONS

The following questions can be used for discussion within a small group, or used for journal reflections by individuals.

1. Jean-Nicholas Grou asks, "Who prevents us from receiving the gift of prayer?" What are some of the hindrances that prevent you from receiving a richer prayer life?

2. Essential to the act of prayer is an acknowledgment of our inability to pray in our own strength. In what ways can we demonstrate an awareness of our need for God in prayer?

3. Sometimes, Grou notes, we work hard in our times of prayer, straining to obtain a spiritual feeling or an extraordinary spiritual experience. According to Grou, what is wrong with this approach?

4. If you were to adopt Grou's advice for the next week, how would your current way of praying be changed?

5. In section 8, the author handles the question, If I am silent, how can I make my requests known to God? Grou replies, "In reality, you have asked for everything, both for yourself and for those whom you love, and far more effectually than if you had made detailed requests." How does this compare with Jesus' teaching in Matthew 6:8? Does this teaching negate the need, at times, to list specific requests?

SUGGESTED EXERCISES

The following exercises can be done by individuals, shared between spiritual friends, or used in the context of a small group. Choose one or more of the following.

1. Try Grou's approach for one week. Pray by exercising a simple attention to God and a simple application of the will.

2. Make your prayer less wordy this week. Keep in mind the point made by Grou that God hears the heart and not the words.

3. Take the strain and stress out of your prayer life for the next several days. Adopt Grou's advice, letting your awareness of your helplessness, not your personal power, establish your relationship with God.

4. Pray the Lord's Prayer this week, but pray it with fresh eyes and a heart that longs to be taught how to pray by the One who calls us to pray.

REFLECTIONS

We live in a wordy world. All too often, we rush into the presence of God with hearts and minds askew and tongues full of words. How much better to settle down into reverential silence and awe before the Holy One of eternity. Jean-Nicholas Grou invites us into just such an experience.

Allow me to share one small experiment I am making in this area. When I pray for others—wife, children, friends, even myself—rather than asking for many things, I am trying to lovingly hold each one in the presence of the Father. And listening. At times, words of encouragement or comfort or guidance are given. At other times, there is no verbal communication at all. But there is always communion for I am most surely in the presence of the living God.

Perhaps my little experiment can give us a glimmering (only a glimmering, I'm sure) of what Grou means when he speaks of "the voice of the heart" that can pray "without any help from words, spoken or conceived."

GOING DEEPER

Grou, Jean-Nicholas. *How to Pray.* Translated by Joseph Dalby. Cambridge: James Clarke, 1982. This book is taken from a much larger work by Grou, *The School of Jesus Christ.* Evelyn Underhill called it "one of the best short expositions of the essence of prayer which has ever been written." The thrust of the book is to draw us into the prayer of silence where, as Grou puts it, "our Savior bids us keep silence and allow our hearts to speak far more eloquently than our lips."

The Virtuous Life

THE HOLINESS TRADITION (the Virtuous Life) is concerned with the personal moral transformation that comes through the development of what the old writers called "holy habits." We are doing what we can (e.g., engaging in spiritual disciplines) in order to receive from God the power to do what we cannot (e.g., love our enemies).

The one thread you will see weaving its way through all these selections is the centrality of love as the motivation for holiness. It is prominent in Richard Rolle's stress on "the vastness and sweetness of love" and the *Theologia Germanica*'s insight into love as the highest impetus for spiritual exercises.

Both Teresa of Avila and Thomas à Kempis deal with temptation and the process involved in overcoming sin. We are fortunate to be able to look at this fundamental issue from both a feminine and a masculine perspective.

Gregory of Nyssa and John Calvin each approach holiness from the perspective of the *athleti dei,* the athletes of God, who are in training for the race of life. Self-denial (the *via negativa*) and vigorous spiritual exercises (the *via positiva*) are both part of a training program appropriate for the development of body, mind, and spirit.

Blaise Pascal reminds us of the dual nature of greatness and wretchedness that hounds our human existence. He does not quickly or easily reconcile the inner contradictions that we all feel, but in the end he does point to a "light for those who desire . . . to see."

Benedict of Nursia focuses his attention on humility and provides simple practical steps we can take to advance in this most excellent of virtues. Finally, William Law reminds us that our faith must, of necessity, produce loving action. Spiritual disciplines are of no value whatsoever unless they make us more loving persons.

These men and women of faith are wise in the ways of holiness. We will do well to linger long over their penetrating words.

Theologia Germanica (ca. 1350)

INTRODUCTION TO THE AUTHOR

Martin Luther, in his 1516 preface to the *Theologia Germanica*, observes that only God knows who wrote the book. As best we can discern, it grew out of the fourteenth-century German renewal movement known as "The Friends of God." Taking its name from Jesus' words in John 15:15, "I have called you friends," this dynamic movement stressed intimacy with God, piety of life, and complete obedience to the commands of Christ.

Written about 1350, the *Theologia* circulated as a kind of "tract" urging people to experience Christ living and present. In 1516 Martin Luther came upon a short version of it and was so impressed that he immediately wrote a brief introduction and had it printed in Wittenberg. Two years later he found a more extensive copy, gave it a more elaborate introduction, and published it in 1518. Luther said that next to the Bible and St. Augustine, he had never read anything as helpful as the *Theologia*.

The driving aim of the *Theologia* is to move our knowledge and experience of God from the "outer person" to the "inner person." It urges us to take quite seriously Jesus' words that out of the heart come the issues of life (Matt. 15:19). Therefore, it brings an important message to us today just as it did to those who lived in the fourteenth and fifteenth centuries.

EXCERPTS FROM THE *THEOLOGIA GERMANICA OF MARTIN LUTHER*

1. God Wills This Ordered Life

One says—and rightly so—that God is above and without rules, measure, and order, yet renders to all things rules, order, measure, and moral integrity.

This should be understood in the following manner: God wills this ordered life. In himself, without the created beings, he cannot have that. For in God, without the relationship to the creature, our human distinctions cannot be made between order and the absence of it, rules for living and lack of them. God, however, has ordained it thus that these structures should be.

For as far as word, work, and deportment are concerned, we always stand in a choice between, on the one hand, rule and righteousness, or, on the other hand, disorder. Now, orderliness and righteousness are better and nobler than the opposite.

2. Sour and Burdensome

Four kinds of people deal with order, command, and rule in four different ways.

Some lead an ordered life neither for God's sake nor out of a particular personal desire, but simply because they are compelled. They do the least possible and it all turns sour and burdensome for them.

A second group observes laws and rules for the sake of reward. That is, people who believe that it is possible to earn the kingdom of heaven and eternal life. They consider that person holy who observes a great many rules. The person who neglects even some little rule, they believe, is lost to the devil. They show great seriousness and diligence in keeping these rules, yet, after a time, it all turns sour and burdensome for them.

The third kind of people are the wicked, false people who think of themselves as perfect and are quick to tell you just how perfect they are. They think that they do not need any rules and laws and, in fact, scoff at any talk about "order."

3. Out of Love

Fourth, we have those who have been illumined by God and guided by the true Light. They do not practice the ordered life in expectation of reward. They do not want to acquire anything with the aid of reward, nor do they hope that they will some day reap some reward because of it. No, they do what they do in the ordered life out of love.

They are not so concerned about the outcome, about how a particular behavior will turn out, how soon, and so on. Their concern is rather that things will work out well, in peace and inner ease. And if sometimes some less important rules have to be neglected, they are not lost in despair.

They know, of course, that order and rectitude are better and nobler than the lack of it. So they want to keep the rules, but they also know that their salvation and happiness are not dependent on the observance of rules. Therefore they are not as anxious as others.

4. Keeping to the Middle

Quite often those in the fourth group are condemned and judged by persons in groups two and three. For instance, the hirelings, also called the "reward folk" (the second group), say of them that they are too careless and sometimes call them unrighteous. The group consisting of "the free spirits" (the third group) will scoff at them: "They believe vain and silly things."

But the "illumined" (the fourth group) keep to the middle which is the best. For a lover of God is better and more pleasing to God than a hundred thousand hirelings. This also applies to their outward actions.

Note, it is the inner person who receives God's law, his word, and all his teachings. These show him how to become united with God. Where this happens, the outer person is structured and tutored by the inner person and learns that no outward law or teaching is needed, for human laws and commands belong to the outer person. They are needed when one knows nothing better. Otherwise people would not know what to do, or what not to do, and so become like dogs or cattle.

5. The Soul of Christ Has Two Eyes

Remember how it is written that the soul of Christ has two eyes, a right eye and a left eye. In the beginning, when these eyes were created, Christ's soul turned its right eye toward eternity and the Godhead and therefore immovably beheld and participated in divine Being and divine Wholeness. This vision continued unmoved and unhampered by all vicissitudes, travail, agitation, suffering, torment, agony—tribulations surpassing anything ever experienced in a person's outer life.

But at the same time the left eye of Christ's soul, his other spiritual vision, penetrated the world of created beings and there discerned the distinctions among us, saw which ones were better and which ones were less good, nobler, or less noble. Christ's outward being was structured in accordance with such inner discrimination.

6. When Hanging on the Cross

Thus Christ's inner being, its vision through the soul's right eye, always participated in full measure in the divine nature, in complete bliss and joy.

But the outer person, the left eye of his soul, was involved in a full measure of suffering, distress, and travail. Yet this took place in such a way that the inner, right eye remained unmoved, unimpeded, untouched by all the travail, suffering, and torment that the outer person had to deal with.

It has been said that Christ, when bound to the pillar and beaten and when hanging on the cross, experienced all this in his outer person while the inner person, the soul in its function as the right eye, rested in the same bliss

and joy as it did after the Ascension or as it does at this very moment.

By this same token Christ's outer person, the soul in its function as the left eye, was never impeded or weakened in its discharge of external duties.

7. To Peer into the Eternal

Now, the created soul of man also has two eyes. One represents the power to peer into the eternal. The other gazes into time and the created world, enabling us to distinguish between the lofty and the less lofty, as I said above.

But these two eyes, which are parts of our soul, cannot carry out their functions simultaneously. If the soul is looking into eternity through its right eye, the left eye must cease all its undertakings and act as if it were dead. If the left eye were to concentrate on the things of this outer world (that is to say, be absorbed by time and created beings), it would hinder the musing of the right eye.

8. Remaining Within

We should note and know what is the simple truth, namely, that no virtue and no good action, not even the confession that God is good, can make man and his soul virtuous, good, or blissful so long as it occurs outside the soul.

Conversely, the same applies to sin and wickedness. It may be commendable to ask, hear about, and gather information concerning good and holy persons, what they have done and suffered, or how they have lived and how God has worked and willed in and through them.

But it is a hundredfold better that people deeply within themselves learn and understand the what and the how of life. They need to learn what God is working and doing in them and how God wishes to use them and not to use them. Thus the saying is still true: No outgoing was ever so good that a remaining within was not better.

9. Only Wait for God

It should also be pointed out that eternal bliss is rooted in God alone and nothing else. And if people are to be saved, this one and only God must be in their soul.

You may ask: "What is that one thing?" I answer: "It is Goodness or that which comes through to us as Goodness." It is neither this nor that particular good that we may name, know, or manifest, but is all good things and that which is above all good things.

This eternal Good does not have to come into the soul, for It is already there, albeit unrecognized. When we say that we should come into the One or that the One should come into the soul, it is the same as saying that we should seek, feel, and taste it. Since it is *one*, it follows that unity and singleness is to be preferred to the manifold.

For bliss or blessedness does not come from the wealth of things, but from God. In other words, bliss or blessedness does not depend on any created thing or on a creature's work, but only on God and his works.

Therefore, I should only wait for God and his work and leave aside all creatures with all their works, first of all my own self.

Let me also say this: No great works and wonders God has ever wrought or shall ever do in or through his created world, not even God himself in his goodness, will make me blessed if they remain outside of me. For blessedness is only present to the extent to which it is within me, as a happening, as an inner knowledge, as love, as feeling and taste.

10. The False Light and the True Light

I have briefly mentioned the false light. I would like to say something further about what it is and how it works.

Look, all that is contrary to the true Light belongs to the false light.

It is an essential quality of the true Light that It does not know deceit, is not inspired by will to deceive, and that It cannot itself be deceived.

But the false light is deceived and constantly pulls others into its deceit.

God does not wish to deceive anyone. He cannot desire that someone be deceived. This is consequently true also about the true Light.

Note now, that the true Light is God, is divine; the false light is nature or natural.

As God is the true Light, void of all I and self and all self-indulgence, so, conversely, the mark of the natural creation and the natural false light is to pamper the I, the Me, and its outgrowths.

Man fancies himself to be what he is not. He fancies himself to be God, yet he is only nature, a created being. From within that illusion he begins to claim for himself the traits that are the marks of God.

Mark this: those who are living in the true light, perceive that everything they might desire or elect is nothing compared to that which has always been desired or elected by all creatures in the depth of their being.

This realization leads them to let go of all desire and reliance on worldly things, surrendering themselves completely to God.

BIBLE SELECTION: JOHN 3:1–8

Now there was a Pharisee named Nicodemus, a leader of the Jews. [2]He came to Jesus by night and said to him, "Rabbi, we know that you are a teacher who has come from God; for no one can do these signs that you do apart from the presence of God." [3]Jesus answered him, "Very truly, I tell you, no one can see the kingdom of God without being born from above." [4]Nicodemus said to him, "How can anyone be born after having grown old? Can one enter a second time into the mother's womb and be born?" [5]Jesus answered, "Very truly, I tell you, no one can enter the kingdom of God without being born of water and the Spirit. [6]What is born of the flesh is flesh, and what is born of the Spirit is spirit. [7]Do not be astonished that I said to you, 'You must be born from above.' [8]The wind blows where it chooses, and you hear the sound of it, but you do not know where it comes from or where it goes. So it is with everyone who is born of the Spirit."

REFLECTION QUESTIONS

The following questions can be used for discussion within a small group, or used for journal reflections by individuals.

1. List the four kinds of people who try to live an ordered, moral life. Which of the four are you most like?
2. The right eye of the soul looks to the eternal, while the left eye looks to the things of this world. Using this metaphor, which is your dominant eye?
3. The author of the *Theologia Germanica* stresses the importance of being motivated from the inside, not merely from the outside. What kinds of inner, and what kinds of outer motivations prompt you to engage in the spiritual disciplines?
4. Our whole world runs on a system of rewards and punishments; e.g., we tend to obey the speed limit for fear of getting a ticket. Yet the author suggests that obedience must be loved for itself, not merely for its rewards or for fear of punishment. How does God's grace fit into this struggle?
5. According to John 3:3, what is the result of being born from above? Which "eye," according to the *Theologia Germanica,* would Nicodemus need in order to understand what Jesus was trying to explain to him?

SUGGESTED EXERCISES

The following exercises can be done by individuals, shared between spiritual friends, or used in the context of a small group. Choose one or more of the following.

1. Begin watching for the motivation behind your actions this week. Use the four categories mentioned in the *Theologia Germanica* as your guide. Are you doing a certain thing out of duty, reward, rebellion, or love?

2. Try going about your tasks this week without being concerned with the outcome of your efforts. Instead, simply enjoy the doing of the task without looking at the "scoreboard."

3. Blessedness, says the author, does not depend on material possessions. This week learn to enjoy God in simple ways, such as taking a walk in a park, viewing a sunset, or spending time with your family. Allow God's presence to season every aspect of your life.

4. The wind, says Jesus, blows where it wills, and you do not know where it came from or where it is going. This week be more open to the gentle breezes of the Spirit, and less controlled by routine. Let the inner motivation of the Spirit empower your actions.

REFLECTIONS

The Friends of God movement (from which the Theologia *came) stood in stark contrast to another popular movement of that day—"The Brothers and Sisters of the Free Spirit." The latter group insisted on following the Spirit without reference to any moral parameters or ethical responsibility. In contrast, the Friends of God insisted on rules and order as essential ingredients in the development of a moral life, and yet without a deadly legalism.*

Their emphasis upon true Christian liberty within the context of clear moral parameters is sorely needed today. Many in our day want to cast aside all moral restraints. Others want to bind us to the letter of the law. The Theologia *is useful in pointing us to a more excellent way—the way of divine grace and mercy that is informed by a clear moral vision.*

GOING DEEPER

Luther, Martin. *Theologia Germanica of Martin Luther.* Translated by Bengt Hoffman. New York: Paulist, 1980. From *The Classics of Western Spirituality* series. The endurance of this book is due in large measure to Luther's warm endorsement of it. There were some twenty editions of it printed in his lifetime. My guess is that Luther's enthusiasm was due more to the Friends of God movement out of which the book came than because of the book itself. The Friends of God was a deeply spiritual movement of heart faith that shared many of the concerns that Luther was later to champion in the Reformation.

The book itself is often disjointed, hard to read, and even harder to understand. Nevertheless, it contains helpful insights into how the individual grows in grace. In particular, it understands how God uses the patient acceptance of trials, the exercise of spiritual disciplines, and the gentle movings of the Spirit to effect the transformation of the individual into the likeness of Christ.

Gregory of Nyssa (331–396)

INTRODUCTION TO THE AUTHOR

Gregory of Nyssa was one of the great "fathers" of the Church. He lived in the fourth century, a time when the persecution of the Christians was coming to an end. Gregory was one of three Greek Cappadocian fathers (the other two were Gregory's brother, St. Basil, and their mutual friend, Gregory of Nazianzus).

He has been called "one of the most powerful and most original thinkers ever known in the history of the Church" (Louis Bouyer). His writings have had a great influence on the spirituality of the Eastern church. He was well versed in Greek philosophy, notably Platonism and Stoicism, but the basis of his thought was rooted in the Bible.

Gregory believed that the main use of the Bible was not for historical reflection but rather for growth in virtue. He and the other Church fathers used the Bible and its characters to teach us how to grow closer to God, how to "elevate" the soul to God. He saw the spiritual life as a race in which we, like St. Paul, "forget . . . what lies behind and strain . . . forward to what lies ahead" (Phil. 3:13).

The following excerpts are taken from Gregory's most famous work, *The Life of Moses*. It was written in response to requests for guidance in living the virtuous life. For Gregory, perfection is discovered in continual striving—a perpetual progress rooted in the infinite grace of God.

EXCERPTS FROM *THE LIFE OF MOSES*

1. The Divine Race

At horse races the spectators intent on victory shout to their favorites in the contest, even though the horses are eager to run. From the stands they participate in the race with their eyes, thinking to incite the charioteer to keener effort, at the same time urging the horses on while leaning forward and flailing the air with their outstretched hands instead of a whip.

They do this not because their actions themselves contribute anything to the victory; but in this way, by their good will, they eagerly show in voice and deed their concern for the contestants. I seem to be doing the same thing myself, most valued friend and brother. While you are competing admirably in the divine race along the course of virtue, lightfootedly leaping and straining constantly for the *prize of the heavenly calling,* I exhort, urge, and encourage you vigorously to increase your speed.

2. Ready Obedience

Since the letter which you recently sent requested us to furnish you with some counsel concerning the perfect life, I thought it only proper to answer your request. Although there may be nothing useful for you in my words, perhaps this example of ready obedience will not be wholly unprofitable to you. For if we who have been appointed to the position as fathers over so many souls consider it proper here in our old age to accept a commission from youth, how much more suitable is it, inasmuch as we have taught you, a young man, to obey voluntarily, that the right action of ready obedience be confirmed in you.

3. The Perfect Life

So much for that. We must take up the task that lies before us, taking God as our guide in our treatise. You requested, dear friend, that we trace in outline for you what the perfect life is. Your intention clearly was to translate the grace disclosed by my word into your own life, if you should find in my treatise what you are seeking.

I am at an equal loss about both things: it is beyond my power to encompass perfection in my treatise or to show in my life the insights of the treatise. And perhaps I am not alone in this. Many great men, even those who excel in virtue, will admit that for them such an accomplishment as this is unattainable. As I would not seem, in the words of the Psalmist, *there to tremble for fear, where no fear was,* I shall put forth for you more clearly what I think.

4. Ever Running the Course of Virtue

The perfection of everything which can be measured by the senses is marked off by certain definite boundaries. Quantity, for example, admits both continuity and limitation. The person who looks at the number ten knows that its perfection consists in the fact that it has both a beginning and an end.

But in the case of virtue we have learned from the Apostle that its one limit of perfection is the fact that it has no limit. For that divine Apostle, great and lofty in understanding, ever running the course of virtue, never ceased *straining toward those things that are still to come.* Coming to a stop in the race was not safe for him. Why? Because no Good has a limit in its own nature but is limited by the presence of its opposite, as life is limited by death and light by darkness. And every good thing generally ends with all those things which are perceived to be contrary to the good.

5. Stopping in the Race

Just as the end of life is the beginning of death, so also stopping in the race of virtue marks the beginning of the race of evil. Thus our statement that grasping perfection with reference to virtue is impossible was not false, for it has been pointed out that what has been marked off by boundaries is not virtue.

I said that it is also impossible for those who pursue the life of virtue to attain perfection. The meaning of this statement will be explained.

The Divine One is himself the Good (in the primary and proper sense of the word), whose very nature is goodness. This he is and he is so named, and is known by this nature. Since, then, it has not been demonstrated that there is any limit to virtue except evil, and since the Divine does not admit of an opposite, we hold the divine nature to be unlimited and infinite. Certainly whoever pursues true virtue participates in nothing other than God, because he is himself absolute virtue. Since, then, those who know what is good by nature desire participation in it, and since this good has no limit, the participant's desire itself necessarily has no stopping place but stretches out with the limitless.

6. The Unattainable Commandment

It is therefore undoubtedly impossible to attain perfection, since, as I have said, perfection is not marked off by limits: The one limit of virtue is the absence of a limit. How then would one arrive at the sought-for boundary when he can find no boundary?

Although on the whole my argument has shown that what is sought for is unattainable, one should not disregard the commandment of the Lord which says, *Therefore be perfect, just as your heavenly father is perfect.* For in the case of those things which are good by nature, even if men of understanding were not able to attain everything, by attaining even a part they could yet gain a great deal.

7. The Attainable Perfection

We should show great diligence not to fall away from the perfection which is attainable but to acquire as much as possible: to that extent let us make progress within the realm of what we seek. For the perfection of human nature consists perhaps in its very growth in goodness.

It seems good to me to make use of Scripture as a counselor in this matter. For the divine voice says somewhere in the prophecy of Isaiah, *Consider Abraham your father, and Sarah who gave you birth.* Scripture gives this admonition to those who wander outside of virtue.

8. Back on Course

Just as at sea those who are carried away from the direction of the harbor bring themselves back on course by a clear sign, upon seeing either a beacon of light raised up high or some mountain peak coming into view, in the same way Scripture by the example of Abraham and Sarah may guide again to the harbor of the divine will those adrift on the sea of life with a pilotless mind.

Human nature is divided into male and female, and the free choice of virtue or of evil is set before both equally. For this reason the corresponding example of virtue for each sex has been exemplified by the divine voice, so that each, by observing the one to which he is akin (the men to Abraham and the women to Sarah), may be directed in the life of virtue by the appropriate examples.

9. The Sheltered Harbor of Virtue

Perhaps, then, the memory of anyone distinguished in life would be enough to fill our need for a beacon light and to show us how we can bring our soul to the sheltered harbor of virtue where it no longer has to pass the winter amid the storms of life or be shipwrecked in the deep water of evil by the successive billows of passion. It may be for this very reason that the daily life of those sublime individuals is recorded in detail, that by imitating those earlier examples of right action those who follow them may conduct their lives to the good.

What then? Someone will say, "How shall I imitate them, since I was not a Chaldean as I remember Abraham was, nor was I nourished by the daughter of the Egyptian as Scripture teaches about Moses, and in general I do not have in these matters anything in my life corresponding to anyone of the ancients? How shall I place myself in the same rank with one of them, when I do not know how to imitate anyone so far removed from me by the circumstances of his life?"

To him we reply that we do not consider being a Chaldean a virtue or a vice, nor is anyone exiled from the life of virtue by living in Egypt or spending his life in Babylon, nor again has God been known to the esteemed individuals in Judea only, nor is Zion, as people commonly think, the divine habitation. We need some subtlety of understanding and keenness of vision to discern from the history how, by removing ourselves from such Chaldeans and Egyptians and by escaping from such a Babylonian captivity, we shall embark on the blessed life.

10. Becoming God's Friend

Since the goal of the virtuous way of life is the very thing we have been seeking, it is time for you, noble friend, to be known by God and to become his friend.

This is true perfection: not to avoid a wicked life because like slaves we servilely fear punishment, nor to do good because we hope for rewards, as if cashing in on the virtuous life by some business-like arrangement. On the contrary, disregarding all those things for which we hope and which have been reserved by promise, we regard falling from God's friendship as the only thing dreadful and we consider becoming God's friend the only thing worthy of honor and desire. This, as I have said, is the perfection of life.

As your understanding is lifted up to what is magnificent and divine, whatever you may find (and I know full well that you will find many things) will most certainly be for the common benefit in Christ Jesus. Amen.

BIBLE SELECTION: PHILIPPIANS 3:12–21

[12]Not that I have already obtained this or have already reached the goal; but I press on to make it my own, because Christ Jesus has made me his own. [13]Beloved, I do not consider that I have made it my own; but this one thing I do: forgetting what lies behind and straining forward to what lies ahead, [14]I press on toward the goal for the prize of the heavenly call of God in Christ Jesus. [15]Let those of us then who are mature be of the same mind; and if you think differently about anything, this too God will reveal to you. [16]Only let us hold fast to what we have attained.

[17]Brothers and sisters, join in imitating me, and observe those who live according to the example you have in us. [18]For many live as enemies of the cross of Christ; I have often told you of them, and now I tell you even with tears. [19]Their end is destruction; their god is the belly; and their glory is in their shame; their

minds are set on earthly things. [20]But our citizenship is in heaven, and it is from there that we are expecting a Savior, the Lord Jesus Christ. [21]He will transform the body of our humiliation that it may be conformed to the body of his glory, by the power that also enables him to make all things subject to himself.

REFLECTION QUESTIONS

The following questions can be used for discussion within a small group, or used for journal reflections by individuals.

1. Gregory of Nyssa compares the spiritual journey to a race. Using that metaphor, what kind of race has your spiritual journey been? A sprint? A marathon? An obstacle course? A downhill coast? An uphill climb?

2. Think of some of the people who have "cheered you on" in your spiritual journey. How did they "exhort, urge, and encourage" you?

3. Does Gregory believe that it is possible to be perfect? Why or why not?

4. Which Bible characters have been "beacons of light" for you? How have their stories inspired you?

5. Paul says that he has not attained perfection or been made perfect yet, but he presses on to take hold of something. For what does he strive? For what are you earnestly striving (what are your goals and desires in life)?

SUGGESTED EXERCISES

The following exercises can be done by individuals, shared between spiritual friends, or used in the context of a small group. Choose one or more of the following.

1. This week cheer someone on in his or her spiritual journey. Send a letter, give that person a phone call, or drop by for a visit, simply to encourage him or her to keep running the race.

2. Chart out one or two areas of your life in which you would like to see some growth. Share your desires and intentions with a friend who can help you grow through the grace of accountability.

3. Do a study of one of the great heroes of the faith (Esther, Moses, Ruth, Abraham, etc.). Let that person's story of courage, faith, and failure redeemed become a source of inspiration to you.

4. True perfection, writes Gregory of Nyssa, consists in becoming a friend of God. This week strengthen your friendship with God by spending time with God, sharing more and more of your life—your hopes and dreams and failures—and allowing God to love you as a cherished friend.

REFLECTIONS

I love the way Gregory's insights are able to cut through all the contemporary debate over perfectionism. He is simply not worried about one doctrine of sanctification over against another.

You see, the cure for an unhealthy perfectionism is not to reject all emphases upon holiness (after all, holy living is God's idea) but rather to insist upon progress in the spiritual life. Gregory's chief concern is that we grow in virtue. For him virtue comes in the trying, the struggling, the running of the race. And the final goal of virtue is that we become the friends of God. That is something worth dedicating our lives to, isn't it!

GOING DEEPER

Gregory of Nyssa. *From Glory to Glory: Texts from Gregory of Nyssa's Mystical Writings.* Edited by Jean Danielou and Herbert Musurillo. London, 1961.

Gregory of Nyssa. *The Life of Moses.* Translated by Abraham J. Malherbe and Everett Ferguson. Edited by Richard J. Payne. New York: Paulist, 1978. From *The Classics of Western Spirituality.*

In this, the best known of his works, Gregory seeks to build a bridge between sophisticated Greeks and the Jewish scriptures. To do this he engages in rather elaborate spiritualizing of the story of Moses in order to focus on the *theoria* or spiritual meaning of the text. This was a common practice in the fourth century; for us it takes a little getting used to.

Richard Rolle (1290–1349)

INTRODUCTION TO THE AUTHOR

Born in the village of Thornton in the diocese of York in England, Richard Rolle was one of the great spiritual leaders of England. He came from humble beginnings and, through the help of a benefactor, was able to attend Oxford. Although he was an outstanding student, he decided to quit before finishing his master's degree because he did not want to get mixed up in the vanity of the academic world.

Rolle returned to Yorkshire and literally ran away from home in order to become a hermit. He made a hermit's habit out of his father's raincoat and left for a nearby church to spend the night in prayer as a preparation. While there he was rapt in a deep experience of prayer so astonishing that onlookers could only marvel as he prayed through the night. When he later preached in that church, it marked the beginning of a powerful ministry.

He lived in different towns and villages throughout his life: sometimes in a monastery, sometimes in a nunnery. He also became famous for his writings, especially his work *The Fire of Love*. Rolle wrote with a kind of passion and energy that few writers have demonstrated. For two hundred years following his death he was highly revered as "St. Richard the Hermit," and his writings were treasured by both religious and nonreligious.

EXCERPTS FROM *THE FIRE OF LOVE*

1. The Spiritual Flame That Feeds the Soul

I cannot tell you how surprised I was the first time I felt my heart begin to warm. It was real warmth, too, not imaginary, and it felt as if it were actually on fire. I was astonished at the way the heat surged up and how this new sensation brought great and unexpected comfort. I had to keep feeling my breast to make sure there was no physical reason for it.

But once I realized that it came entirely from within, that this fire of love had no cause, material or sinful, but was the gift of my Maker, I was absolutely delighted, and wanted my love to be even greater. And this longing was all the more urgent because of the delightful effect and the interior sweetness which this spiritual flame fed into my soul. Before the infusion of this comfort, I had never thought that we exiles could possibly have known such warmth, so sweet was the devotion it kindled. It set my soul aglow as if a real fire was burning there.

2. The Vastness and Sweetness of Love

Yet as some may well remind us, there are people on fire with love for Christ, for we can see how utterly they despise the world and how wholly they are given over to the service of God. If we put our finger near a fire, we feel the heat; in much the same way a soul on fire with love feels, I say, a genuine warmth. Sometimes it is more, sometimes less: it depends on our particular capacity.

What mortal could survive that heat at its peak—as we can know it, even here—if it persisted? We must inevitably wilt before the vastness and sweetness of love so intense and heat so indescribable. Yet at the same time we are bound to long eagerly for just this to happen: to breathe our soul out, with all its superb endowment of mind, in this honeyed flame, and, quit of this world, be held in thrall with those who sing their Maker's praise.

3. Quenching the Flame

But some things are opposed to charity: carnal, sordid things which beguile a mind at peace. And sometimes in this bitter exile physical need and strong human affection obtrude into this warmth, to disturb and quench this flame (which metaphorically I call "fire" because it burns and enlightens). They cannot take away what is irremovable, of course, because this is something which has taken hold of my heart.

Yet because of these things this cheering warmth is for a while absent. It will reappear in time though until it does, I am going to be spiritually frozen, and because I am missing what I have become accustomed to, will feel myself barren. It is then that I want to recapture that awareness of inner fire which my whole being, physical as well as spiritual, so much approves; with it, it knows itself to be secure.

4. The Soul Settled in Devotion

Nowadays I find that even sleep ranges itself against me! The only spare time I have is that which I am obliged to give to slumber. When I am awake, I can try to warm my soul up though it is numb with cold. For I know how to kindle it when the soul is settled in devotion and how to raise it above earthly things with overwhelming desire.

But this eternal and overflowing love does not come when I am relaxing, nor do I feel this spiritual ardor when I am tired out after, say, travelling; nor is it [there] when I am absorbed with worldly interests or engrossed in neverending arguments. At times like these I catch myself growing cold: cold until once again I put away all things external, and make a real effort to stand in my Savior's presence: only then do I abide in this inner warmth.

5. Not Known by Argument

I offer, therefore, this book for the attention, not of the philosophers and sages of this world, not of the great theologians bogged down in their interminable questionings, but of the simple and unlearned who are seeking rather to love God than to amass knowledge. For he is not known by argument but by what we do and how we love.

I think that while the matters contained in such questionings are the most demanding of all intellectually, they are much less important when the love of Christ is under consideration. Anyhow they are impossible to understand! So I have not written for the experts unless they have forgotten and put behind them all those things that belong to the world; unless now they are eager to surrender to a longing for God.

6. Beyond the Things of Time

To achieve this, however, they must, first, fly from every worldly honor; they must hate all vainglory and the parade of knowledge. And then, conditioned by great poverty, through prayer and meditation they can devote themselves to the love of God. It will not be surprising if then an inner spark of the uncreated charity should appear to them and prepare their hearts for the fire which consumes everything that is dark and raises them to that pitch of ardor which is so lovely and so pleasant.

Then will they pass beyond the things of time and sit enthroned in infinite peace. The more learned they are, the more ability they naturally have for loving, always provided of course that they do not esteem themselves highly nor rejoice in being highly esteemed by others. And so, because I would stir up by these means every person to God, and because I am trying to make plain the ardent nature of love and how it is supernatural, the title selected for this book will be *The Fire of Love*.

7. What We Ought to Love

Everyone of us who live in this life of ours knows that we cannot be filled with a love of

eternity or anointed with the sweet oil of heaven unless we are truly converted to God. Before we can experience even a little of God's love, we must be really turned to him, and, in mind at least, be wholly turned from every earthly thing. The turning is indeed a matter of duly ordered love, so that, first, we love what we ought to love and not what we ought not, and, second, our love kindles more towards the former than to the latter.

God is to be loved, of course, most of all: heavenly things too are to be much loved; but little love, or at least no more than is necessary, may be given to earthly things. This surely is the way we turn to Christ: to desire nothing but him. To turn away from those "good things" of the world, which pervert rather than protect those who love them, involves the withering of physical lust and the hatred of wickedness of any sort. So you will find there are people who have no taste for earthly things and who deal with mundane matters no more than is absolutely necessary.

8. Exchanging the Glory

Because those who amass fortunes find comfort in such things—they do not know who will ultimately reap the benefit!—they are not entitled to enjoy even a little cheerful, comforting, heavenly love. Yet they reckon they have had already some experience of future bliss— at least they say so—because of their devotion, a devotion which is feigned, and not genuinely holy.

But surely it is this graceless presumption that will bring about their downfall, for their love of earthly treasure is unlimited. What is more, they will fall from the sweetness with which God delights his lovers. All love which is not God-directed is bad love and makes its possessors bad, too. And this is the reason why those who love worldly splendor with an evil love catch fire of a different sort and separate themselves ever further from the fire of divine love, further, in fact, than the distance separating highest heaven from lowest earth.

Indeed such people become like what they love, for they take their tone from the greed of their day and age. Because they will not give up their old ways, they come to prefer life's specious emptiness to the warmth of happiness. They exchange the glory of incorruptible charity for a fleeting lust of "beauty." And this they could not possibly do were they not blinded by a counterfeit "fire of love" which both devastates virtue at its source and encourages vice in its growth.

9. Destroying the Real Root

Yet on the other hand there are many who, because they care nothing for feminine beauty or riotous living, reckon therefore that they will be sure of salvation. Because of this chastity, outward and visible, they see themselves as saints standing out from the rest. But this is a wrong and silly assumption if they are not at the same time destroying the real root of sin, greed.

As the Bible says, there is nothing worse than the love of money (1 Tim. 6:10), for it means that one's heart is everlastingly bothering about the love of the transitory and not giving itself a chance to acquire devotion. Love for God and love for the world cannot coexist in the same soul: the stronger drives out the weaker, and it soon appears who loves the world, and who follows Christ. The strength of people's love is shown in what they do.

10. Eager to Love God

The devil has got hold of many whom we count good. For he possesses those who are merciful, chaste, and humble—self-confessed sinners to a man, of course, hair-shirted and penance-laden! Very often indeed are mortal wounds obscured by the odor of sanctity.

The devil may have the busy worker, or even the compelling preacher, but not, surely the person whose heart is aglow with charity, ever eager to love God and indifferent to vanity. The eager love of the wicked, on the other hand, is always for what is shameful. They have ceased from all spiritual exercise, or at least are flabby and feeble. Their love has no pattern, being given more to things that are of this world than of the next, more to bodies than to souls.

BIBLE SELECTION: LUKE 11:33–36

[33]"No one after lighting a lamp puts it in a cellar, but on the lampstand so that those who enter may see the light. [34]Your eye is the lamp of your body. If your eye is healthy, your whole body is full of light; but if it is not healthy, your body is full of darkness. [35]Therefore consider whether the light in you is not darkness. [36]If then your whole body is full of light, with no part of it in darkness, it will be as full of light as when a lamp gives you light with its rays."

REFLECTION QUESTIONS

The following questions can be used for discussion within a small group, or used for journal reflections by individuals.

1. Richard Rolle describes his spiritual experiences as being accompanied by a sensation of warmth, which he compares to a fire. Have you ever felt any physical sensations in a time of worship or devotion?

2. What activities fan the flame of devotion in your life? Consider reading, hearing good preaching, praying, being in fellowship with others, enjoying creation, and any other spiritual activities in which you engage.

3. Rolle writes, "People become like what they love." What (or who) are some of your loves, and how have you become like them?

4. The devil, notes Rolle, may have possession of those who appear religious on the outside ("the busy worker, or even the compelling preacher," for example). What three characteristics clearly help us stand in opposition to the devil?

5. Jesus warns us not to hide our light, as a person who lights a candle and then hides it, but instead encourages us to put our light on a stand. How can you as an individual or as a group be a light in a darkened world?

SUGGESTED EXERCISES

The following exercises can be done by individuals, shared between spiritual friends, or used in the context of a small group. Choose one or more of the following.

1. Richard Rolle exhorts us to love Christ with our whole heart, unmixed with love for earthly things. This week examine your loves. Ask yourself if these loves are competing for your devotion to God. Remember Rolle's counsel: "All love which is not God-directed is bad love and makes its possessors bad, too."

2. Worldly honors, notes Rolle, can be a major hindrance in the spiritual life, and he encourages us to fly from them. Look for ways you can avoid being honored this week, and in genuine humility seek to deflect any praise you receive to the God from whom all blessings flow.

3. According to Rolle, love should have a pattern, which is demonstrated in our spiritual exercises. This week make your love for God the center around which all your spiritual exercises are ordered.

4. Endeavor to regain your "eyesight." Jesus said, "Your eye is the lamp of your body. If your eye is healthy, your whole body is full of light; but if it is not healthy, your body is full of darkness" (Luke 11:34). Healthy eyes are eyes that are focused on a single aim: the kingdom of God. Make the kingdom of God the sole focus of your attention this week.

REFLECTIONS

I have not experienced the physical sensations of burning in the heart that Rolle describes, although I have often felt heat in my hands as I have prayed for others. I'm glad, however, for Rolle's witness because the divine Reality he experienced (of which the physical manifestations are only a hint) is so right and true to the ways of God. The divine love of God in Christ both purifies and inflames. Fire is perhaps the best word we have to describe this kind of love.

This love from God is no sentimental slop. It burns away everything that is of a nature contrary to itself. Nothing can abide if it stands in opposition to divine love. Also, this love comforts, draws, nurtures, and inflames us with desire for the Beloved. It is a "love that will not let me go," as the hymn writer aptly confessed. May you and I be more and more drawn in, taken over, and consumed by this love from God.

GOING DEEPER

Rolle, Richard. *English Writings of Richard Rolle, Hermit of Hampole.* Edited by Hope Emily Allen. St. Clair Shores, MI: Scholarly, 1971. This book is not in print but you can dig it out of a good library. It contains meditations on the Psalms and on the Passion of Christ as well as several Epistles. Be aware that it is written in middle English, which is difficult for the modern reader but a delight to the trained ear.

Rolle, Richard. *The Fire of Love.* New York: Penguin, 1972. A wonderfully untidy sort of book: repetitive, energetic, dogmatic, and heartwarming. It is best to think of the book as a great symphony in which the melody is introduced and reintroduced in a variety of ways, and as each movement repeats the melody, it develops fresh themes, adding something new each time around.

John Calvin (1509–1564)

INTRODUCTION TO THE AUTHOR

Born at Noyon, France, and educated at the University of Paris, John Calvin grew up in an atmosphere of wealth and nobility. His father wanted him to study theology, but John felt a yearning to study law. However, he had keen insight as a theologian and the heart of a pastor. Although he was never ordained, he became the curate of St. Martin de Marteville in 1527. In 1534 he was converted to Protestantism, which resulted in two short imprisonments.

In 1536 he wrote his famous *Institutes of the Christian Religion* at the young age of twenty-six. By 1541 he had gone to Geneva, Switzerland, and had influenced that city to the point that he had gained a large following. Under Calvin's leadership, and in spite of opposition to him, Geneva became famous for its high moral standards, economic prosperity, and educational system. Many consider him to have been the father and founder of both the Presbyterian and the Reformed Protestant churches.

He was deeply influenced by the writings of Martin Luther and St. Augustine, especially Augustine's strong predestinarian theology. It is safe to say that no theologian holds a higher or clearer understanding of the sovereignty of God than John Calvin. He was well known for his stern temperament and austere life-style. The following selection deals with self-denial, which Calvin believed to be essential in the life of every Christian. As with other devotional masters, the words of Calvin are sobering to the modern mind-set that sees restraint in wholly negative terms.

EXCERPTS FROM *GOLDEN BOOKLET OF THE TRUE CHRISTIAN LIFE*

1. A Very Excellent Key Principle

The Divine law contains a most fitting and well ordered plan for the regulation of our life; yet it has pleased the heavenly Teacher to direct us by a very excellent key principle. It is the duty of believers to "present your bodies a living sacrifice, holy, acceptable unto God" (Rom. 12:1, KJV); this is the only true worship.

The principle of holiness leads to the exhortation, "Be not conformed to this world; but be ye transformed by the renewing of your mind, that ye may prove what is the will of God" (Rom. 12:2). It is a very important consideration that we are consecrated and dedicated to God. It means that we will think, speak, meditate, and do all things with a view to God's glory.

2. Our Only Legitimate Goal

If we are not our own, but the Lord's, it is clear to what purpose all our deeds must be directed. We are not our own, therefore neither our reason nor our will should guide us in our thoughts and actions. We are not our own, therefore we should not seek what is only expedient to the flesh. We are not our own, therefore let us forget ourselves and our own interests as far as possible.

We are God's own; to him, therefore, let us live and die. We are God's own; therefore let his wisdom and will dominate all our actions. We are God's own; therefore let every part of our existence be directed towards him as our only legitimate goal.

3. The Most Effective Poison

Oh, how greatly we have advanced when we have learned not to be our own, not to be governed by our own reason, but to surrender our minds to God! The most effective poison to lead us to ruin is to boast in ourselves, in our own wisdom and willpower. The only escape to safety is simply to follow the guidance of the Lord.

Our first step should be to take leave of ourselves and to apply all of our powers to the service of the Lord. The service of the Lord does not only include implicit obedience, but also a willingness to put aside our sinful de-sires and to surrender completely to the leadership of the Holy Spirit.

The transformation of our lives by the Holy Spirit, which St. Paul calls the renewal of the mind, is the real beginning of life but foreign to pagan philosophers. These philosophers set up reason as the sole guide of life, of wisdom and conduct. But Christian philosophy demands of us that we surrender our reason to the Holy Spirit. This means that we no longer live for ourselves, but that Christ lives and reigns within us (Eph. 4:23; Gal. 2:20).

4. A Great Advantage

Let us therefore not seek our own, but that which pleases the Lord and is helpful to the promotion of his glory. There is a great advantage in almost forgetting ourselves and in surely neglecting all selfish aspects; for then only can we try faithfully to devote our attention to God and his commandments.

For when Scripture tells us to discard all personal and selfish considerations, it does not only exclude from our minds the desire for wealth, the lust of power, and the favor of others, but it also banishes false ambitions and the hunger for human glory with other more secret evils. Indeed, Christians ought to be disposed and prepared to keep in mind that they have to reckon with God every moment of their lives.

5. Leaving No Room

Christians will measure all of their deeds by God's law and will subject their thoughts to God's will. If we have learned to regard God in every enterprise, we will be delivered from all vain desires. The denial of ourselves (which Christ has so diligently commanded his disciples from the beginning) will at last dominate all the desires of our heart.

The denial of ourselves will leave no room for pride, haughtiness, or vainglory, nor for avarice, licentiousness, love of luxury, wantonness, or any sin born from self-love. Without the principle of self-denial we are either led to indulgence in the grossest vices without the least shame, or, if there is any appearance of virtue in us, it is spoiled by an evil passion for glory. Show me a single person who does not believe in the Lord's law of self-denial who can willingly practice a life of virtue!

6. Nearer to the Kingdom

All who have not been influenced by the principle of self-denial and yet have followed virtue have done so out of a love of praise. Even those philosophers who have contended that virtue is desirable for its own sake have been puffed up with so much arrogance that it is evident they desire virtue for no other reason than to give them a chance to exercise pride.

God is so far from being pleased either with those who are ambitious of popular praise, or with hearts full of pride and presumption, that he plainly tells us "they have their reward" (Matt. 6:5) in this world and that repentant harlots and publicans are nearer to the kingdom of heaven than such persons.

7. The Remedy of All

There is no end and no limit to the obstacles of the one who wants to pursue what is right and at the same time shrinks back from self-denial. It is an ancient and true observation that there is a world of vices hidden in the soul, but Christian self-denial is the remedy of them all. There is deliverance in store only for the one who gives up selfishness and whose sole aim is to please the Lord and to do what is right in his sight.

8. A Well-Regulated Life

The apostle Paul gives a brief summary of a well-regulated life when he says to Titus: "The grace of God that bringeth salvation hath appeared to all, teaching us that denying ungodliness and worldly lusts we should live soberly, righteously, and godly in this present world; looking for that blessed hope, and the glorious appearing of the great God and our Savior Jesus Christ who gave himself for us, that he might redeem us from all iniquity and purify unto himself a peculiar people, zealous of good works" (KJV).

Paul declares that the grace of God is necessary to stimulate us, but that for true worship two main obstacles must be removed: first, ungodliness (to which we are strongly inclined), and second, worldly lusts (which try to overwhelm us).

Ungodliness does not only mean superstitions, but everything that hinders the sincere fear of God. And worldly lusts mean carnal affections. Paul urges us to forsake our former desires which are in conflict with the two tables of the law and to renounce all the dictates of our own reason and will.

9. Sobriety, Righteousness, and Godliness

Paul reduces all the actions of the new life to three classes: sobriety, righteousness, and godliness. Sobriety undoubtedly means chastity and temperance, as well as the pure and frugal use of temporal blessings, and patience under poverty. Righteousness includes all the duties of justice that everyone may receive just dues. Godliness separates us from the pollutions of this world and, by true holiness, unites us to God. When the virtues of sobriety, righteousness, and godliness are firmly linked together, they will produce absolute perfection.

10. Delivering Our Minds from Every Snare

Nothing is more difficult than to forsake all carnal thoughts, to subdue and renounce our false appetites, and to devote ourselves to God and our brethren, and to live the life of angels in a world of corruption. To deliver our minds from every snare Paul calls attention to the hope of a blessed immortality, and encourages us that our hope is not in vain.

As Christ once appeared as a Redeemer, so will he at his second coming show us the benefits of the salvation which he obtained. Christ dispels the charms which blind us and prevent us from longing with the right zeal for the glory of heaven. Christ also teaches us that we must live as strangers and pilgrims in this world, that we may not lose our heavenly inheritance (Titus 2:11–14).

11. Our Conqueror

Let us discuss further how real self-denial makes us more calm and patient. First of all, Scripture draws our attention to the fact that if we want ease and tranquility in our lives, we should resign ourselves and all that we have to the will of God, and at the same time we should surrender our affections to him as our Conqueror.

To crave wealth and honor, to demand power, to pile up riches, to gather all those vanities which seem to make for pomp and empty display, that is our furious passion and our unbounded desire. On the other hand, we fear and abhor poverty, obscurity, and humility, and we seek to avoid them by all means.

We can easily see how restless people are who follow their own mind, how many tricks they try, and how they tire themselves out in their efforts to obtain the objects of their ambition and avarice, and then again to avoid poverty and humility. If God-fearing people do not want to be caught in such snares, they must pursue another course: they should not hope, or desire, or even think of prosperity without God's blessing.

BIBLE SELECTION: PHILIPPIANS 2:1–11

If then there is any encouragement in Christ, any consolation from love, any sharing in the Spirit, any compassion and sympathy, ²make my joy complete: be of the same mind, having the same love, being in full accord and of one mind. ³Do nothing from selfish ambition or conceit, but in humility regard others as better than yourselves. ⁴Let each of you look not to your own interests, but to the interests of others. ⁵Let the same mind be in you that was in Christ Jesus,

> ⁶who, though he was in the form of God,
> did not regard equality with God
> as something to be exploited,
> ⁷but emptied himself,

taking the form of a slave,
being born in human likeness.
[8]And being found in human form,
he humbled himself
and became obedient to the point of
death—
even death on a cross.

[9]Therefore God also highly exalted him
and gave him the name

that is above every name,
[10]so that at the name of Jesus
every knee should bend,
in heaven and on earth and under the
earth,
[11]and every tongue should confess
that Jesus Christ is Lord,
to the glory of God the Father.

REFLECTION QUESTIONS

The following questions can be used for discussion within a small group, or used for journal reflections by individuals.

1. John Calvin points out that "we are not our own." How does this relate to the issue of self-denial?

2. In section 3, Calvin writes about abandoning our reason in favor of following God's will. When have you experienced a clash between your reason and what you felt to be the will of God? How did you respond?

3. A central theme of this selection is the division between those who surrender themselves completely to God and those who do not. Those who do not, writes Calvin, are "restless people." Have you experienced this restlessness? Describe.

4. The key principle of holiness, according to Calvin, is to present our bodies as a living sacrifice, and to be not conformed to this world but transformed by the renewing of our minds (cf. Rom. 12:1–2). In what ways have you been conformed to this world?

5. In what ways does the humility discussed in Philippians 2:1–11 coincide with the self-denial discussed by John Calvin? Are there any ways in which the two ideas differ?

SUGGESTED EXERCISES

The following exercises can be done by individuals, shared between spiritual friends, or used in the context of a small group. Choose one or more of the following.

1. John Calvin writes, "Let every part of our existence be directed towards him as our only legitimate goal." Discover ways that you can make God the goal of all you do this week by doing "all things with a view to God's glory."

2. Pay attention to the ways in which this world tries to conform you to its attitudes and actions. As you watch television, analyze the commercials, asking, "How is this advertisement trying to shape the way I think, feel, and act?"

3. Calvin counsels us to "reckon with God every moment." Allow this practice to become your own this week. Moment by moment, let God be your source of direction and inspiration.

4. Paul encourages the Philippians, "Let each of you look not to your own interests, but to the interests of others" (Phil. 2:4). In an attempt to make self-denial a reality and not merely a good intention, deliberately place the needs and interests of those around you ahead of your own.

REFLECTIONS

Calvin speaks life-giving words when he reminds us that self-denial is an essential part of any genuine life with God. The self-denial of which he speaks has nothing to do with hatred of the body, or with punishment for the sake of punishment, or with earning merit through powers of will and self-control.

The more fitting image is of the athlete who enters a training program appropriate for the development of mind, body, and spirit. And, as we all know, self-denial is a normal part of the regimen of the athlete. We, like the athlete, must experience self-denial as a normal part of our training regimen so that we may "press on toward the goal for the prize of the heavenly call of God in Christ Jesus" (Phil. 3:14).

GOING DEEPER

Calvin, John. *Golden Booklet of the True Christian Life.* Grand Rapids, MI: Baker, 1952. A ninety-six-page summation of Calvin's views on practicing the Christian faith. It covers such topics as holiness, self-denial, crossbearing, the hope of heaven, and the right use of the present.

Calvin, John. *Institutes of the Christian Religion.* 2 vols. Grand Rapids, MI: Eerdmans, 1973. Calvin's magnum opus. There are four books, which come in two volumes. Book 3 deals with living the Christian life. These books are rigorous reading, clearly not for the timid. Calvin also wrote extensive commentaries on many books of the Bible, and these have been published by Baker Book House. Thomas F. Torrance and David W. Torrance have edited and updated the New Testament commentaries, which are available through Eerdmans.

Leith, John H. *John Calvin's Doctrine of the Christian Life.* Philadelphia: Westminster, 1989. A good secondary source that defines Calvin's teaching on the Christian life in the context of his theology.

Blaise Pascal (1623–1662)

INTRODUCTION TO THE AUTHOR

Blaise Pascal is best remembered for his genius in mathematics, but his work as a philosopher and theologian remains perhaps the most insightful of all his works. Born in France in 1623, Pascal was reared by his father and an older sister after his mother's death in 1626. Though he was often ill, he displayed a sharp intellect at an early age.

By the time he was thirty-one he was well known for his contributions in the fields of math and science. However, it was in that year that he visited his sister at a religious community in Port Royal, where he heard a sermon that brought about a profound religious experience. He remembered that day—November 23, 1654—as the key moment in his life. He wrote the following on a piece of paper, sewed it into the lining of his coat, and carried it with him for the rest of his life: "Fire. God of Abraham, God of Isaac, God of Jacob, not of the philosophers and scholars. Certainty, certainty, heartfelt joy, peace. God of Jesus Christ. Joy, joy, joy, oceans of joy!"

Whatever doubts he had before that time had been dispelled. For the next six years he lived with that community (though not as a member), studying the Bible and the Church Fathers. At the age of thirty-seven he began writing a defense of the Christian faith, but his death at age thirty-nine prevented him from finishing. These random notations or "thoughts" were gathered together following Pascal's death and became the world-famous book *Pensées*.

EXCERPTS FROM *PENSÉES*

1. Such Amazing Contradictions

Our greatness and wretchedness are so evident that the true religion must necessarily teach us that there is in us some great principle of greatness and some great principle of wretchedness. It must also account for such amazing contradictions.

To make us happy it must show us that a God exists whom we are bound to love; that our only true bliss is to be in him, and our sole ill to be cut off from him. It must acknowledge that we are full of darkness which prevents us from knowing and loving him, and so, with our duty obliging us to love God and our sin leading us astray, we are full of unrighteousness.

It must account to us for the way in which we thus go against God and our own good. It must teach us the cure for our helplessness and the means of obtaining this cure. Let us examine all the religions of the world at that point and let us see whether any but the Christian religion meets it.

2. Who Can Cure Pride and Lust?

Do the philosophers, who offer us nothing else for our good but the good that is within us? Have they found the cure for our ills? Does it cure our presumption to set us up as God's equal? Have those who put us on the level of the beasts, have the Moslems, who offer nothing else for our good than earthly pleasures, even in eternity, brought us the cure for our lust?

What religion, then, will teach us how to cure pride and lust? What religion, in short, will teach us our true good, our duties, the weaknesses which lead us astray, the cause of those weaknesses, the treatment that can cure them, and the means of obtaining such treatment? All the other religions have failed to do so. Let us see what the wisdom of God will do.

3. Falling into Presumption

"People," says God's wisdom, "do not expect either truth or consolation from other people. It is I who have made you and I alone can teach you what you are. But you are no longer in the state in which I made you. I created you holy, innocent, perfect, I filled you with light and understanding, I showed you my glory and my wondrous works. Your eye then beheld the majesty of God. You were not then in the darkness that now blinds your sight, nor subject to death and the miseries that afflict you.

"But you could not bear such great glory without falling into presumption. You wanted to make yourself your own center and do without my help. You withdrew from my rule, setting yourself up as my equal in your desire to find happiness in yourself, and I abandoned you to yourself. The creatures who were subject to you I incited to revolt and made your enemies, so that today you have become like the beasts, and are so far apart from me that a barely glimmering idea of your author alone remains of all your dead or flickering knowledge.

"The senses, independent of reason and often its masters, have carried you off in pursuit of pleasure. All creatures either distress or tempt you, and dominate you either by forcibly subduing you or charming you with sweetness which is a far more terrible and harmful yoke. That is the state in which people are today. They retain some feeble instinct from the happiness of their first nature, and are plunged into the wretchedness of their blindness and lust which has become their second nature."

4. The Reason for the Many Contradictions

From this principle which I am disclosing to you, you can recognize the reason for the many contradictions which have amazed all mankind and split them into such different schools of thought. Now observe all the impulses of greatness and of glory which the experience of so many miseries cannot stifle, and see whether they are not necessarily caused by another nature.

"It is vain that you seek within yourselves the cure for your miseries. All your intelligence can only bring you to realize that it is not within yourselves that you will find either truth or good. The philosophers made such promises and they have failed to keep them. They do not know what your true good is, nor what your true state is.

"How could they provide cures for ills which they did not even know? Your chief maladies are the pride that withdraws you from God, and the lust that binds you to the earth; all they have done is to keep at least one of these maladies going. If they gave you God as an object of study, it was only to exercise your pride; they made you think you were like him and of a similar nature.

"And those who saw the vanity of such a pretension cast you into the other abyss, by giving you to understand that your nature was like that of the beasts, and they induced you to seek your good in lust which is the lot of the animals. This is not the way to cure you of the unrighteousness which these wise men failed to recognize in you. Only I can make you understand what you are. I do not demand of you blind faith."

5. This Dual Capacity

Adam, Jesus Christ. If you are united to God, it is by grace, and not by nature. If you are humbled, it is by penitence, not by nature. Hence this dual capacity. You are not in the state of creation. With the disclosure of these two states it is impossible for you not to recognize them.

Follow your own impulses. Observe yourself, and see if you do not find the living characteristics of these two natures. Would so many contradictions be found in a simple subject? Incomprehensible. Everything that is incomprehensible does not cease to exist. Infinite number, an infinite space equal to the finite.

Incredible that God should unite himself to us. This consideration derives solely from realizing our own vileness, but, if you sincerely believe it, follow it out as far as I do and recognize that we are in fact so vile that, left to ourselves, we are incapable of knowing whether this mercy may not make us capable of reaching him.

6. To Love and to Know Him

For I should like to know by what right we who are mere animals, which recognize our own weakness, measure God's mercy and keep it within limits suggested by our own fancies. We have so little knowledge of what God is that we do not know what we are ourselves. Disturbed as we are by the contemplation of our own state, we dare to say that God cannot make us capable of communion with him.

But I would ask whether God demands of us anything but that we should love and know him since we are naturally capable of love and knowledge. There is no doubt that we know at least that we exist and love something.

Therefore, if we can see something in the darkness around us, and if we can find something to love among earthly things, why, if God reveals to us some spark of his essence, should we not be able to know and love him in whatever way it may please God to communicate himself to us?

There is undoubtedly an intolerable presumption in such arguments, although they seem to be based on patent humility, which is neither sincere nor reasonable unless it makes us admit that, since we do not know of ourselves what we are, we can learn it only from God.

7. Reconciling These Contradictions

"I do not mean you to believe me submissively and without reason; I do not claim to subdue you by tyranny. Nor do I claim to account to you for everything. To reconcile these contradictions I mean to show you clearly, by convincing proofs, marks of divinity within me which will convince you of what I am, and establish my authority by miracles and proofs that you cannot reject so that you will then believe the things I teach, finding no reason to reject them but your own inability to tell whether they are true or not.

"God's will has been to redeem us and open the way of salvation to those who seek it, but we have shown ourselves so unworthy that it is right for God to refuse to some, for their hardness of heart, what he grants to others by a mercy they have not earned."

8. Light for Those Desiring to See

"If God had wished to overcome the obstinacy of the most hardened, he could have done so by revealing himself to them so plainly that they could not doubt the truth of his essence, as he will appear on the last day with such thunder and lightning and such convulsions of nature that the dead will rise up and the blindest will see him.

"This is not the way he wished to appear when he came in mildness because so many had shown themselves unworthy of his clemency that he wished to deprive them of the good they did not desire. It was therefore not right that he should appear in a manner manifestly divine and absolutely capable of convincing everyone, but neither was it right that his coming should be so hidden that he could not be recognized by those who sincerely sought him. He wished to make himself perfectly recognizable to them.

"Thus wishing to appear openly to those who seek him with all their heart and hidden from those who shun him with all their heart, he has qualified our knowledge of him by giving signs which can be seen by those who seek him and not by those who do not. There is enough light for those who desire only to see, and enough darkness for those of a contrary disposition."

BIBLE SELECTION: JOHN 20:24–31

[24]But Thomas (who was called the Twin), one of the twelve, was not with them when Jesus came. [25]So the other disciples told him, "We have seen the Lord." But he said to them, "Unless I see the mark of the nails in his hands, and put my finger in the mark of the nails and my hand in his side, I will not believe."

[26]A week later his disciples were again in the house, and Thomas was with them. Although the doors were shut, Jesus came and stood among them and said, "Peace be with you." [27]Then he said to Thomas, "Put your finger here and see my hands. Reach out your hand and put it in my side. Do not doubt but believe." [28]Thomas answered him, "My Lord and my God!" [29]Jesus said to him, "Have you believed because you have seen me? Blessed are those who have not seen and yet have come to believe."

[30]Now Jesus did many other signs in the presence of his disciples, which are not written in this book. [31]But these are written so that you may come to believe that Jesus is the Messiah, the Son of God, and that through believing you may have life in his name.

REFLECTION QUESTIONS

The following questions can be used for discussion within a small group, or used for journal reflections by individuals.

1. Blaise Pascal begins this selection by stating that human beings have a dual nature. What are these two aspects, our *first* and *second* natures?

2. Our knowledge of God, says Pascal, comes from the glimpses of God that he allows us to have. What glimpses, or bits of knowledge, has God given you? How did they come together to form the faith you now have?

3. Pascal believes that we were created in glory and innocence and perfection, but that we fell into presumption, desiring to make ourselves the center and do without the help of God, desiring to find happiness in ourselves. How do you deal with the tendency to put yourself at the center, to be independent of God, and to find happiness in yourself?

4. "Observe yourself, and see if you do not find the living characteristics of these two natures," writes Pascal. In looking at your own life, how have you seen both the greatness and the wretchedness, the pure and the impure, the noble and the ignoble?

5. In what ways can you identify with Thomas, who desired evidence in order to believe? Would you describe yourself as a person for whom faith comes easily, or as one who has difficulty believing that which requires a leap of faith?

SUGGESTED EXERCISES

The following exercises can be done by individuals, shared between spiritual friends, or used in the context of a small group. Choose one or more of the following.

1. Blaise Pascal challenges his readers, "Let us examine all the religions of the world . . ." Go to the library this week and check out some books on the major religions of the world. Read them with Pascal's question in mind: How does this religion account for the way we are, and what kind of cure for our problem does it offer?

2. Our chief maladies, notes Pascal, are "the pride that withdraws you from God, and the lust that binds you to the earth." This week make an effort to dismantle your pride by drawing closer to God, and deal firmly with your lust by detaching yourself from the things of this world.

3. God says to us (writes Pascal), "I do not mean you to believe me submissively and without reason." Read a book on apologetics this week, furthering your understanding of the reasonableness of Christianity. C. S. Lewis's *Mere*

Christianity or Paul Little's *Know What You Believe* and *Know Why You Believe* are helpful introductions.

4. Pascal writes, "There is enough light for those who desire only to see, and enough darkness for those of a contrary disposition." The Gospel of John (20:31) tells us that it was written "so that you may come to believe." This week allow the Bible a chance to help you believe; come to the Bible with a desire only to see; this is the proper light in which to read it.

REFLECTIONS

Reflecting on both our creation in the image of God and the Fall, Pascal speaks of the contradictory principles of "greatness" and "wretchedness" that are in us all. How right he is! As far as we know, no one in all creation has a greater capacity for virtue and for depravity than the human species. We invent the microchip and nuclear weapons. We establish orphanages and Auschwitz. Among us is born Mother Teresa and Pol Pot.

And, as Pascal reminds us, only Christianity adequately explains the contradiction and only Christ can lift us above our pride and lust.

GOING DEEPER

Krailsheimer, Alban. *Pascal.* New York: Hill & Wang, 1980. An excellent eighty-page introduction to Pascal: the man of science and the man of faith. Malcolm Muggeridge has a fine chapter on Pascal in his book *The Third Testament.* For a full-blown biography I would suggest you turn to *Pascal: The Emergence of Genius* by Emilie Cailliet (New York: Harper & Row, 1970).

Pascal, Blaise. *Pensées.* Translated by A. J. Krailsheimer. New York: Penguin, 1966. These "thoughts" of Pascal reveal the spiritual genius of this famous man of science. The Krailsheimer translation is the best—he has also translated Pascal's *Provincial Letters* and it is available in a Penguin edition. The Harvard Classics edition of Pascal includes a collection of his minor works, among them an essay on prayer and his "Discourse on the Passion of Love."

Benedict of Nursia (480–543)

INTRODUCTION TO THE AUTHOR

Christianity became the official state religion early in the fourth century, and with this new status began an unfortunate secularization of the Church. When the Christian faith was mixed with the Roman world, the world did not become Christian so much as Christians became worldly. In reaction, many earnest Christians fled to the desert and ultimately to monasteries and convents as a way of escaping the world and living a faithful life. (In time, of course, even these monasteries declined and were in need of renewal.) Into this climate Benedict of Nursia arose to bring new life to the Christian world.

Born into a good family in the Umbrian village of Nursia and educated at Rome, Benedict grew weary of the evils of the city and fled to the mountains of Subiaco to live as a hermit. He became well known for his piety, his wisdom, and his humility. In A.D. 529 he founded a monastery on Monte Cassino, midway between Naples and Rome, and he remained there until his death.

In this monastery Benedict wrote his famous *Rule*, which provided a much needed accountability to the many roving prophets and hermits of the day. In *The Rule* Benedict gives clear, direct, and effective disciplines for living a holy life. His writings inspired an important period of renewal and are still with us today because of their wisdom and insight.

The following passage deals with the subject of humility. Using the metaphor of "Jacob's ladder," Benedict discusses twelve steps of humility. The modern reader may find it hard to hear his austere teaching about the reality of hell and the sinfulness of humankind, but in an age of "feel good" spirituality, we need his words.

EXCERPTS FROM *THE RULE*

1. The Call to Ascend the Ladder of Humility

Friends, the Holy Scriptures cry out to us saying, "Everyone that exalts himself shall be humbled; and he that humbles himself shall be exalted." Therefore, they show us that every exaltation of ourselves is a kind of pride. The Psalmist declares that he guarded against this, saying, "Lord, my heart is not puffed up; nor are my eyes haughty. Neither have I walked in great matters nor in things above me."

If we wish to reach the height of humility in this present life, we must journey up the ladder of Jacob, wherein he saw angels ascending and descending. The way of ascending is humility; the way of descending is pride. If our heart is humble we shall be lifted to heaven. For our body and our soul are two sides of this ladder, and each step is a step in humility. We must first understand the steps of humility and then enter into the disciplines of them.

2. The First Step of Humility: Reverence for God

The first step of humility is to have a constant reverence for God before our eyes. We must shun our tendency of forgetfulness and be always mindful of God's commands. Consider in your mind how those who despise God will burn in hell for their sin, and that life everlasting is prepared for those who have reverence for God.

Let us remember that God sees all from heaven, that the eyes of God are upon us at all times and in all places. The Scriptures teach us that, "The Lord knows all of our thoughts." For this reason we must turn away from evil and ask God in prayer that his will be done in us. Again, the Scriptures say, "There are ways that seem right to us, but in the end will lead us to ruin." So let us live in the faith that God is ever present to us.

3. The Second Step of Humility: Doing God's Will

The second step on the ladder of humility is rejecting our own will and desires and, instead, doing God's will. The Lord Jesus said, "I came not to do my own will, but the will of the One who sent me." It is also said, "Self-will has its

punishment, but the doing of God's will wins the crown."

4. The Third Step of Humility: Obedience to Others

The third step of humility by which we ascend to heaven is when, because of our love for God, we submit ourselves to another in all obedience. By this we imitate the Lord of whom the Apostle Paul said, "He became obedient even unto death."

5. The Fourth Step of Humility: Enduring Affliction

The fourth step of humility is accepting the hardship of the commandments and enduring with patience the injuries and afflictions we face. We are called to endure and not grow weary or give up, but to hold fast. The Scriptures teach us, "They that persevere unto the end shall be saved."

Those who have faith must bear every disagreeable thing for the Lord, keeping in mind the promise, "But in all these things we shall overcome because of Him who loves us." God shall try us by fire just as silver is tried and purified. Our Lord teaches us that when we are struck on one cheek, we must turn the other; when asked for a piece of our clothing, give the whole thing; when asked to go one mile, go two; when we are cursed by others, we must bless them.

6. The Fifth Step of Humility: Confession

The fifth step of humility is to keep no secrets from the one to whom we confess. We must humbly confess all of our evil thoughts and all of our evil actions. Again, the Scriptures teach us, "Reveal your way to the Lord and trust in Him." And it says further, "Confess to the Lord, for He is good. His mercy endures forever." Remember what the Psalmist said, "I have acknowledged my sin to you, O Lord, and my injustice I have not kept hidden. You have forgiven the wickedness of my sins."

7. The Sixth Step of Humility: Contentment

The sixth step of humility is to be content in all things. We are to be content with the meanest and worst of everything. In all things we must be mindful of our own lowliness, considering ourselves to be lowly and meek, knowing that though we have nothing in this life, the Lord is always present with us.

8. The Seventh Step of Humility: Self-Reproach

The seventh step of humility is when we declare with our tongue and believe in our inmost soul that we are the lowliest and vilest of all, humbling ourselves and saying with the Psalmist, "But I am a worm, and I am the reproach of all, the outcast of the people." The Scriptures teach us that it is good to be humbled so that we may learn God's commandments.

9. The Eighth Step of Humility: Obeying the Common Rule

The eighth step of humility is to obey the common rule of the monastery. We do this by doing nothing except what is sanctioned by the rule and example of the elders.

10. The Ninth Step of Humility: Silence

The ninth step of humility is to withhold our tongue from speaking, keeping silence until we are asked. The Scriptures teach us that "in the multitude of words there comes sin." And further, "A person full of speaking is not established in the earth."

11. The Tenth Step of Humility: Seriousness

The tenth degree of humility is when we are not easily provoked to laughter. For the Scriptures remind us, "The fool exalts his voice in laughter."

12. The Eleventh Step of Humility: Simple Speech

The eleventh step of humility is to speak with few and sensible words. We are to speak gently and not with a loud voice. Again, the Scriptures teach us, "The wise man is known by the fewness of his words."

13. The Twelfth Step of Humility: Humble in Appearance

The twelfth step of humility is to be not only humble of heart, but also humble in appearance. No matter where we are—whether doing the work of God, or in the garden, or on a journey—we should adopt the posture of reverence, ever mindful of who we are. Our attitude should be that of the publican in the Gospel who said, with his eyes fixed on the ground, "Lord, I am a sinner and I am not worthy to lift my eyes up to heaven."

14. Humility as a Way of Life

If we ascend all of these steps of humility, we shall arrive at that love of God which, being perfect, casts out all fear. If we persist in observing them, we will begin to keep them without any effort. In time it will no longer be a force of habit, but a way of life. Though we may begin them with a fear of hell, we will begin living them out of a love for Christ, developing habits of good, and taking pleasure in virtue. May the Lord be pleased to manifest all this by his Holy Spirit in you, his laborer, now cleansed from vice and sin.

BIBLE SELECTION: LUKE 18:9–14

[9]He also told this parable to some who trusted in themselves that they were righteous and regarded others with contempt: [10]"Two men went up to the temple to pray, one a Pharisee and the other a tax collector. [11]The Pharisee, standing by himself, was praying thus, 'God, I thank you that I am not like other people: thieves, rogues, adulterers, or even like this tax collector. [12]I fast twice a week; I give a tenth of all my income.' [13]But the tax collector, standing far off, would not even look up to heaven, but was beating his breast and saying, 'God, be merciful to me, a sinner!' [14]I tell you, this man went down to his home justified rather than the other; for all who exalt themselves will be humbled, but all who humble themselves will be exalted."

REFLECTION QUESTIONS

The following questions can be used for discussion within a small group, or used for journal reflections by individuals.

1. In section 1, Benedict states that when we try to exalt ourselves, we are humbled, and when we humble ourselves, we are exalted. Is this true from your experience?

2. While many modern readers may have difficulty accepting Benedict's use of the fear of hell as a motivating factor, it has been a part of Christian theology for centuries, dating back to Jesus himself (cf. Matt. 25). Is the fear of hell a motivating factor for you? Should it be? Why or why not?

3. In section 5, Benedict says that the fourth step in humility is accepting the hardships of life. What are some of the hardships you have faced? In what ways did they help you to develop humility?

4. In looking over the twelve steps of humility, which of them would be the easiest for you to climb? Which would be the most difficult? Why?

5. In the parable of the Pharisee and the tax collector, Jesus tells us that the tax collector (one who was despised in the Jewish culture) went home justified with God, while the Pharisee (one who was respected in the Jewish culture) did not. With Benedict's teaching on humility in mind, what do you think Jesus is trying to tell us?

SUGGESTED EXERCISES

The following exercises can be done by individuals, shared between spiritual friends, or used in the context of a small group. Choose one or more of the following.

1. The first step of humility is "to have a constant reverence for God before our eyes." Cultivate the habit of being mindful of God in all that you do this week.
2. Confession, for Benedict, was closely related to humility. This week make a full and complete confession to God. Take a thorough inventory of your life; leave no stones unturned. Be bold—the mercy of God endures forever.
3. The use of words is also related to humility. This week climb the ninth step of humility by withholding your tongue from speaking, keeping silence until you are asked to speak. Or, climb the eleventh step, learning to speak with few and sensible words.
4. Let the prayer of the tax collector become your own this week: "God, be merciful to me, a sinner!" Pray it often, and let it soften your heart.

REFLECTIONS

In his discussion of humility Benedict says something wonderful that is easy to miss, namely, that there are things we can do that will move us forward in the life of humility.

Humility, of course, is one of those virtues that can never be attained by focusing on it. The idea is ludicrous. As a result, however, many have concluded that we can do nothing to deal with the arrogant, ego-centered drives that plague us moderns. We simply wait for God to pour humility on our heads. Such is the state of the Church in our day.

Benedict has done us a great service by showing us that we can undertake spiritual work in this realm. There are actual activities of mind, body, and spirit that will move us forward. By the grace of God we can strike a blow against pride and increasingly experience the joy of a meek and humble life.

GOING DEEPER

De Waal, Esther. *Seeking God*. Collegeville, MN: Liturgical, 1984. An extraordinarily sensitive book that takes the central insights of *The Rule* and makes them relevant to ordinary people who work in offices, get caught in traffic jams, and shop in supermarkets. De Waal has also developed a two-part tape series, "The Rule of Benedict in a World of Paradox," which can be secured through Raven and Dove Productions, P.O. Box 545, Petersham, MA 01366-0545.

St. Benedict of Nursia. *The Rule of St. Benedict in English*. Edited by Timothy Fry. Collegeville, MN: Liturgical Press, 1982. This slender book (actually it is more like a booklet or handbook) is all that we have from Benedict's pen, but what an influence it has had. Even though it was originally written to give structure to the emerging monasteries of the sixth century, many of the insights are amazingly transferable to contemporary circumstances.

Thomas à Kempis (1380–1471)

INTRODUCTION TO THE AUTHOR

In 1399, at the age of nineteen, Thomas à Kempis became a monk at the Augustinian monastery where he would spend the rest of his life. He was made subprior in 1429, but his outer life was not very eventful; he lived and died a simple monk. His inner life, however, was deep and rich, filled with a genuine devotion to Christ. The lasting achievement of his life came in 1441 when he edited Gerhard Groote's diary.

The following passage comes from *The Imitation of Christ,* the classic that some believe was written by Groote (1340–1384) and edited by Thomas. Although the book's tone is somber and its prescriptions demanding, it continues to bless countless Christians because of its clarity and insight into the human spirit. In the eyes of many, *The Imitation* ranks second only to the Bible in its impact on the worldwide Christian community. The selection that follows addresses a struggle that we all have: temptation. May it give you insight and encouragement as you deal with the various temptations that you must face.

EXCERPTS FROM *THE IMITATION OF CHRIST*

1. Be on the Watch

As long as we live in the world we cannot escape temptations and tribulations. As it is written in Job, "Our life on this earth is warfare." For this reason we must be careful and concerned about our own temptations. We must be watchful in prayer lest the devil be given an opportunity to deceive us. For the devil never sleeps but "goes about seeking whom he may devour." Remember, no one is so holy that he or she does not have to deal with temptations. We can never be free of them.

2. The Usefulness of Temptations

And yet, temptations can be useful to us even though they seem to cause us nothing but pain. They are useful because they can make us humble, they can cleanse us, and they can

184

teach us. All of the saints passed through times of temptation and tribulation, and they used them to make progress in the spiritual life. Those who did not deal with temptations successfully fell to the wayside.

3. The Source of Temptations: Why We Can't Run Away

No one is completely free of temptations because the source of temptation is in ourselves. We were born in sinful desire. When one temptation passes, another is on its way. We will always have temptation because we are sinners who lost our original innocence in the Garden. Many have tried to escape temptations only to find that they more grievously fall into them. We cannot win this battle by running away alone; the key to victory is true humility and patience; in them we overcome the enemy.

If we merely turn away from temptation outwardly and do not strike at the root, we will make very little progress. In fact, you will find that the temptations will return more quickly and powerfully, and you will feel even worse. Little by little, through patient endurance of spirit (with the help of God), you will win a better victory than by your own determination.

4. Temptations Reveal Who We Are

The beginning of all evil temptations is an unstable mind and a small trust in God. Just as a ship without a helm is tossed about by the waves, so a person who lacks resolution and certainty is tossed about by temptations. Temptation reveals our instability and our lack of trust in God; temptations reveal who we are. This is why we must pay attention to them.

5. How Temptations Enter and Overcome Us

We will do better in dealing with temptations if we keep an eye on them in the very beginning. Temptations are more easily overcome if they are never allowed to enter our minds. Meet them at the door as soon as they knock, and do not let them in. One simple thought can enter the mind and start the process.

The process works like this. First, the thought is allowed to enter into our minds. Second, the imagination is sparked by the thought. Third, we feel a sense of pleasure at the fantasy, and we entertain it. Fourth and finally, we engage in the evil action, assenting to its urges. This is how, little by little, temptations gain entrance and overcome us if they are not resisted at the beginning. The longer we let them overcome us, the weaker we become, and the stronger the enemy against us.

6. Never Despair: God Is with You

We must not despair when we are tempted but, instead, seek God more fervently, asking for his help in this time of tribulation. Remember St. Paul's words of assurance, "God will make a way of escape from every temptation so that we may be able to bear it." Let us, therefore, humble ourselves before God and take shelter beneath his hand. God will lift up all who have a humble spirit and save them in all trials and tribulations.

Patience is necessary in this life because so much of life is fraught with adversity. No matter how hard we try, our lives will never be without strife and grief. Thus, we should not strive for a peace that is without temptation, or for a life that never feels adversity. Peace is not found by escaping temptations, but by being tried by them. We will have discovered peace when we have been tried and come through the trial of temptation.

7. The Pain of Temptations

"But," you may say, "what about those who find such pleasure and delight when they give in to temptations?" To be sure, there is pleasure for them, but how long does it last? It is like smoke—it vanishes quickly. Soon even the memory of the joy is gone. They will never find rest, and they will live in bitterness and weariness and fear.

The very thing they think will bring them joy will bring them sorrow; that which they think will bring them pleasure will bring them only pain. Because of their blindness and numbness they may never see or feel how miserable they are. They may not even know that their soul is slowly dying.

8. The Way to True Delight

But, if you want to have true delight, here is the way: have contempt for all worldly things and all lower delights, and rich consolation will, in turn, be given to you. In proportion as you withdraw yourself from the love of these things, so you will find consolations from God much more sweet and potent.

At first this will be difficult. Long-standing habits will resist, but they will be vanquished, in time, by a better habit—if you persevere! The flesh will cry out, but it will be restrained by the Spirit. The devil will try to stir you up and provoke you, but he will run away the moment you begin to pray. And above all, try to engage in useful work. In doing so, the devil is prevented from having access to you.

9. Lay the Axe to the Root

If we made an effort to stand firmly and courageously in the struggle, doubtless we should see the help of our Lord from heaven, for he is ready to help those who trust in his grace; he gives us occasions to fight that we may win. If our spiritual progress relies only on outward observances, our devotion will not last long. Let us lay the axe to the root, so that being purged of unruly passions we may have peace of mind.

If every year we uprooted a single fault, we should soon become perfect. But we often feel that we were better and more pure at the beginning of our spiritual lives than we are now after many years of living our vows! Fervor and progress ought to increase daily, but it is thought to be a fine thing these days if a person can hold on to even a little of those first intense feelings! If we would exercise a little self-discipline at the beginning, then we would later be able to do everything easily and joyfully.

10. Defeating Old Habits

It is hard to give up old habits, but it is even harder to go against one's own will. Yet, if you cannot overcome small, trivial things, when will you overcome difficult ones? Fight the urge when it starts, and break off bad habits, lest perhaps, little by little, they lead you into greater trouble. Oh, if you could only know how much peace for yourself and joy for others your good efforts could bring, I think you would be more anxious for spiritual growth!

11. The Temptation to Gossip

I wonder why we are so eager to chatter and gossip with each other, since we seldom return to the quiet of our own hearts without a damaged conscience? The reason is that by idle chit-chat we seek comfort from one another and we hope to lighten our distracted hearts. And to make matters worse, we chatter most freely about our favorite topics, about what we would like to have, or about those things we especially dislike!

What a mistake! This outside comfort is no small detriment to the inner comfort that comes from God. Therefore, we must watch and pray that we do not waste time. If it is proper to speak, speak of what will benefit others spiritually. Bad habits and neglect of our spiritual progress contribute much to our endless chatter.

12. Putting Troubles to Use

Sometimes it is good for us to have troubles and hardships, for they often call us back to our own hearts. Once there, we know ourselves to be strangers in this world, and we know that we may not believe in anything that it has to offer. Sometimes it is good that we put up with people speaking against us, and sometimes it is good that we be thought of as bad and flawed, even when we do good things and have good intentions. Such troubles are often aids to humility, and they protect us from pride. Indeed, we are sometimes better at seeking God when people have nothing but bad

things to say about us and when they refuse to give us credit for the good things we have done! That being the case, we should so root ourselves in God that we do not need to look for comfort anywhere else.

13. Our Need for God

When a person of good will is troubled or tempted or vexed by evil thoughts, then he better understands his need for God, without whom he can do nothing good at all. In such a state, he is sad and he sighs and prays because of the miseries he suffers; then, he is tired of living any longer and he wishes to die, so that he may be set free to be with Christ. When all that happens, he knows for certain that perfect security and full peace cannot exist in this world.

14. Four Sources of Peace

Finally, I want to teach you the way of peace and true liberty. There are four things you must do. First, strive to do another's will rather than your own. Second, choose always to have less than more. Third, seek the lower places in life, dying to the need to be recognized and important. Fourth, always and in everything desire that the will of God may be completely fulfilled in you. The person who tries this will be treading the frontiers of peace and rest.

BIBLE SELECTION: 1 CORINTHIANS 10:12–13

[12]So if you think you are standing, watch out that you do not fall. [13]No testing has overtaken you that is not common to everyone. God is faithful, and he will not let you be tested beyond your strength, but with the testing he will also provide the way out so that you may be able to endure it.

REFLECTION QUESTIONS

The following questions can be used for discussion within a small group, or used for journal reflections by individuals.

1. According to Thomas à Kempis, can we ever escape temptations? Of what value are temptations in our spiritual life?

2. Temptations, writes Thomas, "reveal who we are." How have temptations revealed who you are?

3. Sin, Thomas admits, does bring pleasure, but the pleasure vanishes quickly and we are left with bitterness, weariness, and fear. "The very thing they think will bring them joy will bring them sorrow," Thomas writes. What things have you sought, thinking they would bring you pleasure, only to find sorrow as their end?

4. According to Thomas, "If every year we uprooted a single fault, we should soon become perfect." The word *soon* may be an overstatement, but given his intention of showing us how we grow little by little, what single fault would you like to uproot in the next year?

5. Like Thomas à Kempis, St. Paul spoke about the importance of temptations, and how we overcome them. According to 1 Corinthians 10:12–13, what happens to us when we think we are standing firm? According to Thomas, what would it mean to "watch out"?

SUGGESTED EXERCISES

The following exercises can be done by individuals, shared between spiritual friends, or used in the context of a small group. Choose one or more of the following.

1. Gossip and idle chatter, says Thomas, are entered into because we think they will "lighten our distracted hearts." But they do not. This week, replace gossip and idle chatter with speech that "will benefit others spiritually."

2. In section 5, Thomas describes the four steps by which temptation becomes sin. Write out those steps on a sheet of paper and carry it with you. Keep tabs on your own temptations, comparing your experience with Thomas's.

3. Note the four keys to peace in section 14. Try them out this week. Keep track of what happens as you make them a part of your life.

4. After reading both this selection and the passage from 1 Corinthians, sum up on a sheet of paper all that you have learned about temptation. Carry it with you; commit it to memory. May its wisdom help you win the battle of temptation.

REFLECTIONS

I wish that I could announce to you that I am beyond temptation. I cannot. To be sure, there are things that no longer have the same alluring power (we do get beyond some things), but that only means that the temptations have become more subtle. We are all tempted.

But the glorious word of Scripture is that we are not left to our own resources in dealing with temptation. The great God of Abraham, Isaac, and Jacob—the One who revealed himself to Moses, David, and Mary—is our ever-present help in times of trouble. Jesus Christ, our ever-living Prophet, is with us—teaching, empowering, loving. The blessed Holy Spirit draws near to us in the hour of temptation—guiding, strengthening, encouraging. "The one who is in you is greater than the one who is in the world," says the Scripture (1 John 4:4), and we can verify the affirmation in experience. And when we do stumble and fall, we have an advocate with the Father in our Savior Jesus.

GOING DEEPER

Thomas à Kempis. *The Imitation of Christ.* Translated by William Creasy. Notre Dame, IN: Ave Maria, 1989. For half a millennium, *The Imitation* has been the unchallenged devotional masterpiece for Christians everywhere. We have been immensely enriched by this simple book, which distills the insights of a dynamic spiritual movement in the fifteenth century known as "The Brethren of the Common Life." There are numerous English translations to choose from. I heartily endorse this fresh one by William Creasy because he has succeeded in creating a text that elicits an experience similar to that of the original reader. You might also want a copy of the fine translation by Professor E. M. Blaiklock.

William Law (1686–1761)

INTRODUCTION TO THE AUTHOR

William Law was a devout Anglican priest. His practical work was as a spiritual director, offering guidance to people who sought a closer, deeper relationship with God. The following excerpt is from his best-known work, *A Serious Call to a Devout and Holy Life*, a book that greatly influenced the English Evangelical Revival. The simplicity and directness of this book have made it a classic among Christian devotional literature.

This particular selection deals with the tendency we all have to separate our religious life from our practical, daily life. Law drives home the point that Christianity is concerned not only with our faith but with our conduct as well. In the spirit of the apostle James, William Law affirms that, like a bow and an arrow, our works and our faith function as one.

EXCERPTS FROM *A SERIOUS CALL TO A DEVOUT AND HOLY LIFE*

1. A Life Devoted

Devotion is neither private nor public prayer, though public and private prayers are a part of devotion. Devotion signifies a life given or devoted to God.

The devout, therefore, are people who do not live to their own will, or in the way and spirit of the world, but only to the will of God. Such people consider God in everything, serve God in everything, and make every aspect of their lives holy by doing everything in the name of God and in a way that conforms to God's glory.

We readily acknowledge that God alone is to be the rule and measure of our prayers. In our prayers we are to look totally unto him and act totally for him, and we must pray in this manner and for such ends as are suitable to his glory.

2. God the Rule and Measure

Now if we conclude that we must be pious in our prayers, we must also conclude that we must be pious in all the other aspects of our lives. For there is no reason why we should make God the rule and measure of our prayers, why we should look wholly unto him and pray according to his will, and yet not make him the rule and measure of all the other actions of our life. For any ways of life, any employment of our talents whether of our bodies, our time, or money that are not strictly according to the will of God, that are not done to his glory are simply absurdities, and our prayers fail because they are not according to the will of God. For there is no other reason why our prayers should be according to the will of God unless our lives may also be of the same nature. Our lives should be as holy and heavenly as our prayers. It is our strict duty to live by reason, to devote all of the action of our lives to God, to walk before him in wisdom and holiness and all heavenly conversation, and to do everything in his name and for his glory. If our prayers do not lead us to this, they are of no value no matter how wise or heavenly. No, such prayers would be absurdities. They would be like prayers for wings though we never intended to fly.

If we are going to pray for the Spirit of God, we must make that Spirit the rule of all our actions. Just as it is our duty to look wholly unto God in our prayers, so it is our duty to live wholly unto God in our lives. But we cannot live wholly unto God unless we live unto him in all the ordinary actions of our life, unless he is the rule and measure of all our ways, just as we cannot pray wholly unto God unless our prayers look wholly unto him.

3. Ridicule in the Life

This is the reason that we see such ridicule in the lives of many people. Many people are strict when it comes to times and places of devotion, but when the service and the church is over, they live like those that seldom or never come there. In their way of life, their manner of spending their time and money, in their cares and fears, in their pleasure and indulgences, in their labors and diversions, they are like the rest of the world. This leads the world to make light of those who are devout because they see their devotion goes no further than their prayers. When their prayers are over, they stop living unto God until the next time they pray. In between they live with the same attitudes and desires as other people. This is the reason why they are scoffed at by worldly people, not because they are really devoted to God, but because they appear to have no other devotion than their occasional prayers.

4. The Failure of Julius

For instance, there is a man named Julius who is very fearful of missing his prayers. Everyone in his church assumes Julius to be sick if he is not at church. But if you were to ask him why he spends the rest of his time playing games, why he spends the rest of his time with worldly people and worldly pleasures, why he is eager to engage in sinful diversion, why he engages in idle, gossiping conversation, or why he never puts his conversation, his time, and money under the rules of religion, Julius has no more to say for himself than the most disorderly person. For the whole tenor of Scripture lies directly against a life of debauchery and intemperance. One who lives in such a manner lives no more according to the religion of Jesus Christ than the person who lives in gluttony and intemperance.

If a person were to tell Julius that he cannot live that way and still remain a Christian, Julius would conclude that the person was not a Christian and reject his company. But if a person tells him that he may live as the rest of the world does, that he may enjoy himself as others do, that he may conform to the rest of the world and gratify his desires and passions as most people do, Julius would never suspect that such a person is not a Christian or that he is doing the devil's work.

And yet if Julius were to read all of the New Testament from the beginning to the end, he would find his course of life condemned in every page of it.

5. The Great Absurdity

And indeed nothing more absurd can be imagined than wise, sublime, and heavenly prayers added to a life where neither work nor play, neither time nor money are under the direction of our prayers. If we were to see a person pretending to act wholly with regard to God in everything that this person did and yet at the same time this person never prayed—whether public or private—wouldn't we be amazed?

Yet this is the same thing as when one is very strict in devotion, being careful to observe times and places of prayer, and yet in the rest of one's life—time, labor, talents, and money—completely neglects the will of God. It is as great an absurdity to offer up holy prayers without a holy life as it is to live a holy life without prayer.

Just as we cannot live a holy life without prayer, so we cannot have prayer without a holy life. To be foolish in the way we spend our time and money is no greater a mistake than to be foolish in relation to our prayers. If our lives cannot be offered to God, how can our prayers?

6. Rules for Daily Life

The simple point is this: either Christianity prescribes rules to live by in our daily lives, or it does not. If it does, then we must govern all our actions by those rules if we are to worship God. For if Christianity teaches anything about eating and drinking, spending our time and money, how we are to live in the world, what attitudes we are to have in daily life, how we are to be disposed toward all people, how we are to behave toward the sick, the poor, the old, and destitute, whom we are to treat with particular love, whom we are to regard with a particular esteem, how we are to treat our enemies, and how we are to deny ourselves, we would be foolish to think that these teachings are not to be observed with the same strictness as those teachings that relate to prayer.

It is very observable that there is not one command in all the gospel for public worship. One could say that it is the duty that is least insisted upon in Scripture. Frequent church attendance is never so much as mentioned in all of the New Testament. But the command to have a faith which governs the ordinary actions of our lives is to be found in almost every verse of Scripture. Our blessed Savior and his Apostles were very intent on giving us teachings that relate to daily life. They teach us: to renounce the world and be different in our attitudes and ways of life; to renounce all its goods, to fear none of its evils, to reject its joys, and have no value for its happiness; to be as newborn babes who are born into a new state of things; to live as pilgrims in spiritual watching, in holy fear, and heavenly aspiring after another life; to take up our cross daily, to deny ourselves, to profess the blessedness of mourning, to seek the blessedness of poverty of spirit; to forsake the pride and vanity of riches, to take no thought for the morrow, to live in the profoundest state of humility, to rejoice in worldly sufferings; to reject the lust of the flesh, the lust of the eyes, and the pride of life; to bear injuries, to forgive and bless our enemies, and to love all people as God loves them; to give up our whole hearts and affections to

God, and to strive to enter through the straight gate into a life of eternal glory.

Isn't it strange that people place so much emphasis upon going to church when there is not one command from Jesus to do so, and yet neglect the basic duties of our ordinary life which are commanded in every page of the Gospels?

7. Walking the Talk

If self-denial is a condition for salvation, all who desire to be saved must make self-denial a part of everyday life. If humility is a Christian duty, then the everyday life of a Christian must show forth humility. If we are called to care for the sick, the naked, and the imprisoned, these expressions of love must be a constant effort in our lives. If we are to love our enemies, our daily life must demonstrate that love. If we are called to be thankful, to be wise, to be holy, they must show forth in our lives. If we are to be new people in Christ, then we must show our newness to the world. If we are to follow Christ, it must be in the way we spend each day.

BIBLE SELECTION: JAMES 2:14–26

[14]What good is it, my brothers and sisters, if you say you have faith but do not have works? Can faith save you? [15]If a brother or sister is naked and lacks daily food, [16]and one of you says to them, "Go in peace; keep warm and eat your fill," and yet you do not supply their bodily needs, what is the good of that? [17]So faith by itself, if it has no works, is dead.

[18]But someone will say, "You have faith and I have works." Show me your faith apart from your works, and I by my works will show you my faith. [19]You believe that God is one; you do well. Even the demons believe—and shudder. [20]Do you want to be shown, you senseless person, that faith apart from works is barren? [21]Was not our ancestor Abraham justified by works when he offered his son Isaac on the altar? [22]You see that faith was active along with his works, and faith was brought to completion by the works. [23]Thus the scripture was fulfilled that says, "Abraham believed God, and it was reckoned to him as righteousness," and he was called the friend of God. [24]You see that a person is justified by works and not by faith alone. [25]Likewise, was not Rahab the prostitute also justified by works when she welcomed the messengers and sent them out by another road? [26]For just as the body without the spirit is dead, so faith without works is also dead.

REFLECTION QUESTIONS

The following questions can be used for discussion within a small group, or used for journal reflections by individuals.

1. According to William Law, in what areas of our lives should our faith have influence? In what areas does your faith influence your life?

2. If, as Law believes, the vitality of one's faith is revealed by one's actions, how would you describe your spiritual health?

3. What are some of the struggles you face as you attempt to demonstrate your faith not merely in words, but in actions?

4. Describe someone you know or have known whose life impressed you. What made that person special to you?

5. In James 2:14–26 the author chastises the members of the church for thinking that faith can exist apart from action. Which do you tend to emphasize in your life, having the right beliefs or engaging in the right kinds of action? How might James respond to you if he were here?

SUGGESTED EXERCISES

The following exercises can be done by individuals, shared between spiritual friends, or used in the context of a small group. Choose one or more of the following.

1. This week take an inventory of your practices and beliefs, noting the extent to which they have been shaped by the world around you. Write them out so that you can get a better idea of how your faith influences your life.

2. This week examine all your purchases. According to William Law, the way we spend our money should be influenced by our faith. Keep a running log so that at the week's end you can see where your money is going. Examine these purchases in light of Jesus' words about not storing up treasures.

3. James 2:14–26 reminds us that our faith becomes real in the way we relate to those who are less fortunate. This week donate some food or clothing to a local shelter, soup kitchen, thrift store, or other ministry program.

4. On a piece of paper make several circles that represent the different areas of your life. Your circles should include vocation, hobbies, family, friends, recreation, and church. Allot a percentage for how much you think your faith influences each of these areas (e.g., vocation = 75 percent), and shade in the amount in that circle. Ask yourself, Is my faith influencing my life? Begin thinking about how Christ can become the center of all the areas of your life.

REFLECTIONS

I am endlessly moved by the writings of William Law because he so obviously believed in prayer and was so utterly committed to living out his faith in the ordinary junctures of daily life. He knew that true prayer never ends at the altar; rather it transforms the inner personality in such a way that we are enabled to love enemies and do good to all people. Prayer that does not profoundly affect daily life is not prayer at all but merely "lip labor," as Law himself put it.

This interpenetration of our spiritual life with our daily life is a winsome combination but one that I easily forget. My temptations are at the extremes: either I want to pray only and watch God act, or I want to go out and do it all myself. Far too seldom do I enter the wonderful equilibrium that the old writers called ora et labora, *prayer and work. I am grateful to William Law for reteaching me this valuable lesson—one that it seems I must learn repeatedly.*

GOING DEEPER

Law, William. *A Serious Call to a Devout and Holy Life.* New York: Paulist, 1978. From *The Classics of Western Spirituality.* This is Law's best-known and most important work. It takes with utmost seriousness the idea of the disciplines of the spiritual life as the means by which God transforms the human personality. There is also a nine-volume edition of his entire works that was first printed in 1762.

Walker, A. K. *William Law: His Life and Work.* London: Society for Promoting Christian Knowledge, 1973. This is the best critical biography available. It helps us to understand Law in the context of the issues of his day and assesses his importance and influence.

Teresa of Ávila (1515–1582)

INTRODUCTION TO THE AUTHOR

Teresa de Cepeda y Ahumada was born in Ávila, Spain, in 1515. At the age of twenty she entered the Carmelite Convent of the Incarnation. While there she battled many serious illnesses, especially between the ages of twenty-eight and thirty. She lived a very devout life at the convent and was known to have occasional supernatural experiences.

In 1555 Teresa experienced what she called a "second conversion," which changed her spiritual life decisively. She began experiencing visions more often, most notably, visions of Christ piercing her heart with a spear. Under the direction of her spiritual counselor, she began working on a project to establish new Carmelite houses that were devoted to the contemplative life. Later John of the Cross worked alongside her in this effort.

Teresa began her writing career with a spiritual autobiography, and it was quickly noticed that she had a gift for writing about the spiritual life in elegant yet simple terms. Her most famous work on prayer is *Interior Castle*, which she wrote following a vision. In it she describes the soul's journey from the outside of a castle and through many rooms as it strives toward the center room where the soul can unite with God completely. In the spirit of Bunyan's *Pilgrim's Progress*, Teresa uses allegory to describe the spiritual journey we all face, with its attendant obstacles and joys.

EXCERPTS FROM *INTERIOR CASTLE*

1. Strive to Escape the Poisonous Sins

This chapter has to do with those who have already begun to practice prayer and who long to leave the first stage, or room. However, they may not have the strength or resolve to leave that first room. They may have difficulty avoiding occasions of sin, which is a very grave condition. It is a great mercy that they should strive to escape the poisonous sins of the first stage of prayer, even if it is short-lived.

In some ways, these people will face more difficulty than those who are content at the beginning level. However, they are further along, and therefore in less danger of falling away, and have a greater hope of going farther in the "castle." God is so anxious that we should grow close to him that he calls us unceasingly to approach him. Many souls at this stage find his voice so sweet that they are grieved at being unable to respond to him immediately. This is why they suffer more than beginners.

2. God Looks into Our Souls

God appeals to us through other good people, through sermons, or through the reading of good books. Sometimes he calls through our sicknesses and our trials as he bids us to pray. However feeble such prayers may be, God values them highly.

God looks into our souls and perceives our desires. If our desires are good, we cannot fail. Nevertheless, the assaults of the devils that are made upon the soul are terrible. Again, this is why the soul suffers more at this stage than does the beginner. Whereas before the soul was somewhat deaf and blind and had no will to resist, now it has begun to hear and see and resist as one who is about to gain victory.

It is at this stage that the devils will attack the soul with the earthly pleasures of this world, like snakes who bite with deadly poison. They trick the soul into thinking that such pleasures will last an eternity; they remind the soul of the high esteem in which it is held in the world; they place before it the many friends and relatives who will disagree with the manner of life you have now begun.

3. Wonderful Capacities

Oh, Jesus! What confusion the devils bring about in the poor soul, and how distressed it becomes, not knowing if it ought to proceed or return to the first room, i.e., the beginning stages of prayer.

But on the other hand, you have blessed us with wonderful capacities to help us along the way! *Reason* tells the soul how mistaken it is in thinking that these earthly pleasures are of the slightest value in comparison with what it is seeking. *Faith* instructs the soul in what it must do to find true satisfaction. *Memory* reminds it how all of those pleasures come to an end, and how all those who once engaged in those pleasures—who seemed to find such enjoyment in them!—are now dead and buried. People who were once prosperous are now beneath the ground, and we trample on their graves.

The *will* inclines the soul to love God, the One in whom it has seen so many acts and signs of love. In particular, the will shows the soul how this True Lover never leaves it, but goes with it everywhere and gives it life and being. Then the *understanding* comes forward and makes the soul realize that, for however many years it may live, it can never hope to have a better friend. For the world is full of falsehood and these pleasures which the devil pictures to it are accompanied by trials and cares and annoyances. It reminds the soul that if it were to go back from this stage, it would never again find security or peace. It is reflections of this kind which vanquish devils.

4. The Vain Habits We Fall Into

But, oh, my God and Lord, how everything is ruined by the vain habits we fall into and the way everyone else follows them! Our faith is so dead that we desire what we see more than what faith tells us about—even though what we see is that people who pursue these things end up with nothing but misfortune!

All this is the work of the venomous snakes of sin that bite us early in our journey. Like one who is bitten by a snake, our whole body swells up with the poison. Only the great mercy of God will preserve us. The soul will certainly suffer great trials at this time, especially if the devil sees that its character and habits are such that it is ready to make further progress: all the powers of hell will combine to drive it back again.

5. We Must Be Resolute

That is why it is very important for us to associate with others who are walking in the right way—not only those who are where we are in the journey, but also those who have gone farther. Those who have drawn close to God have the ability to bring us closer to him, for in a sense they take us with them.

Let us firmly resolve not to lose the battle we fight. For if the devil sees that we are willing to lose our life and our peace, and that nothing can entice us back to the first room, he will soon cease from troubling us. But we must be resolute, for we fight with devils, and thus, there is no better weapon than the Cross.

6. Content with the Consolations

I feel I must repeat this important point: at the beginning we must not become content with the consolations we may receive at the early stages. That would be like building our house on sand. At this stage you are beginning to build a beautiful castle, and you must build it on strong virtues, not temporary consolations.

Neither should we complain about a lack of consolations at this stage. Rather, embrace the Cross which Jesus bore upon his shoulders and realize that this Cross is yours to carry too. We are free in the same measure we are able to suffer.

You may also make the mistake of thinking that you will be better able to bear your trials if God will only grant you inward consolations. Remember that God knows what is best for us, and that we are not capable of asking for what is best for us. All that beginners in prayer must do is this: labor and be resolute, preparing themselves with diligence to bring their will into conformity with the will of God. This ability is the greatest thing that can be accomplished on the spiritual journey.

7. Do Not Lose Heart

If we go astray at the beginning and want the Lord to do our will and lead us as our desires dictate, how can we be building on a firm foundation? I must remind you that it is the Lord's will that we should be tested and that even allows evil vipers to bite us. When we are afflicted with evil thoughts that we cannot cast out, or when we enter a spiritual desert that we cannot find our way out of, God is teaching us how to be on our guard in the future and to see if we are really grieved at having offended him.

If, then, you sometimes fall, do not lose heart. Even more, do not cease striving to make progress from it, for even out of your fall God will bring some good. I know of a man who willingly took poison in order to prove that his antidote was powerful enough to save him. Sometimes God allows us to fall in order to reveal to us our sinfulness and to show us what harm comes as a result of sin. Our sins can have the effect of leading us back to God and striving all the more.

8. Gently Begin a Time of Prayer

Let us, therefore, place our trust in God and not in ourselves, relying heavily on his mercy and not fighting the battle alone. When you feel the beginnings of temptation, do not fight back with strenuous efforts, but rather, gently begin a time of prayer and recollection. At first it will be difficult, but after a while you will be able to do it easily, and for long periods of time.

Do not think that you must stop doing your work in order to pray. The Lord will turn all of our work time into profit as long as we continue in a spirit of prayer. There is no remedy for the temptations that we face except to start at the beginning, and the beginning is prayer. The only way to lose is to turn back.

9. The Door to This Castle Is Prayer

Some of you may think that since turning back is such a terrible thing, then it would have been better not to have begun at all. Remember, it is even more dangerous to have never begun. The door by which we enter this castle is prayer. It is absurd to think that we can enter heaven without first entering into this castle and finding out our own sinfulness and how much we owe to God for our redemption.

For our works have no value unless they are united with faith, and our faith has no value unless it is united with works. May God grant us the ability to see how much we cost him, to see that the servant is not greater than the Master, to see that we must work if we would enjoy his glory. For this reason we must pray, lest we continually enter into temptation.

10. Communion with the Trinity

In this seventh dwelling place the union comes about in a different way: our good God now desires to remove the scales from the soul's eyes and let it see and understand, although in a strange way, something of the favor he grants it. When the soul is brought into that dwelling place, the Most Blessed Trinity, all three Persons, through an intellectual vision, is revealed to it through a certain representation of the truth. First there comes an enkindling in the spirit in the manner of a cloud of magnificent splendor; and these Persons are distinct, and through an admirable knowledge the soul understands as a most profound truth that all three Persons are one substance and one power and one knowledge and one God alone.

Here all three Persons communicate themselves to it, speak to it, and explain those words of the Lord in the Gospel: that he and the Father and the Holy Spirit will come to dwell with the soul that loves him and keeps his commandments.

11. Use No Force

You will not be able to enter all the dwelling places through your own efforts, even though these efforts may seem to you great, unless the Lord of the castle himself brings you there. Hence I advise you to use no force if you meet with any resistance.

Once you get used to enjoying this castle, you will find rest in all things, even those involving much labor, for you will have the hope of returning to the castle, which no one can take from you.

BIBLE SELECTION: TITUS 3:1–8

Remind them to be subject to rulers and authorities, to be obedient, to be ready for every good work, [2]to speak evil of no one, to avoid quarreling, to be gentle, and to show every courtesy to everyone. [3]For we ourselves were once foolish, disobedient, led astray, slaves to various passions and pleasures, passing our days in malice and envy, despicable, hating one another. [4]But when the goodness and loving kindness of God our Savior appeared, [5]he saved us, not because of any works of righteousness that we had done, but according to his mercy, through the water of rebirth and renewal by the Holy Spirit. [6]This Spirit he poured out on us richly through Jesus Christ our Savior, [7]so that, having been justified by his grace, we might become heirs according to the hope of eternal life. [8]The saying is sure.

REFLECTION QUESTIONS

The following questions can be used for discussion within a small group, or used for journal reflections by individuals.

1. "God appeals to us through other good people, through sermons, or through the reading of good books," writes Teresa of Avila. Which people, which sermons, and which books has God used to appeal to you?

2. Teresa speaks of being at different stages in the life of prayer. How would you describe your prayer life? Are you at a beginning, intermediate, or advanced stage?

3. In section 3, Teresa describes how reason, faith, memory, the will, and understanding work together to help us overcome our desire for sin. In your own words, explain what each of these capacities does in its efforts to help us turn from sin.

4. According to Teresa, God actually uses our trials and temptations to teach us "how to be on our guard in the future." What would your spiritual life be like if you had never experienced any kind of temptation?

5. In Titus 3:1–8, Paul contrasts two ways of life. What is the difference between the former life and the life we are to live once we have been washed and renewed by the Holy Spirit? How does this change compare with the movement toward God of which Teresa of Avila writes?

SUGGESTED EXERCISES

The following exercises can be done by individuals, shared between spiritual friends, or used in the context of a small group. Choose one or more of the following.

1. People who are "walking in the right way," writes Teresa, draw us closer to God; in a sense, they actually "take us with them" as they draw close to God. This week resolve to take someone with you as you draw near to God. Do this by sharing some of your experiences with a person who would benefit by hearing of your travels.

2. "May God grant us the ability to see how much we cost him," prays Teresa. This week focus your prayers on how precious you are to God, meditating on the nature of all that Jesus has done for you in order that you might know God's love.

3. Teresa cautions us not to fight temptations, but rather, "gently begin a time of prayer and recollection." As you face temptations this week, use them as opportunities to turn to God in prayer. Little by little this will become a habit.

4. Titus 3:2 exhorts us to "speak evil of no one, to avoid quarreling, to be gentle, and to show every courtesy to everyone." Make this your aim this week, knowing that all you do is an example to others of what Jesus has done in your life.

REFLECTIONS

For some reason, Teresa of Ávila has always been difficult for me to read. Maybe it is her allegory of the castle with its various rooms or stages in the life of prayer, each one drawing us deeper in until we experience habitual union with God and "spiritual marriage." Far from being in the third room or at the fifth stage, I often feel that I'm still on the front porch! She just seems so far beyond anything I would ever hope to experience . . . or even want to experience!

The great thing, though, that we can learn from Teresa is that progress can be made in the spiritual life. As we develop consistent habits of prayer, temptations that once dogged us no longer have the same drawing power. This is a wonderful reality to know, and Teresa of Ávila can help draw us in to this reality.

GOING DEEPER

Ramge, Sebastian. *An Introduction to the Writings of St. Teresa.* Chicago: Henry Regnery, 1963.

Teresa of Ávila. *The Collected Works of St. Teresa of Ávila.* Translated by Kieran Kavanaugh. Washington, DC: ICS, 1976.

Teresa of Ávila. *The Interior Castle.* New York: Paulist, 1979. Teresa received the image of this book in a vision on Trinity Sunday, 1577, in which she beheld "a castle made entirely out of a diamond or of very clear crystal in which there are many rooms, just as in heaven there are many dwelling places." Each room moves us closer to the center where "the King of Glory dwells in the greatest splendor."

The Spirit-Empowered Life

THE CHARISMATIC TRADITION (the Spirit-Empowered Life) focuses on the Holy Spirit who comes alongside us and animates and empowers our efforts. It is one of the great blessings in the Christian walk. The authors in this section explore this divine/human cooperation.

The sense of surrender to the movings of the Spirit is especially evident in Catherine of Genoa's personal witness, "I have given the keys of my house to Love." That same sensitivity is evident in the counsel of Isaac Penington to "wait for the Spirit to move and breathe in us."

Two writers who share a deep sense of the immediacy of the Spirit are Jean-Pierre de Caussade and Thomas Kelly. De Caussade's famous phrase "the sacrament of the present moment" is reinforced by my favorite sentence from his pen: "The soul, light as a feather, fluid as water, innocent as a child, responds to every movement of grace like a floating balloon." And nearly every sentence of Kelly contains this sense of "the continuously renewed immediacy" of the Spirit.

George Fox seemed to walk in constant awareness of the power of God and he urges us to "sing . . . in the Spirit, . . . pray . . . in the Spirit, [and] praise the Lord night and day." Then Ignatius of Loyola gives us sane counsel on the discernment of spirits. And finally, John Bunyan speaks out of personal experience on the identification and exercise of spiritual gifts.

Thomas Kelly (1893–1941)

INTRODUCTION TO THE AUTHOR

Thomas Kelly was born into a Quaker family in Ohio in 1893. He was educated at Haverford and Harvard and acquired a reputation for outstanding scholarship. Kelly was involved in two important ministries in his early years: working with German prisoners in 1917–18 and pastoring a Quaker community in Berlin in 1924–25. Upon his return, he taught at Earlham College and the University of Hawaii. In 1936 he began teaching philosophy at Haverford, where he remained until his death in 1941.

While a student at Haverford, Kelly said to a professor, "I am going to make my life a miracle!" He set high standards for his life, desiring excellence in truth in all areas. Some believed that he was driven to the point of exhaustion until, in 1937, he had an experience that ended the strain and striving. His efforts were now aimed at developing an acquaintance *with* God, not merely acquiring knowledge *about* God.

Kelly was known by his colleagues as a man of genuine devotion, and his writings, in particular *A Testament of Devotion* and *The Eternal Promise*, have made a lasting impact on all who have read them. Rufus Jones said of the former book, "There are a few—a very few—great devotional books . . . and here is a book I can recommend along with the best of the ancient ones."

The book was originally given as a five-part series of addresses, and the following selection is taken from the first address, titled "The Light Within."

EXCERPTS FROM *A TESTAMENT OF DEVOTION*

1. An Amazing Inner Sanctuary

Meister Eckhart wrote, "As thou art in church or cell, that same frame of mind carry out into the world; into its turmoils and fitfulness." Deep within us all there is an amazing inner sanctuary of the soul, a holy place, a Divine Center, a speaking Voice, to which we may continuously return. Eternity is at our hearts, pressing upon our time-torn lives, warming us with intimations of an astounding destiny, calling us home unto Itself.

It is a light within which illumines the face of God and casts new shadows and new glories upon our faces. It is a seed stirring to life if we do not choke it. It is the Shekinah of the soul, the Presence in the midst. Here is the slumbering Christ, stirring to be awakened, to become the soul we clothe in earthly form and action. And he is within us all.

2. The Secret Places of the Heart

The basic response of the soul to the Light is internal adoration and joy, thanksgiving and worship, self-surrender and listening. The secret places of the heart cease to be our noisy workshop. They become a holy sanctuary of adoration and self-oblation, where we are kept in perfect peace if our minds be stayed on Him who has found us in the inward springs of our life. And in the brief intervals of overpowering visitation we are able to carry the sanctuary frame of mind out into the world, into its turmoil and fitfulness. Powerfully are the springs of our will moved to an abandon of singing love toward God; powerfully are we moved to a new and overcoming love toward time-blinded men and all creation.

3. A Subterranean Sanctuary of the Soul

But the light fades, the will weakens, the humdrum returns. Can we endure this fading? No, nor should we try, for we must learn the disciplines of his will, and pass beyond this first lesson of his grace. But the Eternal Inward Light does not die when ecstasy dies, nor exist only intermittently with the flickering of our psychic states.

Continuously renewed immediacy, not receding memory of the Divine Touch, lies at the base of religious living. Let us explore together the secret of a deeper devotion, a more subterranean sanctuary of the soul, where the Light Within never fades, but burns, a perpetual Flame; where the wells of living water of divine revelation rise up continuously, day by day and hour by hour, steady and transfiguring.

4. Secret Habits of Unceasing Orientation

What is here urged are internal practices and habits of the mind. What is here urged are secret habits of unceasing orientation of the deeps of our being about the Inward Light, ways of conducting our inward life so that we are perpetually bowed in worship while we are also very busy in the world of daily affairs. What is here urged are inward practices of the mind at deepest levels, letting it swing like the needle, to the polestar of the soul.

And like the needle, the Inward Light becomes the truest guide of life, showing us new and unsuspected defects in ourselves and our fellows, showing us new and unsuspected possibilities in the power and life of good-will among men. But, more deeply, he who is within us urges, by secret persuasion, to such an amazing Inward Life with him, so that, firmly cleaving to him, we always look out upon all the world through the sheen of the Inward Light, and react toward men spontaneously and joyously from this Inward Center.

5. History Rooted in Eternity

Such practice of inward orientation, of inward worship and listening, is no mere counsel for special religious groups, for small religious orders, for special "interior souls," for monks retired in cloisters. This practice is the heart of religion. It is the secret, I am persuaded, of the inner life of the Master in Galilee. He expects this secret to be freshly discovered in everyone who would be his follower. It creates an amazing fellowship, the church catholic and invisible, and institutes group living at a new level, a society grounded in reverence, history rooted in eternity, colonies of heaven.

The Inner Light, the Inward Christ, is no mere doctrine, belonging peculiarly to a small religious fellowship, to be accepted or rejected as a mere belief. It is the living Center of Reference for all Christian souls and Christian groups.

Practice comes first in religion, not theory or dogma. And Christian practice is not exhausted in outward deeds. They are the fruits, not the roots. A practicing Christian must above all be one who practices the perpetual return of the soul into the inner sanctuary, who brings the world into its Light and rejudges it, who brings the Light into the world with all its turmoil and its fitfulness and re-creates it. To the reverent exploration of this practice we now address ourselves.

6. Behind the Scenes

There is a way of ordering our mental life on more than one level at once. On one level we may be thinking, discussing, seeing, calculating, meeting all the demands of external affairs. But deep within, behind the scenes, at a profounder level, we may also be in prayer and adoration, song and worship and a gentle receptiveness to divine breathings.

Between these two levels is fruitful interplay, but ever the accent must be upon the deeper level, where the soul dwells in the presence of the Holy One, forever bringing all affairs of the first level down into the Light, holding them there in the Presence, reseeing

them in a new and more overturning way and responding to them in spontaneous, incisive, and simple ways of love and faith.

7. Mental Habits of Inward Orientation

How, then, shall we lay hold of that Life and Power and live the life of prayer without ceasing? By quiet, persistent practice in turning all of our being, day and night, in prayer and inward worship and surrender, toward him who calls in the deeps of our souls.

Mental habits of inward orientation must be established. An inner, secret turning to God can be made fairly steady after weeks and months and years of practice and lapses and failures and returns. It is as simple as Brother Lawrence found it, but it may be long before we can achieve any steadiness in the process.

Begin now, as you read these words, as you sit in your chair, to offer your whole selves, utterly and in joyful abandon, in quiet, glad surrender to him who is within. In secret ejaculations of praise, turn in humble wonder to the Light, faint though it may be. Keep contact with the outer world of sense and meanings. Here is no discipline in absentmindedness. Walk and talk and work and laugh with your friends. But behind the scenes, keep up the life of simple prayer and inward worship. Let inward prayer be your last act before you fall asleep and the first act when you awake.

8. Ever Return Quietly

The first days and weeks and months are awkward and painful, but enormously rewarding. Awkward, because it takes constant vigilance and effort and reassertions of the will at the first level. Painful, because our lapses are so frequent, the intervals when we forget him so long. Rewarding, because we have begun to live.

Lapses and forgettings are so frequent. But when you catch yourself again, lose no time in self-recriminations, but breathe a silent prayer for forgiveness and begin again, just where you are. Offer this broken worship up to him and say: "This is what I am except Thou aid me." Admit no discouragement, but ever return quietly to him and wait in his presence.

9. The First Sign of Simultaneity

At first the practice of inward prayer is a process of alternation of attention between outer things and the Inner Light. Preoccupation with either brings the loss of the other. Yet what is sought is not alternation, but simultaneity, worship undergirding every moment, living prayer, the continuous current and background of all moments of life.

The first signs of simultaneity are given when at the moment of recovery from a period of forgetting there is a sense that we have not completely forgotten him. What takes place now is not reinstatement of a broken prayer, but a return to liveliness. The currents of his love have been flowing, but whereas we had been drifting in him, now we swim.

10. Made Pliant in His Holy Will

But periods of dawning simultaneity and steadfast prayer may come and go, lapsing into alternation for long periods and returning in glorious power. And we learn to submit to the inner discipline of withdrawing of his gifts. For if the least taint of spiritual pride in our prayer-growth has come, it is well that he humble us until we are worthy of greater trust.

For though we begin the practice of secret prayer with a strong sense that we are the initiators and that by our wills we are establishing our habits, maturing experience brings awareness of being met and tutored, purged and disciplined, simplified and made pliant in his holy will by a power waiting within us. For God himself works in our souls, in their deepest depths, taking increasing control as we are progressively willing to be prepared for his wonder.

11. No New Technique

There is no new technique for entrance upon this stage where the soul in its deeper levels is continuously at Home in him. The processes of inward prayer do not grow more complex, but more simple. In the early weeks we begin with simple, whispered words. Formulate them spontaneously. "Thine only. Thine only." Or seize upon a fragment of the Psalms: "so panteth my soul after Thee, O God."

Repeat them inwardly, over and over again. For the conscious cooperation of the surface level is needed at first, before prayer sinks into the second level as habitual divine orientation. Longer discipline in this inward prayer will establish more enduring upreachings of praise and submission and relaxed listening in the depths, unworded but habitual orientation of all one's self about him who is the Focus.

And in the X-ray light of eternity we may be given to see the dark spots of life, and divine grace may be given to reinforce our will to complete abandonment in him. For the guidance of the Light is critical, acid, sharper than a two-edged sword. He asks all, but he gives all.

BIBLE SELECTION: JOHN 6:32–40

[32]Then Jesus said to them, "Very truly, I tell you, it was not Moses who gave you the bread from heaven, but it is my Father who gives you the true bread from heaven. [33]For the bread of God is that which comes down from heaven and gives life to the world." [34]They said to him, "Sir, give us this bread always."

[35]Jesus said to them, "I am the bread of life. Whoever comes to me will never be hungry, and whoever believes in me will never be thirsty. [36]But I said to you that you have seen me and yet do not believe. [37]Everything that the Father gives me will come to me, and anyone who comes to me I will never drive away; [38]for I have come down from heaven, not to do my own will, but the will of him who sent me. [39]And this is the will of him who sent me, that I should lose nothing of all that he has given me, but raise it up on the last day. [40]This is indeed the will of my Father, that all who see the Son and believe in him may have eternal life; and I will raise them up on the last day."

REFLECTION QUESTIONS

The following questions can be used for discussion within a small group, or used for journal reflections by individuals.

1. Have you ever experienced what Thomas Kelly describes as "a Light Within," or "a speaking Voice," or "the Divine Center"? Describe.
2. "Continuously renewed immediacy, not receding memory of the Divine Touch, lies at the base of religious living," writes Kelly. Why does the author insist that we have fresh experiences of God each moment, and not subsist on memories of previous experiences?
3. Kelly encourages us to be "perpetually bowed in worship while we are also very busy in the world of daily affairs." If you were to adopt this habit, how would it affect your daily affairs?
4. We may begin this process, notes Kelly, with a sense that we are in control, that we are the initiators, but after a while we realize that it is God who is at work, and has been at work in us all along. What prompts us to think that we are the creator, redeemer, and sustainer of our spiritual life? How have you struggled with this issue?
5. How are eating, drinking, seeing, and believing related in John 6:32–40? Describe yourself in terms of your level of hunger and thirst.

SUGGESTED EXERCISES

The following exercises can be done by individuals, shared between spiritual friends, or used in the context of a small group. Choose one or more of the following.

1. The habit we must develop, writes Kelly, is the ordering of our mental life on more than one level at once—on one level we are thinking and seeing and discussing, but on another level we are in prayer and adoration. Try this for the next week, keeping track of your experiences.

2. Becoming pliable in the hands of the Spirit is a constant theme for Kelly. This week attempt to become more open to the leading of the Spirit as you go about each day. Give ear to the still, small voice in the Inner Sanctuary.

3. Begin this exercise simply, as Kelly advises, by repeating inwardly, over and over, simple, short prayers such as "Thine only. Thine only." Or use a phrase from one of the psalms, such as "The Lord is my Shepherd." Soon this prayer will sink into the second level, and you will enjoy the blessing of "habitual divine orientation."

4. Jesus said that he came not to do his own will, but the will of God. Kelly believes that the secret for Jesus was an inward orientation of worship and listening, and that this secret is waiting to be discovered anew by Jesus' followers. Although you may find this a difficult exercise, try to shift your orientation this week, making worship and listening the central activities of your daily life.

REFLECTIONS

I will always remember my first encounter with the writings of Thomas Kelly. I was waiting for a plane in a Washington, D.C., airport on a rainy February morning and was captivated by these penetrating words: "We have seen and known some people who seem to have found this deep Center of living, where the fretful calls of life are integrated, where No as well as Yes can be said with confidence."

The rain splattered against the window outside; tears splattered against my coat. It was a holy place, an altar, the chair where I sat. I was never to be the same. Quietly, I asked God to give me this ability to say Yes or No out of what Kelly calls "the Divine Center." May God touch you as well from the writings of Thomas Kelly.

GOING DEEPER

Kelly, Richard. *Thomas Kelly: A Biography.* New York: Harper & Row, 1966. Richard Kelly was only six when his famous father died. As a young man he began collecting biographical material, and this book is the result of his many years of devoted research.

Kelly, Thomas. *The Eternal Promise.* New York: Harper & Row, 1966. Not as strong as *Testament*, yet the essays are all useful in developing the spiritual life—which is more than can be said for most books.

Kelly, Thomas. *Reality of the Spiritual World.* Wallingford, CT: Pendle Hill, 1942. A fine little booklet of forty-seven pages that clearly demonstrates Kelly's scholarship as a philosopher as well as his deep spiritual experience.

Kelly, Thomas. *A Testament of Devotion.* San Francisco: Harper San Francisco, 1992. This book is Kelly's great contribution to the world, and he didn't even know he wrote it. These penetrating essays into the spiritual life were compiled after his untimely death.

Catherine of Genoa (1447–1510)

INTRODUCTION TO THE AUTHOR

Catherine was born into a prominent religious family; her father was the viceroy of Naples and two of his family had been popes. In 1463 she married Guiliano Adorno, a wealthy but worldly man with whom she had little in common. After ten years of living a life of worldly vanity, she was converted to the contemplative life. Her husband had lost his fortune so with the remaining income they lived among the poor in Genoa. Guiliano became a member of the Third Order of St. Francis, and both he and Catherine worked among the poor and the sick. In 1479 they began working full time in a nearby hospital. A year later Guiliano died, and Catherine became the matron of the hospital.

Catherine of Genoa was a woman whose spirituality ran deep. Her love for God was matched only by her love for others. Though her writings are full of life and fervor, creative and inspiring, she is best remembered for her acts of charity. Her main work, *Life and Teachings,* along with her *Dialogues,* were her most important literary contributions. The following passage comes from *Life and Teachings.* As you will note, she was a woman who had keen insight into the pure love of God and the human struggle of accepting that love.

EXCERPTS FROM *LIFE AND TEACHINGS*

1. Little by Little

The creature is incapable of knowing anything except what God gives to it from day to day. If it knew beforehand what God intends for it, it would never be at peace. At times I have thought that my love was complete, but later, as my sight grew clearer, I became aware that I had many imperfections. I did not recognize them at first because God's love for me has it planned that I will achieve it little by little for the sake of preserving me and keeping me humble so as to be tolerable to myself and others!

Every day I feel the motes in my eyes being removed as God's pure love casts them out. We cannot see these imperfections because if we saw them, we could not bear the sight. Thus, God lets us imagine that we are complete. But never does God cease to remove them. From time to time I feel that I am growing only to see that I still have a long way to go.

They become visible to me in the mirror of God's Truth, of his Pure Love where everything I thought was straight appears crooked.

2. The Keys of My House

Our self-will is so subtle and so deeply rooted within our own selves and defends itself with so many reasons, that when we try to fight against it, we manage to lose in the end. We end up doing our own will under many covers—of charity, of necessity, or of justice. But God's love wills to stand naked and without any cover since it has nothing to hide.

I have seen this love. Indeed, every day I feel myself more occupied with him, and I feel a greater fire within. It is as if I have given the keys of my house to Love with permission to do all that is necessary. I became so consumed with this love that as I stood contemplating this work within me, I felt that even if I were cast into hell, hell itself would have appeared to me all love and consolation.

3. No Comfort Except in God

I find my mind more restricted upon God every day. It is like a man who at first is free to roam the city, and then is confined to a house, and then to a room, then to a smaller room, then to the cellar, and finally bound and blindfolded until there is no way of escape. With no comfort except in God who was doing this all along through love and great mercy, I came to a place of great contentment.

4. Living Without Self-Will

God and sin cannot live peaceably side by side. After considering things as they truly are, I felt a desire to live without self-will. When God gives light to the soul, it no longer desires to live with that part of it that continues to block the light. The soul desires to offer itself entirely to God so that it can no longer live except in the manner willed by his tender love. In this manner, it will begin to produce works that are pure, full, and sincere. These are the works that are pleasing to God.

Since I am determined to join myself to God, I find that I am also bound to be the enemy of his enemies. And since I find nothing that is more his enemy than the self that is in me, I am constrained to hate this part of me more than any other. Indeed, because of the war that exists between it and the Spirit, I am determined to separate it from myself and treat it as nothing.

5. Renouncing the Care of Ourselves

I then saw others who were fighting against their evil inclinations and forcing themselves to resist them. But I saw that the more they struggled against them, the more they committed them. So I said to them, "You are right in lamenting your sins and imperfections, and I would be lamenting with you if it were not for the fact that God is holding me. You cannot defend yourself and I cannot defend myself. The thing we must do is renounce the care of ourselves unto God who can defend our true self. Only then can God do for us what we cannot do ourselves."

As to the renouncing of ourselves, I told them, "Take a piece of bread and eat it. When you have eaten it, its substance goes into you to nourish the body and the rest is eliminated because your body no longer needs it. For the body is more important than the bread; it was created as a means, but it is not to remain forever with us. Likewise, we must remove all evil inclinations from our bodies; they cannot live on within us, lest we die."

6. Content to Wait upon God

God gives us his light in an instant, allowing us to know all that we need to know. No more is given to us than is necessary in his plan to lead us to perfection. We cannot seek this light; it is given to us from God only as he chooses. Neither do we know how it comes, or how we even know that it is! If we try to know more than we have been made to know, we will accomplish nothing. We simply wait like a stone, with no capacity until he brings us life.

Therefore I will not weary myself with seeking beyond what God wants me to know. Instead I will abide in peace with the understanding God has given me, and I will let this occupy my mind. If we are to see properly, we must pluck out of our eyes our own presumption. If we gaze too long at the sun, we go blind; in this manner, I think, does pride blind many of us who want to know too much.

When God finds a soul that rests in him and is not easily moved, he operates within it in his own manner. That soul allows God to do great things within it. He gives to such a soul the key to the treasures he has prepared for it so that it might enjoy them. And to this same soul he gives the joy of his presence which entirely absorbs such a soul.

7. God's Clever Strategy

The selfishness that is within us, however, is so contrary to God that God cannot induce us to do his will except by a clever strategy: promising us greater things than what the world can give—even in this life—and promising a kind of consolation that the world does not know.

God does this, I think, because he knows how much we are attached to pleasure. He knows that we are the kind who will not leave our one little toy unless we are offered four!

8. Vision of the Life to Come

If we could see what we will receive in the life to come (as a reward for what we have done here), we would cease to occupy ourselves with anything but the things of heaven. But God, who desires that we see by faith and who desires that we not do good because of selfish motives, gives us this vision little by little, sufficient to the level of faith of which we are capable. In this manner, God leads us into a greater vision of that which is to come until faith is no longer needed.

On the other hand, if we were somehow informed that we were about to die, and that the life that awaits us will be miserable because of our sins, and that we would have to suffer eternally, I feel sure that we—for fear of it—would rather let ourselves be killed than commit one single sin! But God—as unwilling as he is that we avoid sin out of the motive of fear and therefore never lets us see it—will show it in part to souls who are clothed and occupied with him.

9. Steadfast Trust

May this be our prayer: "I do not want to turn my eyes from you, O God. There I want them to stay and not move no matter what happens to me, within or without." For those who trust in God need not worry about themselves. As I think about you, my spiritual children, I see that God's pure love is attentive to all of your needs. It is because of this tender love that I need not ask anything of God for you. All I need to do is lift you up before his face.

BIBLE SELECTION: LUKE 16:19–31

[19]"There was a rich man who was dressed in purple and fine linen and who feasted sumptuously every day. [20]And at his gate lay a poor man named Lazarus, covered with sores, [21]who longed to satisfy his hunger with what fell from the rich man's table; even the dogs would come and lick his sores. [22]The poor man died and was carried away by the angels to be with Abraham. The rich man also died and was buried. [23]In Hades, where he was being tormented, he looked up and saw Abraham far away with Lazarus by his side. [24]He called out, 'Father Abraham, have mercy on me, and send Lazarus to dip the tip of his finger in water and cool my tongue; for I am in agony in these flames.' [25]But Abraham said, 'Child, remember that during your lifetime you received your good things, and Lazarus in like manner evil things; but now he is comforted here, and you are in agony. [26]Besides all this, between you and us a great chasm has been fixed, so that those who might want to pass from here to you cannot do so, and no one can cross from there to us.' [27]He said, 'Then, father, I beg you to send him to my father's house— [28]for I have five brothers—that he may warn them, so that they will not also come into this place of torment.' [29]Abraham replied, 'They have Moses and the prophets; they should listen to them.' [30]He said, 'No, father Abraham; but if someone goes to them from the dead, they will repent.' [31]He said to him, 'If they do not listen to Moses and the prophets, neither will they be convinced even if someone rises from the dead.'"

REFLECTION QUESTIONS

The following questions can be used for discussion within a small group, or used for journal reflections by individuals.

1. In section 1, Catherine notes our limitations concerning our self-awareness. As you look back at your own life, were there times when you thought you had attained some level of wisdom only to realize later that you were not as wise as you thought? Describe.

2. "Our self-will is so subtle," writes Catherine, that we often "end up doing our own will under many covers," such as charity or necessity or justice. In what ways have you noticed that your selfless acts done for others were actually selfish acts done mainly for yourself? What was Catherine's solution to this?

3. "When God finds a soul that rests in him and is not easily moved, he operates within it in his own manner. That soul allows God to do great things within it" (section 6). In what ways are you learning to rest in God and not be easily moved? In what ways are you preventing God from doing great things within you?

4. Catherine compares us with children who are attached to one toy and cannot let it go unless offered the prospect of having four. Which "toy" is preventing you from receiving more from God?

5. The rich man thinks that his family would repent if they could only see Lazarus raised from the dead. What is Abraham's reply? What kind of miracle would it take for you to begin investing all your energies in God?

SUGGESTED EXERCISES

The following exercises can be done by individuals, shared between spiritual friends, or used in the context of a small group. Choose one or more of the following.

1. Leave your one toy this week in order to receive an abundance from God. Keep yourself focused on the better blessings of God, which far exceed the temporary pleasure of sin.
2. The way to overcome our subtle self-will, says Catherine, is to give the keys of our house to God, letting him have control. This week give God the keys to all the rooms of your house; do not merely invite him in as an occasional guest, but let him become the Owner of the house.
3. Section 8 deals with our understanding of heaven and hell, as does the parable in Luke 16:19–31. Spend some time meditating on where you will spend eternity. As Catherine warns, do not let fear become your main motivating factor in living a godly life, but rather let your desire for God become more and more central in all that you do.
4. Catherine's closing words indicate how she prayed for others: she did not ask anything of God for them; instead, she lifted them up before God's face. Try this way of praying for others this week.

REFLECTIONS

Catherine went beyond loving God; she loved the ways of God. It is one thing for us to love God's grace and mercy, his power and steadfastness, but it is quite another to love his ways.

Think of the contrast between our ways and God's ways! We seek the spectacular act of devotion, the quantum leap of faith; God focuses on the seemingly insignificant changes that occur "little by little." We are concerned to watch out for number one; God invites us to "renounce the care of ourselves." We want to relegate God to the extracurricular category of our lives; God wants our complete attention. We want things done right now; God possesses eternal patience. These are the ways God chooses to work, and as we come into line with God's ways and operate in constancy with his ways, we learn that they are altogether good.

GOING DEEPER

Catherine of Genoa. Translated by Serge Hughes and edited by Richard J. Payne. New York: Paulist, 1979. From *The Classics of Western Spirituality.* This volume combines two of Catherine's works, which together essentially give us all her written "teachings." There is one other work called simply *The Life,* but its salient points are also covered in this volume and in a more compelling and concise form. Protestants will, of course, have difficulty with the first work, *Purgation and Purgatory,* but even so there are things to learn in it. *The Spiritual Dialogue* carries on a conversation between "body" and "soul" with input from "self-love" and "human frailty." It concludes with a description of Catherine's unusual death.

Baron Friedrich von Hügel wrote a book about Catherine, *The Mystical Element of Religion as Studied in Saint Catherine of Genoa and Her Friends* (London, 1908). To my knowledge, there are no other books about her in English.

George Fox (1624–1691)

INTRODUCTION TO THE AUTHOR

Born and raised in the turmoil of seventeenth-century Puritan England, George Fox became the founder and most prominent leader of the Quakers (the Society of Friends). His famous *Journal* reveals a bold and passionate, even prophetic, man who acted with the certainty of one who knows God firsthand, not by hearsay. He was quick to confront those who "did not possess what they professed." He laid bare pomposity and pretense. He also called thousands to a direct, intimate knowledge of Christ who was present to teach and empower them.

If the *Journal* portrays a fiery public figure, George Fox's *Letters* show us a loving pastor. In forty years, Fox wrote over three thousand letters, mostly to groups. These tender, practical letters display a full range of pastoral concern, from the life of prayer and worship to family life to the life of commerce. The following selections give us a glimpse into Fox's loving call to confident and complete Christian living.

EXCERPTS FROM *THE LETTERS OF GEORGE FOX*

1. The Living God

He is the living God, that clothes the earth with grass and herbs, causes the trees to grow and bring forth food for you, and makes the fishes of the sea to breathe and live. He makes the fowls of the air to breed and causes the buck and the doe, the creatures, and all the beasts to bring forth whereby they may be food for you. He is the living God, that causes the sun to give warmth to you, to nourish you when you are cold. He is the living God, that causes the snow and frost to melt and causes the rain to water the plants. He is the living God, that made heaven and earth, the clouds, causes the springs to break out of the rocks, and divided the great sea from the earth. He divides the light from the darkness, by which it is called day and the darkness night, and divided the great waters from the earth, gathered them together, which great waters he called sea and the dry land earth. He is to be worshiped that does this. He is the living God that gives you breath, life, and strength and gives you beasts and cattle whereby you may be fed and clothed. He is the living God, and he is to be worshiped.

This is the King of kings and Lord of lords, in whose hand is the breath of all mankind. [Letter 292]

2. Walking in the Power of God

My little children in the Lord God Almighty, this is my joy that you all be ordered and guided by the mighty power of God. Know that Voice that speaks, the sound of the words, and the power of them. For words without power destroy the simplicity, bring up into a form and out of obedience of the Truth. Therefore, walk in the power of the Truth that the name of the Lord God may be glorified among you, his renown may be seen in you and among you, and all the world may be astonished, and the Lord admired in the ordering of his people who are guided by his wisdom.

Let no strife be among you. Let none seek for the highest place, but be lowly minded, condescending one to another. Bear with one another in patience.

Therefore all Friends, mind that which is of God in you, to guide you to the Father of life, who gives you food and raiment and strength that you may flourish, your souls delight themselves in fatness, feed and eat of the abundance of riches with him and of the daily bread which comes from above, "the Bread of Life" (John 6:35). [Letter 79]

Dwell in patience and in peace and love and unity one with another. And be subject in the Power, Life, and Wisdom to God and to one another. That in it you may be as a pleasant field to the Lord God, and as the lilies, the flowers, and the buds feeling the pleasant showers and streams of Life from the living God flowing upon you, whereby the presence and blessing of the Lord God Almighty amongst you all may be felt. [Letter 183]

3. Singing in the Spirit

My dear Friends, be not carried away by good words and fair speeches, but everyone have hold of the Truth in yourselves by which you may be stayed upon Christ, your bread of life, the staff of your heavenly and eternal life.

Now Friends, who have denied the world's songs and singing, sing you in the Spirit and with grace, making melody in your hearts to the Lord. You that have denied the world's formal praying, pray always in the Spirit.

You that have denied the world's giving thanks and their saying of grace and living out of it, do you in everything give thanks to the Lord through Jesus Christ.

And you that have denied the world's praising God with their lips, while their hearts are far off, do you always praise the Lord night and day.

And you that have denied the world's fastings, keep the fast of the Lord that breaks the bond of iniquity and lets the oppressed go free, that your health may grow and your Light shine as the morning. [Letter 167]

4. Truth Can Live in the Jails

Dear Friends, who suffer for your testimony and to all the rest in your county, I am glad to hear of your faithfulness and of your standing for the Church which Christ is the head of, which is in God, and [you] are become his living members. And therefore wherever you are, in prison, or out of prison, where two or three are gathered together in his name, there is a Church, and Christ the living Head in the midst of them: a prophet, to open to his Church the things of his Kingdom; and a bishop, to oversee his living members, that they be preserved in his Light, Grace, Truth, Spirit, and Gospel; and he is a shepherd, to feed with heavenly food; and a priest, who has offered himself up a sacrifice for the sins of the whole world, who cleanses, washes and purifies his Church. And therefore feel and see Christ exercising his offices, and ruling in your hearts. [Letter 368]

Sing and rejoice you children of the Day and of the Light. For the Lord is at work in this thick night of darkness that may be felt. Truth does flourish as the rose, the lilies do grow among the thorns, the plants atop of the hills, and upon them the lambs do skip and play.

Never heed the tempests nor the storms, floods or rains, for the Seed, Christ, is over all and does reign.

And so, be of good faith and valiant for the Truth. For the Truth can live in the jails. Fear not the loss of the fleece, for it will grow again. And follow the Lamb, if it be under the beast's horns or under the beast's heels, for the Lamb shall have the victory over them all. [Letter 227]

5. Doing Truth to All

So, this is the word of the Lord God to you all. Do rightly, whether you be tradesmen, of what calling or profession or sort so ever, or husbandmen. Do rightly, justly, truly, holily, equally to all people in all things; and that is according to that of God in everyone, and the witness of God, and the wisdom of God, and the life of God in yourselves.

Whatever your calling, live in the power of Truth and wisdom of God to answer that just principle of God in all people upon the earth. So, let your lives preach, let your light shine, that your works may be seen, that your Father may be glorified. This has the praise of God, and they who do so come to answer that which God requires, to love mercy, do justly, and to walk humbly with God.

So everyone strive to be rich in the Life, and the things of the Kingdom that has no end; for the person that covets to be rich in the things of this world falls into many snares and hurtful lusts. Therefore, let the one that buys, or sells, or possesses, or uses this world be as if he did not. Let them be masters over the world in the power and Spirit of God, and let them know that they owe no one anything but love; yet serve God in Truth, and one another in their generation. [Letter 200]

6. Considering Your Promises

And now dear Friends, in all your words, in all your business and employments, have a care of breaking your words and promises to any people. Consider beforehand, that you may be able to perform and fulfill both your words and promises to people, that your Yea be Yea and Nay, Nay in all things, which Christ has set up instead of an oath.

Therefore all are to consider afore-hand, before they speak their Yea, Yea, what they are able to perform. It will preserve you out of all rash, hasty words and promises, for such kind of inconsiderate and rash speaking is not in the everlasting covenant of light, life, and grace.

Christ says, "If you have not been faithful with the dishonest wealth, who will entrust you the true riches?" (Luke 16:11). Therefore there must be a justness and faithfulness in the outward riches between individuals if you will have a place in your hearts for the true heavenly riches. The inward faithfulness to God brings forth faithfulness to people in outward things. [Letter 380]

7. The Bright Morning Star

All dear Friends everywhere, who have no helper but the Lord, who is your strength and your life, let your cries and prayers be to him, who with his eternal power has kept your heads above all waves and storms. Let none go out of their habitations in the stormy time of the night, those whose habitation is the Lord, the Seed, Christ Jesus.

In this Seed you will see the bright and morning Star appear which will expel the night of darkness, by which morning Star you will come to the everlasting Day which was before night was.

So, everyone feel this bright morning Star in your hearts, there to expel the darkness. [Letter 280] (*Abridged and revised for the modern reader by Howard R. Macy.*)

BIBLE SELECTION: ISAIAH 58:1–9

Shout out, do not hold back!
Lift up your voice like a trumpet!
Announce to my people their rebellion,
to the house of Jacob their sins.
²Yet day after day they seek me
and delight to know my ways,
as if they were a nation that practiced
  righteousness
and did not forsake the ordinance of their
  God;
they ask of me righteous judgments,
they delight to draw near to God.
³"Why do we fast, but you do not see?
Why humble ourselves, but you do not
  notice?"
Look, you serve your own interest on your
  fast day,
and oppress all your workers.
⁴Look, you fast only to quarrel and to fight
and to strike with a wicked fist.
Such fasting as you do today
will not make your voice heard on high.
⁵Is such the fast that I choose,
a day to humble oneself?

Is it to bow down the head like a bulrush,
and to lie in sackcloth and ashes?
Will you call this a fast,
a day acceptable to the LORD?

⁶Is not this the fast that I choose:
to loose the bonds of injustice,
to undo the thongs of the yoke,
to let the oppressed go free,
and to break every yoke?
⁷Is it not to share your bread with the hungry,
and bring the homeless poor into your house;
when you see the naked, to cover them,
and not to hide yourself from your own kin?
⁸Then your light shall break forth like the
  dawn,
and your healing shall spring up quickly;
your vindicator shall go before you,
the glory of the LORD shall be your rear guard.
⁹Then you shall call, and the LORD will
  answer;
you shall cry for help, and he will say, Here
  I am.

REFLECTION QUESTIONS

The following questions can be used for discussion within a small group, or used for journal reflections by individuals.

1. In the first section, George Fox reveals his keen sense that God is intimately and powerfully involved in ordinary life. In what ways do you see "the living God" giving you "breath, life, and strength"?

2. Fox encourages the Christian community to live together so remarkably that it will astonish the world into admiring the Lord. What are the attitudes and actions that make this possible? (See section 2.)

3. In your work and daily business, what would it look like to "do rightly . . . to all people in all things" (section 5)? What would it be like to owe no one "anything but love"?

4. If you were to make only those commitments that you were sure you could keep (letting your yes mean yes and your no mean no), as Fox suggests, how would it affect your economic, social, and family life?

5. In Isaiah 58:6–7, the prophet gives examples of an acceptable fast before God. What actions are a part of God's chosen fast? How can these be regarded as acts of devotion?

SUGGESTED EXERCISES

The following exercises can be done by individuals, shared between spiritual friends, or used in the context of a small group. Choose one or more of the following.

1. God's provision in ordinary life (e.g., plants and animals for food, sunshine for warmth) leads Fox to an attitude of praise. Let the awareness of God's bountiful blessings in creation lead you into worship this week.

2. Patience, peace, love for one another, and carrying one another's burdens are a few examples of how we can demonstrate the love of God in the midst of our communities of faith. This week put some of these actions into practice.

3. Make it your aim to treat others justly this week. As Fox commands us, be careful not to show any prejudice in your dealings with others, but rather treat all people as you would have others treat you.

4. For both Isaiah and George Fox, living peaceably and setting the oppressed free, feeding the hungry and housing the homeless were essential parts of the fast that is acceptable to God. Try this kind of fasting this week, being mindful of the devotional nature of these important acts of charity.

REFLECTIONS

I never tire of hearing the stories of George Fox. He was always so alive to "Christ living and present among you." Even in the most discouraging of circumstances he would declare that "the power of the Lord is over all." On one occasion Fox was preaching in the open air and a drunken soldier stuck a sword to his throat, demanding that he stop preaching. Fox looked straight at the man and declared, "Hack away, your sword is nothing to me but a straw!" Dramatically the power of God fell upon the soldier; he staggered backwards, fell to the ground, and was converted.

Fox's legacy is one of courage and faithfulness. And he would urge us, as he did those of his own day, to be "valiant for the truth upon the earth."

GOING DEEPER

Fox, George. *The Journal of George Fox.* Edited by John L. Nickalls. Cambridge: Cambridge University Press, 1952. Reprinted with corrections, London: London Yearly Meeting, 1986. Fox's *Journal* is the prototype of modern religious journal writing. It is powerful, cryptic, insightful, and compassionate all at the same time.

Fox, George. *No More but My Love.* Edited by Cecil W. Sharman. London: Quaker Home Service, 1980. An attractive, modernized selection from 137 of Fox's letters.

Fox, George. *The Power of the Lord Is Over All.* Edited by T. Canby Jones. Richmond, IN: Friends United Press, 1989. The first complete edition in over 150 years of all George Fox's 421 published letters. Jones has written a helpful introduction and has slightly adapted Fox's writing for modern readers.

Trueblood, D. Elton. *The People Called Quakers.* Richmond, IN: Friends United Press, 1971. This book will give you some historical and theological background on George Fox and the early Quaker movement.

Ignatius of Loyola (1491–1556)

INTRODUCTION TO THE AUTHOR

Ignatius was born in the family castle of Loyola in the Basque country of Spain. His family belonged to a long line of nobility, and Ignatius reflected his refined upbringing throughout his early life. He participated in all the revelry of royalty—gambling, dueling, romance—and worldly attraction.

In 1517 he took service in the army and in May of 1521 received a leg wound in a border skirmish with the French. He returned to Loyola to recuperate and found himself able to do nothing but read. He happened upon a book called *The Life of Christ* and was converted as a result. He also read *The Imitation of Christ* and the stories of St. Francis. He concluded by asking, "Could I not do what Francis did?" He then resolved to make a pilgrimage to Jerusalem, disposed of all his worldly goods, and clothed himself in sackcloth.

His ship was detained in Manresa, however, and he was forced to remain there for a year. During that time he had several profound mystical experiences that led him to begin sharing his faith with others. He also penned a large portion of *The Spiritual Exercises* during his stay in Manresa, and carried these notes with him as he continued the journey to Jerusalem. Ignatius would later become famous for these simple yet profound instructions on how to take a spiritual retreat. His "exercises" became the standard for Jesuit retreats and have remained so to this day.

EXCERPTS FROM *THE SPIRITUAL EXERCISES OF ST. IGNATIUS*

1. Different Movements

The following are some rules for perceiving and understanding the different movements that are produced in the soul—the good that should be accepted; the bad that should be rejected.

The enemy is accustomed ordinarily to propose apparent pleasure to those persons who go from mortal sin to mortal sin. He thus causes them to imagine sensual delights and pleasure in order to hold them more and more easily and to increase their vices and sins. The good spirit acts in these persons in a contrary way, awakening the conscience to a sense of remorse through the good judgment of their reason.

This takes place in those who earnestly strive to purify themselves from their sins and who advance from good to better in the service of God our Lord. For these persons it is common for the evil spirit to cause anxiety and sadness and to create obstacles based on false reasoning, thus preventing the soul from making further progress.

It is characteristic of the good spirit to give courage and strength, consolation, tears, inspiration, and peace, making things easy and removing all obstacles so that the soul may make further progress in good works.

2. Tears Inspired by Love

I call it *consolation* when the soul is aroused by an interior movement which causes it to be inflamed with love of its Creator and Lord and consequently can love no created thing in this world for its own sake, but only in the Creator of all things. It is likewise consolation when one sheds tears inspired by love of the Lord, whether it be sorrow for sins or because of the Passion of Christ our Lord, or for any other reason that is directly connected to his service and praise. Finally, I call consolation any increase of faith, hope, and charity and any interior joy that calls and attracts to heavenly things, and to the salvation of one's soul, inspiring it with peace and quiet in Christ our Lord.

I call *desolation* all that is contrary to the third rule, as darkness of the soul, turmoil of the mind, inclination to low and earthly things, restlessness resulting from many disturbances and temptations which leads to loss of faith, loss of hope, loss of love. It is also desolation when a soul finds itself completely apathetic, tepid, sad, and separated as it were, from its Creator and Lord. For just as consolation is contrary to desolation, so the thoughts that spring from consolation are the opposite of those that spring from desolation.

3. Stand Firm and Constant

In time of desolation one should never make a change, but stand firm and constant in the resolution and decision which guided him the day before the desolation, or to the decision which he observed in the preceding consolation. For just as the good spirit guides and consoles us in consolation, so in desolation the evil spirit guides and counsels. Following the counsels of this latter spirit, one can never find the correct way to a right decision.

Although in desolation we should not change our earlier resolutions, it will be very advantageous to intensify our activity against the desolation. This can be done by insisting more on prayer, meditation, frequent examinations, and by increasing our penance in some suitable manner.

One who is in desolation must strive to persevere in patience which is contrary to the vexations that have come upon him. He should consider, also, that consolation will soon return and strive diligently against the desolation.

4. Why We Are in Desolation

There are three reasons why we are in desolation. The first is because we have been tepid, slothful, or negligent in our Spiritual Exercises, and so through our own fault spiritual consolation is withdrawn from us.

The second is that God may try to test our worth, and the progress that we have made in his service and praise when we are without such generous rewards of consolation and special graces.

The third is that he may wish to give us a true knowledge and understanding so that we may truly perceive that it is not within our power to acquire or retain great devotion, ardent love, tears, or any other spiritual consolation, but that all of this is a gift and a grace of God our Lord. Nor does God wish us to claim as our own what belongs to another, allowing our intellect to rise up in a spirit of pride or vainglory, attributing to ourselves the devotion or other aspects of spiritual consolation.

5. The Sufficient Grace

A person who is in consolation ought to think of how he will conduct himself during a future desolation and thus build up a new strength for that time.

A person who is in consolation should also take care to humble and abase himself as much as possible. He should recall how little he felt he was worth in the previous time of desolation when he was without such grace or consolation.

On the other hand, a person who is in desolation should recall that he can do much to withstand all of his enemies by using the sufficient grace that he has and taking strength in his Creator and Lord.

6. A Show of Determination

The enemy is weak in the presence of strength, but strong if he has our will. He will lose courage and take flight when we make a show of determination. In like manner, if we lose courage and begin to retreat, the anger, rage, and vindictiveness of the enemy becomes great beyond all bounds.

The enemy will lose courage and take flight as soon as a person who is following the spiritual life stands courageously against his temptations and does exactly the opposite of what the enemy suggests. On the contrary, if a person begins to take flight and loses courage in the midst of fighting temptation, no wild beast on earth is more fierce than the enemy as he pursues his evil intention with ever increasing malice.

7. A False Lover

The enemy also behaves like a false lover who wishes to remain hidden and does not want to be revealed. For when this deceitful man pays court, with evil intent, to the daughter of some good father or the wife of a good husband, he wants his words and suggestions to be kept secret. He is greatly displeased if the girl reveals to her father, or the wife to her husband, his deceitful words and depraved intentions, for he then clearly perceives that his plan cannot succeed.

In like manner, when the enemy tempts a just soul with his wiles and deceits, he wishes and desires that they be received and kept in secret. When they are revealed to a confessor or some other spiritual person who understands his deceits and evil designs, the enemy is greatly displeased for he knows that he cannot succeed in his evil design once his obvious deceits have been discovered.

The enemy's behavior is also like that of a military leader who wishes to conquer and plunder the object of his desires. Just as the commander of an army pitches his camp, studies the strength and defenses of a fortress, and then attacks it on its weakest side, in like manner, the enemy of our souls studies from all sides our theological, cardinal, and moral virtues. Wherever he finds us weakest and most in need regarding our eternal salvation, he attacks and tries to take us by storm.

8. An Angel of Light

It belongs to God and his angels to bring true happiness and spiritual joy to the soul and to free it from the sadness and disturbance which the enemy causes. It is the nature of the enemy to fight against such joy and spiritual consolation by proposing (seemingly) serious reasons, subtleties, and continual deceptions.

Also, it is characteristic of the evil one to transform himself into an angel of light, to work with the soul in the beginning, but in the end work for himself. At first he will suggest good and holy thoughts, and then, little by little he strives to gain his own ends by drawing the soul into his hidden deceits.

It is well for a person who has been tempted to examine afterward the course of the good thoughts that were suggested to him. Let him consider their beginning and how the enemy contrived, little by little, to make him fall from the state of sweetness and spiritual delight that he was enjoying until he finally brought him to perverse designs. With the experience and knowledge thus acquired and noted, one may better guard himself in the future against the customary deceits of the enemy.

9. An Open Door

In those who are making spiritual progress, the action of the good angel is gentle, light, and sweet, as a drop of water entering a sponge. The action of the evil spirit is sharp, noisy, and disturbing, like a drop of water falling upon a rock. In those souls that are going from bad to worse, the action of these two spirits is the reverse.

The cause for this difference of action is the disposition of the soul which is either contrary or similar to the spirits mentioned above. When the disposition of the soul is contrary to that of the spirits, they enter it with noise and disturbances that are easily perceived. When the disposition of the soul and that of the spirits are similar, they enter silently as one coming into his own house through an open door.

BIBLE SELECTION: 1 PETER 5:6–11

[6]Humble yourselves therefore under the mighty hand of God, so that he may exalt you in due time. [7]Cast all your anxiety on him, because he cares for you. [8]Discipline yourselves, keep alert. Like a roaring lion your adversary the devil prowls around, looking for someone to devour. [9]Resist him, steadfast in your faith, for you know that your brothers and sisters in all the world are undergoing the same kinds of suffering. [10]And after you have suffered for a little while, the God of all grace, who has called you to his eternal glory in Christ, will himself restore, support, strengthen, and establish you. [11]To him be the power forever and ever. Amen.

REFLECTION QUESTIONS

The following questions can be used for discussion within a small group, or used for journal reflections by individuals.

1. There has always been a lot of discussion (some good, some bad) about the spiritual realms of good and evil. How do you understand the presence and work of angels and demons? How did Ignatius of Loyola clarify or confuse your previous understanding?

2. Feelings of consolation and desolation are one of the main topics of this selection on discerning the spirits. Have you ever experienced either of these in the manner Ignatius describes? Share your experiences.

3. What are the three reasons Ignatius gives for a soul entering into a state of desolation? (See section 4.) Have any of these three been a part of your experience? How did the Spirit move in order to help you grow in that situation?

4. In section 7, the author reveals the enemy's one great fear. What is it? What can we do to ensure that the enemy has that fear?

5. In 1 Peter 5:6–11, especially verse 8, Peter offers us both a warning and some advice when we face temptation. What are they? Compare this counsel with the teachings of Ignatius.

SUGGESTED EXERCISES

The following exercises can be done by individuals, shared between spiritual friends, or used in the context of a small group. Choose one or more of the following.

1. The devil will attack our weakest side, writes Ignatius. However, we can combat this attack by knowing where we are weak and making a move to strengthen that side. This week make it your goal to discover your weakest areas, and resolve to strengthen that side.

2. Pay close attention this week to the inner movements in your soul. Discern the source of your thoughts and feelings by using Ignatius's descriptions.

3. "The enemy is weak in the presence of strength," writes Ignatius. Stand firm in the presence of temptations this week, relying not on your own strength but on the strength of God.

4. 1 Peter 5:7 encourages, "Cast all your anxiety on him, because he cares for you." Be bold this week as you pray, casting all your anxieties on God, knowing that he cares deeply about each of them.

REFLECTIONS

There is a four-part structure to the Ignatian spiritual retreat. The first week is given to the contemplation of our sin in the light of God's love. The second week centers on the life of Christ, the third week on the death of Christ, and the fourth week on the resurrection of Christ.

Many readers would be uncomfortable with various details of The Spiritual Exercises, *but I want to commend this four-part rhythm to you. We need a deeper musing upon our perennial knack for disobedience and God's unbounded habit of mercy. We need a richer contemplation upon that Life that shows us the way so we may follow "in his steps." We need a fuller meditation upon that Death that sets us free. We need a more profound experience of that Resurrection that empowers us to obey Christ in all things.*

GOING DEEPER

Brou, Alexandre. *Ignatian Method of Prayer.* Milwaukee: Bruce, 1949.

Charmot, François. *Ignatius Loyola and Francis de Sales: Two Masters, One Spirituality.* Translated by Sister M. Renelle. St. Louis: B. Herder Book Co., 1966.

Harvey, Robert. *Ignatius Loyola: A General in the Church Militant.* Milwaukee: Bruce, 1936.

Ignatius of Loyola. *The Autobiography of St. Ignatius Loyola.* Translated by Joseph F. O'Callaghan and edited by John C. Olin. New York: Harper & Row, 1974.

Ignatius of Loyola. *The Spiritual Exercises of St. Ignatius.* Translated by Anthony Mottola. New York: Doubleday, 1964. This, of course, is the basis for the thirty-day Ignatian retreat. It is not really a book in the normal sense: better to think of it as a workbook. It sketches out the retreat experience with appropriate meditation exercises. It is best used in the context of a leader who can guide you through the retreat.

Jean-Pierre de Caussade (1675–1751)

INTRODUCTION TO THE AUTHOR

Little is known about the life of the Jesuit Jean-Pierre de Caussade beyond the bare facts of his career. He was born in Toulouse, France, and was ordained a member of the Society of Jesus in 1708. Although he was by no means unrecognized as a scholar and preacher, there is only one mention of him in the Jesuit calendar, and the only book he published, *Spiritual Instructions on the Various States of Prayer*, appeared anonymously and for a time was attributed to a more popular contemporary.

Two key phrases have become identified with his name. The first, "self-abandonment to divine providence," implies a dynamic surrender of ourselves to the will and way of God. The second, "the sacrament of the present moment," awakens us to the requirement of doing our duty, whatever it may be, a carrying out of God's purpose for us not only this day, or this hour, but this minute, this very minute.

We who long to press into the heart of God will find comfort and hope in de Caussade's joyful surrender to God's will and constant discovery of God's loving purpose in the midst of life's trials and tribulations.

EXCERPTS FROM *THE SACRAMENT OF THE PRESENT MOMENT*

1. Sick Doctors and Healthy Patients

God's order, his pleasure, his will, his action and grace; all these are one and the same. The purpose on earth of this divine power is perfection. It is formed, grows, and is accomplished secretly in souls without their knowledge. Theology is full of theories and arguments expounding the miracles it works in each soul. We may be able to understand all these speculations, cogently discuss, write, teach, and instruct souls through them. But with only this in mind in relation to those in whom that divine purpose exists, I suggest we are like sick doctors trying to cure patients in perfect health.

God's order and his divine will, humbly obeyed by the faithful, accomplishes this divine purpose in them without their knowledge in the same way as medicine obediently swallowed cures invalids who neither know nor care how. Just as it is fire and not the philosophy or science of that element and its effects that heats, so it is God's order and his will which sanctify and not curious speculations about its origin or purpose.

To quench thirst it is necessary to drink. Reading books about it only makes it worse. Thus, when we long for sanctity, speculation only drives it further from our grasp. We must humbly accept all that God's order requires us to do and suffer. What he ordains for us each moment is what is most holy, best, and most divine for us.

2. What God Ordains for the Present Moment

All we need to know is how to recognize his will in the present moment. Grace is the will of God and his order acting in the center of our hearts when we read or are occupied in other ways; theories and studies, without regard for the refreshing virtue of God's order, are merely dead letters, emptying the heart by filling the mind. This divine will flowing through the soul of a simple uneducated girl, through her suffering or some exceptionally noble act in adversity, carries out in her heart God's mysterious purpose without thought entering her head. Whereas the sophisticated man, who studies spiritual books out of mere curiosity, whose reading is not inspired by God, takes into his mind only dead letters and grows even more arid and obtuse.

God's order and his divine will is the life of all souls who either seek or obey it. In whatever way this divine will may benefit the mind, it nourishes the soul. These blessed results are not produced by any particular circumstance but by what God ordains for the present moment. What was best a moment ago is so no longer because it is removed from the divine will which has passed on to be changed to form the duty to the next. And it is that duty, whatever it may be, that is now most sanctifying for the soul.

3. The Fruit Ripens

If the divine will ordains that reading is the duty of the present moment, reading achieves that mysterious purpose. If the divine will abandons reading for an act of contemplation, that duty will bring about a change of heart and then reading will be harmful and useless. If the divine will rejects contemplation for confessions and the like (especially if they are lengthy), it will establish Jesus Christ in our heart which all the sweetness of contemplation would only prevent.

The mysterious growth of Jesus Christ in our heart is the accomplishment of God's purpose, the fruit of his grace and divine will. This fruit, as has been pointed out, forms, grows, and ripens in the succession of our duties to the present which are continually being replenished by God, so that obeying them is always the best we can do. We must offer no resistance and blindly abandon ourselves to his divine will in perfect trust.

This divine will is infinitely wise, powerful, and benevolent towards souls who totally and unreservedly put their trust in it, and who love and seek it alone, and who believe with an unshakable faith and confidence that what the divine will ordains each moment is best, who look no further afield for vain comparisons with any material benefits God's order may bring.

4. Jesus Christ in the Center of Our Being

The will of God is the presence, the reality, and the virtue in all things, adjusting them to souls. Without God's direction all is void, emptiness, vanity, words, superficiality, death. The will of God is the salvation, sanity, and life of body and soul whatever else it may bring to either of them. Whether it be vexation and trouble for the mind, or sickness and death for the body, nevertheless that divine will remains all in all. Bread without the divine will is poison, with it true sustenance. Without the divine will reading only blinds and perplexes, with it it enlightens.

The divine will is the wholeness, the good and the true in all things. Like God, the universal Being, it is manifest in everything. It is not necessary to look to the benefits received by the mind and body to judge their virtue. These are of no significance. It is the will of God that gives everything, whatever it may be, the power to form Jesus Christ in the center of our being. This will knows no limits.

5. God's Purpose in the Present Moment

Divine action does not distinguish between creatures, whether they are useless or useful. Without it everything is nothing, with it nothing is everything. Whether contemplation, meditation, prayer, inward silence, intuition, quietude, or activity are what we wish for ourselves, the best is God's purpose for us at the present moment. Souls must look upon everything as though it were a matter of complete indifference, and, seeing only him in all things, must take or leave them as he wishes so as to live, be nourished by, and hope in him alone and not by any power or virtue which does not come from him.

Every moment, and in respect of everything, they must say, like St. Paul, "Lord what should I do?" Let me do everything you wish. The Spirit wants one thing, the body another, but Lord, I wish only to do your divine will. Supplication, intercession, mental or vocal

prayer, action or silence, faith or wisdom, particular sacraments or general grace, all these, Lord, are nothing, for your purpose is the true and only virtue in all things. It alone, and nothing else, however sublime or exalted, is the object of my devotion since the purpose of grace is the perfection of the heart, not of the mind.

6. This Secret Union

The presence of God which sanctifies our souls is the Holy Trinity which dwells in our hearts when they surrender to the divine will. God's presence coming to us through an act of contemplation brings this secret union. Like everything else belonging to God's order and enjoined by the divine will, it must always take first place as the most perfect means of uniting ourselves to God.

It is by being united to the will of God that we enjoy and possess him, and it is a delusion to seek this divine possession by any other means. Being united to God is the only way, not in any specific manner or style, but in a thousand different ways, and the one he chooses for us is the best. But they must all be loved and esteemed since they are all ordained by God and his purpose, chosen for and adapted to each soul to bring about the divine union. And souls must abide by his choice, preferring the way of this blessed will, and must love and respect it just as much in others.

7. We Must Set No Bounds

For example, if God's purpose prescribes for me vocal prayers, loving sentiments, insight into the mysteries, I must love the silence and bareness which a life of faith inspires in others. But for myself, I must make use of my duty to the present and by it unite myself to God. I must not, like the quietists, reduce all religion to a denial of any specific action, despising all other means, since what makes perfection is God's order, and the means he ordains is best for the soul. No, we must set no bounds or limits or shape to the will of God.

We must accept any way he chooses to communicate with us and respect any way it pleases him to unite himself to others. Thus, all simple souls have but one general way, though specific and different in each one, which makes up the diversity of the mystical experience. All simple souls must admire and respect one another, saying: "Let us proceed each one along our path to the same goal, united in purpose and by means of God's order which, in its great variety, is in us all." It is in this light that the lives of the saints and the spiritual books must be read, without ever being misled or going astray.

8. When Will God Be All in All?

It is why it is absolutely essential neither to read nor hold spiritual discourse unless ordained by God. Since his order makes it their duty to the present to do so, far from being misled, souls will find reassurance in the very things which contradict what they have learnt. But if God's order does not make this reading and spiritual discourse the duty to the present moment, they will always emerge troubled and find themselves confused and uncertain.

Without God there can be no order anywhere. How long, then, shall we continue to concern ourselves with our own liberty or our own capacity to suffer the trials and tribulations of the present moment? When will God be all in all to us? Let us see things in their true light and rise above them to live purely in God himself.

BIBLE SELECTION: GENESIS 22:1–12

After these things God tested Abraham. He said to him, "Abraham!" And he said, "Here I am." [2]He said, "Take your son, your only son Isaac, whom you love, and go to the land of Moriah, and offer him there as a burnt offering on one of the mountains that I shall show you." [3]So Abraham rose early in the morning, saddled his donkey, and took two of his young men with him, and his son Isaac; he cut the wood for the burnt offering, and set out and went to the place in the distance that God had shown him. [4]On the third day Abraham looked up and saw the place far away. [5]Then Abraham said to his young men, "Stay here with the donkey; the boy and I will go over there; we will worship, and then we will come back to you. " [6]Abraham took the wood of the burnt offering and laid it on his son Isaac, and he himself carried the fire and the knife. So the two of them walked on together. [7]Isaac said to his father Abraham, "Father!" And he said, "Here I am, my son." He said, "The fire and the wood are here, but where is the lamb for a burnt offering?" [8]Abraham said, "God himself will provide the lamb for a burnt offering, my son." So the two of them walked on together.

[9]When they came to the place that God had shown him, Abraham built an altar there and laid the wood in order. He bound his son Isaac, and laid him on the altar, on top of the wood. [10]Then Abraham reached out his hand and took the knife to kill his son. [11]But the angel of the LORD called to him from heaven, and said, "Abraham, Abraham!" And he said, "Here I am." [12]He said, "Do not lay your hand on the boy or do anything to him; for now I know that you fear God, since you have not withheld your son, your only son, from me."

REFLECTION QUESTIONS

The following questions can be used for discussion within a small group, or used for journal reflections by individuals.

1. "All we need to know," writes Jean-Pierre de Caussade, "is how to recognize [God's] will in the present moment." Have you found this to be easy or difficult in your life? What direction does the author give to help us discern God's will in the present moment?

2. In section 1, de Caussade compares spiritual growth with taking medicine: even though we do not fully understand how it works, and at times are unaware of its working within us, yet it heals us. How has God worked in your life even though, at the time, you were unaware of what was happening?

3. One of the problems the author addresses is the tendency to control our life with God by doing specific exercises at specific times, thus negating the possibility of letting God determine both the what and the when of our spiritual disciplines. Others, however, simply do nothing because they are unsure what God wants them to do. In which of these directions do you tend to lean? Explain.

4. "We must offer no resistance and blindly abandon ourselves to his divine will in perfect trust," writes de Caussade. Which do you find more difficult: discerning God's will or doing it?

5. God's will in the present moment for Abraham was not to sacrifice his son but to be willing to sacrifice his son. What might God be asking you to sacrifice? Are you willing? Why or why not?

SUGGESTED EXERCISES

The following exercises can be done by individuals, shared between spiritual friends, or used in the context of a small group. Choose one or more of the following.

1. "Every moment," writes Jean-Pierre de Caussade, we should say like St. Paul, "Lord what should I do?" Make this your constant prayer this week.

2. Look for the grace in all that happens to you this week. No matter what comes your way, turn to God and ask how each activity—however mundane—can become a sacrament of the present moment.

3. The author believes that God sanctifies our souls when our hearts are surrendered (see section 6). Surrender your heart to God in the next week. Make a daily, even an hourly, commitment of surrender.

4. While Abraham's call was clear, sometimes our call to make a sacrifice is muted by our many distractions. In your times of prayer, focus on God's call for you in the present moment. Begin each time of prayer by saying, "God, whatever you will for me today, I am ready to obey." Such willingness allows God to work in our lives in mighty ways.

REFLECTIONS

I love de Caussade's emphasis on God's activity in the moments of our personal histories. It is this feature in his writings that saves The Sacrament *from the vaporous, ethereal character of so many of the mystical works. The spirituality of de Caussade is so utterly practical and down-to-earth. He takes the moments of our days and the simple duties that make them up and gives them sacramental significance. Obedience to this duty of the present moment constitutes the path to holiness.*

Nor is de Caussade speaking of a way of life beyond the reach of ordinary disciples. He writes, "Let us unceasingly impress upon every soul that the invitation of this gentle, loving Savior expects nothing difficult or extraordinary of them. Indeed, God is only asking for your heart. Everyone can aspire to the same love, the same surrender, the same God and his work." De Caussade offers a spirituality for ordinary folk—people just like you and me.

GOING DEEPER

de Caussade, Jean-Pierre. *The Sacrament of the Present Moment.* Translated by Kitty Muggeridge. San Francisco: Harper & Row, 1982. Usually found under the title *Self-Abandonment to Divine Providence,* this book is a masterpiece of Christian spirituality. Kitty Muggeridge's translation (using a much-improved French text) brings to English readers the original vibrancy and spiritual recklessness of de Caussade. Like many of the great devotional classics, this work must be read slowly and prayerfully. Do not look for linear logic, but for the sudden burst of insight and the unusual turn of phrase.

Isaac Penington (1617–1680)

INTRODUCTION TO THE AUTHOR

Isaac Penington was the son of the mayor of London. In 1658 he joined the Society of Friends (the Quakers). He was such a zealous follower of Christ and filled with such faith that he was jailed six times for proclaiming his unshakable convictions. He spent five years in prison as a result of his desire to worship in a manner other than the one prescribed by the established church. For a Quaker, this meant through silence as opposed to liturgy and sacraments and sermons.

He also refused to take an oath in court (which he believed was forbidden by God in Scripture). As a result, he and his wife lost all their property. The hardships he encountered in the following years helped him to understand the growth that comes through suffering. Penington offers light and truth and comfort for all who suffer and are afflicted today as he was in his day. The following selection comes from some of the letters he wrote to friends. They reveal his own tenderness, sympathy, and unwavering faith.

EXCERPTS FROM *LETTERS ON SPIRITUAL VIRTUES*

1. Wait for Breathings from His Spirit

Friend, it is a wonderful thing to witness the power of God as it reaches to the heart and demonstrates to the soul the pure way to life. Surely the person who partakes of this power will be favored by the Lord. Therefore, we ought to wait diligently for the leadings of the Holy Spirit in everything we do. Thus we will be able to travel through all that is contrary to God and into the things that are of God.

It is also a wonderful thing to witness God's preservation that keeps us from sliding backwards and being entangled in the traps of the enemy. For the enemy has many ways and uses many devices to ensnare our minds and draw it away from the Truth. There our souls are lulled asleep with false hopes and we lose the feeling and enjoyment of the true life and power.

O Friend, do you not have a sense of the way to the Father? Then you must press your spirit to bow daily before God and wait for breathings to you from his Spirit. Pray that he will continue his mercy to you and make his way more and more clear before you every day. Yes, and also pray that he will give you strength in all the trials which may come your way. By his secret working in your spirit, giving you assistance from time to time, you will advance nearer and nearer towards the kingdom.

2. The Way to His Dwelling Place

And do not pay careful attention to the desires of the body, but instead, trust the Lord. Though you are weak and small, and though you may fall into the company of those who are more clever than you and are able to trick you by their reason, and though you may not have an answer to their arguments, you know and can feel God's pure Truth in your spirit. Desire only to have that life brought forth in you and to have your spirit renewed and changed by God's power.

O dear heart, it is in this that you are accepted by God, and here his love and tender care will be over you. His mercy will reach out to you daily and you shall have true satisfaction in your heart. Hold that Truth in your heart where all the devices of the devil and the reasonings of false teachers shall not be able to reach it. You will be able to feel the strength of the Lord helping his child during times of trial, and you will feel the joy of praise during the seasons of his good pleasure.

And so you shall experience the truth of God's promise that the gates of hell will not prevail against you. Therefore, remember, do not look to others or to the reasoning of the wise, but keep yourself where you have felt the Lord visit you that he may visit you again and again—every day—teaching you more and more the way to his dwelling place, drawing you near to the place where there is righteousness, life, rest, and peace—forever!

3. Feed on the Tree of Life

O Friends! Feed on the tree of life; feed on the measure of life, and the pure power which God has revealed and manifested in you. Do you know where your real food comes from, do you remember the taste? Then keep to it, and do not meddle with the kind of food that seems desirable to the *other* eye, the one that promises to make you wise.

O abide in the simplicity that is in Christ Jesus, in the naked truth that you have felt there! It is there that you will be able to know and distinguish your food, which has several names in Scripture but is all one and the same thing: the bread, the milk, the water, the wine, the flesh, and blood of him who came down from heaven. It is all the same food, only it is given to us in different measure—sometimes weaker, sometimes stronger—according to the capacity we have for receiving it. Thus, it is given different names.

4. Dwell in Your Habitation

O keep out of that wisdom which does not know the truth. Rather, keep to the principle of life—keep to the seed of the kingdom—and feed on that which was from the beginning. Is this not the true meat? Is this not the true drink? The Lord has advanced you to this appointment of life and power where things are known and revealed and felt beyond what words can utter.

O dwell in your habitation and feed on the food which God brings into this dwelling place. It is pure and alive, and it will cause your souls and spirits more and more to live in and to God as you eat and drink thereof. May the Lord God preserve you and watch over you, may you feel victory and dominion over all that is contrary to him, and may you triumph over all that stands in the way of your fellowship with him.

5. Helping One Another with a Tender Hand

Friends, our life is love and peace and tenderness. We are called to bear one another's burdens, forgive one another, and never judge or accuse one another. Instead, we must pray for one another, helping one another up with a tender hand if there has been any slip or fall. O! wait to feel this spirit. Wait to be guided and to walk in this spirit that you may enjoy the Lord in sweetness and walk meekly, tenderly, peaceably, and lovingly with one another. Then you will be able to praise the Lord, and anything that has hindered you, you will be able to overcome in the Lamb's dominion. That which is contrary shall be trampled upon as his life rises and begins to rule in you.

So, watch your hearts and ways. Watch over one another in gentleness and tenderness. Know that we cannot help one another out of a snare of our own strength, for only the Lord, who must be waited upon, can do this in all and for all. So, attend to the Truth, to the service and enjoyment and possession of it in your hearts. Walk in such a way that you do not bring disgrace upon it, but instead, let the Truth be a good savor to others in the places where you live. May the meek, innocent, tender, righteous life that reigns within you and governs you, shine through you into the eyes of all with whom you speak.

6. An Eye of Pity

Who is able to undergo the crosses and afflictions—inward or outward—that come upon us? The Lord is able to uphold the one who feels his weakness and daily waits on him for support, even under the heaviness of the cross.

I know, dear heart, that your outward trials are painful and bitter. And I know also that the Lord is able to sustain you through them and make you able to stand your ground. O that you could dwell in the knowledge and sense of this: the Lord sees your sufferings with an eye of pity and also is able to achieve some good through them. He is able to bring life and wisdom to you through your trials. He will one day give you dominion over that which grieves and afflicts you.

Therefore, do not be grieved at your situation or be discontented. Do not look at the difficulty of your condition, but instead, when the storm rages against you, look up to him who can give you patience and can lift your head over it all and cause you to grow. If the Lord did not help us with his mighty arm, how often would we fall! If God helps you in proportion to your problems, you should have no reason to complain, but rather, to bless his name.

God is exceedingly good and gracious and tenderhearted. He does not turn away from the affliction of his people in any way. This I share in tender love towards you, with breathings to our Father, that his pleasant plant may not be crushed in you by the foot of pride or violence, but instead, may overgrow it and flourish the more because of it. (From thy truly loving Friend in the Truth, and for the Truth's sake.)

7. Quickened by the Spirit

Friend, some questions about prayer may arise in your mind as you have begun to sense the Truth, or have been touched by the Truth from God's Holy Spirit. Since you have operated so long from a fleshly mind and ungodly nature and not in the leading of the Spirit, you may have some doubts about the practice of prayer.

Those people who doubt the power of prayer will never have their questions answered until the Lord opens their spirits and teaches it to them. Herein is the truth: all true prayer is in and from the Holy Spirit.

The promise of God concerning prayer (that is, the certainty of prayer being answered) is referring to the kind of prayer that is in faith and to the Holy Spirit. It is not, however, dealing with the prayers that come from the flesh or will or human wisdom. Therefore, the great care and concern in prayer is that it be of God in the quickenings and motions of his own Spirit. For the dead cannot praise God, nor can the dead truly pray to him.

We must not pray in a way that lacks life, that lacks God's Spirit (who calls us to pray, teaches us to pray, and makes intercessions for us). True prayer is not in the time, in the will, or in the power of the person praying. Rather, it is a gift of God that resides in his Spirit. It is not ours, but it is given to us. Therefore, it is ours to wait upon the Spirit, to wait for the Spirit to move and breathe in us, and to give us the ability to call upon the Father and give us the power of prevailing with the Father, in the name and through the life of the Son.

BIBLE SELECTION: JOHN 6:52–59

[52]The Jews then disputed among themselves, saying, "How can this man give us his flesh to eat?" [53]So Jesus said to them, "Very truly, I tell you, unless you eat the flesh of the Son of Man and drink his blood, you have no life in you. [54]Those who eat my flesh and drink my blood have eternal life, and I will raise them up on the last day; [55]for my flesh is true food and my blood is true drink. [56]Those who eat my flesh and drink my blood abide in me, and I in them. [57]Just as the living Father sent me, and I live because of the Father, so whoever eats me will live because of me. [58]This is the bread that came down from heaven, not like that which your ancestors ate, and they died. But the one who eats this bread will live forever." [59]He said these things while he was teaching in the synagogue at Capernaum.

REFLECTION QUESTIONS

The following questions can be used for discussion within a small group, or used for journal reflections by individuals.

1. Isaac Penington counsels his friend to "wait diligently for the leadings of the Holy Spirit." Describe your experiences of being led by the Holy Spirit. Have you sensed any influence or work of the Spirit recently?

2. In sections 3 and 4, the author discusses two kinds of food, one that we eat out of pride and sin in order to become wise (like the fruit in the Garden of Eden), and one that we eat in order to nourish our soul (the Bread, the Wine,

the Water of which Jesus spoke). What are some of the "bad" foods you have eaten? Where do you go to get the "good" food?

3. According to Penington, God not only feels our pain but is also able to use it to help us grow. How has God used your past struggles and your pain as a means to help you grow? Describe.

4. From where does "true prayer" come? (See section 7.) How, according to Penington, can we learn to pray in this manner?

5. Jesus says that we are to feed on him ("whoever eats me will live"; John 6:57). What experiences have you had of feeding on the life and power of Jesus?

SUGGESTED EXERCISES

The following exercises can be done by individuals, shared between spiritual friends, or used in the context of a small group. Choose one or more of the following.

1. The power of God comes to us when we "wait diligently for the leadings of the Holy Spirit in everything we do." Learn the joy of "waiting" this week. In your times of prayer, as well as throughout the day, pause to wait on the leading of the Spirit.

2. Isaac Penington counsels, "Watch over one another in gentleness and tenderness. Know that we cannot help one another out of a snare of our own strength, for only the Lord, who must be waited upon, can do this in all and for all" (section 5). Let your prayers and concerns for others this week be lifted to God in a spirit of trust and patience.

3. If you are facing a difficulty at this time, adopt the author's suggestion: "Do not look at the difficulty of your condition, but instead, when the storm rages against you, look up to him who can give you patience and can lift your head over it all and cause you to grow."

4. Explore ways in which you can feast upon "the bread of life" this week. Read the Gospels with a sense of hunger, go to worship with a desire to feed on Christ's presence, and abide in Christ through times of prayer and contemplation.

REFLECTIONS

The selections you have just read were letters that Penington wrote, sometimes to individuals, sometimes to groups of people. This practice of giving spiritual direction by letter is a time-honored tradition going back to the New Testament epistles and before. But it has been almost entirely lost in our day. We are the less for the loss.

As we follow Penington's counsel to "wait diligently for the leadings of the Holy Spirit" perhaps, just perhaps, we will hear the whispered prompting to write a letter of spiritual counsel and encouragement to someone in need.

GOING DEEPER

Unfortunately, none of Isaac Penington's writings are in print (with the possible exception of the small Pendle Hill booklet entitled *The Inward Journey of Isaac Penington*) and so you will need to scour libraries to find his works. His entire writings, including the collected letters, are contained in a four-volume edition titled *The Works of Isaac Penington*. The fourth edition (1863), printed by Friends Book Store, Philadelphia, was the most recent I could find. There are other small books that contain selections from his writings such as *The Life Hid with God in Christ* (London: Samuel Harris, 1876) and *Letters of Isaac Penington* (Philadelphia: Book Association of Friends, 1879). There is also a small biography written by Joseph Bevan entitled *Memoirs of the Life of Isaac Penington* (Philadelphia: Wm. H. Pile's Sons, 1903).

John Bunyan (1628–1688)

INTRODUCTION TO THE AUTHOR

John Bunyan was born in the parish of Elston, two miles from Bedford, England. His father, like himself, was a poor tinker, but he managed to send John to school for a short time. Later, John served for two years in the Parliamentarian army during the civil war against Charles I.

In 1660 Bunyan was put in the Bedford jail for twelve years for preaching without a license. While in prison he supported his family by making shoelaces. It was in prison that he wrote *Grace Abounding to the Chief of Sinners* (first published in 1666), an autobiographical sketch of his conversion, call to ministry, and subsequent imprisonment. After his release in 1672, Bunyan was appointed pastor of the Baptist church in Bedford but was again sent to prison (on the same charge) for six months. It was then that he wrote his most famous work, *The Pilgrim's Progress*, published in 1678. This book is a monumental classic, second only to the Bible in the number of copies sold since its first printing.

The following passage is Bunyan's own account of his call into ministry. His writings reveal the anguish he endured as one who was called by God to preach the gospel. Bunyan touches on some important themes for anyone engaged in ministry. Like St. Paul, he knew both the pain and the glory of being an instrument in the hands of God.

EXCERPTS FROM *GRACE ABOUNDING TO THE CHIEF OF SINNERS*

1. Called to the Work of the Ministry

I want to speak a word or two about preaching the Word and of God's dealings in calling me to this work. I had been awake to the Lord for five or six years, having seen the great worth of Jesus Christ our Lord, and my need for him, and having been enabled to trust my soul to him.

Some of the saints who had good judgment and holiness of life seemed to feel that God had counted me worthy to understand the blessed Word and that he had given me some measure of ability to express helpfully to others what I saw in it. So they asked me to speak a word of exhortation to them in one of the meetings.

At first this seemed to be an impossible thing for me to do, but they kept at it. I finally consented and spoke twice to small meetings of Christians only, but with much weakness and infirmity. So I tested my gift among them, and it seemed as I spoke that they were being given a blessing. Afterward many told me, in the sight of the great God, that they were helped and comforted. They gave thanks to the Father of mercies for this gift he had given to me.

The church continued to feel that I should preach, and so after solemn prayer to the Lord, with fasting, I was ordained to regular public preaching of the Word among those who believed and also to those who had not yet received the faith.

2. Exercising the Gift

About this time I began to feel a great desire to preach to the unsaved, not for the desire of glorifying myself, for at that time I was particularly being afflicted with the fiery darts of the Devil concerning my eternal state. I could not rest unless I was exercising this gift of preaching, and I was pressed forward into it.

I began to see that the Holy Spirit never intended that people who had gifts and abilities should bury them in the earth, but rather, he commanded and stirred up such people to the exercise of their gift and sent out to work those who were able and ready. And so, although I was the most unworthy of all the saints, I set upon this work.

Though trembling, I used my gift to preach the blessed gospel, in proportion to my faith, as God had showed me in the holy Word of truth. When the word got around that I was doing this, people came in by the hundreds from all over to hear the Word preached.

3. God's Instrument

At first I could hardly believe that God would speak through me to the heart of anyone, and I still counted myself unworthy. Yet those who were quickened through my preaching loved me and had a respect for me. Although I insisted that it was not because of what I had said, still they publicly declared that it was so. They, in fact, blessed God for me, unworthy wretch though I was, and counted me as God's instrument who showed them the way of salvation.

And when I saw that they were beginning to live differently, and that their hearts were eagerly pressing after the knowledge of Christ and rejoicing that God sent me to them, then I began to conclude that God had blessed his work through me. And so I rejoiced. Yes, the tears of those whom God had awakened by my preaching were my solace and my encouragement.

4. Ministering in Chains

In my preaching of the Word I noticed that the Lord led me to begin where his Word begins with sinners; that is, to condemn all flesh and to state clearly that the curse of God is upon all people as they come into the world because of sin. And this part of my work I fulfilled easily for the terrors of the Law and the guilt of my transgressions lay heavy upon my conscience.

I preached what I felt, even that under which my own poor soul groaned and trembled. Indeed, I was as one sent to them from the dead. I went myself in chains, preached to them in chains, and had in my own conscience that fire which I pleaded with them to beware of.

I can honestly say that many a time as I have gone to preach I have been full of guilt and terror right up to the pulpit door, and there it has been taken off and I have been at liberty until my work was done. Then immediately, before I could get down the pulpit stairs, it was upon me as bad as before. Yet God carried me on, but surely with a strong hand.

5. My Heart Full of Concern

In all my preaching, thank God, my heart has earnestly cried out to God to make the Word effectual to the salvation of souls, for I have been fearful that the enemy would take the Word away from the conscience and so it would be unfruitful. I have tried to speak the Word so that a particular person might realize himself guilty of a particular sin.

And after I have preached, my heart has been full of concern to think that the Word might now fall as rain on stony places, and I have often cried out from my heart, "Oh, that those who have heard me speak today will see as I do what sin, death, hell, and the curse of God really are, and that they might understand the grace and love and mercy of God, that it is through Christ to them no matter in what condition they are, even if they are his enemies!"

During those times, especially when I have spoken of the life that is in Christ without works, it has sometimes seemed as if an angel of God were standing behind me to encourage me. With great power and with heavenly evidence upon my soul I have been laboring to unfold this wonderful doctrine, to demonstrate it, and to fasten it upon the consciences of my hearers. For this doctrine seemed to me not only to be true, but more than true!

As sometimes happens, those who were awakened by my ministry afterward fell back into sin. I can say that their loss was more terrible to me than if my own children had gone to their graves. I think I can say this without any offense to the Lord, that nothing has ever hurt

me so much unless it was the fear of the loss of my own salvation.

6. Travailing to Bring Forth Children to God

Sometimes I have noticed that a word cast in, by the way, has done more than all the rest of the sermon. Sometimes when I thought I had done the least, then it developed that the most had been accomplished; and at other times when I thought I had really gotten hold of them, I found that I had fished for nothing.

In my preaching I have actually been in real pain, travailing to bring forth children to God, and I have never been satisfied unless there has been some fruit. If not, it made no difference who complimented me, but if it were fruitful I did not care who might condemn me.

It never pleased me to see people merely drinking in opinions if they were ignorant of Christ and the value of his salvation. When I saw sound conviction for sin, especially the sin of unbelief, and hearts set on fire to be saved by Christ, those were the souls I counted blessed.

7. Temptations Abounding

But in this work, as in any other, I had my different temptations. Sometimes I would suffer from discouragement, fearing that I would not be of any help to anyone and that I would not even be able to speak sense to the people. At such times I have had a strange faintness seize me. At other times I have been assaulted by thoughts of blasphemy before the congregation.

Again, there have been times when I have been about to preach on some searching portion of the Word and I have found the Tempter suggesting, "What! Will you preach this? This condemns you. Your own soul is guilty of this; you must not preach on it. If you do, you must leave the door open for you to escape from the guilt of what you will say. If you preach like this, you will lay that guilt upon your own soul and you will never be able to get out from under it."

I've been kept from consenting to these horrid suggestions and instead have preached against sin and transgression wherever I found it, even though it did bring guilt upon my own conscience. It is far better to bring oneself under condemnation by plain preaching to others, than to save yourself by imprisoning the truth in unrighteousness. Blessed be God for his help also in this.

8. A Sledge Hammer upon the Head of Pride

I have also had the Word come to me with some sharp, piercing sentence concerning the gifts God has given me. For instance, "Though I speak with the tongues of men and of angels, and have not charity, I am become as a sounding brass, or a tinkling cymbal" (1 Cor. 13:1, KJV). Though a tinkling cymbal is a musical instrument that can make heart-inflaming melody, the cymbal does not contain life; though it can make wonderful music, it can be crushed and thrown away.

So are all those who have gifts but do not have saving grace. Christ can use gifted people to affect the souls of the people in his Church, yet when he has finished using them, he can hang them up without life. Such considerations were a sledge hammer upon the head of pride and the desire of vainglory. What! thought I, shall I be proud because I am a sounding brass? Does not the person who has the least of the life of God have more than these instruments?

9. Grace the Forerunner of Glory

I perceived that although gifts are good to accomplish the task they are designed for—the edification of others—yet they are empty and without power to save the soul unless God is using them. And having gifts is no sign of a person's relationship to God. This also made me see that gifts are dangerous things, not in themselves, but because of those evils of pride and vainglory that attend them. Blown up with the applause of ill-advised Christians, the poor creatures who possess these gifts can easily fall into the condemnation of the Devil.

Gifts are desirable, but great grace and small gifts are better than great gifts and no grace. The Bible does not say that the Lord gives gifts and glory, but that he gives grace and glory. Blessed is everyone to whom the Lord gives true grace, for that is a certain forerunner of glory.

BIBLE SELECTION: 1 TIMOTHY 4:9–16

[9]The saying is sure and worthy of full acceptance. [10]For to this end we toil and struggle, because we have our hope set on the living God, who is the Savior of all people, especially of those who believe.

[11]These are the things you must insist on and teach. [12]Let no one despise your youth, but set the believers an example in speech and conduct, in love, in faith, in purity. [13]Until I arrive, give attention to the public reading of scripture, to exhorting, to teaching. [14]Do not neglect the gift that is in you, which was given to you through prophecy with the laying on of hands by the council of elders. [15]Put these things into

practice, devote yourself to them, so that all may see your progress. [16]Pay close attention to yourself and to your teaching; continue in these things, for in doing this you will save both yourself and your hearers.

REFLECTION QUESTIONS

The following questions can be used for discussion within a small group, or used for journal reflections by individuals.

1. In section 2, John Bunyan uses the biblical metaphor of burying one's talents. Although Jesus was referring to money in this parable, the talents are often used as a symbol of spiritual gifts. What are some of the gifts God has given you? Are they buried or are they being put to good use?

2. Bunyan tested his gift by exercising it. Why is testing our gifts important? What did the church do to confirm Bunyan's gift of preaching? What evidence was later shown to confirm that God was using this gift?

3. The devil, writes Bunyan, discouraged him from exercising his gift by accusing him of being unworthy. In what ways have you been discouraged, or felt unworthy, to use your gifts?

4. In sections 8 and 9, the author discusses the dangers associated with spiritual gifts. What, according to Bunyan, is the greatest danger connected with these gifts? Has this been true in your experience?

5. In 1 Timothy 4:14, Paul urges Timothy not to neglect his gift (in Timothy's case, it was the gift of preaching and teaching and administrating). How does the insight we get from John Bunyan help us see why Timothy might have been tempted to neglect his gift? How might Timothy have felt when he read this letter of encouragement from his mentor, Paul?

SUGGESTED EXERCISES

The following exercises can be done by individuals, shared between spiritual friends, or used in the context of a small group. Choose one or more of the following.

1. During the next week examine your spiritual giftedness. Ask others how you have been helpful to them. This is a good starting point. Their answers might surprise you. Many gifts go unnoticed by those who have them.

2. If you sense you have a certain gift but are not sure, test the gift, as Bunyan did. Exercise it, and see if others receive spiritual benefit from your abilities. Like Bunyan, seek the help of the church in this matter; ask others to pray

with you. You may also want to accompany your prayers over this matter with a time of fasting.

3. For those who have been exercising spiritual gifts for some time, be sure to keep a healthy check on the way you are using them. Be careful to note how easily pride can enter in, especially if your gift is a public one (such as preaching). Try not to listen to "the applause of ill-advised Christians, " as Bunyan would put it.

4. Some of you may be more like Timothy, who was feeling discouraged and was in danger of neglecting his gifts. Read through 1 and 2 Timothy, putting yourself in Timothy's place. Imagine that Paul is writing those letters to you.

REFLECTIONS

We must forever lift high the sacredness of all vocation, but in the economy of God the work of proclaiming the gospel is especially significant. Paul stated it succinctly, "How are they to hear without someone to proclaim him?" (Rom. 10:14). It is a high calling, a holy vocation, this proclamation of the gospel. It is a calling worthy of "double honor," says Scripture (1 Tim. 5:17).

Unfortunately, we live in a day when the preaching ministry has been trivialized and demeaned and ridiculed. It is sad indeed, but take courage—God is now raising up new leaders, leaders of integrity and humility, leaders who are

Lone like the Tishbite, like the Baptist, bold;
Cast in a rare and apostolic mold.

GOING DEEPER

Bunyan, John. *Grace Abounding to the Chief of Sinners*. Chicago: Moody Bible Institute, 1959. An intensely introspective autobiography of Bunyan's journey in faith.

Bunyan, John. *The Pilgrim's Progress*. Various editions. This stunningly executed allegory has furnished the Christian imagination with names and situations that have now percolated through most of our literature. Seldom does something so popular manage also to be so accurate.

The Compassionate Life

THE SOCIAL JUSTICE tradition (the Compassionate Life) is not a set of pious exercises for the devout, but a trumpet call to a freely gathered people who seek the total transformation of persons, institutions, and societies. We are to combine suffering love with courageous action. We are to stand against all oppressions and for all liberations. We are to become the voice of the voiceless, pleading their cause in the halls of power and privilege. The authors in this section on social justice show us the way.

William Temple and John Woolman both saw themselves as agents of change in their societies. Woolman called people off the "desire of wealth" in order to "break the yoke of oppression." Temple saw the method of change to be twofold: clearly articulate "Christian principles" and "then pass on to Christian citizens, acting in their civic capacities, the task of reshaping the existing order in closer conformity to the principles."

John Wesley warns us of the "sins of omission" whereby we fail to do the good that we can do. Hannah Whitall Smith urges us to serve not out of the "Must I?" of duty but the "May I?" of love. Jeremy Taylor counsels, "Never be ashamed of your birth, of your parents, your occupation, or your present employment, or the lowly status of any of them." And Elizabeth O'Connor takes up the hard issue of money, urging us to reclaim for "ourselves the energy with which we have endowed money."

Two authors in this section—Catherine of Siena and Dietrich Bonhoeffer—deal with Christian community. Catherine helps us see how God's people, the Church, "is there to serve the bread of life and blood lest the journeying pilgrims, my creatures, grow weary and faint on the way." And Bonhoeffer teaches us that "Christianity means community through Jesus Christ and in Jesus Christ. No Christian community is more or less than this."

All these authors write out of lived experience. We have much to learn from each one.

William Temple (1881–1944)

INTRODUCTION TO THE AUTHOR

William Temple was born in The Palace, in Exeter, the son of Frederick Temple, who later became the archbishop of Canterbury. Educated at Rugby and at Balliol College, Oxford, he was a Fellow lecturer in philosophy at Queen's College, Oxford, from 1904 to 1910 and the chaplain to the archbishop of Canterbury from 1910 to 1921. He then served as bishop of Manchester, 1921–28; archbishop of York, 1928–42; and archbishop of Canterbury from 1942 until his death in 1944.

Many have considered Temple an outstanding leader of modern Protestantism. He was regarded by all who knew him as a great, yet humble, man. His premature death prevented even greater accomplishments, but he managed to influence multitudes of people through his lecturing, preaching, and writing.

He was a pioneer of the ecumenical movement and a tireless church reformer. He gave excellent leadership to Christian social movements and stood as a prophetic voice to the world. He once said, "In our dealings with one another let us be more eager to understand those who differ from us than either to refute them or press upon them our own tradition."

The following selection addresses a very important issue: the role of the Church in society. In it, Temple shows his keen insight into human nature and social structures.

EXCERPTS FROM *CHRISTIANITY AND SOCIAL ORDER*

1. The Church's Impact upon Society

The method of the Church's impact upon society at large should be twofold. First, the Church must announce Christian principles and point out where the existing social order is in conflict with them. Second, it must then pass on to Christian citizens, acting in their civic capacities, the task of reshaping the existing order in closer conformity to the principles.

At this point, technical knowledge and practical judgments will be required. For example, if a bridge is to be built, the Church may remind the engineer that it is his obligation to provide a safe bridge, but is not entitled to tell him how to build it or whether his design meets this requirement.

A particular theologian may also be a competent engineer, and in this case he may be entitled to make a judgment on its safety. But he may do so because he is a competent engineer, and not because he is a theologian. His theological skills have nothing whatsoever to do with it.

2. Christian Principles

This is a point of first-rate importance, and it is frequently misunderstood. If Christianity is true at all, it is a truth of universal application; all things should be done in the Christian spirit and in accordance with Christian principles.

"Then," say those who want reform, "produce your Christian solution for unemployment." But there neither is nor could be such a thing. The Christian faith does not by itself enable its members to see how a vast number of people within an intricate economic system will be affected by a particular economic or political idea.

"In that case," say those who want to uphold the status quo, "keep off the turf! By your own confession you are out of place here." Here the Church must reply, "No; I cannot tell you what is the remedy. But I can tell you that a society with chronic unemployment is a diseased society. If you are not doing all that you can to find the remedy, you are guilty before God."

The Church is likely to be attacked from both sides if it does its duty. It will be told that it has become "political" when in fact it has merely stated its principles and pointed out when they have been breached. The Church will be told by advocates of particular policies

that it is futile because it does not support theirs. If the Church is faithful to its commission, it will ignore both sets of complaints and continue as far as it can to influence all citizens and permeate all parties.

3. In the Center of Our Own World

We are dealing here with Original Sin, the least popular part of traditional Christianity. It may be expressed in simple terms as follows: Our standard of value is the way things affect us. Each of us takes our place in the center of our own world. But I am not the center of the world, or the standard of reference between good and bad. I am not, but God is.

In other words, from the beginning I put myself in God's place. This is my original sin. I was doing it before I could speak, as has everyone else. I am not "guilty" on this account because I could not help it. But I am in a state, from birth, in which I shall bring disaster on myself and everyone else unless I escape it.

Education may make my self-centeredness less disastrous by widening my horizons. But this is like climbing a tower which widens the horizons of my vision while leaving me still the center of reference. The only way to deliver me from my self-centeredness is by winning my entire heart's devotion, the total allegiance of my will to God—and this can only be done by the Divine Love of God disclosed by Christ in his life and death.

4. No Such Thing as a Christian Social Ideal

Political issues are often concerned with people as they are, not with people as they ought to be. Part of the task of the Church is to help people to order their lives in order to lead them to what they ought to be. Assuming they are already as they ought to be always leads to disaster.

It is not my belief that people are utterly bad, or even that they are more bad than good. What I am contending here is that we are not wholly good, and that even our goodness is infected with self-centeredness. For this reason, we are exposed to temptation as far as we are able to obtain power.

The Church's belief in Original Sin should make us intensely realistic and should free us from trying to create a Utopia. For there is no such thing as a Christian social ideal to which we should try to conform the society we live in as closely as possible. After all, no one wants to live in "the ideal society" as depicted by anyone else.

Moreover, there is the desperate problem of getting there. When I read a description of the Ideal Society and think how we might begin transforming our own society into it, I am reminded of the Englishman in Ireland who asked an Irishman, "Which way to Roscommon?" "Is it Roscommon you want to go to?" said the Irishman. "Yes," said the Englishman, "that's why I asked the way." "Well," said the Irishman, "if I wanted to go to Roscommon, I wouldn't be starting from here."

Although Christianity supplies no ideal, it does supply something of far more value, namely, principles on which we can begin to act in every possible situation. It is to these principles I now want to turn our attention.

5. Not with Man, but with God

All Christian thinking must begin not with man, but with God. The fundamental conviction is that God is the creator of the world which could not begin or continue except by his will. The world is not necessary to God in the same way God is necessary to the world. If there were no God, there would be no world; if there were no world, God would still be what he is (presumably about to make the world). For God is impelled to make the world because of his love. The world is not necessary to God, but it results from his love.

In making the world he brought into existence vast numbers of things, like electrons which always have to obey his law for them and do so. But he made creatures—men and women—who could disobey his law for them and often do so. He did this in order that among his creatures there might be some who answer his love with theirs by offering to him a free obedience.

This involved a risk in that they would naturally take the self-centered outlook on life, and then, increasingly become hardened in that selfishness. This is what has happened. To win them out of this, he came on earth and lived out the divine love in human life and death. He is increasingly drawing us to himself by the love thus shown.

Lord Acton, who knew more history than any other Englishman of the last generation, deliberately declared: "The action of Christ who is risen on mankind whom he redeemed fails not, but increases." But this task of drawing all people to himself will not be complete until the end of history. The kingdom of God is a reality here and now but can be perfect only in the eternal order.

6. Our True Value

The fundamental facts about human beings are two: first, we are made "in the image of God"; and second, that image has been stamped upon an animal nature. Between these two there is constant tension resulting in perpetual tragedy.

Our dignity is that we are children of God, capable of communion with God, the object of the love of God—displayed to us on the Cross—and destined for eternal fellowship with God. Our true value is not what we are worth in ourselves, but what we are worth to God, and that worth is bestowed upon us by the utterly gratuitous love of God.

All of our lives should be ordered and conducted with this dignity in view. The State must not treat us as having value only in so far as we serve its end as totalitarian States do. The State exists for its citizens, not the citizens for the State. But neither must we treat ourselves, or conduct our lives, as if we were ourselves the center of our own value. We are not our own ends. Our value is our worth to God, and our end is "to glorify God and enjoy him forever."

7. The Image of Holiness and Love

We are self-centered, but we always carry with us abundant proof that this is not the whole truth about our nature. We have to our credit both capacities and achievements that could never be derived from self-interest alone.

The image of God—the image of holiness and love—is still there, though defaced. It is the source of our aspirations. It is even—because of its defacement—the source of our perversities. It is capable of response to the Divine Image in its perfection. It enables us to see "the light of the knowledge of the glory of God in the face of Jesus Christ," and so "with unveiled face, reflecting as a mirror the glory of the Lord," we may be "transformed into the same image from glory to glory."

That is our destiny. And our social life, so far as it is deliberately planned, should be ordered with that destiny in view. We must be treated as what we actually are but always with a view to what in God's purpose we are destined to become. For the law, the social order, is our schoolmaster to bring us to Christ.

BIBLE SELECTION: ROMANS 13:1–7

Let every person be subject to the governing authorities; for there is no authority except from God, and those authorities that exist have been instituted by God. [2]Therefore whoever resists authority resists what God has appointed, and those who resist will incur judgment. [3]For rulers are not a terror to good conduct, but to bad. Do you wish to have no fear of the authority? Then do what is good, and you will receive its approval; [4]for it is God's servant for your good. But if you do what is wrong, you should be afraid, for the authority does not bear the sword in vain! It is the servant of God to execute wrath on the wrongdoer. [5]Therefore one must be subject, not only because of wrath but also because of conscience. [6]For the same reason you also pay taxes, for the authorities are God's servants, busy with this very thing. [7]Pay to all what is due them—taxes to whom taxes are due, revenue to whom revenue is due, respect to whom respect is due, honor to whom honor is due.

REFLECTION QUESTIONS

The following questions can be used for discussion within a small group, or used for journal reflections by individuals.

1. The method of the Church's impact on society should be twofold, according to William Temple. First, the Church should make its principles known, and second, the Church should equip its members to reshape the existing order. In your opinion, how well has the Church done in achieving these two goals?

2. Any political involvement by Christians, notes Temple, will be attacked from two sides: one side will say that Christians have no business in political matters, and the other side will tell Christians that their efforts are futile. How have you experienced this opposition in your attempts to take a stand politically?

3. Temple is careful to point out that there is not only a responsibility but also a limitation for those Christians who wish to make an impact on the public square: Christians are not necessarily equipped to have all the answers to all the questions. What, then, can Christians say?

4. If you were to begin all your political thinking from God's viewpoint, as Temple suggests, how might you look at certain issues differently than you do now?

5. Look up Romans 12:2. Reading that verse in conjunction with Romans 13:1–7, what are some of the things you might be both responsible for and limited in doing?

SUGGESTED EXERCISES

The following exercises can be done by individuals, shared between spiritual friends, or used in the context of a small group. Choose one or more of the following.

1. Examine an important political issue this week. Read the editorials in your newspaper to clarify the differing opinions, but read them with Temple's counsel of looking at the issue from God's vantage point.

2. While Christians are not, by virtue of their faith alone, experts in every field, they are on solid ground when they combine their faith with their area of expertise. Ask yourself how your beliefs and your vocational skill might work together for the common good.

3. Treat everyone you meet this week with the dignity he or she deserves as a person who is created in the image of God.

4. Paul encouraged the Romans to live peaceably under the existing government, seeing the government as ministers of God. While this counsel does not prevent us from speaking for or against certain causes, it does presuppose a certain attitude that we should adopt, even when we protest. This week strive to make a difference in the world around you, but go about your task with courtesy and respect.

REFLECTIONS

The really big idea in this essay of Temple's is that the social order is to be influenced and shaped by a Christian ethical and moral environment. This is to be done by a clear articulation of Christian principles rather than through a specific political agenda.

And what are these Christian principles? Let me list a sampling: the supremacy of the law of love, the reality of original sin, the infinite value of all human life. It is easy to see how these, along with others, could help shape life in the public square.

GOING DEEPER

Temple, William. *Christianity and Social Order.* New York: Seabury, 1977. Provides a helpful and balanced discussion of the social implications of the gospel.

Temple, William. *Daily Readings from William Temple.* Compiled by Hugh C. Warner. London: Oxford University Press, 1981.

Temple, William. *Hope of a New World.* Salem, NH: Ayer, 1940.

Temple, William. *Nature, Man and God.* London: Macmillan, 1960. These essays are the Gifford Lectures that were delivered at the University of Glasgow in the academic years 1932–33 and 1933–34. The book is a serious theological and philosophical work and shows the keen mind of Temple.

Temple, William. *Religious Experience and Other Essays and Addresses.* Edited by A. E. Baker. Greenwood, SC: Attic, 1959.

John Woolman (1720–1772)

INTRODUCTION TO THE AUTHOR

John Woolman was a quiet man whose faithfulness spoke loudly in tempestuous times. Born in New Jersey to a Quaker farm family, Woolman lived in the ferment of colonial America. It was a time of impending revolt against England, a time of rampant slave trade and of war with Indians, a time when many suffered the hardships of poverty. Woolman's life of simple, steady obedience addressed them all. It would have surprised him that later writers would call him a "saint" and a "prophet," for he was only trying to follow Christ, the True Shepherd, as closely as possible.

Woolman begins his *Journal*, "I have often felt a motion of love to leave some hints in writing of my experience of the goodness of God." Over the sixteen years that *The Journal* was written, we can see how Woolman becomes increasingly aware of the broad scope of God's love and how his own tenderness grows toward all people and the whole creation. In love he lived a life of rigorous integrity and courageous witness, a life that challenges us still. The following selections only begin to illustrate his wide and thorough integration of God's goodness into his living.

EXCERPTS FROM *THE JOURNAL OF JOHN WOOLMAN*

1. The Voice of the True Shepherd

My mind through the power of Truth was in a good degree weaned from the desire of outward greatness, and I was learning to be content with real conveniences that were not costly, so that a way of life free from much entanglements appeared best for me, though the income was small. I had several offers of business that appeared profitable, but did not see my way clear to accept them, believing the business proposed would be attended with more outward care and cumber than was required of me to engage in. I saw that a humble man with the blessing of the Lord might live on a little, and that where the heart was set on greatness, success in business did not satisfy the craving, but that in common with an increase of wealth the desire of wealth increased. There was a care on my mind to so pass my time as to things outward that nothing might hinder me from the most steady attention to the voice of the True Shepherd.

2. The Fear of Man Brings a Snare

I find that to be a fool as to worldly wisdom and commit my cause to God, not fearing to offend men who take offense at the simplicity of Truth, is the only way to remain unmoved at the sentiments of others.

The fear of man brings a snare. By halting in our duty and giving back in the time of trial, our hands grow weaker, our spirits get mingled with the people, our ears grow dull as to hearing the language of the True Shepherd, that when we look at the way of the righteous, it seems as though it was not for us to follow them.

There is a love that clothes my mind while I write which is superior to all expressions, and I find my heart open to encourage a holy emulation to advance forward in Christian firmness. Deep humility is a strong bulwark, and as we enter into it, we find safety and true exaltation. The foolishness of God is wiser than man, and the weakness of God is stronger than man. Being unclothed of our own wisdom and knowing the abasement of the creature, therein we find that power to arise which gives health and vigor to us.

3. Dwell in Humility

First, my dear friends, dwell in humility and take heed that no views of outward gain get too deep hold of you, that so your eyes being single to the Lord, you may be preserved in the way of safety.

Where people let loose their minds after the love of outward things and are more engaged in pursuing the profits and seeking the friendships of this world than to be inwardly acquainted with the way of true peace, such walk in a vain shadow while the true comfort of life is wanting. Their examples are often hurtful to others, and their treasures thus collected do many times prove dangerous snares to their children.

But where people are sincerely devoted to follow Christ and dwell under the influence of his Holy Spirit, their stability and firmness through a divine blessing is at times like dew on the tender plants round about them, and the weightiness of their spirits secretly works on the minds of others.

4. Freely Cease from Fighting

It requires great self-denial and resignation of ourselves to God to attain that state wherein we can freely cease from fighting when wrongfully invaded, if by our fighting there were a probability of overcoming the invaders. Whoever rightly attains to it does in some degree feel that spirit in which our Redeemer gave his life for us, and through divine goodness many of our predecessors and many now living have learned this blessed lesson. But many others, having their religion chiefly by education and not being enough acquainted with that cross which crucifies to the world, do manifest a temper distinguishable from that of an entire trust in God.

5. Justice Without Delay

[*The following is taken from a speech of Woolman that helped lead the Quakers to reject the institution of slavery years before the American Revolution.*]

My mind is often led to consider the purity of the Divine Being and the justice of his judgments, and herein my soul is covered with awe.

Many slaves on this continent are oppressed, and their cries have reached the ears of the Most High! Such is the purity and certainty of his judgments that he cannot be partial in our favor. In infinite love and goodness he has opened our understandings from one time to another concerning our duty towards this people, and it is not a time for delay.

Should we now be sensible of what he requires of us, and through a respect to the private interest of some persons or through a regard to some friendships which do not stand on an immutable foundation, neglect to do our duty in firmness and constancy, still waiting for some extraordinary means to bring about their deliverance, it may be that by terrible things in righteousness God may answer us in this matter.

6. This Precious Habitation

The place of prayer is a precious habitation, for I now saw that the prayers of the saints were precious incense. And a trumpet was given me that I might sound forth this language that the children might hear it and be invited to gather to this precious habitation, where the prayers of the saints, as precious incense, arise before the throne of God and the Lamb. I saw this habitation to be safe, to be inwardly quiet when there were great stirrings and commotions in the world.

Prayer at this day in pure resignation is a precious place. The trumpet is sounded; the call goes forth to the church that she gather to the place of pure inward prayer, and her habitation is safe.

7. Searching Questions

Do I use food and drink in no other sort and in no other degree than was designed by him who gave these things for our sustenance? Do I never abuse my body by inordinate labor, striving to accomplish some end which I have unwisely proposed?

If I go on a visit to the widows and fatherless, do I go purely on a principle of charity, free from any selfish views? If I go to a religious meeting, it puts me on thinking whether I go in sincerity and in a clear sense of duty, or whether it is not partly in conformity to custom, or partly from a sensible delight which my animal spirits feel in the company of other people, and whether to support my reputation as a religious man has no share in it.

8. Say Neither More nor Less

It was my concern from day to day to say neither more nor less than what the spirit of truth opened in me, being jealous over myself lest I should say anything to make my testimony look agreeable to that mind in people which is not in pure obedience to the cross of Christ.

9. Break the Yoke of Oppression

I was renewedly confirmed in my mind that the Lord (whose tender mercies are over all his works, and whose ear is open to the cries and groans of the oppressed) is graciously moving in the hearts of people to draw them off from the desire of wealth and to bring them into such an humble, lowly way of living that they may see their way clearly to repair to the standard of true righteousness, and may not only break the yoke of oppression, but may know him to be their strength and support in times of outward affliction.

10. John Woolman Is Dead

[*The following is excerpted from Woolman's account of a vision he had during a time of serious illness.*]

I then heard a soft, melodious voice, more pure and harmonious than any I had heard with my ears before; I believed it was the voice of an angel who spoke to the other angels. The words were, "John Woolman is dead." I greatly wondered what that heavenly voice could mean.

I was then carried in spirit to the mines, where poor oppressed people were digging rich treasures for those called Christians, and heard them blaspheme the name of Christ, at which I was grieved, for his name to me was precious. Then I was informed that these heathens were told that those who oppressed them were the followers of Christ, and they said among themselves, "If Christ directed them to use us in this way, then Christ is a cruel tyrant."

All this time the song of the angel remained a mystery, and I was very desirous to get so deep that I might understand this mystery.

[After some physical recovery] . . . at length I felt divine power prepare my mouth that I could speak, and then I said, "I am crucified with Christ, nevertheless I live; yet not I, but Christ liveth in me, and the life I now live in the flesh [is] by faith in the Son of God, who loved me and gave himself for me" (Gal. 2:20, KJV). Then the mystery was opened, and I perceived there was joy in heaven over a sinner who had repented, and that the language "John Woolman is dead" meant no more than the death of my own will. (*Abridged for the modern reader by Howard R. Macy.*)

BIBLE SELECTION: PSALM 40:4–8

[4]Happy are those who make
the LORD their trust,
who do not turn to the proud,
to those who go astray after false gods.
[5]You have multiplied, O LORD my God,
your wondrous deeds and your thoughts
    toward us;
none can compare with you.
Were I to proclaim and tell of them,
they would be more than can be counted.

[6]Sacrifice and offering you do not desire,
but you have given me an open ear.
Burnt offering and sin offering
you have not required.
[7]Then I said, "Here I am;
in the scroll of the book it is written of me.
[8]I delight to do your will, O my God;
your law is within my heart."

REFLECTION QUESTIONS

The following questions can be used for discussion within a small group, or used for journal reflections by individuals.

1. After early success as a merchant, John Woolman decided that to continue to expand his business would divert too much of his energy and attention from God. For this reason he turned to a more quiet life as a tailor and an orchardist. What actions could help you keep a "steady attention to the voice of the True Shepherd" in the midst of your vocation?

2. In what ways, both obvious and subtle, do you find that the sentiments of others hinder you in following God's way? How can humility become both health and safety for you?

3. What entices you to "let loose" your mind "after the love of outward things"? Catalogs and advertisements? Social pressures? Lotteries? Also, how does humility help you to keep your eyes "single to the Lord"?

4. In his day, John Woolman was deeply concerned about the institution of slavery. What cries of oppression do you think God is hearing today? What actions might be required of you?

5. With the prophets, the psalmist says that religious practices are less important than doing God's will, a will that Micah describes as "to do justice, and to love kindness, and to walk humbly with your God" (Mic. 6:8). What would that look like in your life this week?

SUGGESTED EXERCISES

The following exercises can be done by individuals, shared between spiritual friends, or used in the context of a small group. Choose one or more of the following.

1. Like John Woolman, endeavor to be content with "real conveniences" that are not costly. When making purchases this week, let this attitude be your guide.

2. Our material treasures, says Woolman, can easily become dangerous snares. Experience the joy of giving things away this week. As you de-accumulate, be sure to give freely to those who are in need.

3. Woolman became sensitive to the fact that many of his material possessions came from the sweat and labor of people who were oppressed (see section 10). As a follower of Christ, avoid buying goods that are the product of oppression.

4. Reflect, like the psalmist, on the "wondrous deeds" and the attention God has focused on you. Recount specific occasions as you compose your own litany of God's gracious acts.

REFLECTIONS

I do not know when I first read The Journal of John Woolman, *nor how many times I have read it, nor how many editions of it I have read. I do know that no writing outside of the Bible has meant more to me than Woolman's* Journal. *The issues Woolman pinpointed are the issues we wrestle with today: militarism, racism, consumerism. And he dealt with these issues in a striking combination of compassion and courage, tenderness and firmness.*

I have gained many things from John Woolman, but by far the most important is an understanding of the profound social implications of the Christian walk. But Woolman not only warns us of the large idolatries; he also nurtures us in the small fidelities, whether we are dealing with the problem of overcommitments or the ethics of business conduct. In all these matters Woolman teaches us to have our hearts "enlarged in love."

GOING DEEPER

Over the last two hundred years there have been many editions and abridgments of John Woolman's *Journal,* as well as several biographies. The following may be helpful:

Whitney, Janet. *John Woolman: American Quaker.* Boston: Little, Brown, 1942. A standard and useful account of Woolman's life.

Woolman, John. *The Journal and Major Essays of John Woolman.* Edited by Phillips P. Moulton. New York: Oxford University Press, 1971; Richmond, IN: Friends United Press, 1989. This is the definitive edition of the *Journal* and the one from which the selections here were taken. Fine introduction and helps.

Woolman, John. *"The Journal of John Woolman" and "A Plea for the Poor."* Edited by Frederick B. Tolles. New York: Corinth, 1961. A paperback reprint of the classic John Greenleaf Whittier edition of *The Journal* with a brief but excellent introduction by Tolles.

Hannah Whitall Smith (1832–1911)

INTRODUCTION TO THE AUTHOR

Hannah Whitall Smith was a Quaker born in Philadelphia in 1832. Her book, *The Christian's Secret of a Happy Life,* from which the following excerpts are taken, has become a classic. Published in 1870, it was a beacon of encouragement in the age in which it was written, and continues to inspire men and women to a more joyful life with Christ. It has sold nearly two million copies.

Whitall Smith was by no means a dour servant of Jesus, but rather, her life expressed the joy that is found in complete surrender. The "secret" to a happy life, according to Whitall Smith, is to trust implicitly in the promises of the Bible. Her goal was not to impress the scholar, but to elevate the simple man or woman who longed for a more consecrated way of living.

Deeply practical, her writings deal directly with the day-to-day struggles of ordinary people. She weaves her scriptural theology in and out of the stories of people's lives. In the following selection she deals frankly with the problem of feeling burdened by Christian service. What can be done when our work for God has lost its joy? Hannah Whitall Smith offers us excellent counsel.

EXCERPTS FROM *THE CHRISTIAN'S SECRET OF A HAPPY LIFE*

1. The "Must I?" of Duty

There is, perhaps, no part of Christian experience where a greater change occurs, upon entering into this life hid with Christ in God, than in the matter of service.

In all the ordinary forms of Christian life, service is apt to have more or less of bondage in it; that is, it is done purely as a matter of duty, and often as a trial and a cross. Certain things, which at the first may have been a joy and a delight, become after a while weary tasks, performed faithfully, perhaps, but with much secret disinclination, and many confessed or unconfessed wishes that they need not be done at all, or at least that they need not be done so often.

The soul finds itself saying, instead of the "May I?" of love, the "Must I?" of duty. The yoke, which was at first easy, begins to gall, and the burden feels heavy instead of light.

2. The Treadmill of Daily Christian Work

One dear Christian expressed it once to me in this way: "When I was first converted," she said, "I was so full of joy and love that I was only too glad and thankful to be allowed to do anything for my Lord, and I eagerly entered every open door. But after a while, as my early joy faded away, and my love burned less fervently, I began to wish I had not been quite so eager; for I found myself involved in lines of service that were gradually becoming very distasteful and burdensome to me.

"Since I had begun them, I could not very well give them up without exciting great remark, and yet I longed to do so increasingly. I was expected to visit the sick, pray beside their beds. I was expected to attend prayer-meetings, and speak at them. I was expected, in short, to be always ready for every effort in Christian work, and the sense of these expectations bowed me down continually.

"At last it became so unspeakably burdensome to me to live the sort of Christian life I had entered upon, and was expected to live, that I felt as if any kind of manual labor would have been easier; and I would have infinitely preferred scrubbing all day on my hands and knees to being compelled to go through the treadmill of my daily Christian work. I envied," she said, "the servants in the kitchen, and the women at the washtubs."

3. A Constant Burden

This may seem to some like a strong statement; but does it not present a vivid picture of some of your own experiences, dear Christian? Have you never gone to work as a slave to his daily task, believing it to be your duty and that therefore you must do it, but rebounding like an Indian-rubber ball back into your real interests and pleasures the moment your work was over?

You have known of course that this was the wrong way to feel, and have been thoroughly ashamed of it, but still you have seen no way to help it. You have not *loved* your work; and, could you have done so with an easy conscience, you would have been glad to give it up altogether.

Or, if this does not describe your case, perhaps another picture will. You do love your work in the abstract, but in the doing of it you find so many cares and responsibilities connected with it, and feel so many misgivings and doubts as to your own capacity or fitness, that it becomes a very heavy burden, and you go to it bowed down and weary before the labor has even begun. Then also you are continually distressing yourself about the results of your work, and greatly troubled if they are not just what you would like; and this of itself is a constant burden.

4. The Things We Want to Do

Now, from all these forms of bondage the soul that enters fully into the blessed life of faith is entirely delivered. In the first place, service of any sort becomes delightful to it, because, having surrendered its will into the keeping of the Lord, He works in it to will and to do His good pleasure, and the soul finds itself really *wanting* to do the things God wants it to do.

It is always very pleasant to do the things we *want* to do, even if they are difficult to accomplish, or make our bodies tired. If our *will* is really set on a thing we view the obstacles that lie in the way of reaching it with a sublime indifference, and we laugh to ourselves at the idea of any opposition or difficulties which might hinder us. How many men have gone gladly to the ends of the world in search of worldly fortunes, or to fulfill worldly ambitions, and have scorned the thought of any "cross" connected with it! How many mothers have congratulated themselves, and rejoiced over the honor done their sons in seeing them promoted to some place of power and usefulness in their country's service, although it has involved perhaps years of separation, and a life of hardship for their dear ones! And yet these same men, and these very mothers, would have felt and said that they were taking up crosses too heavy almost to be borne, had the service of Christ required the same sacrifice of home, and friends, and worldly ease.

5. Constraining Us by Love

It is altogether the way we look at things, whether we think they are crosses or not. And I am ashamed to think that any Christian should ever put on a long face and shed tears over doing a thing for Christ which a worldly person would be only too glad to do for money.

What we need in the Christian life is to get believers to *want* to do God's will as much as other people want to do their own will. And this is the idea of the Gospel. It is what God intended for us; and it is what He promised. In describing the new covenant in Hebrews 8:6–13, He says it shall no more be the old covenant made on Sinai,—that is, a law given from the outside, controlling a man by force,— but it shall be a law written *within*, constraining us by love.

"I will put my laws," He says, "into their minds, and write them on their hearts." This can mean nothing but that we shall *love* His law; for anything written in our hearts we must love. "And putting it into our minds" is

surely the same as God working in us to "will and to do of his good pleasure," and means that we shall will what God wills, and shall obey His sweet commands, not because it is our duty to do so, but because we ourselves want to do what He wants us to do.

6. God's Way of Working

Nothing could possibly be conceived more effectual than this. How often have we thought, when dealing with our children, "Oh, if I could only get inside of them, and make them *want* to do just what I want, how easy it would be to manage them then!" How often in practical experience we have found that to deal with cross-grained people we most carefully avoid suggesting our wishes to them, but must in some way induce them to suggest the thing themselves, sure that there will then be no opposition with which to contend. And we, who are by nature a stiff-necked people, always rebel more or less against a law from outside of us, while we joyfully embrace the same law springing up within.

God's way of working, therefore, is to get possession of the inside of us, to take the control and management of our will, and to work it for us. Then obedience is easy and a delight, and service becomes perfect freedom, until the Christian is forced to explain, "This happy service! Who could dream earth had such liberty?"

7. Entire Control

What you need to do, then, dear Christian, if you are in bondage in the matter of service, is to put your will over completely into the hands of your Lord, surrendering to Him the entire control of it. Say, "Yes, Lord, YES!" to everything, and trust Him so to work in you to will as to bring your whole wishes and affections into conformity with His own sweet, and lovable, and most lovely will.

I have seen this done often in cases where it looked beforehand an utterly impossible thing. In one case, where a lady had been for years rebelling fearfully against a little act of service which she knew was right, but which she hated, I saw her, out of the depths of despair, and without any feeling whatever, give her will in that matter up into the hands of her Lord, and begin to say to Him, "Thy will be done; *Thy will be done!*" And in one short hour that very thing began to look sweet and precious to her.

8. The Lord Is Our Burden-Bearer

Many Christians, as I have said, love God's will in the abstract, but carry great burdens in connection with it. From this also there is deliverance in the wonderful life of faith. For in this way of life no burdens are carried, no anxieties felt. The Lord is our burden-bearer, and upon Him we must lay off every care. He says, in effect, "Be careful for nothing, but make your requests known to me, and I will attend to them all."

Be careful for *nothing,* He says, not even your service. Why? Because we are so utterly helpless that no matter how *careful* we were, our service would amount to nothing! What have we to do with thinking whether we are fit or not fit for service? The Master-workman surely has a right to use any tool He pleases for His own work, and it is plainly not the business of the tool to decide whether it is the right one to be used or not. He knows; and if He chooses to use us, of course we must be fit. And in truth, if we only knew it, our chief fitness is in our utter helplessness. His strength is made perfect, not in our strength, but in our weakness. Our strength is only a hindrance.

BIBLE SELECTION: HEBREWS 8:6–13

[6]But Jesus has now obtained a more excellent ministry, and to that degree he is the mediator of a better covenant, which has been enacted through better promises. [7]For if that first covenant had been faultless, there would have been no need to look for a second one.

[8]God finds fault with them when he says:

"The days are surely coming, says the Lord,
when I will establish a new covenant with the
    house of Israel
and with the house of Judah;
[9]not like the covenant that I made with their
    ancestors,
on the day when I took them by the hand to
    lead them out of the land of Egypt;
for they did not continue in my covenant,
and so I had no concern for them, says the Lord.

[10]This is the covenant that I will make with the
    house of Israel
after those days, says the Lord:
I will put my laws in their minds,
and write them on their hearts,
and I will be their God,
and they shall be my people.
[11]And they shall not teach one another
or say to each other, 'Know the Lord,'
for they shall all know me,
from the least of them to the greatest.
[12]For I will be merciful toward their iniquities,
and I will remember their sins no more."

[13]In speaking of "a new covenant," he has made the first one obsolete. And what is obsolete and growing old will soon disappear.

REFLECTION QUESTIONS

The following questions can be used for discussion within a small group, or used for journal reflections by individuals.

1. At what point in your life did you first feel the joy of serving God?
2. How does your life compare or contrast with the experience of the woman whose level of vitality waxed and then waned?
3. What, according to Hannah Whitall Smith, is the solution to this common problem?
4. Many people can relate to the author's observation that service becomes a drudgery when we feel inadequate to do the job. What call to service have you left unheeded because you did not feel qualified?
5. Hebrews 8:6–13 tells us that the new covenant has been established by Jesus. This new covenant, according to Whitall Smith, transforms service from a duty into a desire. How does this happen in our lives?

SUGGESTED EXERCISES

The following exercises can be done by individuals, shared between spiritual friends, or used in the context of a small group. Choose one or more of the following.

1. Make a list of all the things you do. Use two headings: "Things I have to do" and "Things I want to do." What does the length of the lists teach you about yourself?
2. Meditate on Hebrews 8:6–13 sometime this week. Turn your meditation into prayer, asking Christ to liberate you from the *have to's* of duty to the *want to's* of desire.
3. Rank yourself on a scale of one to ten in the following category: "Eagerness to Serve Others for God." Now, ask the following questions:
   a. Am I serving mainly out of a sense of duty?
   b. Do I feel inadequate to serve?
   If you answered yes to one or both, go back and reflect on Whitall Smith's counsel regarding these two issues.
4. Allow yourself to be a "tool" this week. As the author has noted, the tool does not question the builder but simply allows itself to be used. Pay attention to the many ways in which God can use you—even with your imperfections. Consciously try to become weak, for as Hannah Whitall Smith notes, "His strength is made perfect, not in our strength, but in our weakness. Our strength is only a hindrance."

REFLECTIONS

In this reading Hannah Whitall Smith has touched an almost universal experience. At one time or another all of us have felt the heavy weight of duty. We are bowed low with the burden of integrity. Service drags and drains rather than uplifts and encourages.

Her answer: fall in love with Jesus over and over again. Let him work from the inside, giving us the grace-filled "want to" of love to replace the "have to" of duty. Her answer may not be complete but it certainly is central. Nothing is more at the heart of our discipleship to Jesus Christ than an ongoing, ever-deepening love relationship. This, in turn, draws us to love all peoples and gives us the desire to do his works upon the earth.

GOING DEEPER

Whitall Smith, Hannah. *The Christian's Secret of a Happy Life.* Old Tappan, NJ: Fleming H. Revell, 1962. To my knowledge this is the only book Hannah Whitall Smith ever wrote. It was enough. In simple language she describes the journey of the soul through doubts, failures, and temptations, into the joy of obedience, and finally up into divine union. Threading its way throughout this book is a rhapsodic joy that is a marked contrast to the tone of many ascetical works. Whitall Smith found life good and invited her readers into the merry mercy of God.

Jeremy Taylor (1613–1667)

INTRODUCTION TO THE AUTHOR

Born and educated in Cambridge, England, Jeremy Taylor soon became famous for his scholarly abilities. He was ordained in 1633 and later became the chaplain to Charles I. This relationship led to his subsequent imprisonment by the Parliamentarians in 1645. He moved to Ireland in 1658 and, after the Restoration, was consecrated bishop of Down and Connor.

He was a vivid, illustrative, prolific writer who left behind enough works to fill fifteen octavo volumes. He wrote the first English narrative of Christ's life as well as a number of devotional and scholarly books. He is best known for his *Holy Living* and *Holy Dying*, two practical manuals that guide the reader into a deeper life of sacrifice and humility by drawing on classical as well as Christian writers.

The following selection reveals Taylor's extensive insight into human behavior. He sees with great clarity our inner struggles for recognition, and the many stratagems we employ to get it. His "rules" may sound foreign or offensive to some modern readers who are more at ease with the language of self-esteem, but Taylor's understanding of the importance of humility is a much needed word for us today.

EXCERPTS FROM *THE RULE AND EXERCISES OF HOLY LIVING*

1. A Realistic Opinion of Yourself

The grace of humility is exercised in the following rules.

First, Do not think better of yourself because of any outward circumstance that happens to you. Although you may—because of the gifts that have been bestowed upon you—be better at something than someone else (as one horse runs faster than another), know that it is for the benefit of others, not for yourself.

Remember that you are merely human and that you have nothing in yourself that merits worth except your right choices.

Second, Humility does not consist in criticizing yourself, or wearing ragged clothes, or walking around submissively wherever you go. Humility consists in a realistic opinion of yourself, namely, that you are an unworthy person. Believe this about yourself with the same certainty you believe that you are hungry when you have gone without food.

2. Do Good Things in Secret

Third, When you hold this opinion of yourself, be content that others think the same of you. If you realize that you are not wise, do not be angry if someone else should agree! If you truly hold this opinion of yourself, you should also desire that others hold this opinion as well. You would be a hypocrite to think lowly of yourself, but then expect others to think highly of you.

Fourth, Nurture a love to do good things in secret, concealed from the eyes of others, and therefore not highly esteemed because of them. Be content to go without praise, never being troubled when someone has slighted or undervalued you. Remember, no one can undervalue you if you know that you are unworthy. Once you know that, no amount of contempt from another person will be able to hurt you.

3. Never Be Ashamed

Fifth, Never be ashamed of your birth, of your parents, your occupation, or your present employment, or the lowly status of any of them. When there is an occasion to speak about them to others, do not be shy, but speak readily, with an indifference to how others will regard you. It is said of Primislaus, the first king of Bohemia, that he kept his old work shoes by his side so that he would always remember his humble upbringing.

Sixth, Never say anything, directly or indirectly, that will provoke praise or elicit compliments from others. Do not let your praise be the intended end of what you say. If it so hap-

pens that someone speaks well of you in the midst of a conversation, you are not to stop the conversation. Only remember this: do not let praise for yourself be the design of your conversations.

4. Reflect It Back to God

Seventh, When you do receive praise for something you have done, take it indifferently and return it to God. Reflect it back to God, the giver of the gift, the blesser of the action, the aid of the project. Always give God thanks for making you an instrument of his glory for the benefit of others.

Eighth, Make a good name for yourself by being a person of virtue and humility. It is a benefit for others who hear of you to hear good things about you. As a model, they can use your humility to their advantage. But be careful among your own circle of friends, and do not let your good reputation be the object of your gaze. Use it as an instrument to help your neighbor, but do not use it for your own gain. Be like Moses, whose face shined brightly for others to see but did not make it a looking-glass for himself.

5. The Waters of Vanity

Ninth, Do not take pride in any praise given to you. Rejoice in God who gives gifts others can see in you, but let it be mixed with a holy respect, so that this good does not turn into evil. If praise comes, put it to work by letting it serve other ends than yourself. But be cautious and on guard that pride never enters in, thereby rendering your praise a loss.

Tenth, as in the Sixth rule, Do not ask others your faults with the intent or purpose being to have others tell you of your good qualities. Some will speak lowly of themselves in order to make others give an account of their goodness. They are merely fishing for compliments, and yet, it is they who end up swallowing the hook, until by drinking the waters of vanity they swell up and burst.

6. The Devil's Whispers

Eleventh, When you are slighted by someone, or feel undervalued, do not harbor any secret anger, supposing that you actually deserved praise and that they overlooked your value, or that they neglected to praise you because of their own envy. Do not try to seek out a group of flatterers who will take your side, in whose vain noises and empty praises you may try to keep up your high opinion of yourself.

Twelfth, Do not entertain any of the devil's whispers of pride, such as that of Nebuchadnezzar: "Is not this great Babylon, which I have built for the honor of my name, and the might of my majesty, and the power of my kingdom?"

Some people spend their time dreaming of greatness, envisioning theaters full of people applauding them, imagining themselves giving engaging speeches, fantasizing about having great wealth. All of this is nothing but the fumes of pride, exposing their heart's true wishes. Although there is nothing directly evil in this, it is the offspring of an inner evil and has nothing whatsoever to do with the obtaining of humility.

7. The Desire to Disparage

Thirteenth, Take an active part in the praising of others, entertaining their good with delight.

In no way should you give in to the desire to disparage them, or lessen their praise, or make any objection. You should never think that hearing the good report of another in any way lessens your worth.

Fourteenth, Be content when you see or hear that others are doing well in their jobs and with their income, even when you are not. In the same manner, be content when someone else's work is approved and yours is rejected.

8. Focus on the Strengths

Fifteenth, Never compare yourself with others unless it be to advance your impression of them and lower your impression of yourself. St. Paul encouraged us to think more highly of others than we do of ourselves. Thus, it is beneficial to focus on the strengths of those around us in order to see our weaknesses more clearly.

When I look around, I see that one person is more learned than I, another person more frugal, another person more chaste, and yet another person who is more charitable, or perhaps less proud. If I am to be humble, I will not overlook their good virtues, or dismiss it, but rather, I will reflect upon them.

The truly humble person will not only look admirably at the strengths of others, but will also look with great forgiveness upon the weaknesses of others. The truly humble person will try to see how the sinful deeds done by others were committed because the person was unenlightened or misled, concluding that if the person had the same benefits and helps that he had, they would not have committed any such evil, but rather, would have done much good.

St. Paul said of himself, "I am the chief of all sinners." This is how we should all view ourselves. But this rule is to be used with caution:

do not say it to others, but keep it to yourself. Why? Because the reasons you have for feeling this way (the knowledge of your sins) is not known to others the way it is known to you, and it may make them doubt the praise you give to God for all he has done for you. If you keep these thoughts to yourself, you will be much more able to give God praise and thanks publicly.

9. Virtue Scorns a Lie for Its Cover

Sixteenth, Do not constantly try to excuse all of your mistakes. If you have made a mistake, or an oversight, or an indiscretion, confess it plainly, for virtue scorns a lie for its cover. If you are not guilty (unless it be scandalous), do not be overly concerned to change everyone's opinion about the matter. Learn to bear criticism patiently, knowing the harsh words of an enemy can be a greater motivator than the kind words of a friend.

Seventeenth, Give God thanks for every weakness, fault, and imperfection you have. Accept it as a favor of God, an instrument to resist pride and nurse humility. Remember, if God has chosen to shrink your swelling pride, he has made it that much easier for you to enter in through the narrow way!

10. What Is Most Important to God

Eighteenth, Do not expose others' weaknesses in order to make them feel less able than you. Neither should you think on your superior skill with any delight, or use it to set yourself above another person.

It is told of Cyrus that he would never compete in any sport with his friends in which he knew himself to be superior to them. Instead, he would always compete in sports in which he was less skillful than his opponents. He did not want to prove his superiority by winning, but rather, placed more importance on learning from those who were more skilled while at the same time sharing in the joy of their success.

Nineteenth, Remember that what is most important to God is that we submit ourselves and all that we have to him. This requires that we be willing to endure whatever his will brings us, to be content in whatever state we are in, and to be ready for every change.

11. Increased by Exercising

Humility begins as a *gift* from God, but it is increased as a *habit* we develop. That is, humility is increased by exercising it. Taken all together, these rules are good helps and instruments for the establishing and increasing of the grace of humility and the decreasing of pride.

12. An Exercise for Increasing the Grace of Humility

Confess your sins often to God and don't think of them as scattered offenses in the course of a long life; a burst of anger here, an act of impatience there. Instead, unite them into one continuous representation of your life. Remember that a person may seem rather good if his faults are scattered over large distances throughout his lifetime; but if his errors and follies are placed next to one another, he will appear to be a vicious and miserable person. Hopefully this exercise, when really applied to your soul, will be useful to you for increasing the grace of humility.

BIBLE SELECTION: LUKE 14:7–11

[7]When he noticed how the guests chose the places of honor, he told them a parable. [8]"When you are invited by someone to a wedding banquet, do not sit down at the place of honor, in case someone more distinguished than you has been invited by your host; [9]and the host who invited both of you may come and say to you, 'Give this person your place,' and then in disgrace you would start to take the lowest place. [10]But when you are invited, go and sit down at the lowest place, so that when your host comes, he may say to you, 'Friend, move up higher'; then you will be honored in the presence of all who sit at the table with you. [11]For all who exalt themselves will be humbled, and those who humble themselves will be exalted."

REFLECTION QUESTIONS

The following questions can be used for discussion within a small group, or used for journal reflections by individuals.

1. Humility, writes Jeremy Taylor, begins with a realistic assessment of ourselves, namely, that we are unworthy. How does this contrast with the modern emphasis on having high self-esteem?

2. "Some people spend their time dreaming of greatness," Taylor observes. "Although there is nothing directly evil in this," he goes on to say, "it is the offspring of an inner evil." How have your dreams of greatness been a hindrance in your spiritual life?

3. Taylor encourages us not to be ashamed of our birth, economic position, or vocation. In what ways have you been made to feel ashamed concerning these areas?

4. Look over the whole list of Taylor's rules. Which of them comes easiest for you? Which is the hardest?

5. In Luke 14:7–11, Jesus tells a parable to a group of people because he noticed how they chose places of honor for themselves. In what ways does this parable coincide with Taylor's teaching on humility?

SUGGESTED EXERCISES

The following exercises can be done by individuals, shared between spiritual friends, or used in the context of a small group. Choose one or more of the following.

1. "Nurture a love to do good things in secret" this week (rule 4). Let your acts of kindness go unnoticed. Simply do them for the sake of others, not for the praise you would receive.

2. Avoid manipulating conversations so as to receive praise or compliments from others this week (rules 6 and 10). As Taylor exhorts, "do not let praise for yourself be the design of your conversations." Also, when you do receive praise, "reflect it back to God" (rule 7).

3. Taylor believes that a thorough confession best helps us gain humility (see section 12). As you make your confession this week, be careful not to see your faults and failings as random and sporadic actions in an otherwise good life, but rather "unite them into one continuous representation of your life." This exercise, notes Taylor, when really applied to your soul, will be useful for increasing the grace of humility.

4. As Jesus commands, as you go about your week do not try to take a place of honor, but be content with the lowest place. Humble yourself, and let others do the exalting.

REFLECTIONS

In his preface to Holy Living *Taylor speaks of the "instruments of virtue" that are to be utilized in the ongoing development of a holy life. Activities of engagement and abstinence that produce humility are just such instruments.*

These are God-ordained means for the development of virtue, and we cannot expect the spirit of humility to grow in us without regular use of them. Indeed, this is true with all the virtues. Hence, according to Taylor, one of our enduring tasks is to continually seek out and "make use of the proper instruments of virtue."

GOING DEEPER

Jeremy Taylor wrote extensively (e.g., *The Great Exemplar* [1649] and *The Worthy Communicant* [1668]), but he is best remembered for *The Rule and Exercises of Holy Living* (1650) and *The Rule and Exercises of Holy Dying* (1651). I have not found a good modern edition of either *Holy Living* or *Holy Dying* and so most likely you will need to utilize old ones you can find in a library. There is an 1875 edition (Boston: Estes and Lauriat). Just to give you an idea of what these books cover, here are a few chapter titles from *Holy Dying*: "Reflections on the Vanity and Shortness of Life"; "Reasons for a Daily Examination of Our Actions"; "Rules for the Practice of Patience"; "An Exercise Against Despair in the Day of Our Death."

Elizabeth O'Connor (1921–)

INTRODUCTION TO THE AUTHOR

In 1947 a movement of the Spirit produced the founding of the Church of the Saviour in Washington, D.C. Pastored by Gordon Cosby, this church demonstrated a radical faith witness to the rest of the world. Elizabeth O'Connor was one of the church's early members and would later join the church staff. Her writings would chronicle their story, letting the rest of the world know of the amazing work God was doing in their midst.

O'Connor is a gifted writer whose insights into the spiritual journey have helped countless women and men grow deeper in their own walk with God. Her writings challenge and confront, as well as encourage and inspire. The following selection comes from a book that comprises several letters written to the early faith communities of the Church of the Saviour. Although these letters were written to stir and nurture the faith and commitment of these young churches, they speak a fresh word of exhortation to all scattered pilgrims on the very important subject of money.

EXCERPTS FROM *LETTERS TO SCATTERED PILGRIMS*

1. The Handling of Money

"Filthy lucre," as money is sometimes called, has been a favorite topic of conversation for us since the early days of The Church of the Saviour. We talk about it probably as much as Jesus did. When the founding members, young and poor, were forming themselves into a properly incorporated community of faith, they struggled for a discipline of membership that would help them and future church members to deal concretely with at least some aspects of the handling of money. In its first writing the discipline read, "We commit our-selves to giving 10 percent of our gross income to the work of the Church."

While there was some precedence in biblical history for the 10 percent figure, our first members felt that this kind of giving would enable them to begin to tackle the injustices of society in a way that would be meaningful to themselves, as well as to others. Their proposed constitution and disciplines were submitted to Reinhold Niebuhr, an eminent theologian of the last generation who had agreed to read them and comment. His only suggestion concerned the discipline on money. "I would suggest," Niebuhr said, "that you commit yourselves not to tithing but to proportionate giving, with tithing as an economic floor beneath which you will not go unless there are some compelling reasons." The discipline was rewritten and stands today in each of the six new faith communities:

We covenant with Christ and one another to give proportionately beginning with a tithe of our incomes.

2. Proportionate Giving

None of us has to be an accountant to know what 10 percent of a gross income is, but each of us has to be a person on his knees before God if we are to understand our commitment to proportionate giving.

Proportionate to what? Proportionate to the accumulated wealth of one's family? Proportionate to one's income and the demands upon it, which vary from family to family? Proportionate to one's sense of security and the degree of anxiety with which one lives? Proportionate to the keenness of our awareness of those who suffer? Proportionate to our sense of justice and of God's ownership of all wealth? Proportionate to our sense of stewardship for those who follow after us? And so on, and so forth. The answer, of course, is in proportion to all of these things.

Proportionate giving has kept us from mistaking our churchgoing for Christianity, and from looking at our neighbor to see what we should be doing. In our better moments we desire that each member and intern member work under the guidance of the Holy Spirit to determine what proportionate giving means in his or her individual situation. We have, of course, hoped for ourselves and for others that the proportion of giving would increase as we identified with the oppressed and learned to trust God at deeper levels for our own future.

3. The Borders Have Been Pushed Out

By and large the discipline has served us well. Over the years we have kept the 10 percent floor for members and the 5 percent floor for our intern members. Many have struggled with the minimum giving, and some have turned away. Others have broken loose and showered our community with riches. The borders of the mission have been pushed out, and the suffering of our city has been eased a bit.

Sometimes the giving has been excessive and ecstatic, and sometimes impulsive—a diamond engagement ring dropped in the offering plate, a silver service set appearing at the door, a check for several thousand dollars representing the total accumulated wealth of a young couple.

4. Blessed Be the Tithe

I first heard the tithing discipline explained in a class in Christian Growth that I was taking when I was new to The Church of the Saviour and the Christian faith. Following the class we met with the members of other classes for a short worship service. The small chapel rang with the words, "Blessed be the tie that binds our hearts in Christian love." My untutored ears heard the words as "Blessed be the tithe. . . ." I went home to explain the discipline to my nonreligious household, and commented, "They even sing about it."

The next Sunday we all went to see those strange people, and to hear about the things they were planning. Gordon Cosby was preaching his annual sermon on money, which was as spellbinding then as now. Before the year was over my household was tithing, and when the time came to purchase a retreat farm, we threw caution to the wind and went with everyone else to borrow what we could toward the down payment. It was not that our souls were so quickly converted, but that we sensed that something important was going on, and we wanted to be a part of it. We had been captured by a man's vision of what a community might do if it really cared about the oppressed and the suffering.

5. Reclaiming Ourselves

In a recent sermon on money Gordon said as forcefully as ever that to give away money is to win a victory over the dark powers that oppress us. He talked about reclaiming for ourselves the energy with which we have endowed money: "Money is a hang-up for many of us. We will not be able to advance in the Christian faith until we have dealt at another level with the material. It is a matter of understanding what it means to be faithful to Jesus Christ."

He went on to say that the poor suffer because they are not able to give. Without any doubt Gordon's teaching-sermons on money have influenced the whole orientation of the new communities toward the material area of life. Each of them began on a sound financial basis because each began with a small nucleus of tithing members. All contributions of the communities are used to further the work of the missions within the year they are given. Nothing has ever been put aside for a rainy day. We have followed faithfully the injunction given by Moses to his people as he led them out of bondage, "No one must keep any of it for tomorrow" (Exod. 16:19, JB).

6. Stabilizing Our Standard of Living

Despite our corporate style and our exposure to the issues that are raised around the subject of money, we know that we have not gained much "downward mobility." While we have succeeded in stabilizing our standard of living, most of us cling to what we have known. Though the budgets of our faith communities are large by traditional standards, we are fully aware that they represent only a fraction of the potential giving of the congregation.

We still wrestle with fear when we consider abandoned giving. Our wills, with rare exceptions, look like the wills of those who have never been committed to the building of a faith community, or who have never had the poor in mind. This may indicate that, in the face of the threat caused by consideration of our deaths, we regress to old definitions of family and narrower spheres of identity. In any case, most of us would probably say that we are not as free as we would like to be where the material things of life are concerned. What may have looked like radical obedience to us a quarter of a century ago, no longer seems radical today.

7. Faces That We Know

Coming to know some of our suffering sisters and brothers in the Third World and in the ghettoes of Washington has made all the difference in the way we view the earth. The unemployment statistics are made up of faces that we know. We behold the plight of the poor not only with fresh eyes, but with the awareness that our faithfulness in the past gave God one way of performing veritable miracles.

Scattered throughout our new faith communities are persons who ask with increasing uneasiness what it means to be faithful in this time in their individual treks and in our slow migration as a people out of the old orders of "necessity and death." In a personal and in a corporate way we are wrestling once more with the question of what we are to do with our money. Some of us experience an inner division, for our hearts so often tell us one thing and our heads another.

When we begin to take the Scriptures seriously, "You cannot serve God and Money" (Matt. 6:24, NEB) becomes a personal address. One would expect God to applaud our small efforts at faithfulness; instead a Spirit comes and takes us where we are not yet prepared to go.

8. The Worship of Idols

As we become exposed to the poor and their needs, the rich young ruler and the widow and her mite lose the storybook quality of our childhood faith, and become figures in the counterculture literature of a revolutionary leader—the very one whom we call Saviour. The First Commandment and all the Scriptures on the worship of idols begin to lay bare our own primitive selves. Some of us have looked into the face of our idols and found that one of them is money.

Though we along with millions of other churchgoers are saying that Jesus saves, we ask ourselves if we are not in practice acting as though it were money that saves. We say that money gives power, money corrupts, money talks. Like the ancients with their molten calf we have endowed money with our own psychic energy, given it arms and legs, and have told ourselves that it can work for us. More than this we enshrine it in a secret place, give it a heart and a mind and the power to grant us peace and mercy.

9. Individual Answers

Do we believe that money and possessions have a way of coming between people who want to be in community with each other? Do we really believe that every life has resources more priceless than gold, and that our hearts, minds and labor are adequate for any task? What if the world is right and there are things that only money can buy, gifts of the spirit that only money can unlock, and blocks that only money can push aside?

The questions continue to be raised, and we continue to struggle for the answers that in the end have to be individual answers, for we are each at a different place in our spiritual trek with different understandings of what the Gospel has to say to us about what we do with our money.

BIBLE SELECTION: MATTHEW 6:19–24

[19]"Do not store up for yourselves treasures on earth, where moth and rust consume and where thieves break in and steal; [20]but store up for yourselves treasures in heaven, where neither moth nor rust consumes and where thieves do not break in and steal. [21]For where your treasure is, there your heart will be also.

[22]"The eye is the lamp of the body. So, if your eye is healthy, your whole body will be full of light; [23]but if your eye is unhealthy, your whole body will be full of darkness. If then the light in you is darkness, how great is the darkness!

[24]"No one can serve two masters; for a slave will either hate the one and love the other, or be devoted to the one and despise the other. You cannot serve God and wealth."

REFLECTION QUESTIONS

The following questions can be used for discussion within a small group, or used for journal reflections by individuals.

1. After reading this selection, what are some of your "gut-level" reactions to this strong word about how we spend money?
2. Gordon Cosby urged his listeners to reclaim for "ourselves the energy with which we have endowed money." In what ways have you endowed money with energy? What would be gained by reclaiming that energy?
3. O'Connor quotes Cosby as preaching, "To give away money is to win a victory over the dark powers that oppress us." Has money ever seemed like a "dark power" that oppresses you? Explain.
4. How possible is it in a properly disciplined spiritual life to invest and use money for the greater good of others and the advancement of the kingdom of God?
5. Jesus preached that we cannot serve God and wealth (Matt. 6:24), because he perceived that Mammon (the spirit of wealth) functions as a false god for many. How has money tried to gain your allegiance? What struggles have you encountered in trying to "serve two masters"?

SUGGESTED EXERCISES

The following exercises can be done by individuals, shared between spiritual friends, or used in the context of a small group. Choose one or more of the following.

1. Explore tithing for a month if you do not already practice this principle. Without becoming legalistic, look for ways to curb your unnecessary spending in order to give more lavishly to the poor.
2. Begin to identify with the "faces" of the poor. O'Connor notes that the Church of the Saviour was able to give so much to the poor because the poor were no longer "them" but "us." Spend an afternoon at an urban ministry center. Look carefully at the faces of those you meet, and listen to their voices.
3. Take a weekend to do a personal financial inventory. Look over your checkbook ledger for the past year, identifying the ways you spend your money. Take this information into your prayer chamber, asking God to help you gain victory over the power of money.
4. Jesus counsels us, "Do not store up for yourselves treasures on earth" (Matt. 6:19). In an attempt to de-accumulate, put on a garage sale, giving all or a portion of your proceeds to the poor, or to some other ministry effort.

REFLECTIONS

I am deeply indebted to the ministry of the Church of the Saviour. At one point when I was all but ready to abandon the gospel ministry, Gordon Cosby, in a serendipitous one-hour visit, spoke life-giving words into my spirit. And, over the years, the writings of Elizabeth O'Connor have nurtured hope in me for the future of the Church. When I would see so many churches rushing after the little tin gods of self-aggrandizement and prosperity, I was sorely tempted to cry "Icabod!" over all outward religion. But O'Connor told another story—a story of discipleship and commitment amid honest struggle. I was encouraged to believe that the Church could actually be a redemptive fellowship rather than a religious equivalent of secular promotion. I am deeply thankful to God for the Church of the Saviour and to Elizabeth O'Connor, who has been led to chronicle its story.

GOING DEEPER

O'Connor, Elizabeth. *Call to Commitment.* New York: Harper & Row, 1963. This was the first book to tell the unusual story of the Church of the Saviour. At the time it was written, the church was in the forefront of defining new wineskins of Christian renewal—a position that it occupies to this day. You may also wish to read *Journey Inward, Journey Outward,* which continues to record the development of this incendiary fellowship.

O'Connor, Elizabeth. *Letters to Scattered Pilgrims.* New York: Harper & Row, 1979. These letters to the six faith communities of the Church of the Saviour have a way of calling us forward into uncharted waters of discipleship. Her discussion of money, from which the present selection is taken, is a penetrating analysis of one of the most persistent idols in Western culture.

John Wesley (1703–1791)

INTRODUCTION TO THE AUTHOR

John Wesley was one of nineteen children born to Samuel and Susanna Wesley. His father was an Anglican clergyman and his mother was devoted both to God and to her children. John attended Christ Church College at Oxford, was ordained an Anglican minister, and was made a Fellow of Lincoln College. While he was at Oxford, he and a group of friends banded together to encourage one another to live a holy life. Their methodical approach to holiness led others at the college to refer to them as "Methodists."

Although Wesley grew up a deeply religious man, something was lacking in his heart. On May 24, 1738, he attended a prayer meeting at which the leader read Luther's preface to the book of Galatians. It was then, Wesley wrote, that he first understood that God loved him—even him—and the gospel became rooted in his heart. With his heart "strangely warmed," Wesley embarked on an unusual preaching ministry, especially to the common folk in the English countryside.

Historians have said that by evangelizing the common people of eighteenth-century England, Wesley saved the country from a bloody revolution. His impact upon England was dramatic during his lifetime, and even more dramatic on America after his death as many Methodist preachers crisscrossed the frontier with his message.

The following excerpts come from his famous work *Christian Perfection*. In that book, Wesley gives practical advice to those who want to move toward perfection, which for Wesley did not mean a state of sinlessness, but a desire to be fully in love with God with one's whole heart, soul, mind, and strength.

EXCERPTS FROM *CHRISTIAN PERFECTION*

1. The Danger of Pride

The first advice I would give to those who have been saved from sin by grace is to watch and pray continually against pride. For it is pride not only to ascribe what we have to ourselves, but also to think we have what we do not. One man, for instance, ascribed his knowledge to God and was therefore humble. But then he thought he had more than everyone else which is dangerous pride.

We often think that we have no need of anyone else's advice or reproof. Always remember, much grace does not imply much enlightenment. We may be wise but have little love, or we may have love with little wisdom. God has wisely joined us all together as the parts of a body so that we cannot say to another, "I have no need of you."

Even to imagine that those who are not saved cannot teach you is a very great and serious mistake. Dominion is not found in grace. Not observing this has led some into many mistakes and certainly into pride. Beware even the appearance of pride! Let there be in you that lowly mind which was in Christ Jesus. Be clothed with humility. Let modesty appear in all your words and actions.

One way we do this is to own any fault we have. If you have at any time thought, spoken, or acted wrong, do not refrain from acknowledging it. Never dream that this will hurt the cause of God—in fact, it will further it. Be open and honest when you are rebuked and do not seek to evade it or disguise it. Rather, let it appear just as it is and you will thereby not hinder but adorn the gospel.

2. The Danger of Enthusiasm

Also, beware of the daughter of pride: enthusiasm. By enthusiasm I mean the tendency to hastily ascribe everything to God, supposing dreams and voices and visions to be special revelations that God has given to you. While they may be from God, they may also be from the devil. Therefore, "believe not every spirit, but test the spirits to see whether they be of God." Test all things by the written word of God, and let all bow down before it.

You are in danger of enthusiasm every time you depart even a little from the Scriptures. We must never depart from the plain meaning of

Scripture, and we must always take it in the context in which it was written. But keep in mind that we must not despise reason, knowledge, or human learning, every one of which is a gift of God and was given to serve a purpose.

One general inlet to enthusiasm is expecting the end without the means: expecting knowledge, for instance, without searching the Scriptures and consulting with the people of God, or expecting spiritual strength without constant prayer and steady watchfulness, or expecting God to bless you without hearing the word of God at every opportunity.

Another inlet to enthusiasm may be the very desire to "grow in grace." For some people this will continually lead them to seek "new" grace and thereby lead us to seek something other than new degrees of loving God and our neighbor. Some will think they have come upon a new grace when they have discovered what it means to be "one with Christ" or to "die with Christ." When we take a fresh teaching from the Scriptures to heart, we must not conclude that it is a "new" gift. We have all of these things when we are justified; all that remains is that we experience them in higher degrees.

We should always remember that love is the highest gift of God. All of our revelations and gifts are little things compared to love. There is nothing higher in religion. If you are looking for anything else, you are looking wide of the mark. Settle in your heart that from this moment on you will aim at nothing more than that love described in the thirteenth chapter of 1 Corinthians. You can go no higher than this.

3. The Danger of Antinomianism, or Lawlessness

Third, I caution you to beware of antinomianism, which is the belief that there is no need for laws in the life of the believer. That great truth that "Christ is the end of the law" may betray us into this belief if we do not consider that Christ himself adopted every point of the moral law! Beware of thinking, "Because I have the love of God I do not need holiness," or "Since I pray all the time I have no need for set times of private prayer," or "Because I am spiritual I have no need for self-examination."

Instead, let this be our thought: "I prize thy commandments above gold or precious stones. O, what love I have found in your laws! All the day long I will study in it." We must beware of self-indulgence, or of mocking self-denial, fasting, or abstinence. We cannot cry out, "Only believe, believe!" and call others "legalists" who are trying to live as Scripture teaches. We must remember that "by works our faith is made perfect."

4. The Danger of Sins of Omission

Sins of omission are avoiding to do good of any kind when we have the opportunity. We must beware of these sins and, instead, be zealous of good works. Do all the good you possibly can to the bodies and souls of your neighbors. Be active. Give no place to laziness. Be always busy, losing no shred of time. Whatever your hand finds to do, do it with all your might.

Also, be slow to speak. It is said, "In a multitude of words sin abounds." Try not to talk too much, or for a long period of time. Not many people can converse profitably beyond an hour's time. Especially avoid pious "chit-chat" or religious gossip.

5. The Danger of Desiring Anything but God

Also, beware of desiring anything other than God. Jesus said, "If your eye remains single your whole body shall be full of light." Do not allow the desire for tasteful food or any other pleasure of the senses, the desire of pleasing the eye or the imagination, the desire for money or praise or power, to rule you. While you have the ability to feel these desires, you are not compelled to feel them. Stand fast in the liberty wherewith Christ has made you free!

Be an example to all of denying yourself and taking up your cross daily. Let others see that you are not interested in any pleasure that does not bring you nearer to God, nor regard any pain which does. Let them see that you simply aim at pleasing God in everything. Let the language of your heart sing out with regard to pleasure or pain, riches or poverty, honor or dishonor, "All's alike to me, so I in my Lord may live and die!"

6. The Danger of Schism

Beware of schism, of making a tear in the Church of Christ. Ceasing to have a reciprocal love "for one another" (1 Cor. 12:25), is inner disunity which is at the very root of all outward separation. Beware of everything which leads to this separation. Beware of a dividing spirit.

Therefore, do not say, "I am of Paul," or "I am of Apollos." This is the very thing which caused the schism at Corinth. Do not say, "This is my preacher, the best preacher in England. Give me him and you can have all the rest." All this tends to breed division, to disunite those whom God has joined.

Do not despise or run down any preacher. Do not exalt anyone above the rest lest you hurt both him and the cause of God. Do not bear hard upon any preacher because of some inconsistency or inaccuracy of expression; no, not even for some mistake, even if you are right.

Do not even give a single thought of separating from your brethren, whether their opinions agree with yours or not. Just because someone does not agree with everything you say does not mean that they are sinning. Nor is this or that opinion essential to the work of God. Be patient with those who disagree with you. Do not condemn those who do not see things just as you do, or who think it is their duty to contradict you, whether in a great thing or a small.

O, beware of touchiness, of testiness, of an unwillingness to be corrected. Beware of being provoked to anger at the least criticism, and avoiding those who do not accept your word.

BIBLE SELECTION: 1 CORINTHIANS 13:1–8

If I speak in the tongues of mortals and of angels, but do not have love, I am a noisy gong or a clanging cymbal. [2]And if I have prophetic powers, and understand all mysteries and all knowledge, and if I have all faith, so as to remove mountains, but do not have love, I am nothing. [3]If I give away all my possessions, and if I hand over my body so that I may boast, but do not have love, I gain nothing.

[4]Love is patient; love is kind; love is not envious or boastful or arrogant [5]or rude. It does not insist on its own way; it is not irritable or resentful; [6]it does not rejoice in wrongdoing, but rejoices in the truth. [7]It bears all things, believes all things, hopes all things, endures all things.

[8]Love never ends. But as for prophecies, they will come to an end; as for tongues, they will cease; as for knowledge, it will come to an end.

REFLECTION QUESTIONS

The following questions can be used for discussion within a small group, or used for journal reflections by individuals.

1. John Wesley begins this selection by discussing the dangers of pride. He lists some of them: ascribing to ourselves what comes from God; thinking too highly of our gifts; thinking we have no need of correction; believing that we have no need of others in the church; imagining that nonbelievers have nothing to teach us; and being reluctant to admit our faults. Which of these do you struggle with the most?

2. In section 2, Wesley writes of the tendency of some to expect a spiritual blessing (e.g., knowledge, spiritual strength) without any spiritual work on their part (e.g., prayer, reading the Bible, hearing the preached Word, Christian fellowship). As you look at your life, what spiritual blessings would you like to have from God? What spiritual means might help you to receive those blessings?

3. Wesley discusses in section 4 the danger of sins of omission (not doing things we ought to have done). What are your most nagging sins of omission?

4. In section 6, Wesley deals with the problem of schism. Have you experienced this problem in your local church? In a small group? In your family? According to Wesley, how should we deal with this problem?

5. In 1 Corinthians 13:1–8, Paul urges the believers at Corinth to aim toward love above all else. It seems that the Corinthians had been placing too much emphasis on their individual gifts and not enough emphasis on the right use of their gifts, which is to build one another. In what ways have you struggled with this same problem?

SUGGESTED EXERCISES

The following exercises can be done by individuals, shared between spiritual friends, or used in the context of a small group. Choose one or more of the following.

1. John Wesley urges us, "Be active." This week endeavor to "do all the good you possibly can." Shift your focus from your sins of commission to your sins of omission.

2. Wesley strongly recommends that we not "run down any preacher." Avoid the easy tendency toward schism that comes from becoming a fan of one preacher or teacher to the detriment of another. Learn to say, "I am for Paul, *and* I am for Apollos."

3. Schism happens not only when we seek to follow a popular leader who suits our fancy, but also when we separate from fellow members over a difference of opinion on a nonessential matter. This week strive to make amends where this has occurred, and as Wesley counsels, "Be patient with those who disagree with you."

4. Both Wesley and Paul urged their listeners to pursue love above all else. Examine your own life this week, asking, "How much love is demonstrated in my life?" List what you need to change about your attitudes and actions toward those around you.

REFLECTIONS

I am always impressed with the balance in Wesley's counsel. He encourages zeal and warns of its excesses. He advocates disciplines of the spiritual life and cautions against legalism. Even in the small selection in this devotional reading he has many insights for us. Let me mention just one.

Wesley tells us to beware of wanting God to do things for us that he has ordained we should do for ourselves. Sometimes people hanker after direct revelations about issues that can be fully resolved by an honest study of Scripture. At other times people expect to progress and mature in holiness by "spiritual highs" when God's ordained means involve regular disciplines of prayer, fasting, and solitude. God, you see, wants us to be "co-laborers" with him as we discover this gracious life of "righteousness and peace and joy in the Holy Spirit" (1 Cor. 3:9; Rom. 14:17).

We would do well to pay close attention to Wesley's counsel—in it are words of life.

GOING DEEPER

Snyder, Howard A. *The Radical Wesley and Patterns for Church Renewal.* Downers Grove, IL: Inter-Varsity, 1980. Snyder gives us the innovative insights and methodologies of Wesley and shows why they transformed eighteenth-century England and how they can transform contemporary society as well.

Wesley, John. *The John Wesley Reader.* Compiled by Al Bryant. Waco, TX: Word, 1983. Devotional meditations drawn from Wesley's journal, sermons, and letters.

Wesley, John. *The Journal of John Wesley.* Edited by Percy Livingstone Parker. Various editions. This paperback abridged edition of *The Journal* is good for someone making a first acquaintance with Wesley. Various publishers carry this edition: Lion, Moody, STL, and others.

Wesley, John. *The Works of John Wesley.* Edited by Albert C. Outler. 32 vols. Nashville: Abingdon, 1984. If you are looking for the very best and most complete material of Wesley, this is the set. Outler is the finest Wesley scholar of the twentieth century. The set is expensive—$50.00 per volume.

Catherine of Siena (1347–1380)

INTRODUCTION TO THE AUTHOR

Caterina di Giacomo di Benincasa was born in the Fontebranda district of Siena, Italy, the twenty-fourth of twenty-five children. She was reared in a poor but devout Catholic family in an age of class feuds and religious wars. At the age of seven she vowed her virginity to God, and at fifteen she cut off her hair in defiance of her parents' efforts to see her married. At eighteen she became a Dominican nun and began to live in solitude and silence, going out of her room only for mass.

At twenty-one she decided to return to her family and spend her life helping the poor, serving as a nurse in homes and hospitals. Even though her fame spread from poor beggars to powerful popes, she managed to maintain a deep interior life of silence and devotion to God. Catherine was called upon to help settle political disputes and social unrest until her death in 1380.

A popular form of religious writing during the Middle Ages involved the use of a metaphor to portray the spiritual life. Ladders and castles and dark nights—all have been employed as ways of describing the indescribable. In the following selection, Catherine adopts the metaphor of a "bridge," using it as a way of describing the work of Christ and the way to heaven. Modern readers who are "literal" minded may find it obscure. She wrote of things that defy words; therefore we would do well to read her works with our heart as well as our mind.

EXCERPTS FROM *THE DIALOGUE*

1. The Bridge

(Then God the eternal One responded to her soul): I want to describe the Bridge for you. It stretches from heaven to earth by reason of my having joined myself with your humanity which I formed in the earth's clay. This bridge has three stairs. Two of them were built by my Son on the wood of the most holy cross, and the third even as he tasted the bitterness of the gall and vinegar they gave him to drink. You will recognize in these three stairs three spiritual stages.

2. The Feet of Affection

The first stair is the feet which symbolize the affections. For just as the feet carry the body, the affections carry the soul. My Son's nailed feet are a stair by which you can climb to his side where you will see revealed his inmost heart. For when the soul has climbed up on the feet of affection and looked with her mind's eye into my Son's open heart, she begins to feel the love of her own heart in his consummate and unspeakable love. (I say consummate because it is not for his own good that he loves you; you cannot do him any good since he is one with me.)

Then the soul, seeing how much she is loved, is herself filled to overflowing with love. So, having climbed the second stair, she reaches the third. This is his mouth where she finds peace from the terrible war she has had to wage because of her sins.

3. Divinity Kneaded into the Clay of Humanity

At the first stair, lifting the feet of her affections from the earth, she stripped herself of sin. At the second she dressed herself in love for virtue. And at the third stage she tasted peace.

So the bridge has three stairs, and you can reach the last by climbing the first two. The last stair is so high that the flooding waters cannot strike it—for the venom of sin never touched my Son.

But though the bridge has been raised up so high, it still is joined to the earth. Do you know when it was raised up? When my Son was lifted up on the wood of the most holy cross he did not cut off his divinity from the lowly earth of your humanity. So though he was raised so high, he was not raised off the earth. In fact, his divinity is kneaded in the clay of your

humanity like one bread. Nor could anyone walk on that bridge until my Son was raised up. This is why he said, "If I am lifted up high I will draw everything to myself" (John 12:32).

4. Drawn by Love

When my goodness saw that you could be drawn in no other way, I sent him to be lifted onto the wood of the cross. I made of that cross an anvil where this child of humankind could be hammered into an instrument to release humankind from death and restore it to the life of grace. In this way he drew everything to himself: for he proved his inspeakable love, and the human heart is always drawn by love. He could not have shown you greater love than by giving his life for you (John 15:13). You can hardly resist being drawn by love, then, unless you foolishly refuse to be drawn.

I said that, having been raised up, he would draw everything to himself. This is true in two ways: First, the human heart is drawn by love as I said, and with all its powers: memory, understanding, and will. If these three powers are harmoniously united in my name, everything else you do, in fact or intention, will be drawn to union with me in peace through the movement of love, because all will be lifted up in the pursuit of crucified love. So my Truth indeed spoke truly when he said, "If I am lifted up high, I will draw everything to myself." For everything you do will be drawn to him when he draws your heart and its powers.

What he said is true also in the sense that everything was created for your use to serve your needs. But you who have the gift of reason were made not for yourselves but for me, to serve me with all your heart and all your love. So when you are drawn to me, everything is drawn with you because everything was made for you. It was necessary, then, that this bridge be raised high. And it had to have stairs so that you would be able to mount it more easily.

5. The Stones of True Virtue

This bridge has walls of stone so that travelers will not be hindered when it rains. Do you know what stones these are? They are the stones of true solid virtue. These stones were not, however, built into walls before my Son's passion. So no one could get to the final destination even though they walked along the pathway of virtue. For heaven had not yet been unlocked with the key of my Son's blood, and the rain of justice kept anyone from crossing over.

But after these stones were hewn on the body of the Word, my gentle Son (I have told you that he is the bridge), he built them into walls, tempering the mortar with his own blood. That is, his blood was mixed into the mortar of his divinity with the strong heat of burning love.

By my power the stones of virtue were built into walls on no less a foundation than himself, for all virtue draws life from him, nor is there any virtue that has not been tested in him. So no one can have any life-giving virtue but from him, that is, by following his example and his teaching. He perfected the virtues and planted them as living stones built into walls with his blood. So now all the faithful can walk without hindrance and with no cringing fear of the rain of divine justice because they are sheltered by the mercy that came down from heaven through the incarnation of this Son of mine.

6. The Key of His Blood

And how was heaven opened? With the key of his blood. So, you see, the bridge has walls and a roof of mercy. And the hostelry of holy Church is there to serve the bread of life and blood lest the journeying pilgrims, my creatures, grow weary and faint on the way. So has my love ordained that the blood and body of my only-begotten Son, wholly God and wholly human, be administered.

At the end of the bridge is the gate (which is, in fact, one with the bridge), which is the only way you can enter. This is why he said, "I am the light of the world; whoever walks with me walks not in darkness but in light" (John 8:12). And in another place my Truth said that no one could come to me except through him, and such is the truth (John 14:6).

7. The Light Undimmed by Falsehood

I explained all this to you because I wanted to let you see the way. So when he says that he is the Way, he is speaking the truth. And I have already shown you that he is the Way, in the image of a bridge. He says he is the Truth, and so he is, and whoever follows him goes the way of truth. And he is Life. If you follow his truth, you will have the life of grace and never die of hunger, for the Word has himself become your food.

Nor will you ever fall into darkness, for he is the light undimmed by any falsehood. Indeed, with his truth he confounds the lie with which the devil deceived Eve. That lie broke up the road to heaven, but Truth repaired it and walled it up with his blood.

Those who follow this way are children of the truth because they follow the truth. They pass through the gate of truth and find themselves in me. And I am one with the gate and the way that is my Son, eternal Truth, a sea of peace. But those who do not keep to this way travel below the river—a way not of stones, but of water. And since there is no restraining the water, no one can cross through it without drowning.

8. Continually Running On

Such are the pleasures and conditions of the world. Those whose love and desire are not grounded in the rock, but are set without order on created persons and things apart from me (and these, like water, are continually running on), run on just as they do. Though it seems to them that it is the created things they love that are running on by while they themselves remain firm, they are, in fact, continually running on to their end in death.

They would like to preserve themselves (that is, their lives and the things they love) and not run away to nothingness. But they cannot. Either death makes them leave all behind, or by my decree these created things are taken away from them. Such as these are following a lie by going the way of falsehood. They are children of the devil, who is the father of lies (John 8:44).

9. Every Bitterness Sweet, Every Burden Light

How foolish and blind are those who choose to cross through the water when the road has been built for them! This road is such a joy for those who travel on it that it makes every bitterness sweet for them, and every burden light. Though they are in the darkness of the body, they find light; and though they are mortal, they find life without death. For through love and the light of faith they taste eternal Truth, with the promise of refreshment in return for the weariness they have borne for me.

Your tongue could never tell, nor your ears hear, nor your eyes see the joy they have who travel on this road, for even in this life they have some foretaste of the good prepared for them in everlasting life. Now you have heard and seen what this bridge is like. I have told you all this to explain what I meant when I said that my only-begotten Son is a bridge, as you see he is, joining the most high with the most lowly.

BIBLE SELECTION: JOHN 14:1–11

"Do not let your hearts be troubled. Believe in God, believe also in me. [2]In my Father's house there are many dwelling places. If it were not so, would I have told you that I go to prepare a place for you? [3]And if I go and prepare a place for you, I will come again and will take you to myself, so that where I am, there you may be also. [4]And you know the way to the place where I am going." [5]Thomas said to him, "Lord, we do not know where you are going. How can we know the way?" [6]Jesus said to him, "I am the way, and the truth, and the life. No one comes to the Father except through me. [7]If you know me, you will know my Father also. From now on you do know him and have seen him."

[8]Philip said to him, "Lord, show us the Father, and we will be satisfied." [9]Jesus said to him, "Have I been with you all this time, Philip, and you still do not know me? Whoever has seen me has seen the Father. How can you say, 'Show us the Father'? [10]Do you not believe that I am in the Father and the Father is in me? The words that I say to you I do not speak on my own; but the Father who dwells in me does his works. [11]Believe me that I am in the Father and the Father is in me; but if you do not, then believe me because of the works themselves."

REFLECTION QUESTIONS

The following questions can be used for discussion within a small group, or used for journal reflections by individuals.

1. Describe the three stairs in your own words. In what ways have you experienced any of these?
2. The cross, for Catherine of Siena, is the bridge between God and humanity. Does Catherine believe that the cross of Jesus is the only way to God? Do you believe that the cross of Jesus is the only way? Explain.
3. While we cannot get to heaven on the merits of our personal virtues, they are of value in the Christian life once they are "mortared by the blood of Christ." In the area of personal behavior, how was your life changed as a result of your relationship to the saving blood of Christ?
4. In section 6, Catherine gives us a glimpse of the importance of the Church in the spiritual journey. What role does it play? In what ways does your church provide this benefit to travelers like yourself?
5. Catherine labored to explain the enigmatic phrase of Jesus, "I am the way." In the Bible passage above, Thomas tells Jesus that he, too, does not understand and asks to know the "way" to where Jesus is going. How does Jesus respond? If Catherine were present, how might she help Thomas understand?

SUGGESTED EXERCISES

The following exercises can be done by individuals, shared between spiritual friends, or used in the context of a small group. Choose one or more of the following.

1. Meditate on the heart of God. Take time this week to consider all that you mean to God. Allow yourself to bask in the glow of God's unending and unconditional love for you.
2. Although we cannot "get to the final destination" along the pathway of virtue, the solid stones of holiness need to be built into the bridge in order to keep the rains from destroying our pathway. Make it your aim this week to build a solid foundation by developing a new habit of holiness.
3. God uses his Church to provide sustenance for us along the way, notes Catherine. This week come to worship with an empty stomach, longing to receive the nourishment for your soul that God wants to provide through his Church.
4. Jesus said, "Let not your hearts be troubled." As you face any struggles this week, or feel any anxiety, lean on Jesus through faith. Trust that he knows what you are going through, and is able to care for you beyond your expectations.

REFLECTIONS

Catherine's kind of writing with its rich symbols and metaphors and allegories is hard for me to hear, trained as I am in historical/grammatical hermeneutics. Perhaps you found the reading difficult, too.

And yet, with all its excesses, there is something good here. God revealed his truth to her in this simple picture of Christ as a bridge "over troubled waters"—to use the words of a twentieth-century song. The gate on the bridge that proclaims Christ as the only way, the stairs that lead us more deeply into sanctification, the wall of virtues mortared by the blood of Christ—all these and more speak truth and life to us. So, while I, with my post-Reformation heritage, must work to hear her words, I can see that it is with good reason that the Roman Catholic church granted Catherine the title, "Doctor of the Church."

GOING DEEPER

Catherine of Siena. *The Dialogue.* Edited by Richard J. Payne. New York: Paulist, 1980. From *The Classics of Western Spirituality.* This is Catherine's major work, written two years before her death. (She called it simply "my book.") It is more an intimate conversation than a treatise. In it Catherine presents a series of questions or petitions to God the Father, and each time she receives a response and amplification.

Catherine of Siena. *Selected Letters of Catherine Benincasa: Saint Catherine of Siena as Seen in Her Letters.* Translated and edited by Vida D. Scudder. New York: Dutton, 1927.

da Capua, Raimonda. *The Life of St. Catherine of Siena.* Translated by George Lamb. New York: P. J. Kenedy, 1960.

Levasti, Arrigo. *My Servant, Catherine.* Translated by Dorothy M. White. Westminster, MD: Newman, 1954.

Dietrich Bonhoeffer (1906–1945)

INTRODUCTION TO THE AUTHOR

Bonhoeffer was born into a family of seven children in Breslau, Germany. He grew up in Berlin, where his father worked as a physician. His boyhood friends included the great scholar Adolf von Harnack and the historian Hans Delbrück.

At sixteen Bonhoeffer began his study of theology at Tübingen and presented his doctoral thesis at the age of twenty-one. He spent one year on the faculty of Union Theological Seminary in New York, where he became acquainted with American Christianity. His popularity as a teacher and writer grew when he returned to Germany, but in 1933 he delivered a radio broadcast denouncing the German public for its blind obedience to a "leader" (Hitler) whom he saw as dangerous. When Hitler came to power, Bonhoeffer left for England and served as the pastor of two churches. While preparing for a trip to visit with Mahatma Gandhi, he received a call to go back to Germany and serve as the head of a seminary to train young pastors. It was there, at Finkenwälde, that Bonhoeffer refined his understanding of Christian community. In April 1943 he was arrested and sent to prison and later implicated in a plot to assassinate Adolf Hitler. On April 8, 1945, he was hanged in Flossenbürg.

His writings live on today, inspiring men and women with his insights into the grace of God and the cost of discipleship. The following selection deals with the subject of Christian community, especially the role of Jesus Christ in the life of the Church.

EXCERPTS FROM *LIFE TOGETHER*

1. In and Through Jesus Christ

Christianity means community through Jesus Christ and in Jesus Christ. No Christian community is more or less than this. Whether it be a brief, single encounter or the daily fellowship of years, Christian community is only this. We belong to one another only through and in Jesus Christ.

What does this mean? It means, first, that a Christian needs others because of Jesus Christ. It means, second, that a Christian comes to others only through Jesus Christ. It means, third, that in Jesus Christ we have been chosen from eternity, accepted in time, and united for eternity.

First, the Christian is the man who no longer seeks his own salvation, his deliverance, his justification in himself, but in Jesus Christ alone. He knows that God's Word in Jesus Christ pronounces him guilty, even when he does not feel his guilt, and God's Word pronounces him righteous, even when he does not feel that he is righteous at all. The Christian no longer lives of himself by his own claims and of his own justification, but by God's claims and God's justification. He lives wholly by God's Word pronounced upon him whether that Word declares him guilty or innocent.

2. Alien Righteousness

The death and the life of the Christian is not determined by his own resources; rather he finds both only in the Word that comes to him from the outside, in God's Word to him. The Reformers expressed it this way: Our righteousness is an "alien righteousness," a righteousness that comes from outside of us (*extra nos*). They were saying that the Christian is dependent on the Word of God spoken to him. He is pointed outward, to the Word that comes to him.

The Christian lives wholly by the truth of God's Word in Jesus Christ. If somebody asks him, Where is your salvation, your righteousness? he can never point to himself. He points to the Word of God in Jesus Christ which assures him salvation and righteousness. He is as alert as possible to this Word. Because he daily hungers and thirsts for righteousness, he daily desires the redeeming Word.

And it can come only from the outside. In himself he is destitute and dead. Help must come from the outside, and it has come and comes daily and anew in the Word of Jesus Christ, bringing redemption, righteousness, innocence, and blessedness.

3. Christ in the Word of Another

But God has put this Word into the mouth of others in order that it may be communicated to us. When one person is struck by the Word, he speaks it to others. God has willed that we should seek and find his living Word in the witness of a brother, in the mouth of a man. Therefore, the Christian needs another Christian who speaks God's Word to him. He needs him again and again when he becomes uncertain and discouraged, for by himself he cannot help himself without belying the truth.

He needs his brother as a bearer and proclaimer of the divine word of salvation. He needs his brother solely because of Jesus Christ. The Christ in his own heart is weaker than the Christ in the word of his brother; his own heart is uncertain, his brother's is sure.

And that also clarifies the goal of all Christian community: they meet one another as bringers of the message of salvation. As such, God permits them to meet together and gives them community. Their fellowship is founded solely upon Jesus Christ and this "alien righteousness." All we can say, therefore, is: the community of Christians springs solely from the Biblical and Reformation message of the justification of man through grace alone; this alone is the basis of the longing of Christians for one another.

4. Christ Opened the Way

Second, a Christian comes to others only through Jesus Christ. Among people there is strife. "He is our peace," says Paul of Jesus Christ (Eph. 2:14). Without Christ there is discord between God and man and between man and man. Christ became the Mediator and made peace with God and among men.

Without Christ we should not know God, we could not call upon him, nor come to him. But without Christ we also could not know our brother, nor could we come to him. The way is blocked by our own ego. Christ opened the way to God and to our brother. Now Christians can live with one another in peace; they can love and serve one another; they can become one. But they can continue to do so only by way of Jesus Christ. Only in Jesus Christ are we one, only through him are we bound together. To eternity he remains the one Mediator.

5. We Are in Him

Third, when God's Son took on flesh, he truly and bodily took on, out of pure grace, our being, our nature, ourselves. This was the eternal counsel of the triune God. Now we are in him. Where he is, there we are too, in the incarnation, on the Cross, and in his resurrection. We belong to him because we are in him. That is why the Scriptures call us the Body of Christ.

But if, before we could know and wish it, we have been chosen and accepted with the whole Church in Jesus Christ, then we also belong to him in eternity *with* one another. We who live here in fellowship with him will one day be with him in eternal fellowship.

He who looks upon his brother should know that he will be eternally united with him in Jesus Christ. Christian community means community in and through Jesus Christ. On this presupposition rests everything that the Scriptures provide in the way of directions and precepts for the communal life of Christians.

6. Made Ready to Forgive

"But as touching brotherly love ye need not that I write unto you: for ye yourselves are taught of God to love one another. . . . but we beseech you, brethren, that ye increase more and more" (1 Thess. 4:9, 10, KJV). God himself has undertaken to teach brotherly love; all that men can do to add to it is to remember this divine instruction and the admonition to excel in it more and more. When God was merciful, when he revealed Jesus Christ to us as our Brother, when he won our hearts by his love, this was the beginning of our instruction in divine love.

When God was merciful to us, we learned to be merciful with our brethren. When we received forgiveness instead of judgment, we, too, were made ready to forgive our brethren. What God did to us, we then owed to others. The more we received, the more we were able to give; and the more meager our brotherly love, the less were we living by God's mercy and love. Thus God himself taught us to meet one another as God has met us in Christ. "Wherefore receive ye one another, as Christ also received us to the glory of God" (Rom. 15:7, KJV).

7. The Basis of Our Community

In this wise does one, whom God has placed in common life with other Christians, learn what it means to have brothers. "Brethren in the Lord," Paul calls his congregation (Phil. 1:14). One is a brother to another only through Jesus Christ. I am a brother to another person through what Jesus Christ did for me and to me; the other person has become a brother to me through what Jesus Christ did for him.

The fact that we are brethren only through Jesus Christ is of immeasurable significance.

Not only the other person who is earnest and devout, who comes to me seeking brotherhood, must I deal with in fellowship. My brother is rather that other person who has been redeemed by Christ, delivered from sin, and called to faith and eternal life.

Not what a man is in himself as a Christian, his spirituality and piety, constitutes the basis of our community. What determines our brotherhood is what that man is by reason of Christ. Our community with one another consists solely in what Christ has done to both of us. This is true not merely at the beginning, and though in the course of time something else were to be added to our community; it remains so for all the future and to all eternity.

I have community with others and I shall continue to have it only through Jesus Christ. The more genuine and the deeper our community becomes, the more will everything else between us recede, the more clearly and purely will Jesus Christ and his work become the one and only thing that is vital between us. We have one another only through Christ, but through Christ we do have one another, wholly, and for all eternity.

That dismisses once and for all every clamorous desire for something more. One who wants more than what Christ has established does not want Christian brotherhood. He is looking for some extraordinary social experience which he has not found elsewhere; he is bringing muddled and impure desires into Christian brotherhood. Christian brotherhood is not an ideal which we must realize; it is rather a reality created by God in Christ in which we may participate.

BIBLE SELECTION: EPHESIANS 2:11–22

[11]So then, remember that at one time you Gentiles by birth, called "the uncircumcision" by those who are called "the circumcision"—a physical circumcision made in the flesh by human hands—[12]remember that you were at that time without Christ, being aliens from the commonwealth of Israel, and strangers to the covenants of promise, having no hope and without God in the world. [13]But now in Christ Jesus you who once were far off have been brought near by the blood of Christ. [14]For he is our peace; in his flesh he has made both groups into one and has broken down the dividing wall, that is, the hostility between us. [15]He has abolished the law with its commandments and ordinances, that he might create in himself one new humanity in place of the two, thus making peace, [16]and might reconcile both groups to God in one body through the cross, thus putting to death that hostility through it. [17]So he came and proclaimed peace to you who were far off and peace to those who were near; [18]for through him both of us have access in one Spirit to the Father. [19]So then you are no longer strangers and aliens, but you are citizens with the saints and also members of the household of God, [20]built upon the foundation of the apostles and prophets, with Christ Jesus himself as the cornerstone. [21]In him the whole structure is joined together and grows into a holy temple in the Lord; [22]in whom you also are built together spiritually into a dwelling place for God.

REFLECTION QUESTIONS

The following questions can be used for discussion within a small group, or used for journal reflections by individuals.

1. According to Dietrich Bonhoeffer, why do we need other Christians? Along those same lines, how should we evaluate other Christians?

2. If someone were to ask you, "From where does your righteousness, your salvation, come?" how would you answer? How does Bonhoeffer tell us we should answer that question? (See section 2.)

3. Bonhoeffer believes that God has chosen to use people as a means of communicating the Word to us. Describe a time when God used someone else to speak to you.

4. When we are forgiven, says Bonhoeffer, we are made ready to forgive. Describe your ability to forgive. Does it match your understanding of how much God has forgiven you? Explain.

5. Why, according to Paul in Ephesians 2:11–22, does the blood of Christ make unity possible between Jew and Gentile? What are some practical ways in which you can begin showing unity in your church, or campus, or neighborhood, or fellowship group?

SUGGESTED EXERCISES

The following exercises can be done by individuals, shared between spiritual friends, or used in the context of a small group. Choose one or more of the following.

1. This week begin viewing other Christians as Bonhoeffer has described them. Focus on the fact that Christ is in them, and that you are able to experience Christ in that brother or sister.

2. As you go to church this week, put an end to the incessant desire for an "extraordinary social experience," and instead look upon others as bringers of salvation. Focus on Christ, not on the skills of those leading worship.

3. All of us, writes Bonhoeffer, will be eternally united with Christ and with one another. Therefore, make an effort this week to tear down any walls of hostility. Let Christ be the Mediator as you make peace with those in your community of faith.

4. Paul encouraged the Ephesians to remember the former time when they were separated from Christ and each other. Set aside some time this week to reflect on your life before Christ. Use this reflection as a way of developing a sense of gratitude.

REFLECTIONS

In Life Together *Bonhoeffer makes crystal clear the fundamental difference between radical Christian fellowship and the community of natural desire. With sadness I have had to recognize that the very way we arrange our lives in middle America effectively excludes us from life together. To take Bonhoeffer seriously would mean such a total rethinking of the life of faith that the entire socioeconomic structures of our lives would be revolutionized.*

Life Together is a salty book to dig into if you are tired of "sweetness and light for God's little flock" and are prepared for "costly grace."

GOING DEEPER

Bethge, Eberhard. *Costly Grace: An Illustrated Introduction to Dietrich Bonhoeffer.* New York: Harper & Row, 1979. A brief but excellent biography by a friend and colleague of Bonhoeffer. Bethge has also written a definitive biography (over eight hundred pages) titled simply *Dietrich Bonhoeffer.*

Bonhoeffer, Dietrich. *The Cost of Discipleship.* New York: Macmillan/Collier, 1963. This practical study of the Sermon on the Mount has had a tremendous influence on the Church. It is from this book that Bonhoeffer gave to the world his powerful term *cheap grace.* You should also be aware of two devotional-style books, *Psalms: The Prayer Book of the Church* and *Meditating on the Word.*

Bonhoeffer, Dietrich. *Ethics.* New York: Macmillan, 1955. Bonhoeffer's most important work and one that still has an influence today. You may also want to read his *Letters and Papers from Prison.*

Bonhoeffer, Dietrich. *Life Together.* San Francisco: Harper & Row, 1954. Must reading. The seminary at Finkenwälde was primarily a male sfellowship which, in part, accounts for the masculine-dominated language, so don't be turned away from the book on that account. It gives practical advice on how life together in Christ can be sustained in families and in groups.

The Word-Centered Life

THE EVANGELICAL TRADITION (the Word-Centered Life) has two foci: the centrality of Scripture and the importance of evangelism. In following this tradition, we are taking seriously both the Reformation call of *Sola Scriptura* (the Scripture alone) and the Pietist experience of "the warm heart," or conversion.

Two of our authors give special attention to the value of Scripture— E. Stanley Jones and Madame Guyon. Jones calls us to three simple habits: "First, the habit of reading the Word of God daily," "Second, pray in private by habit," and "Third, pass on to others what you have found." Guyon invites us all into the experience of "praying the Scripture" and "beholding the Lord."

John Chrysostom deals with the subject of conversion but he does so in a broader, more expansive way than that to which we are usually accustomed. Francis of Assisi describes his own calling to the work of evangelism, and Watchman Nee gives us practical counsel in the work of evangelism. Sadhu Sundar Singh's whole life was one of evangelism. Charles Spurgeon helps us see our great need for spiritual revival, both individually and as a Church.

Some of us may find these topics a bit threatening, and yet our mentors write in such natural and inviting ways that we can feel safe exploring these important issues.

E. Stanley Jones (1884–1973)

INTRODUCTION TO THE AUTHOR

E. Stanley Jones devoted his whole life to the subject of conversion. He was one of the best-known missionaries and religious writers in the first half of the twentieth century. Beginning in 1908, Jones worked among the high-caste Hindus and Muslims in India. Later in his life, he divided his time between missionary work in India and evangelistic missions in the United States.

One of his great accomplishments was the establishment of the Ashram, a Hindu word that means "retreat." This movement spread across the United States in the middle part of this century and continues in some measure today. The Ashram is a week-long structured Christian retreat that focuses on solitude and community building.

E. Stanley Jones had a keen understanding of the spiritual life and the means of spiritual renewal. The following selection discusses the delicate balance between the activity of God and the response of his children in the establishment and cultivation of conversion.

EXCERPTS FROM CONVERSION

1. Receptivity and Response

Conversion is a gift and an achievement. It is the act of a moment and the work of a lifetime. You cannot attain salvation by disciplines—it is the gift of God. But you cannot retain it without disciplines. If you try to attain salvation by disciplines, you will be trying to discipline an unsurrendered self. You will be sitting on a lid. The result will be tenseness instead of trust. "You will wrestle instead of nestle." While salvation cannot be attained by discipline around an unsurrendered self, nevertheless when the self is surrendered to Christ and a new center formed, then you can discipline your life around that new center—Christ. Discipline is the fruit of conversion—not the root.

This passage gives the double-sidedness of conversion: "As therefore you received Christ Jesus the Lord, so live in him, rooted and built up in him and established in the faith" (Col. 2:6–7, RSV). Note, "received"—receptivity; "so live"—activity. It appears again, "rooted"—receptivity; "built up in him"—activity.

The "rooted" means we take from God as the roots take from the soil; the "built up" means we build up as one builds a house, a character and life by disciplined effort. So we take and try; we obtain and attain. We trust as if the whole thing depended on God and work as if the whole thing depended on us. The alternate beats of the Christian heart are receptivity and response—receptivity from God and response in work from us.

2. Simple Habits

The best Man that ever lived on our planet illustrated this receptivity and response rhythm. No one was so utterly dependent on God and no one was more personally disciplined in his habits.

He did three things by habit: (1) "He stood up to read as was his custom"—he read the Word of God by habit. (2) "He went out into the mountain to pray as was his custom"—he prayed by habit. (3) "He taught them again as was his custom"—he passed on to others by habit what he had and what he had found.

These simple habits were the foundation habits of his life. They are as up-to-date as tomorrow morning. No converted person can live without those habits at work vitally in his life.

3. God Interpreting Himself

First, the habit of reading the Word of God daily, preferably in the morning. The New Testament is the inspired record of the Revelation—the revelation is the person of Jesus Christ. He moves out of the pages of this Book and meets us with the impact of his person on our persons. That impact is cleansing. "Now you are clean through the word which I have spoken unto you." When you "expose your all to his everything," then you submit yourself to

a daily cleansing of the mind, of motive, of emotions.

I know two brilliant Christians who come to the daily morning devotions without their Bibles. They can meditate, they say. They are both shallow. For they mediate God to themselves through their own thinking—they become the medium. They do not go to God direct as they imagine—they go through their own thinking; they become the mediator. That is why we have to have the revelation of God through the Word. It is God interpreting himself to us. His interpretation of himself is Jesus. When you expose your thinking to him, you expose yourself to God. These words of the New Testament have been in such close contact with the Word that they are vibrant with Life.

Dr. Howard Atwood Kelly, professor of gynecological surgery at Johns Hopkins, says of reading the Bible, "Such reading applied with an honest heart transforms the nature, enables the prostitute to love holiness and become an angel of mercy, and raises the beggar and the drunkard to set them among the princes of the earth." He said again: "The Bible vindicates itself because it is such excellent medicine. It has never failed to cure a single patient if only he took his prescription honestly."

Take the prescription of the Word of God daily. No Christian is sound who is not scriptural.

4. Perennially Fresh with God

Second, pray in private by habit. When we read the Scripture, God speaks to us. In prayer we speak to God. Then God speaks to us, no longer through the Word only, but directly in words to us.

Carlyle says: "Prayer is and remains the native and deepest impulse of the soul of man." Lincoln said: "I have been driven many times to my knees by the overwhelming conviction that I had nowhere else to go; my own conviction and that of those around me seemed insufficient for the day."

Lincoln practiced prayer. A gentleman with an appointment to meet Lincoln at five A.M. arrived fifteen minutes early. He heard a voice in the next room and asked the attendant: "Who is in the next room? Someone with the President?" "No, he is reading the Bible and praying." "Is that his habit so early in the morning?" "Yes, sir, he spends each morning from four to five in reading the Scriptures and praying." No wonder we cannot forget Lincoln. He is perennially fresh with God.

There is no experience of conversion which will make you immune against the lack of reading the word of God and prayer. When prayer fades out, power fades out. We are as spiritual as we are prayerful; no more, no less.

5. The Converted Convert

Third, pass on to others what you have found. The third habit is the habit of passing on to others what has been given to us in the reading of the Word and prayer. It is a law of the mind that that which is not expressed dies. If you don't share it, you won't have it.

Paul says, "He who supplies seed to the sower" (2 Cor. 9:10, RSV). He gives seed only to those who sow it. If you don't sow it, you will have nothing to sow. Those who do not pass on to others are themselves empty. The converted convert, or they don't stay converted. Unless you are evangelistic, you don't remain evangelical.

These three things are basic in the cultivation of the converted life. Without them the converted life will fade out. In addition to them certain auxiliary suggestions must be made.

6. Keep the Fire Burning

First, cultivate the new life by daily disciplines. Commissioner Brengle of the Salvation Army, a center of great spiritual power, suggests three things to keep the fire burning: "Keep the draught open; clean the ashes out; keep putting in fuel."

Second, keep honest at any cost. A South African boy had won a swimming championship, but he was six months over age when he won it. Then he was converted. He brought his beloved trophy in his hands and made a clean breast of it before the committee.

Third, keep confessing your sins after conversion. Don't be afraid to say: "I am sorry. I was wrong." The rule about confessing your sins should be, the circle of confession should be the circle affected by the sin. If the sin has been against an individual, confess it to that individual; if against a family, to a family; if against a group, then to a group; if against a church, to a church.

7. Conversions, Unlimited

Fourth, pray for those who have wronged you. That will be an antidote for resentments and bitterness. A theological professor keeps a card index of nasty letters he receives and prays for their writers every day. No wonder his spirit has an extraordinary sweetness. A friend of mine was shot at by a youth, who because of it was sent to prison for twelve years. My friend kept in touch with him through those prison years, and now that his term of sentence is over, he has taken him into his home.

Fifth, constantly enlarge the area of your conversion. Make your conversion take in more and more areas of your life. In the Sat Tal Ashram in India we gave the servants, including the sweeper, a holiday one day each week, and we volunteered to do their jobs for them. The sweeper's work included the cleaning of the latrines before the days of flush toilets. No one would touch that job but an outcaste, but we volunteered.

One day I said to a Brahmin convert who was hesitating to volunteer: "Brother C., when are you going to volunteer?" He shook his head slowly and said: "Brother Stanley, I'm converted, but I'm not converted that far." Some of our conversions are "Conversions, Limited," and some are "Conversions, Unlimited." Some take in the individual life, but not the social and economic. Some let their conversion function within their class and race, but not among all classes and all races.

A little girl was kneeling on her father's lap and was telling him how much she loved him, but she was looking over her father's shoulder and making faces at her little brother. The mother saw it and said: "You little hypocrite, you telling your father you love him and then making faces and sticking out your tongue at your little brother." Christians who hold race prejudices do just that. They tell God the Father they love him and then look over his shoulder and tell his other children they despise them. How can we love God whom we have not seen unless we love his children whom we do see?

8. Habits That Cannot Be Christianized

Sixth, give up habits that cannot be Christianized. In Africa a Christian teacher used to go off on weekends and drink. He became drunk and went into a native hut and slept. When he woke up, an old man was seated looking at him. The old man asked him who he was, and was told that he was a Christian. When he asked the old man who he was, he replied, "I'm not a Christian, but if I were, I wouldn't be living the way you are—I'd really live as a Christian." This awakened the teacher; he was really converted and lived a Christian life afterwards—converted by an unconverted man!

Why should children of God cut their life expectancy in half by deliberately taking poison into their systems in smoking? This is the finding of those who have investigated. Why try to prove yourself an exception? Why hasten the process of decay by smoking?

9. Seven Vital Virtues

After partaking of the divine nature add these things:

> . . . supplement your faith with virtue, and virtue with knowledge, and knowledge with self-control, and self-control with steadfastness, and steadfastness with godliness, and godliness with brotherly affection, and brotherly affection with love. (2 Pet. 1:5b–7)

Sit down every day and go over these seven things and ask yourself if you are adding them to your basic faith—virtue, knowledge, self-control, steadfastness, godliness, brotherly affection, and love. Check up to see whether you are going up or down in each of these qualities—especially the last one. All growth in Christian living is a growth in love. You may add the other six to your faith, but if you don't add love, then you are going down as a Christian.

Enlarge the area of your conversion, taking in fresh territory every day.

BIBLE SELECTION: COLOSSIANS 2:6–7

⁶As you therefore have received Christ Jesus the Lord, continue to live your lives in him, ⁷rooted and built up in him and established in the faith, just as you were taught, abounding in thanksgiving.

REFLECTION QUESTIONS

The following questions can be used for discussion within a small group, or used for journal reflections by individuals.

1. Conversion, writes E. Stanley Jones, is both receiving the work of God and responding to this gift by disciplined effort. How have you learned to keep both of these in balance? Have there been times when you leaned too far in one direction? Describe.
2. The Bible is a central medium of communication between God and his people, especially in regard to personal transformation. Jones even compares the daily reading of the Bible to taking medicine. How has the Bible shaped your thoughts, your actions, and your beliefs?
3. "In prayer we speak to God. Then God speaks to us," writes Jones. Does God speak to you in your times of prayer? Describe.
4. According to Jones, what will happen to us if we do not pass on to others the insights and teachings that God has given us? Have you experienced this miracle of "seed supply"?
5. According to Colossians 2:6–7, our life with Christ is like a tree. Using this metaphor, how would you describe the tree of your spiritual life? How are its roots? Its branches? Its fruit?

SUGGESTED EXERCISES

The following exercises can be done by individuals, shared between spiritual friends, or used in the context of a small group. Choose one or more of the following.

1. Develop the habit, if you have not already done so, of reading the Word of God daily. Establish a consistent time, place, and pattern. Make this habit a high priority this week.

2. In similar fashion, if you have not already done so, begin a regular habit of praying in private. You may have to rise early in order to make time, but remember, "When prayer fades out, power fades out."

3. Scatter some "seeds" this week by passing on to others some of the things God has been teaching you. This kind of personal sharing is always a benefit to others. Do not worry about it being wise or intellectual enough, simply share what God is doing in your life, and watch others warm up to the good news.

4. Try E. Stanley Jones's exercise found in section 9. Using 2 Peter 1:5b–7 as your checklist, go over these seven virtues on a daily basis, noting whether you are seeing an increase or a decrease.

REFLECTIONS

You may have found yourself struggling with this selection by E. Stanley Jones because his way of speaking of conversion is not common today. We are accustomed to hearing about conversion in the context of assenting to certain statements and reciting a certain prayer. Jones, on the other hand, sees conversion as the activity of God on our behalf that results in the transformation and reordering of the total life. That is, we accept Christ as our Life!

I would suggest to you that Jones has a fuller, more biblical understanding of conversion than that promulgated today in popular religion. Conversion does not make us perfect, but it does catapult us into a total experience of discipleship that affects—and infects—every sphere of our living. When we begin our pilgrimage of faith, we may not know all that conversion to Christ will mean, but we can be assured that no corner of our lives will be left untouched.

GOING DEEPER

Jones, E. Stanley. *The Christ of Every Road*. New York: Abingdon, 1930. Perhaps Jones's best-known book, this useful study of Pentecost discusses a great variety of topics, e.g., "Pentecost and Sex," "Pentecost and Personality."

Two other books in the series are worth noting: *The Christ of the Mount* and *The Christ of the Indian Road*.

Jones, E. Stanley. *Conversion*. New York: Abingdon, 1959. Clearly E. Stanley Jones understood conversion in a much larger, more biblical context than is common today. That alone makes this book worthwhile. Add to it Jones's missionary breadth from years of working with Hindus, Muslims, and a host of other groups and you have a book that deserves to endure.

Jones, E. Stanley. *Growing Spiritually.* New York: Abingdon-Cokesbury, 1953. Jones wrote a series of daily devotional guides, of which this is one. Others in the series include *How to Be a Transformed Person, Christian Maturity,* and *Abundant Living.*

Sadhu Sundar Singh (1889–1933?)

INTRODUCTION TO THE AUTHOR

Sadhu Sundar Singh has been called the St. Paul of India. His conversion to Christ is one of the great stories of the faith. Sundar was raised a Sikh and so had studied intently the holy book of the Sikh religion, the Granth Sahib, and also the Hindu sacred book, the Gita. His piety even as a child was known throughout the region.

Sundar's mother died when he was just a teenager, and her death threw the young man into overwhelming grief. He railed at God, even publicly burning the Bibles of the Christian missionaries of the area.

Finally, Sundar's despair led him to plan his own death. For three days and nights he stayed in his room. "If God wants me to live, let him say so," he exclaimed. "Oh God, if there be a God, reveal yourself to me tonight." His plan was simple and carefully thought out: if God did not speak to him before morning, he would go out to the railway line, lay his head on the rails, and wait in the darkness for the 5:00 A.M. train from Ludhiana to end his misery. For seven hours he waited in silent meditation. At 4:45 A.M., witnesses Sundar, a bright cloud of light suddenly filled his room and out of the brightness came the face and figure of Jesus. Sundar had been expecting Krishna or one of his own gods, but not Jesus. Yet, he was certain it was Jesus. He spoke to Sundar in Hindustani: "How long are you going to persecute me? I died for you. For you I gave my life. You were praying to know the right way; why don't you take it? I am the Way."

As a result of this vision, Sundar's life was dramatically and irrevocably changed and he was led into one of the most remarkable ministries of the twentieth century.

EXCERPTS FROM *WITH AND WITHOUT CHRIST*

1. A Hidden and Inexhaustible Mine

It is very difficult to explain the deep experience of the inner life. As Goethe has said: "The highest cannot be spoken." But it can be enjoyed and put into action. This is what I mean. One day, during my meditation and prayer, I felt his presence strongly. My heart overflowed with heavenly joy. I saw that in this world of sorrow and suffering there is a hidden and inexhaustible mine of great joy of which the world knows nothing, because even those who experience it are not able to speak of it adequately and convincingly.

I was anxious to go down to the neighboring village to share that joy with others. But, because of my physical illness, there arose a conflict between my soul and my body. The soul wanted to go but the body lagged behind. But finally I overcame and dragged my sick body and told the people in the village what Christ's presence had done for me and would do for them.

They knew that I was ill and that there was some inner compulsion which urged me to speak to them. Thus, though I was unable to explain all that Christ's presence had meant to me, that deep experience had been translated into action and people had been helped. Where the tongue is lacking, life, through action, reveals the reality. As St. Paul says: "The letter kills, but the Spirit gives life" (2 Cor. 3:6, NIV).

2. God's Sweet and Life-Giving Presence

As some insects with their antennae feel their surroundings and distinguish between hurtful and useful things, so spiritual people, through their inner senses, avoid dangerous and destructive influences and enjoy God's sweet and life-giving presence; they are constrained by their blissful experience to bear witness to God. As Tertullian has said: "Whenever the soul comes to itself and attains something of its natural soundness, it speaks of God."

Almost everyone has an inner capacity— some more, some less—to sense spiritual truths without knowing how they have attained them. As someone has said: "They know without knowing how." For instance, Colburn, when six years old, was asked how many seconds there are in eleven years. In four seconds he gave the correct answer. When questioned as to how he had arrived at the answer, all he could say was that the answer had come to his mind. Just so God reveals spiritual realities to those who seek to live according to his will.

3. Those Without the Joyful Inner Life in God

The will to live, which is present in every person, is an impulse urging us to carry life to its perfection, that is, to that state in which the purpose of God for each life will be fulfilled, so that we will be eternally happy in Him. On the other hand, to those who are without the experience of the joyful inner life in God, life is a burden. Schopenhauer was one of these; he said: "Life is hell."

There is nothing strange in such people wanting to commit suicide. As a result of the teaching of the Greek philosopher, Hegesias, many young men committed suicide. Also, several philosophers like Zeno, Empedocles, and Seneca, put an end to their lives. But the strange thing is that their philosophy did not show them how to remove those things which made them unhappy instead of destroying their lives.

Such is the philosophy of the world (James 3:15). Although some, who are tired of this life on account of its struggles and anxieties, may repress the will-to-live, but cannot repress the will-to-believe. Even if they have no belief in God or in any other spiritual reality, they have at least a belief in their unbelief, though Pyrrho said: "We cannot even be sure that we are not sure."

4. Satisfying the Inner Craving

The inner life cannot be freed by changing the place or by killing the body, but only by putting off the "old person" and putting on the new person, thus passing from death to life. Those who go astray, instead of satisfying their inner craving in the Creator, try to satisfy it in their own crooked ways. The result is that, instead of being happy and satisfied, they become miserable.

For instance, a thief who is stealing and hoarding things as a means of happiness is not only missing his happiness, but by his acts of theft is destroying the very capacity for it. That capacity is deadened by his sinful conduct. And if he loses the sense of the sinfulness of theft and his conscience does not feel remorse, he has already committed spiritual suicide. He has not only killed the capacity but has killed the soul which had the capacity.

5. Satisfying This Tiny Heart

Real joy and peace do not depend on power, kingly wealth, or other material possessions. If this were so, all people of wealth in the world would be happy and contented, and princes like Buddha, Mahavira, and Bhartari would not have renounced their kingdom. But this real and permanent joy is found only in the Kingdom of God, which is established in the heart when we are born again.

The secret and reality of this blissful life in God cannot be understood without receiving, living, and experiencing it. If we try to understand it only with the intellect, we will find our effort useless. A scientist had a bird in his hand. He saw that it had life, and, wanting to find out in what part of the bird's body the life was, he began dissecting the bird. The result

was that the very life of which he was in search disappeared mysteriously. Those who try to understand the inner life merely intellectually will meet with a similar failure. The life for which they are looking will vanish in the analysis.

In comparison with this big world, the human heart is only a small thing. Though the world is so large, it is utterly unable to satisfy this tiny heart. Our ever growing soul and its capacities can be satisfied only in the infinite God. As water is restless until it reaches its level, so the soul has no peace until it rests in God.

6. The Eternally Growing Soul

The material body cannot keep company forever with the spirit. After fulfilling its purpose for some time as the instrument of the soul for its work in the world, the body begins to refuse, through weakness and old age, to go along with the spirit any further. This is because the body cannot keep pace with the eternally growing soul.

Although the soul and body cannot live together forever, the fruits of the work which they have done together will remain forever. So it is necessary to lay carefully the foundation of our eternal life. But the pity of it is that we, by the misuse of freedom, can lose it forever. Freedom means the capacity to do either good or bad deeds. By constantly choosing to do bad deeds, we become slaves of sin and destroy our freedom and life (John 8:21, 34).

By giving up our sins, on the other hand, and by following the truth, we are made free forever (John 8:32). The works of those who are thus made free and spend all their life in God's service, that is, of those who die in the Lord, will follow them (Rev. 14:13). To die in the Lord does not mean death, for the Lord is "the Lord of the living and not of the dead," but to die in the Lord means losing oneself in his work. As the Lord said: "Those who want to save their life will lose it, and those who lose their life for my sake will save it" (Luke 9:24).

7. The Habit Formed Now

We ought to make the best possible use of God-given opportunities and should not waste our precious time by neglect or carelessness. Many people say: there is plenty of time to do this or that; don't worry. But they do not realize that if they do not make good use of this short time, the habit formed now will be so ingrained that when more time is given to us, this habit will become our second nature and we shall waste that time also. "Whoever is faithful in a very little is faithful also in much" (Luke 16:10).

8. One Spirit, Different Results

Now it is right that every one of us should fulfill in our life the purpose of our Creator and spend that life for the glory of God and the good of others. Each of us should follow our calling and carry on our work according to our God-given gifts and capacities. "There are diversities of gifts but the same Spirit" (1 Cor. 12:4, 11, KJV).

The same breath is blown into the flute, cornet, and bagpipe, but different music is produced according to the different instruments. In the same way the one Spirit works in us, God's children, but different results are produced, and God is glorified through them according to each one's temperament and personality.

BIBLE SELECTION: ACTS 9:1–19

Meanwhile Saul, still breathing threats and murder against the disciples of the Lord, went to the high priest [2]and asked him for letters to the synagogues at Damascus, so that if he found any who belonged to the Way, men or women, he might bring them bound to Jerusalem. [3]Now as he was going along and approaching Damascus, suddenly a light from heaven flashed around him. [4]He fell to the ground and heard a voice saying to him, "Saul, Saul, why do you persecute me?" [5]He asked, "Who are you, Lord?" The reply came, "I am Jesus, whom you are persecuting. [6]But get up and enter the city, and you will be told what you are to do." [7]The men who were traveling with him stood speechless because they heard the voice but saw no one. [8]Saul got up from the ground, and though his eyes were open, he could see nothing; so they led him by the hand and brought him into Damascus. [9]For three days he was without sight, and neither ate nor drank.

[10]Now there was a disciple in Damascus named Ananias. The Lord said to him in a vision, "Ananias." He answered, "Here I am, Lord." [11]The Lord said to him, "Get up and go to the street called Straight, and at the house of Judas look for a man of Tarsus named Saul. At this moment he is praying, [12]and he has seen in a vision a man named Ananias come in and lay his hands on him so that he might regain his sight." [13]But Ananias answered, "Lord, I have heard from many about this man, how much evil he has done to your saints in Jerusalem;

[14]and here he has authority from the chief priests to bind all who invoke your name." [15]But the Lord said to him, "Go, for he is an instrument whom I have chosen to bring my name before Gentiles and kings and before the people of Israel; [16]I myself will show him how much he must suffer for the sake of my name." [17]So Ananias went and entered the house. He laid his hands on Saul and said, "Brother Saul, the Lord Jesus, who appeared to you on your way here, has sent me so that you may regain your sight and be filled with the Holy Spirit." [18]And immediately something like scales fell from his eyes, and his sight was restored. Then he got up and was baptized, [19]and after taking some food, he regained his strength.

REFLECTION QUESTIONS

The following questions can be used for discussion within a small group, or used for journal reflections by individuals.

1. Sadhu Sundar Singh writes that even though our words cannot convey our experiences of God, our actions can. If someone were to look at your life (and not merely your words), what would it be telling that person?

2. In section 5, the author tells the story of a scientist who dissected a bird to find out its source of life. What happened? To what does Sundar compare this?

3. Making use of our time, and avoiding procrastination, was important to Sundar. In what areas of your life would you like to begin using your time more effectively?

4. Each of us, writes the author, is inspired by the same Spirit, but we produce different results, as the same breath makes different sounds with different musical instruments. What is your contribution to the Christian community? What "sound" is God producing in your life?

5. God stopped Saul on the road to Damascus and changed the course of his life. Has God's call ever stopped you in your tracks, changing the course of your life? Describe.

SUGGESTED EXERCISES

The following exercises can be done by individuals, shared between spiritual friends, or used in the context of a small group. Choose one or more of the following.

1. Sadhu Sundar Singh acted on his desire to share with neighbors the joy he had experienced. This week look for ways to share your joy. Do not worry too much about your words; simply share the delights in your heart.

2. Increase your capacity to receive God's blessings by putting an end to sinful conduct, as the author encourages us to do. Put off the "old person," as the Bible urges, by paying no attention to the distractions that have hindered you.

3. Learn to be faithful in the little things, as Jesus said (Luke 16:10). Make good use of time, redeeming the moments by taking advantage of your opportunities to share your faith, to pray, or to read Scripture.

4. Use the coming week to examine the course of your life. Like Saul who would become Paul, be open to the call and ready to make a change if necessary.

REFLECTIONS

I love the many stories about Sundar Singh. Even his teachings, of which the selections you read are a part, have stories tied to them. Following his remarkable conversion, he adopted the yellow saffron robe of the sadhus, the holy men of India. But he was a sadhu with a difference—traveling from village to village proclaiming the good news of life in Jesus Christ. Like his Master he had no home, no possessions. He belonged to the road, sharing the suffering of his people, eating with those who gave him shelter, and telling all who would listen of the love of God. Even his death is a story shrouded in mystery and adventure. More than once he had sought to bring the gospel message into the great mountains of Tibet, with each attempt ending in failure. In April 1929, Sadhu Sundar Singh was seen on a high mountain trail that leads into Tibet. He has never been heard from or seen since.

GOING DEEPER

I do not think any of Sadhu Sundar Singh's writings are in print. There are two excellent biographies: one by Mrs. Arthur Parker (*Sadhu Sundar Singh: Called of God*), published during the Sadhu's lifetime and with his permission, and the other by C. F. Andrews (*Sadhu Sundar Singh: A Personal Memoir*), published soon after his death and the result of a long and penetrating friendship. The Sadhu's own writings are mainly meditations and transcriptions of addresses. The best known are *At the Master's Feet, Visions of the Spiritual World, Reality and Religion, The Spiritual Life, The Search After Reality, The Cross Is Heaven,* and *With and Without Christ.*

Francis of Assisi (1182–1226)

INTRODUCTION TO THE AUTHOR

Born Giovanni Francesco di Pietro di Bernardone, the legendary St. Francis of Assisi is said to have been the first of the Italian mystics. His family was both worldly and wealthy, and young Francis was a product of this environment, but upon conversion his life changed dramatically.

He heard God's call to "rebuild" the Church, in particular, the little church at San Damiano. (In time he came to understand the call in a larger, deeper sense.) In 1209 he felt a strong desire to "imitate Christ" by living a life of poverty, chastity, and obedience. He literally took the fancy and expensive clothes off his back and handed them to his father, thereby marking the new life he was about to live. He began a ministry to lepers and those who were ill until his death in 1226.

From Francis's deeply spiritual life arose the Franciscan order, which seeks to follow his life-style even today. He was the most beloved of saints of the Middle Ages, captivating those who have read of him. He had the marvelous talent of seeing all the world—every living thing—as a beautiful gift from God. He called the sun, the moon, and all the creatures of the earth his brothers and sisters.

Though he wrote little, his friends and followers recorded much of his life and thought. The following selection is taken from the classic biography *The Little Flowers of St. Francis,* a collection of enchanting tales of Francis and his "Friars Minor" and their merry abandonment to the ministry of Jesus.

EXCERPTS FROM *THE LITTLE FLOWERS OF ST. FRANCIS*

1. Great Agony of Doubt

The humble servant of Christ, St. Francis, at the beginning of his conversion when he had already gathered many companions and received them in the Order, was placed in great agony of doubt as to what he should do: whether to give himself only to continual prayer or to preach sometimes.

He wanted very much to know which of these would please our Lord Jesus Christ most. And as the holy humility that was in him did not allow him to trust in himself or in his own prayers, he humbly turned to others in order to know God's will in this matter.

2. Show Me What Is Best

So he called Brother Masseo and said to him: "Dear Brother, go to Sister Clare and tell her on my behalf to pray devoutly to God, with one of her more spiritual companions, that he may deign to show me what is best: either that I preach sometimes or that I devote myself only to prayer. And then go also to Brother Silvester, who is staying on Mount Subasio, and tell him the same thing."

This was that Lord Silvester who had seen a cross of gold issuing from the mouth of St. Francis which extended in length to heaven and in width to the ends of the world. And this Brother Silvester was so devout and holy that God immediately granted or revealed to him whatever he asked in prayer.

The Holy Spirit had made him remarkably deserving of divine communications, and he had conversed with God many times. And, therefore, St. Francis was very devoted to him and had great faith in him.

3. A Harvest of Souls

Brother Masseo went and, as St. Francis had ordered him, gave the message first to St. Clare and then to Brother Silvester. When the latter received it, he immediately set himself to praying. And while praying he quickly had God's answer.

He went out at once to Brother Masseo and said: "The Lord says you are to tell Brother Francis this: that God has not called him to this state only on his own account, but that he may

reap a harvest of souls and that many may be saved through him."

After this Brother Masseo went back to St. Clare to know what she had received from God. And she answered that both she and her companion had had the very same answer from God as Brother Silvester.

4. Aflame with Divine Power

Brother Masseo therefore returned to St. Francis. And the saint received him with great charity: he washed his feet and prepared a meal for him. And after he had eaten, St. Francis called Brother Masseo into the woods. And there he knelt down before Brother Masseo, and baring his head and crossing his arms, St. Francis asked him: "What does my Lord Jesus Christ order me to do?"

Brother Masseo replied that Christ had answered both Brother Silvester and Sister Clare and her companion and revealed that "He wants you to go about the world preaching, because God did not call you for yourself alone but also for the salvation of others."

And then the hand of the Lord came over St. Francis. As soon as he heard this answer and thereby knew the will of Christ, he got to his feet, all aflame with divine power and said to Brother Masseo with great fervor: "So let's go—in the name of the Lord!"

5. Like a Bolt of Lightning

And he took as companions Brother Masseo and Brother Angelo, holy men. And he set out like a bolt of lightning in this spiritual ardor, not paying any attention to the road or path.

They arrived at a village called Cannara. And St. Francis began to preach, first ordering the swallows who were twittering to keep quiet until he had finished preaching. And the swallows obeyed him. He preached there so fervently that all the men and women of that village, as a result of his sermon and the miracle of the swallows, in their great devotion wanted to follow him and abandon the village.

But St. Francis did not let them, saying to them: "Don't be in a hurry and don't leave, for I will arrange what you should do for the salvation of your souls." And from that time he planned to organize the Third Order of the Continent for the salvation of all people everywhere.

6. The Multitude of Birds

And leaving them much consoled and disposed to penance, he left there and came between Cannara and Bevagna. And while going with the same fervor through that district with his companions, he looked up and saw near the road some trees on which there was such a countless throng of different birds as he had never seen before in that area. And also a very great crowd of birds was in a field near those trees. While he gazed and marveled at the multitude of birds, the Spirit of God came over him and he said to his companions: "Wait for me here on the road. I am going to preach to our sisters, the birds."

And he went into the field toward the birds that were on the ground. And as soon as he began to preach, all the birds that were on the trees came down toward him. And all of them stayed motionless with the others in the field, even though he went among them, touching many of them with his habit. But not a single one of them made the slightest move, and later they did not leave until he had given

them his blessing, as Brother James of Massa, a holy man, said, and he had all the above facts from Brother Masseo, who was one of those who were the companions of the holy Father at that time.

7. Strive Always to Praise God

The substance of St. Francis' sermon to those birds was this: "My little bird sisters, you owe much to God your Creator, and you must always and everywhere praise him, because he has given you a double and triple covering, and your colorful and pretty clothing, and your food is ready without your working for it, and your singing was taught to you by the Creator, and your numbers that have been multiplied by the blessing of God—and because he preserved your species in Noah's ark so that your race should not disappear from the earth.

"And you are also indebted to him for the realm of the air which he assigned to you. Moreover, you neither sow nor reap, yet God nourishes you, and he gives you the rivers and springs to drink from. He gives you high mountains and hills, rocks and crags as refuges, and lofty trees in which to make your nests. And although you do not know how to spin or sew, God gives you and your little ones the clothing which you need. So the Creator loves you very much since he gives you so many good things. Therefore, my little bird sisters, be careful not to be ungrateful, but strive always to praise God."

8. They Sang a Wonderful Song

Now at these words of St. Francis, all those birds began to open their beaks, stretch out their necks, spread their wings, and reverently bow their heads to the ground, showing by their movements and their songs that the words which St. Francis was saying gave them great pleasure. And when St. Francis noticed this, he likewise rejoiced greatly in spirit with them, and he marveled at such a great throng of birds and at their very beautiful variety and also at their attention and familiarity and affection. And therefore he devoutly praised the wonderful Creator in them and gently urged them to praise the Creator.

Finally, when he had finished preaching to them and urging them to praise God, St. Francis made the Sign of the Cross over all those birds and gave them permission to leave. Then all the birds rose up unto the air simultaneously, and in the air they sang a wonderful song. And when they had finished singing, according to the form of the Cross which St. Francis had made over them, they separated in an orderly way and formed four groups. And each group rose high into the air and flew off in a different direction: one toward the east, another toward the west, the third toward the south, and the fourth toward the north. And each group sang marvelously as it flew away.

9. To the Four Quarters of the World

Thereby they signified that, just as St. Francis—who was later to bear the marks of Christ's Cross—had preached to them and made the sign of the Cross over them, so they had separated in the form of a cross and had flown away, singing, toward the four quarters of the world, thus suggesting that the preaching of the Cross of Christ, which had been renewed by St. Francis, was to be carried throughout the world by him and by his friars, who, like birds, possess nothing of their own in this world and commit themselves entirely to the Providence of God.

And so they were called eagles by Christ when he said, "Wherever the body shall be, there eagles will gather." For the saints who place their hope in the Lord will take on wings like eagles and will fly up to the Lord and will not die for all eternity.

To the praise of Christ. Amen.

BIBLE SELECTION: LUKE 12:13–21

[13]Someone in the crowd said to him, "Teacher, tell my brother to divide the family inheritance with me." [14]But he said to him, "Friend, who set me to be a judge or arbitrator over you?" [15]And he said to them, "Take care! Be on your guard against all kinds of greed; for one's life does not consist in the abundance of possessions." [16]Then he told them a parable: "The land of a rich man produced abundantly. [17]And he thought to himself, 'What should I do, for I have no place to store my crops?' [18]Then he said, 'I will do this: I will pull down my barns and build larger ones, and there I will store all my grain and my goods. [19]And I will say to my soul, Soul, you have ample goods laid up for many years; relax, eat, drink, be merry.' [20]But God said to him, 'You fool! This very night your life is being demanded of you. And the things you have prepared, whose will they be?' [21]So it is with those who store up treasures for themselves but are not rich toward God."

REFLECTION QUESTION

The following questions can be used for discussion within a small group, or used for journal reflections by individuals.

1. Francis was "in great agony of doubt as to what he should do." At what points in your life were you in doubt as to which way your life should turn? What did you do? What, or who, helped you to make a decision?

2. Francis was afraid that his own inner desires might get in the way of hearing God's answer, and thus he asked his friends to pray and listen on his behalf. If you were caught in a difficult dilemma, which friends would you ask to pray and listen for you? Why?

3. What was the first thing Francis did after receiving confirmation of what he should do? Do you struggle with the problem of hesitation, feeling that you are not prepared to do ministry?

4. As a result of Francis's sermon, the people were greatly moved to deepen their commitment to God. Have there been sermons, or perhaps classes or seminars, that God used to inspire you to a deeper commitment?

5. In Jesus' parable, a rich man stores up his wealth only to soon die and find that his wealth was of no value. Jesus commands us instead to become "rich toward God" in this life. What are some ways a person can become "rich toward God"?

SUGGESTED EXERCISES

The following exercises can de done by individuals, shared between spiritual friends, or used in the context of a small group. Choose one or more of the following.

1. If you are facing a dilemma of some importance this week, humbly turn to a few friends to help you make a decision. Ask them to pray and listen, and, like Francis, receive their words as if they were the words of Jesus.

2. Learn the joy of creation this week. In the spirit of Francis, take time to be with the birds and the animals, seeing them not as dumb animals but as creatures who are an important part of God's creation.

3. As you listen to a sermon this week, strive to be a good listener. Do not merely hear the words, but listen closely with an ear to how you might apply some of the principles to your life. Ask the Spirit to give you "ears to hear."

4. Both Jesus and Francis caution us not to "store up earthly treasures" but rather to be "rich toward God." Strive to increase your godly wealth this week.

REFLECTIONS

Two things immediately strike me about the life of St. Francis: his merry abandonment and his instant obedience.

Francis was called "God's troubadour," so marked was he by a carefree, happy, exuberant abandonment to God. He tramped the villages and towns of his day, joyfully announcing the presence of the kingdom of God and wonderfully demonstrating its life and power. He also obeyed, without hesitation, any word he believed to be the command of Jesus Christ. The two are connected, of course. Only as we let go of all other loyalties and securities are we free to live obedient lives. Merry abandonment, instant obedience: excellent virtues for us to strive for in our world of a thousand competing loyalties.

GOING DEEPER

Chesterton, Gilbert K. *St. Francis of Assisi.* New York: George H. Doran, 1924. In a style that is classic Chesterton, this book seeks to engage we who are the products of the Enlightenment with the story of a pre-Enlightenment man who somehow seems to span all centuries and who both delights and disturbs us.

Green, Julien. *God's Fool: The Life and Times of Francis of Assisi.* Translated by Peter Heinegg. San Francisco: Harper & Row, 1985. This book, which has been a runaway best-seller in France, is a popular, emotionally gripping portrait of the "little poor man of Assisi."

Ugolino di Monte Santa Maria, Brother. *The Little Flowers of St. Francis.* Garden City, NY: Double-day, 1958. As you read these wonderful stories, I would counsel you not to worry overly much about whether these things happened exactly as they are recorded or about ascertaining the theological accuracy of every jot and tittle. Instead, read for the sheer delight . . . and challenge.

Zeffirelli, Franco. *Brother Sun, Sister Moon.* Great Britain/Italy: Paramount/Vic Films/Euro International, 1972. Though somewhat romantic, this film is nevertheless a gripping introduction to St. Francis. The music is haunting and the photography stunning. Ask for it at local video stores.

Madame Guyon (1648–1717)

INTRODUCTION TO THE AUTHOR

Madame Jeanne Guyon was born at Montargis, France. When she was only fifteen, she married an invalid who was thirty-eight years old. Unhappy in her marriage, she sought happiness in her devotional life. She lived in a convent under royal order for a year and then was imprisoned in Vincennes and the Bastille because of her religious beliefs. Almost twenty-five years of her life were spent in confinement. Many of her books were written during that period.

Writing that compels the reader to move into a living experience of Jesus Christ is Madame Guyon's great contribution to devotional literature. The following excerpts come from her book *Experiencing the Depths of Jesus Christ* (sometimes titled *A Short and Very Easy Method of Prayer*). This book has had a wide influence: Watchman Nee saw that it was translated into Chinese and made available to every new convert in the Little Flock; François Fénelon, John Wesley, and Hudson Taylor all highly recommended it to the believers of their day.

EXCERPTS FROM *EXPERIENCING THE DEPTHS OF JESUS CHRIST*

1. Two Ways to Meet Jesus

I would like to address you as though you were a beginner in Christ, one seeking to know him. In so doing, let me suggest two ways for you to come to the Lord. I will call the first way "praying the Scripture"; the second way I will call "beholding the Lord" or "waiting in his presence."

2. Praying the Scripture

"Praying the Scripture" is a unique way of dealing with the Scripture; it involves both reading and prayer. Turn to the Scripture; choose some passage that is simple and fairly practical. Next, come to the Lord. Come quietly and humbly. There, before him, read a small portion of the passage of Scripture you have opened to.

Be careful as you read. Take in fully, gently, and carefully what you are reading. Taste it and digest it as you read. In the past it may have been your habit, while reading, to move very quickly from one verse of Scripture to another until you have read the whole passage. Perhaps you were seeking to find the main point of the passage.

3. Reading Slowly

But in coming to the Lord by means of "praying the Scripture," you do not read quickly; you read very slowly. You do not move from one passage to another, not until you have *sensed* the very heart of what you have read. You may then want to take that portion of Scripture that has touched you and turn it into prayer.

After you have sensed something of the passage, and after you know that the essence of that portion has been extracted and all the deeper sense of it is gone, then, very slowly, gently, and in a calm manner begin to read the next portion of that passage. You will be surprised to find that when your time with the Lord has ended, you will have read very little, probably no more than half a page.

4. Penetrating into the Depths

"Praying the Scripture" is not judged by *how much* you read but the *way* you read. If you read quickly, it will benefit you little. You will be like a bee that merely skims the surface of a flower. Instead, in this new way of reading with prayer, you become as the bee who penetrates into the *depths* of the flower. You plunge deeply within to remove its deepest nectar.

Of course, there is a kind of reading the Scripture for scholarship and for study—but not here. That studious kind of reading will not help you when it comes to matters that are *divine!* To receive any deep, inward profit from the Scripture you must read as I have described. Plunge into the very depths of the words you read until revelation, like a sweet aroma, breaks out upon you. I am quite sure that if you will follow this course, little by little you will come to experience a very rich prayer that flows from your inward being.

5. Beholding the Lord

Let us move now to the second kind of prayer which I mentioned earlier. The second kind of prayer which I described as "beholding the Lord" or "waiting on the Lord," *also* makes use of Scripture, but it is actually not a time of reading.

Remember, I am addressing you as if you were a new convert. Here is your second way to encounter Christ. And this second way, although you will be using the Scripture, has a purpose altogether different from "praying the Scripture." For that reason you should set aside a separate time when you can come just to wait upon Christ.

In "praying the Scripture" you are seeking to find the Lord in what you are reading, in the very words themselves. In this path, therefore, the content of the Scripture is the focal point of your attention. Your purpose is to take everything from the passage that unveils the Lord to you.

6. Quieting the Mind

In "beholding the Lord" you come to the Lord in a totally different way. Perhaps at this point I need to share with you the greatest difficulty you will have in waiting upon the Lord. It has to do with your mind. The mind has a very strong tendency to stray away from the Lord. Therefore, as you come before the Lord to sit in his presence, beholding him, make use of the Scripture to *quiet* your mind.

The way to do this is really quite simple. First, read a passage of Scripture. Once you sense the Lord's presence, the content of what you have read is no longer important. The Scripture has served its purpose; it has quieted your mind; it has brought you to him.

7. Turning Inward by Faith

So that you can see him more clearly, let me describe the way in which you come to the Lord by the simple act of beholding him and waiting upon him. You begin by setting aside a time to be with the Lord. When you do come to him, come quietly. Turn your heart to the presence of God. How is this done? This, too, is quite simple. You turn to him by *faith*. By faith you believe you have come into the presence of God.

Next, while you are before the Lord, begin to read some portion of Scripture. As you read, *pause*. The pause should be quite gentle. You have paused so that you may set your mind on the Spirit. You have set your mind *inwardly*— on Christ.

You should always remember that you are not doing this to gain some understanding of what you have read; rather, you are reading in order to turn your mind from outward things to the deep parts of your being. You are not there to learn or to read, but you are there to experience the presence of your Lord!

While you are before the Lord, hold your heart in his presence. How? This you also do by faith. Yes, by faith you can hold your heart in the Lord's presence. Now, waiting before him, turn all your attention toward your spirit. Do not allow your mind to wander. If your mind begins to wander, just turn your attention back again to the inward parts of your being. You will be free from wandering—free from any outward distractions—and you will be brought near to God. The Lord is found *only* within your spirit, in the recesses of your being, in the Holy of Holies; this is where he dwells.

8. The Lord Will Meet You

The Lord once promised to come and make his home within you (John 14:23). He promised there to meet those who worship him and do his will. The Lord *will* meet you in your spirit. It was St. Augustine who once said that he had lost much time in the beginning of his Christian experience by trying to find the Lord outwardly rather than by turning inwardly.

Once your heart has been turned inwardly to the Lord, you will have an impression of his presence. You will be able to notice his presence more acutely because your outer senses have now become very calm and quiet. Your attention is no longer on outward things or on the surface thoughts of your mind; instead, sweetly and silently, your mind becomes occupied with what you have read and by that touch of his presence.

Oh, it is not that you will think about what you have read, but you will *feed* upon what you have read. Out of a love for the Lord you exert your will to hold your mind quiet before him. When you have come to this state, you must allow your mind to rest.

In this very peaceful state, *swallow* what you have tasted. At first this may seem difficult, but perhaps I can show you a simple way. Have you not, at times, enjoyed the flavor of a very tasty food? But unless you were willing to swallow the food, you received no nourishment. It is the same with your soul. In this quiet, peaceful, and simple state simply take in what is there as nourishment.

9. Distractions

What about distractions? Let us say your mind begins to wander. Once you have been deeply touched by the Lord's Spirit and are distracted, be diligent to bring your wandering mind back to the Lord. This is the easiest way in the world to overcome external distractions.

When your mind has wandered, don't try to deal with it by changing what you are thinking. You see, if you pay attention to what you are thinking, you will only irritate your mind and stir it up more. Instead, *withdraw* from your mind! Keep turning within to the Lord's presence. By doing this you will win the war with your wandering mind and yet never directly engage in the battle!

10. Disciplining the Mind

As you begin this new venture you will, of course, discover that it is difficult to bring your mind under control. Why is this? Because through many years of habit your mind has acquired the ability to wander all over the world, just as it pleases, so what I speak of here is something that is to serve as a discipline to your mind.

Be assured that as your soul becomes more accustomed to withdrawing to inward things, this process will become easier. There are two reasons that you will find it easier each time to bring your mind under the subjection of the Lord. One is that the mind, after much practice, will form a new habit of turning deep within. The second is that you have a gracious Lord!

11. The Lord's Chief Desire

The Lord's chief desire is to reveal himself to you and, in order for him to do that, he gives you abundant grace. The Lord gives you the experience of enjoying his presence. He touches you, and his touch is so delightful that, more than ever, you are drawn inwardly to him.

BIBLE SELECTION: GENESIS 28:10–19

[10]Jacob left Beer-sheba and went toward Haran. [11]He came to a certain place and stayed there for the night, because the sun had set. Taking one of the stones of the place, he put it under his head and lay down in that place. [12]And he dreamed that there was a ladder set up on the earth, the top of it reaching to heaven; and the angels of God were ascending and descending on it. [13]And the LORD stood beside him and said, "I am the LORD, the God of Abraham your father and the God of Isaac; the land on which you lie I will give to you and to your offspring; [14]and your offspring shall be like the dust of the earth, and you shall spread abroad to the west and to the east and to the north and to the south; and all the families of the earth shall be blessed in you and in your offspring. [15]Know that I am with you and will keep you wherever you go, and will bring you back to this land; for I will not leave you until I have done what I have promised you." [16]Then Jacob woke from his sleep and said, "Surely the LORD is in this place—and I did not know it!" [17]And he was afraid, and said, "How awesome is this place! This is none other than the house of God, and this is the gate of heaven."

[18]So Jacob rose early in the morning, and he took the stone that he had put under his head and set it up for a pillar and poured oil on the top of it. [19]He called that place Bethel; but the name of the city was Luz at the first.

REFLECTION QUESTIONS

The following questions can be used for discussion within a small group, or used for journal reflections by individuals.

1. Madame Guyon uses the image of a bee that either skims the surface of a flower or penetrates deeply into it to illustrate the difference between our usual way of reading the Bible and the way she is encouraging us to read the Bible. Which way best describes your approach to the Scripture?

2. Of the two methods she describes ("praying the Scripture" and "beholding the Lord"), which one might best help you in your spiritual journey? Why?

3. Madame Guyon places great emphasis on our level of desire for God. Over the past two years, what has helped to increase your desire for God?

4. If Madame Guyon came to your home for a cup of coffee and conversation, what one question would you most want to ask her?

5. In the Bible selection for this week (Gen. 28:10–19), the place called Haran became sacred to Jacob because it was there that he had a profound encounter with God. What are some of the sacred places in your life, places where you have encountered God in a meaningful way?

SUGGESTED EXERCISES

The following exercises can be done by individuals, shared between spiritual friends, or used in the context of a small group. Choose one or more of the following.

1. This week set aside fifteen minutes to "pray the Scripture." Using Madame Guyon's approach, remember to:
   • Choose a simple passage.
   • Read it slowly.
   • Try to sense the heart of each verse before moving on.
   • When something strikes you as particularly meaningful, turn it into prayer.

2. Set aside fifteen minutes each day this week to "behold the Lord." Keep in mind the simple steps the author suggests:
   • Use a passage of Scripture to help you focus on God's presence.
   • Read the words until you are able to focus on God's presence.
   • Keep your heart and mind fixed on the presence of God.
   • When your mind wanders, come back to the Bible passage to help you refocus.

3. Madame Guyon writes, "The Lord's chief desire is to reveal himself to you." This week pay close attention to the different ways in which God makes himself known to you.

4. Just as Jacob erected a pillar to honor the place where God had met him in a special way, make a list of the people and places that have touched your life, and give thanks to God as you look over this list. If possible, write a letter of thanks to those who helped make your life special (e.g., camp directors, college chaplains, pastors, staff workers).

REFLECTIONS

The strength of Jeanne Guyon's writing is its simplicity. We must not despise this quality in her, thinking that because it is simple it must therefore be simplistic. Far from it! Her words are profound indeed and will lead us into rich encounters with the living Christ if, with humility of heart, we are willing to learn. In The Imitation of Christ *Thomas à Kempis urges us to read "devout and simple books" as willingly as we do those that are "lofty and profound" for we should always be attracted to "the love of pure truth."*

But what a book! It wins us over by its unpretentiousness. It exposes the shallowness of our own spirituality. And it invites us deeper in. It welcomes us into the Holy of Holies. Most of all, it makes the life of prayer so delightful, so refreshing, that we are drawn into "experiencing the depths of Jesus Christ" for ourselves.

GOING DEEPER

Guyon, Jeanne. *Experiencing the Depths of Jesus Christ.* Edited by Gene Edwards. Goleta, CA: Christian Books, 1975. This book is a delight to read. It provides simple and profound counsel on deepening your prayer life. This edition is an abridged and rewritten version of Guyon's *Short and Very Easy Method of Prayer.* The Little Flock movement has also published her *Spiritual Writings* and *Union with God* in similar fashion.

Guyon, Jeanne. *Madame Guyon: An Autobiography.* Chicago: Moody Press, n.d. While Madame Guyon was in prison for her love of God, her spiritual director asked her to commit to writing the details of her life. The result is this book.

Upham, T. C. *The Life of Madame Guyon.* Greenwood, SC: Attic, 1961. A sympathetic biography with an emphasis on the spiritual life.

John Chrysostom (345–407)

INTRODUCTION TO THE AUTHOR

Born the son of a wealthy Roman general, young John was destined to become one of the finest preachers in the early Church. He would later be known as Chrysostom, "the golden-mouthed." At the age of twenty he studied rhetoric at Antioch. His original intention was to use his skills in the practice of law, but later he rejected law because of its secular nature.

He turned his attention to the study of Scripture and in A.D. 368 was baptized into the Church. Soon afterward he went into solitude with an old Syrian monk, living in a mountain cave near Antioch for four years. His extreme asceticism led to health problems, and he was forced to return to Antioch and temper his discipline. In A.D. 386 he was ordained a priest, and twelve years later he was named patriarch of Constantinople.

In his later life Chrysostom was much maligned for his agreement with much of Origen's theology and for his constant criticism of the apathy he saw in the clergy. His plain speaking and rigid rule of life quickly made enemies with the worldly clergy and the sensual court. He was exiled by Empress Eudoxia to Armenia, a region of Asia Minor. During his exile he continued to write forceful and influential letters to his friends and was known for his ability to endure hardship for the sake of God. Chrysostom died on the journey to a more remote region in 407.

Like Augustine who would follow, Chrysostom's rhetorical skills, learned before his baptism, made him one of the finest preachers in the history of Christianity. It is for this reason that we have chosen one of his sermons for the following selection.

EXCERPTS FROM A SERMON TITLED "DEAD TO SIN"

1. Baptized into His Death

"Know ye not my brethren, that so many of us as were baptized into Jesus Christ were baptized into his death? Therefore we are buried with him by baptism into death" (Rom. 6:3–4, KJV). What does being baptized into his death mean? It has to do with our dying as he did.

We do this by our baptism, for baptism is the cross. What the cross is to Christ, baptism is to us. Christ died in the flesh; we have died to sin. Both are deaths, and both are real.

But if it is real, what is our part, what must we contribute? Paul goes on to say, "As Christ was raised up from the dead by the glory of the Father, even so we also should walk in newness of life" (Rom. 6:4, KJV). Here Paul tells of the importance of the resurrection.

Do you believe that Christ was raised from the dead? Believe the same of yourself. Just as his death is yours, so also is his resurrection; if you have shared in the one, you shall share in the other. As of now the sin is done away with.

Paul sets before us a demand: to bring about a newness of life by a changing of habits. For when the fornicator becomes chaste, when the covetous person becomes merciful, when the harsh become subdued, a resurrection has taken place, a prelude to the final resurrection which is to come.

How is it a resurrection? It is a resurrection because sin has been mortified, and righteousness has risen in its place; the old life has passed away, and new, angelic life is now being lived.

2. The Old Age of Sin

But tears come into my eyes when I think of how much Paul is asking of us and how little we have changed after our baptism, yielding ourselves to sin, going back to the oldness we had before, returning to Egypt, and remembering the onions after the manna. We undergo a change for only ten or twenty days after our baptism, but then take up former things again.

But we must see that it is not for a few days that we are required to change, but rather, for a whole lifetime. The youth of grace must not lead to the old age of sin. The love of money, the slavery to wrong desires, or any sin whatsoever, makes us grow old in soul and body. Our souls become rheumatic, distorted, decayed, and tottering with many sins.

Such, then, are the souls of sinners. Not so those of the righteous, for they are youthful and strong, always in the prime of life, ready for any fight. Not so for the sinners, for they are subject to fall at the least resistance. The sinful lose their ability to see, to hear, and to speak, for they spew forth words that are foul.

3. Suddenly Young

Like the prodigal son, the sinful end up in the mire of the pig's slop, reduced to the greatest wretchedness, and are in a worse state than any disordered person. But when the prodigal was willing, he became suddenly young by his decision. As soon as he had said, "I will return to my Father," this one word conveyed to him all the blessings; or rather, not the word alone, but the deed which he added to the word. He did not say, "I will return," and then stay where he was.

Thus, let us also do this, no matter how far we have gotten carried away in our journey. Let us go back to our Father's house, not lingering over the length of the journey. For we shall find, if we be willing, that the way back again is very easy and very speedy. Only let us leave this strange land of sin where we have been drawn away from the Father. For our Father has a natural yearning toward us and will honor us if we are changed. He finds great pleasure in receiving back his children.

4. The Easier It Will Be

And how am I to go back again? Start back by avoiding vice, going no farther into it, and you have come home. When a person who is sick does not get any worse it is a sign that he is getting better, and so is the case with vice. Go no further and your deeds of wickedness will have an end.

If you do so for two days, you will keep off on the third more easily; and after three days you will add ten, then twenty, then a hundred, then your whole life. For the further you journey back the easier it will be to see how you should be, and the more you will begin to see of your great rewards.

So it was with the prodigal who, when he returned, was greeted with flutes and harps and dancing and feasts. His father who might have chided him for his ill-timed extravagance did nothing of the sort. He did not even mention it, but rather, looked at him as without stain, throwing himself upon him and kissing him.

5. God's Exceeding Desire

Let us, then, as we have such examples before us, be of good cheer and keep from despair. For God is not so well pleased with being our Master as he is with being our Father; he is not so pleased with our being his slaves as he is with our being his children. This is what God truly wants. This is why he did all that he has done, not sparing his only begotten Son, that we, as adopted sons and daughters, might love him as a Father.

God's exceeding desire to be loved comes from loving exceedingly. This is why Jesus said, "Anyone who loves their father or mother more than me, is not worthy of me." He even calls us to esteem that which is most precious to us—our soul—as second to the love of God, for our Father wishes to be loved by us entirely.

When we do not love a person we do not wish to be with them, no matter how great or noble that person may be. But when we love

someone, we want to be with them, and we view their love for us with great honor even if they are not a person of great rank. For this reason—and not because of our great rank—God values our love. So much, in fact, that he suffered greatly on our behalf.

6. What Is There to Fear?

Let us, then, incur dangers for him, running as if for the greatest of crowns. Let us have no fear of poverty or disease, nor hardship or even death itself. For what is there to fear? Losing all of your money? If you bear it nobly, it will be as great a reward to you as if you gave it all to the poor—as long as you freely lose it because you know you have a greater reward in heaven.

What else is there to fear? Having people revile and persecute you? If so, those people have weaved a great crown for you if you bear it meekly. Rejoice and be glad, Jesus said, when people speak evil against you falsely, for great is your reward in heaven. And even if they speak the truth against us, it is to our advantage if we bear it humbly, just as the Pharisee spoke rightly about the publican, but only the publican went home justified because he bore it in humility.

Why do we seek profit? What did Judas profit for being with Christ? Or what profit was the law to the Jews? Or paradise to Adam? Or the promised land to the Israelites? We should keep our mind fixed on one point only: how we may do what is best with the resources we have been given.

7. A Serpent Nestling in Our Bed

If we do this, not even the devil himself will get the better of us. We must remember that we deal with a crafty enemy. If we were suddenly aware of a serpent nestling in our bed, we would go to great lengths to kill it. But when the devil nestles in our souls, we tell ourselves we are in no danger, and thus we lie at ease. Why? Because we do not see him and his intent with our mortal eyes.

This is why we must rouse ourselves and be more sober. Fighting an enemy we can see makes it easy to be on guard, but one that cannot be seen we will not easily escape. Also, know that the devil has no desire for open combat (for he would surely be defeated), but rather, under the appearance of friendship, intends to insinuate the venom of his malice.

For example, he used Job's wife under the guise of love for her husband; Jephtha, too, he persuaded under the pretext of religion to slay his daughter, offering a sacrifice the law forbade. It was the same with Adam, for he put on the air of being concerned for his well-being, saying that his eyes "shall be opened" by eating from the tree.

Be on your guard, and arm yourself with weapons of the Spirit. Become acquainted with the devil's plans that you may keep from getting caught in his traps, and instead, expose him. Paul got the better of him because he was "not ignorant of his devices." Learn and avoid the devil's stratagems, so that after obtaining victory over him, we may, whether in this present life or in that which is to come, be proclaimed conquerors and obtain those unalloyed blessings.

BIBLE SELECTION: LUKE 15:11–32

[11]Then Jesus said, "There was a man who had two sons. [12]The younger of them said to his father, 'Father, give me the share of the property that will belong to me.' So he divided his property between them. [13]A few days later the younger son gathered all he had and traveled to a distant country, and there he squandered his property in dissolute living. [14]When he had spent everything, a severe famine took place throughout that country, and he began to be in need. [15]So he went and hired himself out to one of the citizens of that country, who sent him to his fields to feed the pigs. [16]He would gladly have filled himself with the pods that the pigs were eating; and no one gave him anything. [17]But when he came to himself he said, 'How many of my father's hired hands have bread enough and to spare, but here I am dying of hunger! [18]I will get up and go to my father, and I will say to him, "Father, I have sinned against heaven and before you; [19]I am no longer worthy to be called your son; treat me like one of your hired hands."' [20]So he set off and went to his father. But while he was still far off, his father saw him and was filled with compassion; he ran and put his arms around him and kissed him. [21]Then the son said to him, 'Father, I have sinned against heaven and before you; I am no longer worthy to be called your son.' [22]But the father said to his slaves, 'Quickly, bring out a robe—the best one—and put it on him; put a ring on his finger and sandals on his feet. [23]And get the fatted calf and kill it, and let us eat and celebrate; [24]for this son of mine was dead and is alive again; he was lost and is found!' And they began to celebrate.

[25]"Now his elder son was in the field; and when he came and approached the house, he heard music and dancing. [26]He called one of the slaves and asked what was going on. [27]He replied, 'Your brother has come, and your father has killed the fatted calf, because he has got him back safe and sound.' [28]Then he became angry and refused to go in. His father

came out and began to plead with him. [29]But he answered his father, 'Listen! For all these years I have been working like a slave for you, and I have never disobeyed your command; yet you have never given me even a young goat so that I might celebrate with my friends. [30]But when this son of yours came back, who has devoured your property with prostitutes, you killed the fatted calf for him!' [31]Then the father said to him, 'Son, you are always with me, and all that is mine is yours. [32]But we had to celebrate and rejoice, because this brother of yours was dead and has come to life; he was lost and has been found.'"

REFLECTION QUESTIONS

The following questions can be used for discussion within a small group, or used for journal reflections by individuals.

1. Reflect on your baptism. What did it mean to you (or, if you were baptized as an infant, what has it meant to you)? According to this sermon, what does it mean to God?

2. Have you struggled with sin after your baptism? According to John Chrysostom, what is the cause and what is the cure for this problem?

3. Chrysostom seems to be saying that the body and the soul "age" because of sin. Does this metaphor describe the effects of sin in your life? With that question in mind, how do we become "suddenly young"? How have you felt this?

4. According to this sermon, the devil is particularly difficult to defeat because he refuses to engage in "open combat" and instead deceives us under more positive appearances (friendship, religion, the prospect of gain, and so on). In what ways have you experienced this deception? How, according to Chrysostom, can we find victory?

5. Chrysostom uses the parable of the prodigal son to illustrate how we journey away from God and how we can get back home. In what ways have you journeyed away from God in the past? What made you want to come home?

SUGGESTED EXERCISES

The following exercises can be done by individuals, shared between spiritual friends, or used in the context of a small group. Choose one or more of the following.

1. Meditate on the biblical image that Paul uses for the new life in Christ: resurrection with Christ. As you reflect, keep Chrysostom's words in mind: "Do you believe that Christ was raised from the dead? Believe the same of yourself."

2. We can return to the Father's house, writes Chrysostom, by avoiding vice. Put an end this week to a vice that has been "aging" you. Know that for each day you find success, the next day will be easier.

3. Chrysostom encourages us to "keep our mind fixed on one point only: how we may do what is best with the resources we have been given." Make this point the subject of your reflections this week.

4. Resolve to leave the far land of sin and return to the Heavenly Father. Accompany your return home with a celebration. The angels rejoice when we return to God, so why not join in their choruses of praise!

REFLECTIONS

The title of this sermon, "Dead to Sin," which is of course taken from Paul's letter to the Romans, has been a difficult one for me to deal with. It is just that the image of death seems so final, so absolute, so once-for-all. My experience feels much different. Sin has a way of returning—many resurrections if you will! I think Chrysostom understands this because he seems to indicate that we experience many little deaths to sin.

But how do we become dead to sin? "Start . . . by avoiding vice," says the preacher. Do it for two days, then the third day will be easier. Go for ten days, "then twenty, then a hundred, then your whole life." He, of course, is calling us to the development of "holy habits" that in time will take over our lives and bring death to sin. So basic, yet so important. All habits become habits by simple repetition, and holy habits are no exception. And as we experience more and more deeply the ingrained character of these holy habits, we learn what the moral philosophers mean when they say, "Virtue is easy."

GOING DEEPER

Chrysostom, John. *The Nicene and Post-Nicene Fathers.* Edited by Philip Schaff. Vols. 9–14. Grand Rapids, MI: Eerdmans, 1989. This is the most authoritative material on the writings of Chrysostom that you will find in English. It contains major essays on the priesthood, ascetic treatises, letters, and a myriad of homilies on the Gospels, Acts, Romans, Corinthians, Galatians, Hebrews, and more.

The best I can do for you by way of biography is to direct you to three older works: W. Maggilory's *John of the Golden Mouth* (London, 1871); W. R. W. Stephens's *St. John Chrysostom: His Life and Time* (London, 1872); and R. W. Bush's *Life and Times of Chrysostom* (London, 1885).

Charles Spurgeon (1834–1892)

INTRODUCTION TO THE AUTHOR

Described as "a burning and shining light that suddenly burst upon the moral world," Charles Haddon Spurgeon was one of the most remarkable phenomena of his day, captivating (and often infuriating) audiences with his powerful and convicting sermons. Spurgeon was born and reared in Essex, England, the descendant of several generations of Independent ministers. He became a Baptist in 1850 and in that same year preached his first sermon. In 1852 he was appointed pastor of the Baptist congregation at Waterbeach. In 1854 he went to Southwark, where his popularity grew so much that a new church facility—the Metropolitan Tabernacle—had to be built to house all who came to hear him.

Apart from his preaching—for which he is known best—he founded a pastors' college, an orphanage, and an institution designed to promote uplifting literature. He was a strong Calvinist, and his tenacity concerning certain doctrines caused much controversy outside his church and occasional estrangement within. His fame continued to grow, owing much to his outstanding oratorical skill, his imaginative use of illustration, his sense of humor, and his shrewd common sense.

The following selection comes from one of Spurgeon's many sermons. His sermons were always biblical and doctrinally sound, and this one is ample evidence of his skill in convicting, exhorting, and encouraging his hearers to make changes in their lives.

EXCERPTS FROM "SPIRITUAL REVIVAL THE WANT OF THE CHURCH"

1. Entirely God's Work

Scripture Text: "O LORD, revive thy work" (Hab. 3:2, KJV).

All true religion is the work of God. God is indeed the author of salvation in the world, and religion is the work of grace. If there is anything good or excellent found in his Church, it, too, is entirely God's work, from first to last.

It is God who quickens a soul which was dead, and it is God who maintains the life of that soul; God who nurtures and perfects that life in the Church. We ascribe nothing to ourselves and everything to God. We do not dare for a single moment to think that our conversion or our sanctification is effected by our own efforts or the efforts of another. True, there are means by which we are converted and sanctified, but they are entirely God's work.

2. A Revival of Piety

Therefore, trusting that it is the Spirit of God who helps me, I shall endeavor to apply this principle first to our own souls personally, and second, to the Church at large.

First, then, to ourselves. We too often flog the Church when the whip should be laid on our own shoulders. We should always remember that we are a part of the Church, and that our own lack of revival is in some measure the cause of the lack of revival in the Church at large. I will lay this charge before us: we Christians need a revival of piety in our lives. I have abundant grounds to prove it.

3. No Guarantee

In the first place, look at the *conduct and conversation* of too many of us who profess to be children of God.

It has become very popular to join the Church in our day. Many people have recently joined the Church in our country. But are there any fewer cheats than there used to be? Are there less frauds committed? Do we find morality more extensive? Do we find vice coming to an end? No, we do not. Our age is as immoral as any that preceded it. There is still as much sin, though perhaps it is more cloaked and hidden.

It is well known that it is no guarantee of a man's honesty that he is a member of the Church. The lives of too many of the men and women of the Church give the world cause to wonder if there is godliness in any of us. We reach after money, we covet, we follow the wicked ways of this world, we oppress the poor and deny rights to the working class—and yet we profess to be people of God! The Church lacks revival in the lives of its members.

4. What Will They Talk About

Second, let us take a look at the conversation of many professing Christians. Pay attention to the conversation of the average professing Christian. You might spend from the first of January to the end of December and never hear them speak about their faith. They will scarcely even mention the name of Jesus Christ at all. On Sunday afternoon what will they talk about at the dinner table? It will not be about the minister's sermon, unless they want to point out some faults.

Do they ever talk about what Jesus said and did? What he suffered for us? When we go to each other's houses, what will we talk about? I have concluded this: you will not know how to get to heaven simply by eavesdropping on the conversations of the members of the Church! We talk too little about our Lord. Is this not the truth? Many of us need to pray, "O Lord, revive your work in my soul, that my conversation may be more Christ-like, seasoned with salt, and kept by the Holy Spirit."

5. Holy Fellowship with Jesus

But even if our conduct and conversation were more consistent with our faith, I would still have this third charge against us: there is *too little real communion with Jesus Christ.* If, by the grace of God, our conduct and conversation were consistent and our lives were unblemished, many of us are still sorely lacking in that area we call holy fellowship with Jesus.

Men and women, let me ask you, How long has it been since you have had an intimate conversation with Jesus Christ? Some of you may be able to say, "It was only this morning that I last spoke with him; I beheld his face with joy." But I fear that the great majority of you will have to say, "It has been months since I have been with the Lord."

What have you been doing with your life? Is Christ living in your home and yet you have not spoken to him for months? Do not let me condemn you or judge; only let your conscience speak: Have we not all lived too much without Jesus? Have we not grown contented with the world to the neglect of Christ?

6. Groan for Your Revival

I have in some degree substantiated my claim that we are in need of revival, but now I must turn to the solution of this great problem that we face. Habakkuk prayed, "O LORD, revive thy work." Do you hear his groaning for revival? Our problem is this: there are many who say they want revival but they do not groan for it, they do not long for it.

The true believer, when he is confronted with his need for revival, will long for it. He will not be happy, but will at once begin to strain after it. The true believer will pray day and night, "O LORD, revive thy work!"

And what is it that will make that true Christian groan for revival? When he reflects on what Christ has done for him, he will groan for his own revival. When he hears someone tell a story about a fellow believer who is experiencing great joy in the Lord, he will groan for his own revival. When he attends a lively fellowship and feels no emotion in his heart, he will groan for his own revival.

Those of you who feel you are in need of revival, I would ask you only this: Can you groan for your revival? If you can, do it! May God be pleased to give you grace to continue to do it. And may you turn your groanings into prayers.

7. Make No Resolutions

Make sure that you turn your groanings into prayers. Do not say, "Sir, I feel my need of revival; I intend to get to work on it later this afternoon—then I shall begin reviving my soul." Make no resolutions as to what you will do; your resolutions will surely be broken as they are made. Instead of trying to revive yourself, offer prayers. Do not say, "I will revive myself," but cry, "O LORD, revive *thy work.*"

To say, "I will revive myself," reveals that you do not know your true state. If you knew your own true state, you would just as soon expect a wounded soldier on the battlefield to heal himself without medicine, or get himself to hospital when his arms and legs have been shot off as you would expect to revive yourself without the help of God.

I urge you: do nothing until you have first prayed to God, crying out, "O LORD, revive thy work." Begin, then, by humbling yourself—giving up all hope of reviving yourself, but beginning at once with firm prayer and earnest supplication to God: "O LORD, what I cannot, you do for me. O LORD, revive thy work!"

8. The Absence of Earnestness

And now I come to the second part of the subject upon which I shall be more brief. In the Church itself we must pray this incessant, urgent prayer: "O LORD, revive thy work!"

In this present era there is *a sad decline of the vitality of godliness.* This age has become too much the age of form instead of the age of life. We have preachers who read their sermons out of manuscripts—a pure insult to almighty God! It may sound beautiful and eloquent, but where is the fervent preaching such as that of George Whitefield.

Whitefield's sermons were not eloquent, but were rough and unconnected. But it was not in the words themselves, but in the manner in which he delivered them, the earnestness with which he felt them, the pouring out of his soul as he preached them. When you heard him preach, you felt like you were listening to a man who would die if he could not preach. Where, where is such earnestness today? One sad proof that the Church is in need of revival is the absence of earnestness which was once seen in Christian pulpits.

9. An "Ology" Which Has Cast Out God

Second, I believe that *the absence of sound doctrine* is another proof that the Church is in need of revival. Sound doctrine has to a great degree ceased. It happened when ministers in the pulpit stopped preaching sound doctrine for fear of how it would be received. They stopped talking about "election" and "depravity" and "free grace" because they thought people might stop coming to listen.

Then they decided if it was not fit to preach, it might not be true. They then offered a "new theology," but it is anything but a *theol-*

ogy. It is an "ology" which has cast out God utterly and enthroned man.

In similar fashion, the members of the Church became weak in their doctrine. Today's Church members change their doctrine as often as they change the company they are in. They are hardly the kind of people who would die for their beliefs. Look at their laxity! They have what they call "prayer meetings"; "spare meetings" they ought to be called, for they are sparely attended.

All of this shows me that the Church has swerved from its course. Why do I know this? Because it has begun to be honored in the eyes of the world. The Church must be despised and cast out until the Lord comes, in whose eyes we are to find true honor.

10. Light a Fire

There will be some who will agree with me that the Church needs reviving. But let me ask that instead of complaining about your minister, instead of finding fault with certain parts of the Church, cry out, "O LORD, revive thy work!"

"O!" says one person, "if we had another minister. O! if we had another kind of worship. O! if we had a different sort of preaching." You do not need new ways or new people, you need life in what you have. If you want to move a train, you don't need a new engine, or even ten engines—you need to light a fire and get the steam up in the engine you now have!

It is not a new person or a new plan, but the life of God *in them* that the Church needs. Let us ask God for it! Perhaps he is ready to shake the world at its very foundations. Perhaps even now he is about to pour forth a mighty influence upon his people which shall make the Church in this age as vital as it ever was in any age that has passed.

BIBLE SELECTION: HABAKKUK 3:1–6

A prayer of the prophet Habakkuk according
to Shigionoth.

[2]O LORD, I have heard of your renown,
and I stand in awe, O LORD, of your work.
In our own time revive it;
in our own time make it known;
in wrath may you remember mercy.
[3]God came from Teman,
the Holy One from Mount Paran.   *Selah*
His glory covered the heavens,

and the earth was full of his praise.
[4]The brightness was like the sun;
rays came forth from his hand,
where his power lay hidden.
[5]Before him went pestilence,
and plague followed close behind.
[6]He stopped and shook the earth;
he looked and made the nations tremble.
The eternal mountains were shattered;
along his ancient pathways
the everlasting hills sank low.

REFLECTION QUESTIONS

The following questions can be used for discussion within a small group, or
used for journal reflections by individuals.

1. All revival, writes Charles Spurgeon, must begin with a sense that God, not
   we, is responsible for any real spiritual advance—even the means by which
   we grow. What means of grace (e.g., reading the Bible, prayer, fasting, fellowship, devotional books) has God been pleased to use most in your spiritual
   journey?

2. "We too often flog the Church when the whip should be laid on our own
   shoulders," writes Spurgeon. Why is it so easy to blame "the Church" for its
   lack of piety and not ourselves when, in fact, we are the Church?

3. Spurgeon asks a question that cuts deeply into the heart of the matter. How
   would you answer his revealing question: "How long has it been since you
   have had an intimate conversation with Jesus Christ?"

4. The true believer, writes Spurgeon, when confronted with his or her need for
   revival, will long for it. Did this sermon confront you with your need for revival? How did you react?

5. Habakkuk drew on the past, much as Spurgeon did, as a way of encouraging
   his hearers in the present. What people or events in your past serve as inspiration for you?

SUGGESTED EXERCISES

The following exercises can be done by individuals, shared between spiritual friends, or used in the context of a small group. Choose one or more of the following.

1. Be careful in both your conduct and your conversation this week. Be mindful of the fact that others are watching to see if our faith has truly set us free.

2. Set aside some time for an intimate conversation with Jesus this week. Endeavor to engage in this blessed communion on a regular basis.

3. The answer to our problem, writes Spurgeon, is not trying to reform ourselves, but crying to God in prayer, asking as Habakkuk did, "LORD, revive thy work." Make this your prayer this week.

4. Put an end to the tendency to criticize the Church, especially the clergy, this week. Each time you begin to place blame on the Church, consider how you are part of the problem. Become a part of the solution by keeping your focus on your own personal revival of piety.

REFLECTIONS

I like the perspective that Spurgeon has on "revival." To begin with, he understands that this is God's work and not ours. We cannot simply get up meetings to push and shove and make revival happen. Having made that clear, he goes on to indicate that there is work for us to do: changes in conduct, in conversation, in spiritual communion, and, most of all, in our need to "groan for revival."

But the minute we understand our role, he once again indicates that we must not "try" to make revival happen by good resolutions and other efforts, but only by simple prayer to God. The work is all of God, but strangely we have a part to play; a paradox to be sure, but one that gives us proper balance.

GOING DEEPER

Spurgeon, Charles Haddon. *Lectures to My Students.* Grand Rapids, MI: Zondervan, 1962. This is a book on homiletics for those going into the preaching ministry, but it has had such a wide influence that I wanted you to be aware of it. Beyond the technical material on the art of preaching it also contains helpful counsel on the development of the pastor's spiritual life; e.g., "The Minister's Self-Watch" and "The Pastor's Private Prayer."

Spurgeon, Charles Haddon. *Morning and Evening.* Grand Rapids, MI: Zondervan, 1960. These are one-page devotional readings—one for morning and one for evening—for each day of the year. I have never liked books of devotional readings much, but this is one of the better ones.

Spurgeon, Charles Haddon. *Spurgeon's Sermons.* 10 vols. Grand Rapids, MI: Baker, 1989. This is a reprint of an 1883 set entitled *Sermons of Rev. C. H. Spurgeon of London.* The typesetting is not the best, but it is bound well. Spurgeon is best known as a preacher, and this is an excellent collection of his sermons. The sermon you just read is taken from this collection (vol. 3, Sermon V).

Watchman Nee (1903–1972)

INTRODUCTION TO THE AUTHOR

Watchman Nee (Ni To-sheng) was one of the great Christian leaders of the twentieth century. Like George Muller and Hudson Taylor before him, Nee sought a life of abandonment and faith that few know. Eventually he came to head up a dynamic movement of the Spirit known as the "Little Flock," which was one of the early efforts to forge an indigenous Chinese Christian witness independent of foreign missions and the traditional denominations. It flourished in the 1930s and 1940s with large gatherings of thousands in Shanghai and elsewhere. Perhaps it succeeded too well, for it was severely criticized by the more static missionary establishment.

In 1952 Watchman Nee was arrested by the Chinese Communist government on trumped-up charges and was sentenced to fifteen years of imprisonment. The fifteen years were actually extended to twenty and in all those long years he never betrayed his Lord. On June 1, 1972, while still in prison, he passed into the welcoming presence of God.

Like all of us, Nee made mistakes. Most notably, his "one locality, one church" principle led him into separatism and a denunciation of all churches other than his own, and this inevitably caused deep division in the Christian community. On the other hand, his use of vocational migration evangelism—in which every believer was viewed as an unpaid worker, and the home of every person moving to a new city became a place of prayer and a fresh center of witness—was sheer genius.

Leslie Lyall wrote of Watchman Nee, "When the history of the Chinese church comes to be written it will be impossible to ignore the life and work of an outstanding leader whose influence will last and whose legacy may well be a Christian fellowship (Little Flock) which will survive the fires of persecution and the attempts being made to destroy the Christian church in China" (in the foreword to Angus I. Kinnear, *Against the Tide: The Story of Watchman Nee*, Fort Washington, PA, Christian Literature Crusade, 1973, p. ix).

EXCERPTS FROM *WHAT SHALL THIS MAN DO?*

1. Leading the Individual Soul to Christ

How do people press into the Kingdom? We have considered at some length how a preacher of the Gospel needs to be personally prepared in spirit for the task. But what of the hearers? What is the minimum requirement in the sinner if he or she is to find the Lord and be saved? This question now claims our attention, for it is as important for us to know what we are attempting to do as it is for us to be prepared in spirit to do it.

In the discussion which follows we can only deal with a single point in the preaching of the Gospel. I take it for granted that you know the facts of redemption through the atoning death of Christ, and that you are also born of the Spirit. I assume also that you know how to present those facts clearly and with power. I am concerned here not with the substance of your preaching, but rather with the principles that should guide in the actual task of leading the individual soul to Christ.

What is necessary for a person to be saved? How can a person be prevailed upon to come to the door of the Kingdom and enter? How do we bring people who have only the absolute minimum of knowledge or desire for God into a living touch with Him? These are our questions, and I am going to lay down four guiding principles that will, I hope, be found to go a long way towards answering them.

2. A Threefold Provision, and One Condition Demanded

God has made, from His side, a threefold provision for every person in that person's hour of crisis: Firstly, Jesus has come as the Friend of sinners; secondly, it is He personally (and no intermediary) whom we are called to meet; and thirdly, the Holy Spirit has been poured out on all flesh, to bring to pass in us the initial work of conviction of sin, repentance, and faith, and, of course, all that follows. Then, finally, from the side of the sinner, one condition and one only is demanded. We are *not* required—*in the first place*—to believe, or to repent, or to be conscious of sin, or even to know that Christ died. We are required only to approach the Lord with an honest heart.

This last statement may at first startle you, but as we go on, I think you will see how helpful it is. We will, however, take these points in order, beginning from the side of God's provision.

3. The Friend of Sinners

In the Gospels the Lord Jesus is presented as the Friend of sinners, for historically He was found, first of all, moving among the people as their Friend before He became their Savior. But do you realize that today He is still in the first place our Friend, in order that He may become our Savior?

It is clear from the New Testament that the Lord Jesus came as a Friend, *in order to help sinners to come to Him.* Our coming to Him was made possible by His first coming to us. At the hour of crisis there are many practical difficulties that face the sinner. For example, in the Scriptures we are often told to **believe.** The Word lays stress on the necessity of faith. But you say, "I have not got faith." A girl once said to me, "I can't believe. I would like to believe but I can't! It is no use; I haven't got it in me. The desire is there, but I find faith lacking. It is *impossible* to believe." "That is all right," I said, "You can't believe. But you can ask the Lord to *give* you faith. He is prepared to help you to that extent. You pray: 'Lord, help Thou my unbelief.'"

4. What the Savior Is at Hand to Do

Or again, the Word tells us that we are to **repent.** What if we have no desire whatever to repent? I met a student once who said it was too early for him to come to the Lord. He wanted more time in which to taste the pleasures of sin and to enjoy himself. He said to me, "The thief on the cross was saved, but he had his fling, and it was high time that he repented. But I—I am young." "Well, what do you want to do?" I asked him. He replied, "I want to wait another forty years and have a good time, and then I will repent."

So I said, "Let us pray." "Oh, I can't pray," he answered. "Yes, you can," I said. "You can tell the Lord all you have told me. He is the Friend of unrepentant sinners like you." "Oh, I couldn't say *that* to Him." "Why not? Whatever is in your heart, you tell it to Him. He will help you." Finally he prayed, and told the Lord that he did not want to repent and be saved, but that he knew he needed a Savior; and he just cried to Him for help. The Lord worked repentance in him and he got up a saved man.

I repeat these incidents just to emphasize that what the sinner cannot do the Savior is at hand to do for him. It is for this reason that we can tell people that they need not wait for anything, but can come to Him immediately. Whatever their state, whatever their problem, let them bring it and tell it to the Friend of Sinners.

5. Meeting Christ

What is salvation? Many think that to be saved we must first believe that the Lord Jesus died for us, but it is a strange fact that nowhere in the New Testament does it say precisely that. We are told to believe *in* Jesus, or to believe *on* Him; not to believe *that He died* for us. "Believe on the Lord Jesus Christ and thou shalt be saved," were Paul's words. We are to believe first of all in *Him;* not specifically in what He has done.

I *do* believe in the necessity of His atonement. I trust you will not misunderstand me therefore when I say that the appreciation of that work may not be the *first* step in the sinner's initial contact with the Lord. That appreciation must follow, but the main question is whether or not we have the Son, and not, first of all, whether or not we understand the whole plan of salvation. The first condition of salvation is not knowledge, but *meeting* Christ.

I have come to see that all that is needed for the *initial* step is that there should be a personal touch with God, and when that is so the rest will surely follow. It does not matter, therefore, which verses God elects to use for that first step. After all, we do not need to study the theory of electricity and to understand it thoroughly before we can turn on the electric light. The light does not say, "I am not going to shine for you, for you know nothing of the principle on which I work." And God does not set understanding as the condition of our approach to Him. "This is life eternal, that they should know thee, the only true God, and Jesus Christ whom thou hast sent."

6. It Only Requires a Touch

Let us take three examples from the Gospels. First, the thief on the cross. When he asked the Lord to remember him when Jesus came into His kingdom, Jesus did not remind him of his evil life, nor did He explain the plan of redemption—no, the Lord had only one answer: "Today you shall be with me in paradise." The thief recognized who Jesus was, and he believed *in the Lord*, and that was enough.

Consider the woman who was bleeding and was trying to touch Jesus. There were many pressing in on Him, but only one was healed. She was healed because with a special intention she "touched" Him. And it only required a touch; for in her it represented a reaching out in spirit to God for help in her deep need.

Or recall the incident of the Pharisee and the publican at prayer in the temple. The Pharisee understood all about offerings and sacrifices and tithes, but there was from him no cry of the heart to God. But the publican cried out, "Lord have mercy upon me!" Something went out from him to God which met with an immediate response, and the Lord Jesus singles him out as the one whom God reckoned as righteous. For what is it to be reckoned righteous? It is *to touch God*. That is why our first object must be to lead people to meet Him.

7. A Cry from the Heart

We have said that a cry to God from the heart is sufficient. Because the Holy Spirit has been poured out upon all mankind, a cry is enough.

I always believe that the Holy Spirit is *upon* a person when I preach to that person. I do not mean that the Spirit is *within* the hearts of unbelievers, but that He is outside. What is He doing? He is waiting, waiting to bring Christ into their hearts. He is like the light.

Open the window-shutters even a little, and it will flood in and illuminate the interior. Let there be a cry from the heart to God, and *at that moment* the Spirit will enter and begin His transforming work of conviction and repentance and faith.

Perhaps the biggest condition of success in bringing people to Christ is to remember that the same Holy Spirit, who came to our help in the hour of darkness, is at hand waiting to enter and illumine their hearts also, and to make good the work of salvation to which, in crying to God, they have opened the door.

8. Not a Question of Points

We come now to the single requirement demanded from us. Quite often people preach the Gospel to a person by using a number of "points," only to find that the next day the person will say, "I have forgotten the third point. What was it?" Salvation is not a question of *points!* Salvation is not even a question of understanding or of will. It is, as we have seen, a question of meeting God—of people coming into first-hand contact with Christ the Savior. So what, you ask me, is the minimum requirement in a person to make that contact possible?

The basic condition of a sinner's salvation is not belief or repentance, but just honesty of heart towards God. God requires nothing of us except that we come in that attitude. For it is a *fact* of the Gospel, making possible the initial touch with Jesus Christ, that saves the sinner, and not the sinner's understanding of it.

BIBLE SELECTION: MARK 5:25–34

[25]Now there was a woman who had been suffering from hemorrhages for twelve years. [26]She had endured much under many physicians, and had spent all that she had; and she was no better, but rather grew worse. [27]She had heard about Jesus, and came up behind him in

the crowd and touched his cloak, [28]for she said, "If I but touch his clothes, I will be made well." [29]Immediately her hemorrhage stopped; and she felt in her body that she was healed of her disease. [30]Immediately aware that power had gone forth from him, Jesus turned about in the crowd and said, "Who touched my clothes?" [31]And his disciples said to him, "You see the crowd pressing in on you; how can you say, 'Who touched me?'" [32]He looked all around to see who had done it. [33]But the woman, knowing what had happened to her, came in fear and trembling, fell down before him, and told him the whole truth. [34]He said to her, "Daughter, your faith has made you well; go in peace, and be healed of your disease."

REFLECTION QUESTIONS

The following questions can be used for discussion within a small group, or used for journal reflections by individuals.

1. When did God become real to you? Describe.
2. Of the three provisions of God, which one was the most significant for you in coming to faith in Christ (the friendship of God; the personal touch of Christ; or the convicting work of the Spirit)? Describe.
3. Watchman Nee uses three examples—the thief on the cross, the woman with a hemorrhage who reaches out to Jesus, and the publican—to illustrate what point?
4. How has Jesus' touch healed you in the past? Where do you need Jesus' healing touch at this point in your life?
5. Watchman Nee hoped to make us more effective as we attempt to share our faith with others. What are some of the things he mentions that you think might be helpful to you as you endeavor to draw people to Christ?

SUGGESTED EXERCISES

The following exercises can be done by individuals, shared between spiritual friends, or used in the context of a small group. Choose one or more of the following.

1. Use this week as an opportunity to strengthen your friendship with Christ. As with any friendship, the relationship grows when you share more and more of yourself.
2. Ask God to lead you to people who need to know Jesus as their Friend. Using Nee's counsel, allow Jesus to meet them right where they are. Share with them that Jesus is their Friend, who understands their lack of faith and their lack of desire to repent.

3. Pray that the Holy Spirit will open the "window-shutters" of someone you know who has been closed to the things of God. Keep your eyes open for an opportunity to share the good news of the gospel.

4. Watchman Nee began this selection by saying that he assumed his readers knew the basic principles (not rules and points) of the gospel. Try writing out the basic message of the Christian faith on a sheet of paper. This exercise will be a helpful primer for you as you prepare to share your faith with others.

REFLECTIONS

Watchman Nee was a great evangelist. He was a faithful witness to Jesus Christ through years of abounding and years of abasement. In twenty years of imprisonment he never betrayed his Lord. He endured to the end as seeing Him who is invisible.

Throughout his life Nee retained a passion that people would meet Jesus. I like that. It becomes easy in our sophistication to miss the simplicity of inviting people to Jesus Christ. We do not need elaborate plans or erudite speeches. We need only love.

GOING DEEPER

Nee, Watchman. *The Spiritual Man.* 3 vols. New York: Christian Fellowship, 1968. Watchman Nee himself wrote only this three-volume work; however, many of his sermons and lectures were taken down in shorthand and later transcribed into various books. In my own personal library I have over thirty such books, and there are more. Nee's best-known book is *The Normal Christian Life.* The book from which this selection is taken (*What Shall This Man Do?*) studies the lives of Peter, Paul, and John for practical spiritual application in the threefold ministry of evangelism, church building, and recovery of spiritual life. Some of my favorite Nee volumes include: *Sit Walk Stand, Spiritual Reality or Obsession,* and *The Prayer Ministry of the Church.* There is an excellent biography of Watchman Nee by Angus Kinnear aptly titled *Against the Tide.* Most of Nee's books are published by Christian Literature Crusade.

Acknowledgments

Grateful acknowledgment is made to the following for permission to reprint material copyrighted or controlled by them:

Abingdon Press for excerpts from *Prayer*, by George A. Buttrick. Copyright © 1942 by Whitmore & Stone; copyright renewal © 1969 by George A. Buttrick. For excerpts from *Conversion*, by E. Stanley Jones. Copyright © 1959 by Abingdon Press; copyright renewal © 1987 by Eunice Matthews. For the following excerpts taken from *The Fellowship of the Saints: The Rule and Exercises of Holy Living*, by Jeremy Taylor, *Lancelot Andrews and His Private Devotions*, from the Alexander Whyte translation, and *Christian Perfection*, by John Wesley. *The Fellowship of the Saints*, compiled by Thomas S. Kepler. Copyright © 1947 by Stone & Pierce; copyright renewal © 1976 by Florence Tennant Kepler. Excerpted by permission of the publisher, Abingdon Press.

Baker Book House for excerpts from *The Golden Booklet of the True Christian Life* by John Calvin, translated by Henry J. Van Andel. Copyright © 1952 by Baker Book House. Reprinted by permission of the publisher.

Bantam Doubleday Dell Publishing Group for excerpts from *Introduction to the Devout Life*, by St. Francis de Sales, translated by John K. Ryan. Copyright © 1950 by Harper & Brothers. For excerpts from *The Spiritual Exercises of St. Ignatius*, translated by Anthony Mottola. Copyright © 1964 by Doubleday, a division of Bantam, Doubleday, Dell Publishing Group, Inc. For excerpts from *The Little Flowers of St. Francis*, by Brother Ugolino di Monte Santa Maria, translated by Raphael Brown. Copyright © 1958 by Beverly H. Brown. Used by permission of Doubleday, a division of Bantam, Doubleday, Dell Publishing Group, Inc.

Benedictine College for excerpts from *The Holy Rule of Our Most Holy Father Benedict*, translated by Rev. Boniface Verheyen, O.S.B., 1906. Reprinted by permission of Benedictine College.

Christian Books for excerpts from *Experiencing the Depths of Jesus Christ* by Madame Jeanne Guyon, edited by Gene Edwards. Copyright © 1975 by Gene Edwards. Reprinted by permission of The Seedsowers, P. O. Box 3568, Beaumont, TX 77704, (409) 838-3774.

Cistercian Publications and The Merton Legacy Trust for excerpts from *The Climate of Monastic Prayer,* by Thomas Merton. Copyright © 1969 by Cistercian Publications, Inc., Kalamazoo, Michigan—Spencer, Massachusetts. This work also appears in paperback under the title *Contemplative Prayer.* Used by permission.

Friends United Press for excerpts from *Prayer and Worship,* by Douglas V. Steere, 1978. For excerpts from *"The Power of the Lord Is Over All": The Pastoral Letters of George Fox,* edited by T. Canby Jones. Copyright © 1989 by Friends United Press. Reprinted by permission of Friends United Press, Richmond, IN 47374.

HarperCollins Publishers for excerpts from *The Spirit of the Disciplines: Understanding How God Changes Lives,* by Dallas Willard. Copyright © 1989 by Dallas Willard. For excerpts from *Making All Things New: An Invitation to the Spiritual Life,* by Henri J. M. Nouwen. Copyright © 1981 by Henri J. M. Nouwen. For excerpts from *A Testament of Devotion,* by Thomas Kelly. Copyright © 1941 by Harper & Brothers, copyright renewed © 1969 by Lois Lael Kelly Statler. For excerpts from *The Sacrament of the Present Moment,* by Jean-Pierre de Caussade, translated by Kitty Muggeridge. English translation copyright © 1981 by William Collins Sons & Co., Ltd. Introduction copyright © 1982 by Harper & Row Publishers. For excerpts from *Letters to Scattered Pilgrims,* by Elizabeth O'Connor. Copyright © 1979 by Elizabeth O'Connor. For excerpts from *Life Together,* by Dietrich Bonhoeffer, translated by John W. Doberstein. Copyright © 1954 by Harper & Brothers. For excerpts from *With and Without Christ,* by Sundar Singh. Copyright © 1929 by Harper & Brothers, copyright renewed © 1957 by Sadhu Sundar Singh. For excerpts from *Christian Perfection: Reflections on the Christian Life,* by François de Salignac de La Mothe Fénelon. Copyright © 1947 by Charles Whitson. Reprinted by permission of HarperCollins Publishers and William Collins Sons & Co., an imprint of HarperCollins Publishers Limited.

HarperCollins Publishers UK and Curtis Brown Group Ltd. for excerpts from *Mere Christianity,* by C. S. Lewis. Copyright © 1943, 1945, 1952 by The Macmillan Company. Used by permission of Collins Fount, an imprint of HarperCollins Publishers Limited, and Curtis Brown Group Ltd.

James Clarke and Co. for excerpts from *How to Pray,* by Jean-Nicholas Grou, translated by Joseph Dalby. Copyright © 1955 by James Clarke and Co. The Attic Press edition published in 1982. Reprinted by permission.

Kingsway Publications Ltd. and Tyndale House Publishers for excerpts from *What Shall This Man Do?,* by Watchman Nee. Copyright © 1961 by Angus I. Kinnear. American edition published in 1978 by Tyndale House Publishers, Inc. Used by permission of Kingsway Publications, Ltd., Sussex, England. All rights reserved.

Macmillan Publishing Company and Oxford University Press for excerpts from *A Diary of Private Prayer,* by John Baillie. Copyright © 1949 by Charles Scribner's Sons, copyright renewed © 1977 by Ian Fowler Baillie. Reprinted with the permission of Charles Scribner's Sons, an imprint of Macmillan Publishing Company, and Oxford University Press.

Phillips P. Moulton for excerpts from *The Journal and Major Essays of John Woolman,* edited by Phillips P. Moulton. Published 1971 by Oxford University Press. Reprinted by permission.

New England Province of the Society of Jesus for excerpts from *On the Love of God* by Bernard of Clairvaux, translated by Terence L. Connolly, 1937. Reprinted by permission.

New Reader's Press for excerpts from *Letters by a Modern Mystic,* by Frank Laubach, copyright © 1955, New Reader's Press, Publishing Division of Laubach Literacy International, reproduced by permission.

Paulist Press for excerpts from the following, all texts part of *The Classics of Western Spirituality* series: *The Dark Night of the Soul,* by John of the Cross, edited by E. Allison Peers. Image Books edition published 1959 by special arrangement with The Newman Press. *The Life of Moses,* by Gregory of Nyssa, translated by Abraham J. Malherbe and Everett Ferguson. Copyright © 1978 by The Missionary Society of St. Paul the Apostle in the State of New York. *The Theologia Germanica of Martin Luther,* translated by Bengt Hoffman, preface by Bengt Hägglund. Copyright © 1980 by The Missionary Society of St. Paul the Apostle in the State of New York. *A Serious Call to a Devout and Holy Life / The Spirit of Love,* by William Law, edited by Paul G. Stanwood (paraphrased). Copyright © 1978 by The Missionary Society of St. Paul the Apostle in the State of New York. *The Interior Castle,* by Teresa of Ávila, translated by Kiernan Kavanaugh and Otilio Rodriguez (paraphrased). Copyright © 1979 by the Washington Province of Decalced Carmelites, Inc. *The Dialogue* by Catherine of Siena, translated by Suzanne Noffke. Copyright © 1980 by The Missionary Society of St. Paul the Apostle in the State of New York. Used by permission of Paulist Press.

Paulist Press and The Society for Promoting Christian Knowledge for excerpts from *Showings,* by Julian of Norwich, translated by Edmund Colledge and James Walsh (paraphrased), part of *The Classics of Western Spirituality* series. Copyright © 1978 by The Missionary Society of St. Paul the Apostle in the State of New York. Used by permission of Paulist Press and The Society for Promoting Christian Knowledge.

Penguin Books Ltd. for excerpts from *Confessions* by St. Augustine, translated by R. S. Pine-Coffin. Copyright © 1961 by R. S. Pine-Coffin. For excerpts from *The Fire of Love,* by Richard Rolle, translated by Clifton Wolters. Copyright © 1971 by Clifton Wolters. For excerpts from *Pensées,* by Blaise Pascal, translated by A. J. Krailsheimer. Copyright © 1966 by A. J. Krailsheimer. For excerpts from *Christianity and Social Order,* by William Temple. Copyright © 1942 by Penguin Books, Inc. Reproduced by permission of Penguin Books Ltd.

Thomas Nelson, Inc., for excerpts from *The Imitation of Christ,* by Thomas à Kempis, translated by E. M. Blaiklock. Copyright © 1979 by E. M. Blaiklock. Reprinted by permission.

University of Chicago Press for excerpts from *The Prayers of Kierkegaard,* edited by Perry D. LeFevre. Copyright © 1956 by The University of Chicago. Reprinted by permission of the publisher.

The Westminster/John Knox Press for excerpts from *A Compend of Luther's Theology,* edited by H. T. Kerr. Reprinted by permission.

Yale University Press for excerpts from *Religious Affections,* by Jonathan Edwards, edited by John E. Smith, Volume 2 of *The Works of Jonathan Edwards,* Perry Miller, General Editor. Copyright © 1959 by Yale University Press, Inc. Used by permission.

Indexes

ALPHABETICAL INDEX OF DEVOTIONAL WRITERS

CHRONOLOGICAL INDEX OF DEVOTIONAL WRITERS

1915
Merton, Thomas, 61–67

1921
O'Connor, Elizabeth, 275–80

1932
Nouwen, Henri J. M., 94–99

1935
Willard, Dallas, 13–18

SCRIPTURE INDEX